ICE AND WATER

ALSO IN THE
History *of* Canada Series

ICE AND WATER

POLITICS, PEOPLES, AND THE ARCTIC COUNCIL

JOHN ENGLISH

General Editors
MARGARET MacMILLAN and ROBERT BOTHWELL

ALLEN
LANE

ALLEN LANE
an imprint of Penguin Canada Books Inc.

Published by the Penguin Group
Penguin Canada Books Inc.
90 Eglinton Avenue East, Suite 700, Toronto, Ontario, Canada M4P 2Y3

Penguin Group (USA) Inc., 375 Hudson Street, New York, New York 10014, U.S.A.
Penguin Books Ltd, 80 Strand, London WC2R 0RL, England
Penguin Ireland, 25 St Stephen's Green, Dublin 2, Ireland (a division of Penguin Books Ltd)
Penguin Group (Australia), 707 Collins Street, Melbourne, Victoria 3008, Australia
(a division of Pearson Australia Group Pty Ltd)
Penguin Books India Pvt Ltd, 11 Community Centre, Panchsheel Park,
New Delhi – 110 017, India
Penguin Group (NZ), 67 Apollo Drive, Rosedale, Auckland 0632, New Zealand
(a division of Pearson New Zealand Ltd)
Penguin Books (South Africa) (Pty) Ltd, 24 Sturdee Avenue, Rosebank,
Johannesburg 2196, South Africa

Penguin Books Ltd, Registered Offices: 80 Strand, London WC2R 0RL, England

First published 2013

1 2 3 4 5 6 7 8 9 10 (RRD)

Copyright © John English, 2013

Author representation: Westwood Creative Artists
94 Harbord Street, Toronto, Ontario M5S 1G6

Manufactured in the U.S.A.

Library and Archives Canada Cataloguing in Publication data
available upon request to the publisher.

ISBN: 978-0-670-06538-7

Visit the Penguin Canada website at **www.penguin.ca**

Special and corporate bulk purchase rates available; please see
www.penguin.ca/corporatesales or call 1-800-810-3104, ext. 2477.

To Irene

Some of the chapters of this book are based on lectures I delivered in 2011 at the annual Joanne Goodman Lecture Series at Western University in London, Ontario. The Joanne Goodman Lecture Series was established by Joanne's family and friends to perpetuate the memory of her wonderful spirit, her quest for knowledge, and the rewarding years she spent at Western.

CONTENTS

INTRODUCTION TO THE HISTORY OF CANADA SERIES

Canada, the world agrees, is a success story. We should never make the mistake, though, of thinking that it was easy or foreordained. At crucial moments during Canada's history, challenges had to be faced and choices made. Certain roads were taken and others were not. Imagine a Canada, indeed imagine a North America, where the French and not the British had won the Battle of the Plains of Abraham. Or imagine a world in which Canadians had decided to throw in their lot with the revolutionaries in the thirteen colonies.

This series looks at the making of Canada as an independent, self-governing nation. It includes works on key stages in the laying of the foundations as well as the crucial turning points between 1867 and the present that made the Canada we know today. It is about those defining moments when the course of Canadian history and the nature of Canada itself were oscillating. And it is about the human beings—heroic, flawed, wise, foolish, complex—who had to make decisions without knowing what the consequences might be.

We begin the series with the European presence in the eighteenth century—a presence that continues to shape our society today—and conclude it with an exploration of the strategic importance of the Canadian Arctic. We look at how the mass movements of peoples, whether Loyalists in the eighteenth century or Asians at the start of the twentieth, have profoundly influenced the nature of Canada. We also look at battles and their aftermaths: the Plains of Abraham, the 1866 Fenian raids, the German submarines in the St. Lawrence River during World War II. Political crises—the 1891 election that saw Sir John A. Macdonald battling Wilfrid Laurier; Pierre Trudeau's triumphant patriation of the Canadian Constitution—provide rich moments of storytelling. So, too, do the Expo 67 celebrations, which marked a time of soaring optimism and gave Canadians new confidence in themselves.

We have chosen these critical turning points partly because they are good stories in themselves but also because they show what Canada was like at particularly important junctures in its history. And to tell them we have chosen Canada's best historians. Our authors are great storytellers who shine a spotlight on a different Canada, a Canada of the past, and illustrate links from then to now. We need to remember the roads that were taken—and the ones that were not. Our goal is to help our readers understand how we got from that past to this present.

Margaret MacMillan
Warden at St. Antony's College, Oxford

Robert Bothwell
May Gluskin Chair of Canadian History
University of Toronto

Mercator's Arctic insert that misled many sailor and inspired dreams of easy passages and a warm pole. It shows the discoveries of Frobisher and David (1595). *Septentrionallium terrarium cum privilegio Per Gerardium Mercatorem cum privilegio.* (LAC 004414662)

Meeting between Captain John Ross and Lieutenant William Edward Parry with Greenland indigenous traders, August 10, 1818, as sketched by John Sacheuse (Sackhouse). John Ross, *A Voyage of Discovery Made under the Orders of the Admiralty in his Majesty's Ships Isabella and Alexander* (London: Longman, Hurst, Rees, Orme and Brown, 1819)

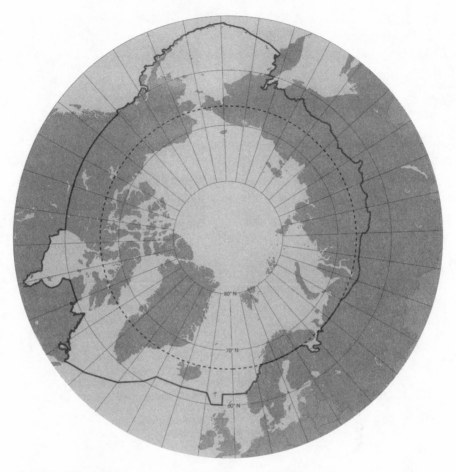

Boundaries of the Arctic

------- Arctic Circle

——— AMAP Area

Geological coverage of the Arctic Monitoring and Assessment Programme area. The
Arctic Circle is also marked (Arctic Monitoring and Assessment Programme, "The
Impact of Black Carbon on Arctic Climate," 2011, p. 20).

PROLOGUE:
CLINTON LOOKS NORTH

Snow glistened in the midday sun as Hillary Clinton strode briskly out of the rustic mansion above Quebec's Meech Lake on March 29, 2010. Her dark suit created a sharp contrast with Canada's late-winter whiteness as the American secretary of state critically appraised the gathering of five foreign ministers that had just ended. The ministers represented the five Arctic coastal states—the United States, Canada, Denmark, Norway, and Russia—but Clinton spoke up for the excluded: Arctic Council member states Finland, Sweden, Iceland, and the Arctic indigenous peoples, who were Permanent Participants in the Arctic Council created in 1996 to assure Arctic cooperation and coordination. Even before the meeting began at Willson House, a fertilizer baron's summer home in the Gatineau Hills north of Ottawa, Clinton had rebuked her Canadian hosts. "Significant international discussions on Arctic issues should include those who have legitimate interests in the region," she declared. "I hope the Arctic will always showcase our ability to work together, not create new divisions."[1]

Silver-haired Lawrence Cannon, Canada's foreign minister and the target of Clinton's stinging comments, sputtered unconvincingly as he denied that his actions were divisive. Foreign minister for only seventeen months in a Conservative government dominated by Prime Minister Stephen Harper, he faced the press alone. He disagreed with Clinton's charge that the invitation to the five coastal states and the absence of three members and the indigenous representatives on the Arctic Council created "new divisions." Sensing Cannon's discomfort, reporters gleefully jabbed at him and pointed out the embarrassment of Canada's major ally criticizing its Arctic policy. Harper had been an outspoken supporter of American foreign policy throughout his political career, and now the American secretary of state had thrown diplomatic reserve aside and rebuked his government.

To the surprise of many, Cannon soon found an articulate, if unusual, supporter: Russian foreign minister Sergei Lavrov. Multilingual, sophisticated, and wily, Lavrov had acquired his many diplomatic skills decades earlier when the Soviet Union confronted Canada and the United States across the Arctic Cold War divide. He found he could still deploy them on Canada's behalf, even though relations between Canada and Russia had recently been tense. Cannon's predecessor as foreign minister, Peter MacKay, had denounced a Russian politician–explorer's placing of a Russian flag 4,300 metres beneath the Arctic Ocean at the North Pole in August 2007. "This isn't the 15th century," MacKay declaimed in angry words that appeared to imply that the North Pole lay in Canadian waters, a claim the Russians quickly and correctly denied.[2] In February 2009, MacKay, by then Canada's defence minister, alleged that two Soviet-era bombers had penetrated Canadian airspace. Canadian fighter jets scrambled to meet them in Cold War fashion, and an apparently furious MacKay appeared on the evening news, warning the Russians to "back off" and "stay away."[3] Showing a delicately honed ability to ignore these recent disputes, Lavrov vigorously defended Cannon and Canada by declaring that the meeting at Meech Lake of the "Arctic Five" did not infringe upon the interests of the Arctic Council. He considered the gathering fully justified by the need of the coastal states to consider how their differing claims to the Arctic might be resolved. Far from undermining Arctic collaboration, the Meech meeting had supported that important purpose.*

In this geopolitical rearranging of the chairs, others more predictably attacked MacKay and Canada. Greenpeace, the controversial non-governmental organization, took Clinton's side but went further, charging that the Arctic Five were "focusing on carving up the petroleum pie rather than ensuring a sustainable future for the Arctic."[4] Climate change, they argued, made the Arctic more important than ever and meant that more voices were needed at the table. Indeed, reporters travelling from the Ottawa airport on the way to Meech Lake passed along Ottawa's celebrated Rideau Canal outdoor rink but saw no skaters: an unusually warm winter in the world's second coldest capital (Ulan Bator is first) had forced the early closing of the rink.[5]

Clinton's presence in Ottawa symbolized the new American and international interest in the Arctic. Senior American officials paid little attention to the Arctic Council until it issued an Arctic Climate Impact Assessment (ACIA) in 2004. In dire prose and with striking illustrations of shrinking glaciers, melting ice, and threatened wildlife, the ACIA warned that the Arctic was becoming warmer than ever before, a transformation with enormous global implications.[6] Although funded principally by American donors, the report roiled the political waters in Washington on the eve of the 2004 presidential election and annoyed the Bush campaign. Bush won, but the Republicans fell in 2008, the

---

*The coastal states are those that directly bound the Arctic Ocean. The Arctic Council membership is defined by states through which the Arctic Circle (66° 33′) passes, which includes the coastal states plus Sweden, Finland and (barely) Iceland. Scientists tend to use other definitions such as the treeline or, more usually, the 10 degrees Celsius isotherm. The latter is defined by those areas where the temperature in July does not rise above 10 degrees Celsius. Climate change, however, is affecting temperatures and the treeline, thus making the scientific definitions increasingly uncertain. For its purposes, the United States Congress has declared that the Arctic extends to all of the Bering Sea, thus extending its southern boundary to 53° latitude. Parts of Canada below the Arctic Circle possess Arctic conditions, and Canadians tend to use a "north of 60" definition for political purposes.

same year in which the United States Geological Survey released a survey indicating that the Arctic held undiscovered riches of 90 billion barrels of oil and 1,669 trillion cubic feet of natural gas.[7] Democrat Hillary Clinton's presence at the meeting of Arctic foreign ministers was testimony to a new American interest in the Arctic and the Arctic Council. In the stern voice the world knew well, Clinton warned that the Arctic had been too long ignored. "Only now," she declared, was it receiving the attention it deserved.[8]

Canadians shunning Scandinavians, smaller countries, and indigenous people; Russian diplomats embracing Canadian Conservatives; and the second most powerful American Democrat politician attacking Canada—irony, paradox, and even comedy abounded in the topsy-turvy of the Arctic Five meeting. For many decades after 1945, the United States and Canada had closely collaborated in the defence of the Arctic against the menace of Soviet Communism and Soviet nuclear bombers coming in over the ice. They had stood together as the Distant Early Warning outposts were strung throughout the North to provide first warning of a Soviet nuclear attack. Now it was the Russian foreign minister who supported his Canadian colleague while his American counterpart issued that country's strongest rebuke of Canada since Canada's 2003 refusal to join the Iraq War.[9]* But the Arctic has often created mists that cloud the international atmosphere.

When Prime Minister Harper, a strong critic of the "anti-Americanism" of the previous Liberal government and a stern foe of Communism, held a press conference on February 6, 2006, immediately after he was sworn in by Governor General Michaëlle Jean, he unexpectedly attacked United States Ambassador David Wilkins for apparently

---

*The Reuters report indicated that "Clinton's statement was the first open official rebuke of Ottawa since the months leading up to the 2003 Iraq War, which Canada refused to participate in." Cannon, it was reported, "spent much of his closing news conference responding to questions about Clinton's statement and insisting he was not trying to marginalize the Arctic Council."

questioning Canada's claims to sovereignty over the Northwest Passage. "We have significant plans for national defence," Harper declared, "and for defence of our sovereignty, including Arctic sovereignty." He bluntly proclaimed that his mandate came from the Canadian people, "not from the ambassador from the United States."[10] Harper's harshness towards the American ambassador underlined a northern dimension to the Conservative Party's political program that Harper had set out as an opposition leader in 2005. In 2008 the normally reserved and prosaic prime minister became rhapsodic at Inuvik, claiming that "The True North is our destiny, for our explorers, for our entrepreneurs, for our artists. And to not embrace its promise now at the dawn of its ascendancy would be to turn our backs on what it is to be Canadian."[11] The Department of National Defence responded quickly to the prime minister's enthusiasm for Arctic sovereignty and placed the Arctic in the forefront of its strategic plans. But the embrace of the Arctic did not immediately extend to the Arctic Council, with its Liberal origins and benign multilateralist flavour. The Conservatives' new approach to foreign policy, Harper asserted, would have a pointy edge. Soldiers had preference over diplomats.

What did it all mean? David Jacobson, President Obama's new ambassador to Ottawa, mocked Harper's Arctic toughness in a 2010 cable publicized soon after by WikiLeaks. Jacobson mischievously suggested that Harper's declaration that the "North has never been more important to our country" could be "paraphrased" to read the "North has never been more important to our Party."[12] And Clinton, of course, thought Harper's regard for the North was tainted by the focus on the five coastal states and his apparent disdain for the Arctic Council, the more inclusive body that focused less on the claims to Arctic resources and sovereignty and more on the environmental and human aspects of the Arctic. But here again there was considerable irony. When the Arctic Council took form in the mid-1990s, the American administration of Bill Clinton, more than any other Arctic nation, expressed reservations about its usefulness and breadth, while Canada, backed by European Arctic states, pushed hard to give the new body life, broad purpose, and a focus on human sustainability in the North.

What sparked the movement towards an Arctic Council? It had many ancestors, but the immediate impetus for its creation came from the general secretary of the Communist Party of the Soviet Union, Mikhail Gorbachev, in Murmansk on the northern shore of the Kola Peninsula on October 1, 1987. In the largest Arctic city, the lifeline for allied assistance to the Soviets in World War II and subsequently the base for the powerful Soviet fleet threatening the West throughout the Cold War, Gorbachev presented a program for Arctic demilitarization and collaboration. His address came a year after the astonishing Reykjavik summit in which he and American president Ronald Reagan came close to a total renunciation of nuclear weapons.[13] In his Murmansk address, Gorbachev lamented the failure of Reykjavik and the continuing build-up of arms in the Arctic. He pointed specifically and critically to a new radar station in Greenland, the testing of American cruise missiles in the Canadian North, and the development by the Canadian government of "a vast programme for a build-up of forces in the Arctic." It was time, he urged, for "a radical lowering of the level of military confrontation in the region. Let the North of the globe, the Arctic, become a zone of peace. Let the North Pole be a pole of peace."

Gorbachev presented a six-point program that included a demilitarization of the Arctic through the use of observers and disarmament, enhanced scientific cooperation, "an integrated comprehensive plan for protecting the natural environment of the North," and the opening of the Northern Sea Route from Europe to the Pacific through the provision of Soviet icebreakers. He also recognized the importance of the indigenous peoples in the Soviet North who had been so long cut off from contact with those in Scandinavia and North America. In his conclusion, he stressed that "the main thing is to conduct affairs so that the climate here is determined by the warm Gulf Stream of the European process

and not by the Polar chill of accumulated suspicions and prejudices."
With these remarkable words, the spark of Arctic cooperation ignited. It
was a speech of great courage and historical significance.[14]

Gorbachev provided the spark, and the end of the Cold War in the
late 1980s and early 1990s ignited the flame, but when it flickered, the
peoples who had dwelt in the North for centuries kept it burning. Their
history explains their effort. When the Europeans, the Russians, and
North Americans extended their sway to the north, the Inuit of Alaska,
Canada, Greenland, and the Soviet Union and the Saami of Finland,
Norway, and Sweden were ignored, pushed aside, and frequently used as
servants for the southerners' ambitions. The tremendous force of change
in the twentieth century profoundly affected the indigenous peoples of
the North. Many in the Soviet Union worked and died in Joseph Stalin's
ruthless attempt to exploit the Soviet North's rich resources. In the
West the change was also momentous, difficult, and sometimes brutal.
Manufactured homes in towns replaced the fabled igloos and nomadic
existence; trapping and hunting skills became less valuable; and young
people learned southern languages, often in schools far distant from
their families. As it was for indigenous people throughout the world, the
shock of the encounter with modern technology and beliefs shattered
social life and caused serious dislocations. The greater contact between
North and South, combined with a growing concern for individual and
group rights after mid-century throughout the West and eventually the
Soviet Union, had unexpected effects.

In Canada, for example, many people in the North took a new
name,* turned their traditional tasks into celebrated forms of artistic

---

*The term "Eskimo" is thought to have been a European derivation of a Cree Indian word
meaning "eaters of raw meat." In the 1960s, Canadian Arctic indigenous peoples rejected the
term in favour of "Inuit," which means in Inuktitut "the people." An "Inuk" is an individual.
Inuit is now used in Greenland, although some prefer "Kalaalit," a more specific indigenous
term, and one also hears "Greenlander," perhaps a reflection of the self-confidence now that
autonomy has been achieved. In Alaska, however, the Inupiat of the north and the Yu'pik

expression, and, by the 1980s, had acquired a powerful voice in public affairs. The character of the transformation was captured by a 1963 National Film Board documentary, *Eskimo Artist: Kenojuak*. Kenojuak Ashevak is shown initially in a dogsled travelling to the settlement at Cape Dorset on Baffin Island. There, she draws upon her rich imagination and knowledge of her people and their ways to produce sketches that soon find admirers in metropolitan galleries in the South where the distant and unknown North had caught the mid-century fascination with the new and exotic. Her 1960 print, *The Enchanted Owl*, became iconic, appearing on a Canadian postage stamp in 1970 and in homes and public buildings across Canada and in Canadian embassies abroad. Her difficult life during which her trapper father was murdered, her children died, and she fought tuberculosis and loneliness in a faraway Quebec City for three years, was obscured by the joyfulness of her art.

"I like to make people happy and everything happy," she said in 1978. "I am the light of happiness and I am a dancing owl."[15]

Kenojuak, who was born in an igloo, expressed an authentic Arctic and Inuit voice, but there were other younger voices in the late sixties and early seventies which had a different tone that began to resonate in the South. Kenojuak, like most of her contemporaries, did not learn English, but many of their children did, often at residential schools away from their families where they sometimes endured physical and sexual abuse that left deep wounds. For Canadian aboriginals, education opened new worlds while simultaneously exposing the harsh realities of their lives. Expo 67, Canada's centennial celebration, featured an elegant, stylized Indian teepee with totem poles and chanting drummers outside. Inside,

---

of the south reject "Inuit" and retain "Eskimo." Although related to the Inuit of Canada, they argue that only the term "Eskimo" properly describes the related peoples of the North who stretch from Russia through to Greenland. The *American Heritage Dictionary* agrees, but Canadian government manuals now insist on Inuit, and place names in the Canadian North and Greenland have frequently been changed to reflect this preference. (For example, Frobisher Bay became Iqaluit in 1987, and Godthab became Nuuk in 1979.)

however, there was, in the words of an August 1967 CBC report, "a different story: one of poverty, unfulfilled treaties, forced religion, and the unhappy experiences of children in residential schools."[16] Yet, in a parallel seen in other colonial experiences, education brought not only Western values and ways but also the tools to criticize them and build a counter-narrative.

One such younger person was Mary Simon, who turned twenty years old in 1967, one of eight children born in a Northern Quebec town that has now become Nunavik. Her non-indigenous father had been a Hudson's Bay Company fur trader who had learned six dialects in Inuktitut and had two children before he decided to marry Mary's Inuk mother. The Hudson's Bay Company told him such a marriage to an indigenous woman would cause his dismissal. He remained with his wife and left the company. In Mary's early years, she and her family lived "on the land ... travelling by dog team, hunting, fishing, trapping and gathering." She graduated from high school by correspondence and then worked as a northern broadcaster for the CBC in the early seventies. In the Inuit tradition, she grew up respecting the knowledge of her elders, but, as she later recalled, they lacked the language to communicate with the government officials, resource developers, and others who were transforming the North.

Articulate in English, attractive, and wily, Simon attended the historic 1977 gathering of Inuit in Barrow, Alaska, which created the Inuit Circumpolar Conference (ICC). This was to become the principal circumpolar organization, and was central to the creation of the Arctic Council almost two decades later. The Barrow attendees came from Canada, Greenland, and Alaska. For Simon, it was "one of the most exciting times of my life." The meeting of Inuit from across the North American Arctic brought back memories for her of being in the bush with her grandmother listening to the BBC, which played Greenlandic Inuit songs. Her grandmother told her, "Those are our relatives who live in faraway lands." Some lived in the Soviet Union's Chukotka

Peninsula, completely cut off by the Cold War from their relatives in North America. In 1986, the Cold War thaw allowed Simon, then the ICC president, to travel to Chukotka, meet Inuit and speak to them in their language. Carried away by the experience, she "wept with joy." In 1995 she became Canada's first ambassador for circumpolar affairs, and in that capacity became the first chair of the Arctic Council in 1996. This Inuit leader was, in the view of the Canadian foreign minister, the Arctic Council's principal architect.[17]

Kenojuak's art reflected the South's growing interest in the North and its idealization of the Arctic as the world's final frontier, the last imaginary place with its enchanted owls, icy white splendour, and mystical light and darkness. Simon and her generation of Inuit leaders responded to these images by accepting the extraordinary character and charm of the Arctic while emphasizing the profound dangers that "outside forces" had for indigenous peoples in the North. For her and the increasingly influential ICC, "the most devastating effect of the outside world" was "a legacy of environmental destruction, including oil spills, toxic contaminants, large-scale resource development, and previous commercial over-exploitation by European and American whalers."[18] By the 1970s, the environmental movement was a powerful force in international and domestic politics throughout the West. The nuclear meltdown at Chernobyl in the spring of 1986 dramatically raised environmental concerns in eastern Europe, and Gorbachev in his historic Murmansk address signalled that the fragile Arctic environment deserved much more careful attention. But there would be tensions as the environmental movement defined its place in the Arctic. On the one hand, indigenous northerners and southern environmental activists could deplore oil spills from tankers or wells and contaminants in Arctic water, but they often disagreed about whaling or the trapping of animals. What the North regarded as essential to their economic and cultural survival, southern environmentalists attacked as cruelty or threats to endangered species. Nevertheless, the concern for the despoliation of the Earth, which gained initial force in the sixties and developed strong political support in the seventies, gave strength to the movement for a multilateral Arctic forum in the North that could develop a joint response to Arctic environmental challenges.

Environmental concern, the growing force of circumpolar indigenous activism, and Gorbachev's willingness to break down the barriers between East and West were the principal catalysts to the creation of the Arctic Council. As noted above, Gorbachev's speech provided the spark, but it is a mark of the deep chill that the Cold War produced that the initial response in many quarters was dismissive. Radio Free Europe published a report asserting that Gorbachev's "words were primarily aired at currying favor among certain segments of the Western public."[19] Military analysts in Washington were similarly dismissive, especially since Gorbachev's "zone of peace" excluded the great Soviet base at Murmansk.[20] The Canadian government persisted in the "build-up" of Canadian forces decried by Gorbachev, and Secretary of State for External Affairs Joe Clark brushed aside the speech.[21] But there were others outside of official circles who harkened to the Soviet leader's call. Specifically the anti-nuclear movement, which had swelled in opposition to President Reagan's Star Wars program that proposed a shield against nuclear missiles over America, was greatly intrigued. In Canada, the Walter and Duncan Gordon Foundation, which had had a long-term interest in the Arctic and nuclear disarmament, immediately grasped the positive implications of Gorbachev's words. On behalf of the Gordon Foundation, Tom Axworthy, the former principal secretary to Canadian prime minister Pierre Trudeau, approached Canada's Science for Peace and asked three of its leaders—former diplomat George Ignatieff, Nobel laureate John Polanyi, and University of Toronto professor Anatol Rapoport—"to take up the invitation of Gorbachev for new thinking on arms control in the North."[22]

The Finns also responded quickly. They knew the Soviets well and kept a precarious neutrality in which they possessed the glitter and wealth of the West while lying in the dark shadows of Soviet military power. The immense nuclear build-up so near to their waters terrified them, and they responded quickly to the promise of environmental responsibility in Gorbachev's speech. The nuclear meltdown at Chernobyl and its radioactive aftermath had already spurred Finnish and Scandinavian efforts to denuclearize the North. Others who warmly responded to the Murmansk initiative were the indigenous peoples of Canada, Greenland, and Alaska. Finally, scientists from Canada and elsewhere, who had met at international congresses and established working relationships during the détente of the 1970s, quickly accepted Gorbachev's invitation to collaborate more closely. From these positive forces, the momentum towards an Arctic Council began to build.

The two strongest initiatives came from the Finns, who pressed for a body concentrating on environmental protection, and from the Canadians, who tended to focus on the security issues and the indigenous peoples of the North. Each had long been a small neighbour of a superpower, and although their immediate motivations and historical relationships were different, the approach to creating a multilateral Arctic institution reflected the way both countries had responded to the challenge of living beside a giant.

Ice and Water is a history of the Arctic Council, a study of how a twenty-first-century institution has roots in the human, ecological, and political development of the most northern region of the planet. Yet one must not be overly ambitious in seeking its roots. As a history of "human rights" has argued, scholars are wrong to seek precursors to our current ideas and institutions in Greek philosophy, Renaissance humanism, and even the United Nations Universal Declaration of Human Rights. Pointing to a brilliant essay on the precursors to Kafka by Jorge Luis Borges, historian Samuel Moyn relates how Borges finds that Kafka's idioms, style, and even obsessions were present in earlier writers, but these "sources" did not make Kafka possible, and if Kafka had not lived, no precursors would have meaning. Following Borges, Moyn argues that "if the past is read as preparation for a surprising recent event, both are distorted." The past becomes the future waiting to happen.[23]

The Arctic Council was far from inevitable. American obstinacy, Russian turmoil, or a Canadian government wary of indigenous participants and environmental activism would surely have squashed the sprouts of Arctic cooperation and coordination emerging in the mid-nineties. At the time of its creation—after the fall of the Berlin Wall, the end of the Cold War, the publication of the Brundtland Report with its concept of sustainable development, and the birth of the internet—those who attended its birth cast few glances towards the past while they concentrated upon future possibilities. The sense that the Council had significance in international politics was faint when representatives of eight Arctic nations created the Arctic Council in September 1996. The Ottawa Declaration of September 19, 1996, attracted little attention. The *Globe and Mail* (Toronto), for example, gave it a brief note and incorrectly reported that all nations were represented by "Cabinet" level officials, while the *New York Times* completely ignored the event. Compared with the celebrated Ottawa treaty banning anti-personnel landmines signed just over one year later, the Ottawa Declaration seemed a sideshow.

The Arctic and the Arctic Council are no longer at the side of international politics and economics. In the new millennium, dubbing the Arctic as "hot" has become a publisher's cliché.[24] In recent years, the Arctic Council has begun to attract Cabinet ministers to its meetings, and the Arctic itself is prominent in international media. The Council's future appears to be diverging sharply from its early days in which its impact upon government policy was limited and non-Arctic nations, peoples, and institutions paid little attention to its work. And yet, while recalling Borges's warning about placing the past's imprint carelessly on the present, a historian of the Arctic Council must recognize that the institution reflects particular fundamental and enduring characteristics of the history of the Arctic and of international organizations. In the case of the former, the Arctic Council has become firmly identified with one of the two dominant narratives of Arctic history, articulated well by Hillary Clinton in her attack on the exclusiveness and resource focus of the Gatineau ministerial meeting. In Clinton's narrative, the Arctic Council symbolized the willingness to "work together" and reject division and confrontation.

With its presence of indigenous peoples unique among Arctic state-based institutions, its symbolic inclusion of Cold War enemies, its focus on the environment and the human dimension of the Arctic, and with the explicit exclusion of "security" from its purview in its founding document, the Council takes its place alongside earlier representations of the Arctic as benign, unthreatened, and unthreatening. Perhaps the most remarkable literary expression of this representation of the Arctic was the Canadian–American explorer Vilhjalmur Stefansson's 1921 book, *The Friendly Arctic: The Story of Five Years in Polar Regions.*[25] The odd but charismatic Stefansson followed the book with a lecture series in which he used photographs principally from the Canadian Arctic Expedition to support his argument for Arctic "friendliness." "Eskimos" were captured dancing and singing, while Caucasians obviously shared in the mirth. Arctic pastures were verdant, ice homes romantic winter abodes. Stefansson does identify by name the indigenous peoples he photographed, and the photographs suggest that he did have the acceptance of the subjects.[26] His openness to Inuit ways was famously reflected in his demonstration for the American Medical Association of the effectiveness of the indigenous low-carbohydrate diet of meat and fish. After a year of such a diet he was as healthy as when he began, a fact cited by later advocates of "paleolithic diets."[27]

And yet Stefansson's own biography and experience scarcely suggest the Arctic was "friendly." The Canadian Arctic Expedition (1913–1918), which Stefansson organized and directed, was marked by one of the greatest Arctic disasters, the loss of the lead ship, the *Karluk,* to crushing Arctic ice in January 1914. Eleven of twenty-five expedition members died. The extreme conditions the survivors faced and later described in articles and memoirs contradict Stefansson's notion of "friendliness." Fellow Arctic explorer Roald Amundsen, the first to reach the South Pole and to traverse the Northwest Passage, thought Stefansson's views "entertaining, and highly plausible to one who has not been 'up there.'" Fundamentally, however, it was "fantastic rot" and a "dangerous distortion" of Arctic conditions.[28]

Despite the condemnation by Amundsen and others, Stefansson's "message" that the North is not "hostile" continues to resonate with many contemporary students of the Arctic. Sherrill Grace, an eminent literary scholar who argues that "the idea of North" or "nordicity" is central to the Canadian imagination, considers Stefansson's writings of enduring importance. As an explorer, an anthropologist with extensive contact with indigenous people, and an enthusiast for the importance of indigenous knowledge, Stefansson complements those Canadian poets, authors, and playwrights who have evoked the magic and monumentality of the North. Far from "rot," *The Friendly Arctic* represents an attempt to understand the Arctic in itself, without the technical and cultural baggage of earlier explorers who have exaggerated the harshness of the North. Grace writes: "By the time the reader has reached the final chapters of this 800 page tome, she must be persuaded by Stefansson's rhetoric and sheer narrative skill, if not by his facts, tables, photographs, and the header 'The Friendly Arctic' at the top of every page, that 'the polar regions are ... friendly and fruitful.'"[29]

The similar narratives of Stefansson and Grace flow from a broad stream whose sources emerged five centuries earlier when Europeans encountered the north and south ends of the western hemisphere. Stefansson's acceptance of the importance of local knowledge and Grace's nordicity find antecedents in the great Spanish priest Bartolemé de las Casas's insistence on the humanity of the colonized and the possibility of a different form of colonization than the exploitative and punitive ways of the Spanish. Later they are reflected in scholars, environmentalists, and political leaders who emphasize the grandeur, sensitivity, and human character of the Arctic and its peoples and who fear the imprint of rapacious development and national rivalries upon the North. For them, the Arctic Council is much favoured because it embodies the values of cooperation, human development, and peaceful resolution of disputes that they espouse.

But there is an alternative narrative that its supporters argue is more historically convincing, one that pays power its due. One encounters the differences between the narratives in intellectual encounters of the late medieval and early modern period when the first explorers reached the New World with European notions of the relationship between nature and human beings, the former to be mastered, the latter to be defined.

From the Elizabethan voyages of Martin Frobisher to the twentieth-century quest for resources and sovereignty, the treatment of indigenous peoples and the interests of national states have created tension. Frobisher garnered support for his voyages by appealing to England's swelling ambitions, the zeal of its commercial world, and its rivalry with others. Seeking the Northwest Passage and the fabled riches of the Indies, Frobisher first regarded the Inuit he encountered as potential guides and curiosities, but when five men disappeared on his first voyage and he took an Inuk hostage to England, the five missing men became proof of the evil and deceit of the indigenous peoples. For centuries, their humanity vanished almost completely for Western adventurers in the North. Frobisher's narrative of national security, the search for resource riches, and indifference or hostility to indigenous presence persisted.

And yet neither of the two principal Arctic narratives has completely dominated. Roald Amundsen, probably the greatest Polar explorer, whose Arctic successes rested upon his close knowledge of Inuit ways, expressed a blend of awe, generosity, paternalism, and cynicism in his account of his voyages and Arctic people. He later wrote that "the seven members of [his ship] the *Gjøa* formed different opinions" of the indigenous peoples they encountered.[30] And opinions changed, as they often did in encounters between Europeans and others. Hillary Clinton, after all, embraced the Arctic Council that Bill Clinton's administration in the 1990s had only reluctantly accepted, whereas the Harper government initially ignored the Council because of its Liberal Party origins and "soft" character, to pursue "harder" forms of power and Canadian "sovereignty." But the Arctic changes too—its people, its climate, and its place.

We begin with its place.

ONE

Place:
Ice and Water

The Arctic is a place like no other. Its polar counterpart, Antarctica, is clearly a continent, even if water does not lap up on the land as it does with Africa and Australia. These other places, unlike the Arctic, have long had specific definition. Schoolchildren know "where they are" and can trace the outline of the shapes of the continents. When the Arctic Environmental Protection Strategy's working group on Conservation of Arctic Flora and Fauna met in 1994, the American delegation noticed that each Arctic nation was following its own definition of what or where the Arctic was. This variation appeared, notably, among the many scientists present. Geographers simply applied the name "Arctic" to those areas north of the Arctic Circle, while others seemed to use the existence of permafrost as the defining characteristic. Climatologists, of course, used temperature, usually an average of 10 degrees Celsius in July, while biologists looked to the treeline, and social scientists were, characteristically, more willing to have flexible southern boundaries that reflected political interests or the presence of indigenous populations. In the absence of clear separations between ice, land, and water, or temperature zones, ambiguity thrived. The Americans recommended that a group be formed to resolve the issue. It was never formed, although Arctic Council scientists today use a map that reflects its members' political interests as well as the traditional definitions.[1]

The contemporary confusion mirrors a past in which the most northern parts of the globe have been seen through various lenses, darkly, distantly, and without the clarity of other zones. The Arctic's place, in short, was uncertain, and that uncertainty had intellectual and other impacts. For the ancients in the West, place defined character, physique, colour, and life, but the Arctic tested the limits of their knowledge and even their imaginations. As the western Europeans began their age of exploration in the last decades of the fifteenth century, their guides were the texts of the great civilizations of the Mediterranean littoral. Among the most influential was the second-century C.E. Alexandrian Ptolemy's *Geography*, which used the concept of latitude as explanation for differences: "All animals and plants that are on the same parallels or equidistant from either pole ought to exist in similar combinations in accordance with the similarities of their environments."[2] Where you were defined what you were. Thus Christopher Columbus wrestled in his journal with the colour of the new peoples he discovered whenever their skins lacked the hues that latitude had predicted. American historian Nicolás Wey Gómez has described how completely Columbus's announcement of his discovery bore the intellectual constructs of his times:

> Columbus underscored the fact that the lands he had just discovered stood directly across from the Canaries, by linking latitude, as he had in the *Diario,* with the skin color of local people. As Columbus put it, his "Indians" were not "monstrous men," as many believed were to be found in the farthest reaches of the inhabited world; nor were they "black as in Guinea": nor did they seem to be born "where the aspect of the solar rays is too strong ..."

Their appearance and character did not fit what Columbus had been taught to believe, but he was able to accept them as human. Farther to the south, however, Columbus encountered the Caribes, the indigenous people of the Caribbean. They were, he believed, the predicted "monstrous men," and accordingly he did not hesitate to make them his victims, either through slavery or death.[3]

As the learning of the Greeks and Romans passed down to the West during the twelfth and thirteenth centuries, the concept of a world machine encompassing the human race emerged, one whose peoples reflected their geography and whose governance was defined by their place. In fact, Ptolemy's world did not extend beyond 65° latitude, and his *Geography* ignored the North entirely. In this classical geopolitics, the temperate zone was inhabited by those peoples who were by nature gifted to govern themselves well, and, in a fateful corollary, to rule over others who lacked their moderation. As maps following classical notions of symmetry and geography appeared in the fourteenth and fifteenth centuries, the Earth was divided into five zones, with the frigid North and the torrid South usually considered uninhabitable, although some considered them the abode of horrendous, wild peoples with whom civil intercourse was impossible.

The Far North was more unknowable than the South, yet some memories and myths about it endured, cosseted in monasteries or spun out in popular legends of encounters with frozen lands and odd peoples. Pytheas of Massilia (Marseille), for example, named the region Ultima Thule, a term that endured for centuries. He claimed he sailed to Ultima Thule in the fourth century B.C.E., discovering a world where the midsummer sun never set.[4] Where Pytheas journeyed remains obscure because the memory of his travels is derived from others who later reported, mostly skeptically, on his tales of endless days and of a "mare concretum," where his small ship encountered a hardened sea, perhaps ice or frozen slush. Despite others' doubts, the evidence surely suggests that Pytheas did travel north.

Pytheas's stories mingled rather uneasily with Greek myths, which claimed that beyond the cold Riphean Mountains and the north wind Boreas lay a blessed land where the Hyperboreans, a giant and glorious race lived in continuous sunlight and bountiful peace.[5] This sense that somewhere beyond the cold was a northern Shangri-La persisted, although imagination was altered by experience when Irish monks sailed westward in the sixth century C.E. in search of paradise. Instead of the northern Utopia they had anticipated, they encountered ice, whales, and perhaps Iceland. St. Brendan's *Navigatio*, the record of this historic voyage in about 500 C.E., served as a guide to lands beyond the western horizon.[6]

In the cartography of the Romans, land often appears northwest of the European continent, and the word "Arctic" itself derives from the Greek word for "bear." The constellations Ursa Major and Ursa Minor are, of course, the "Great Bear" and the "Little Bear," with the latter containing Polaris or the North Star. The Romans had shown interest in the North after the conquest of Britain and the Gauls. However, after 300 C.E., the Empire shifted towards the east, and European awareness of the lands to the northwest all but vanished until the Norse began their extraordinary voyages, first to Greenland and then to North America in the tenth century. With the 1960 discovery of the Norse settlement at L'Anse aux Meadows in Newfoundland, we know now that the Norse, popularly called the Vikings, did reach North America around the end of the first millennium. With their navigational skills in northern waters first honed by their experience sailing eastwards to the White Sea and westwards to Iceland where they first settled at the end of the ninth century, the Norse expanded the limits of European imagination in the next century.

These journeys and settlements occurred at a time of warming in the Northern Hemisphere that made possible agricultural settlements in Greenland that endured until the fifteenth century.

The Norse left not only material evidence in Newfoundland and Greenland, but also the magnificent Icelandic sagas that recorded the voyages of Erik the Red to Greenland and his sons to North America. The North American settlements were brief, but the eastern and western settlements on Greenland were an extension of Europe into the North. The settlers built Catholic churches, paid tithes to Rome, and traded ivory and even polar bears with Europe. A bishopric was established at Gardar in the eastern settlements at the beginning of the thirteenth century, and reports flowed regularly to Rome. But then the Greenland settlements vanished in the early fifteenth century. Why they did remains uncertain. In *Collapse,* an influential study of societies that failed or disappeared, geographer Jared Diamond argues that the Norse clung to their European ways as their agricultural pursuits became increasingly fruitless as the climate cooled. Others disagree, claiming that the appearance of elephant ivory in Europe undermined the trade in walrus tusks. The Hanseatic League pushed out the Norse from their dominant position in northern Europe, and a financial crisis engulfed Norway and Bergen, the port that provided a lifeline to the settlements. In this view, the Greenland colony's fate reflected economic and environmental challenges.[7]

The Norse were not alone in the North. They encountered others in Greenland and to the west on what is now the coast of Canada. The Norse called these people Skraelings, and the scattered descriptions of them convey curiosity and puzzlement, but also sometimes contempt. The longest description is in the twelfth-century Latin *Historia Norvegiae,* where Skraelings are described as "small" people who when struck by a weapon, had wounds that turned white. They were said to bleed endlessly when they were killed, and, the account continued, "lack iron completely; they use whales' teeth for missiles, sharp stones for knives." Archaeological evidence supports this description—except, of course, for the white blood—and provides confirmation of trade between the Norse and the Skraelings, who exchanged tusks for the metals of the Europeans. But the Norse could not situate the people and their place. Greenland, the *Historia* declared, "was the western boundary of Europe, almost touching the African islands where the waters of the oceans flood in."[8] Anthropologists have identified the Skraelings as the Tuniit people who had come to the North American Arctic across the Bering Strait almost 4,000 years earlier. They were not the first. Archaeologist Robert McGhee finds evidence of hunters, settlements, and even artists across the Eurasian Arctic. In a haunting passage, he speculates: "Given the tendency of traditional northerners to rapidly expand the size of their local group during times of plenty, to suddenly move into new and distant hunting grounds, and to face extinction or near-extinction in inevitable famines, it seems likely that many of the peoples who left archaeological evidence of early Arctic occupations have no descendants in the present world."[9]

McGhee's research persuades him that, although they may have left no descendants, Arctic peoples, even those who left no trace, shared three major traits: large families, mobility, and "a predilection for killing as many animals of prey species as possible" based upon a traditional perception of the world where the hunters see no link "between overkilling and a drop in the population of prey animals." The killing of an animal, McGhee writes, "is universally seen as a consensual act between the hunter and hunted."[10] While not the natural conservationists of later popular, romantic fables, the Arctic peoples' relationship with animals had a spiritual and material aspect fundamentally different from that of European explorers. The Tuniit had lived for thousands of years in the North American Arctic when the Norse initially encountered them, probably on what is today's Baffin Island. The Skraelings were surely a shock for the Europeans (and vice versa), although classical mythology and travellers' lore had spun tales of northern peoples. They were neither superhuman Hyperboreans nor wild and threatening subhumans. The "small" Skraelings in their animal skins, whose hunters eventually supplied the treasured walrus tusks to the Norse traders, fitted no earlier myths or preconceptions.

But the Tuniit and European worlds were so different. The Norse took advantage of the medieval warming period to settle in the Arctic, replicating European agricultural and industrial life, complete with its intellectual and governance structures through the Roman Catholic Church and the link with the kingdom of Norway. They lived, as much as possible, as they had done before. The Tuniit, however, had adapted to their environment through the skins they wore, the seals and whales they ate, and the extraordinary miniature sculptures they carved from tusks and soapstone. These carvings are evidence of a complex society based upon a shamanic world view very different from that of late-medieval Christian Europe. The carvings illustrate the role of the shaman who mediated between a sky world and the underworld, and suggest the adaptation of belief to fit the High Arctic world in which they dwelt. There was a relationship between the human and animal worlds that was essential in a hunting society: animals and humans equally possessed souls. While shamanism was not at all exclusive to northern indigenous peoples, Europe's animist traditions were vestigial at the moment of contact with the Tuniit. The complexity of the Tuniit world view and its expression in utilitarian hunting objects evaded the Norse who carried the passion of recent Christian conversion. We gain a sense of the hostility to shamanism in the *Historia Norvegiae* description of the northern "Lapp" people: "Their intolerable ungodliness will hardly seem credible nor how much devilish superstition they exercise in the art of magic. For some of them are revered as soothsayers by the foolish multitude because whenever asked they can employ an unclean spirit, which they call a *gandus*, and make many predictions for many people which later come to pass." It was a world Christian Europeans had come to despise.[11]

The Tuniit's fate, however, was not decided by the Norse presence, as startling and disorienting as it was to them. They faced two greater threats. The first was the warming that occurred after the tenth century C.E., which had made the agricultural settlements in Greenland possible. What benefited the European agriculturalists and traders harmed the nomadic Tuniit. They had constructed their world around hunting on ice and land, and the melting of ice shattered customary practices and beliefs. The second threat was the arrival in Tuniit lands of the Inuit, a much more aggressive people who swept across the North from Alaska with dogsleds. With their Mongolian bows, the most powerful in the world at the time, they overwhelmed the Tuniit in the twelfth and thirteenth century. They soon became the predominant people of the High Arctic and, according to some Norse writings, they were responsible for the destruction of the Norse western settlement on Greenland. Whatever the reason, the Norse were gone from Greenland by the mid-fifteenth century following an Arctic cooling period while the Tuniit survived in settlement fragments. The last Tuniits died in a small settlement on Southampton Island in Hudson Bay in 1902 after a whaling crew brought a disease that finally annihilated them.[12]

The Inuit conquest of the Tuniit meant that the North American High Arctic was dominated by a people who had still wider linguistic and cultural ties from Greenland to Siberia, a fact of enormous significance to those who created the Arctic Council in the late twentieth century. It also meant that the Inuit later avoided the term aboriginal since they had conquered and displaced the "original" Arctic people. But the continuing Inuit presence in the polar North has a broader significance. The Arctic, unlike the Antarctic, was populated continuously by people who had adapted to one of the harshest climates in the world. As in the south, the presence of non-European peoples would fundamentally affect the Europeans who encountered them.

From those early encounters, three key forces that would shape the Arctic future became apparent. First, the peoples of the North had successfully adapted to their circumstances in diet, clothing, and beliefs. The greatest threats to their continued existence would come from outside. Second, the first encounters by Westerners with the Arctic did not reflect a willingness on their part to adapt to altered material and climatic differences. As noted above, the eastern and western settlements on Greenland were thoroughly European from their religious practices to their incorporation within the emerging European system of governance to their emphasis on commercial exchange, the basis for modern capitalism. These differences would persist through future centuries. Third, the failure of the Norse settlement in Greenland meant that the Arctic, unlike the New World in the south, never attracted settlers and almost always was a place through which, or by which, other European goals were achieved—a passage to the riches of the East or a place to prove manliness and courage. It became and remained, for Europe on the eve of its world empire, a sideshow.

As the Norse presence in Greenland ended, other Europeans expanded their presence dramatically around the world, with, for example, Vasco da Gama in the Indian Ocean, Columbus in the Caribbean, and John Cabot (Giovanni Caboto) in Newfoundland. A revolution in the building of ships meant that Europeans could sail more easily to distant shores, and the tremendous burst of individualism accompanying the Renaissance and the Protestant Reformation meant that individual adventure and heroism were ever more highly prized. Moreover, science based upon experiment not only challenged traditions, as when Galileo overturned long-held ideas about the universe, but also strengthened the capacity of adventurers. By the mid-sixteenth century, the Europeans had sketched out a world they hoped to profit from and to dominate. The famous 1569 world map of Gerhard Mercator reflects the impact of the age of reconnaissance when Europeans streamed out beyond their world and brought home great riches, new understandings, and fresh prejudices.

Although the navigational importance of the Mercator projection has never been questioned, its exaggeration of the Northern Hemisphere whereby Greenland is approximately the size of Africa has generated an understandable complaint of Eurocentrism. On the whole, however, the map is notable for charting the new lands fairly accurately for the first time—with the important exception of the North. The northern regions remain mainly mythical in cartographical inspiration. Because inclusion of the Arctic was technically impossible in his projection, Mercator created an insert of the Arctic for his map, which he described in a remarkable letter to John Dee, an astrologer, navigator, and consultant to Elizabeth I. He told Dee that the Arctic insert was derived from a text by Jacobus Croyen, who had based his description on an earlier travelogue. According to Mercator, Croyen had made "some citations from the Gest of Arthur of Britain; however, the greater and most important part he learned from a certain priest at the court of the king of Norway in 1364. He was descended in the fifth generation from those whom Arthur had sent to inhabit these lands, and he related that in the year 1360 a certain Minorite friar, an Englishman from Oxford, a mathematician, went to those islands." And so, the Norse expeditions become linked to the Arthurian legend, and the discoverer of the New World was not simply an Englishman but an Oxford graduate! The map is fascinating, and was profoundly influential in its time and beyond. Whatever its origins and fanciful notions, Mercator's "North" does reflect the Norse experience. More importantly, it suggested that Europeans could reach Asia through the Northwest and the Northeast.

But the Arctic insert possessed more ancient lore than contemporary understanding. In the midst of the Arctic island is, in Mercator's words, "a Whirlpool into which there empty these four Indrawing Seas which divide the North." In the middle is the Pole and a bare and glistening black rock that reaches beyond the clouds. Maps can matter greatly, and John Dee had a prominent place in the English court and could influence the monarch. He had known Mercator when he studied at Louvain and had acquired knowledge of significant navigational aids yet unknown in Britain. After Frobisher finally acquired financing to set out through the north to "Cathay [as Europeans called China] and India," Dee went on board Frobisher's ship to advise on the new geographical and cosmological knowledge he had acquired on the continent. Seven years after Mercator wrote his letter to Dee, Elizabeth I stood on the balcony of her palace at Greenwich on June 7, 1576, and graciously waved to Martin Frobisher as he passed on the first of his three historic Arctic voyages.[13]

Frobisher was a man of his times: in the words of a biographer, his "rise in prestige and worldly influence followed the pattern of Elizabethan England's myriad daredevil, swashbuckling, fortune-seeking marine careerists." He had sailed the African coast, been taken hostage in Guinea, captured Spanish gold in the Caribbean, and eventually became a commander under Sir Francis Drake when English sailors defeated the Spanish Armada, for which glorious deed Elizabeth knighted him. Frobisher had first considered sailing east, north of Russia, where the Muscovy Company had supported several voyages that, while not reaching Cathay, had brought tantalizing evidence of animal and mineral wealth. But the Northwest beckoned more, and he finally got sufficient support for three ships to sail north to Cathay and India. As they neared Greenland, which Frobisher mistakenly identified as "Frisland," a fictional island that Mercator and others placed in the Northwest, one ship was so buffeted by storms it turned back. But Frobisher persisted, first naming one bit of land "Queen Elizabeth's Foreland" and then encountering a passage that he thought akin to the one discovered in 1520 by Ferdinand Magellan in the south. Just as Magellan left his name upon the strait that leads from Atlantic to Pacific, Frobisher dubbed the body of water "Frobisher Strait." He believed it reached to Asia. It did not: we still know it today as Frobisher Bay on Baffin Island.[14]

Frobisher expected to meet other peoples, although contemporary notions of what to expect varied wildly and the memories of the Norse encounters were exceedingly vague. The experience of other explorations had thrown traditional notions of the kind of people that would be found topsy-turvy. When, in August 1576, some Inuit came upon his ship, Frobisher reacted with caution and curiosity: "Afterwards he had sundry conferences with them, and they came aborde his ship, and brought him salmon and raw fleshe and fish, and greedily devoured the same before our mens faces." They played with the ship's ropes and demonstrated they were "very strong of their armes and nimble of their bodies." They then exchanged beads and seal coats with the English sailors and received "belles, looking-glasses and other toys in recompense." Frobisher thought they could guide him through the strait towards the passage to Cathay, but he remained wary. Others were not: "After great courtesie and many meetings, our mariners, contrairie to theyr captaines direction, began more easily to trust them, and five of oure men going ashoare, wer by them intercepted with theyre boate, and were never since heard of to this day againe." An angry Frobisher seized some Inuit as hostages but to no avail. He soon sailed back to England with one hostage and a piece of ore.[15]

His return caused a great stir in London, not least because the ship that had sailed back earlier had reported that Frobisher's ship had been lost. With his own flamboyance matched by the bluster of his major sponsor, Michael Lok, Frobisher became the sensation of the late London fall of 1576. The Inuk and his kayak were, reportedly, "a wonder onto the whole city and to the rest of the realm." He became the talk of London's salons and the court with his kayak's speedy passage through waters. But he died within a month.[16] The black ore's fascination lasted longer, particularly after one assayer declared that he had found gold flecks within it. That judgment was sufficient to cause investors to rush to fund a second Frobisher expedition, with Elizabeth herself providing £1,000, an amount equivalent to about £80 million in 2013.[17] The ore's promise obscured thoughts of passages to Cathay and other discoveries. The 1577 summer voyage returned with 200 tons of ore and an Inuk male, his wife, and child, and the following year 2,000 tons were to be brought to England by Frobisher's third voyage. With gold flowing from the Americas through the Spanish empire, England's greatest foe, the chance of Arctic riches inspired investors and sailors. The Spanish even managed to place a spy on Frobisher's second voyage. But the black stones ultimately proved worthless, and the thought of a permanent mining colony vanished after Frobisher's third voyage in 1578. Frobisher proved to be a poor geographer; he did not recognize Hudson Bay and took too long to admit his treasured ore was fool's gold. And yet, as historian L.H. Neatby writes, "he pierced the barrier of the realms of frost and opened a breach for more skilled navigators to exploit."[18]

Frobisher's discoveries barely changed the later edition of Mercator, which appeared in 1595, shortly after his death. It retained the four large islands surrounding the pole and even included the fictional island of Frisland which Frobisher had mistaken for Greenland. In the next few years, however, explorations in the eastern and western North transformed the Arctic map. In the east, Willem Barentsz began in 1594 his journeys in search of a Northeast Passage. Supported by wealthy Amsterdam merchants in the Netherlands (which had freed itself from Spanish rule in 1581), Barentsz reshaped the map of the Northeast before he and most of his crew died on the third and final voyage. He nevertheless reached and went beyond Novaya Zemlya and discovered Spitsbergen. Barentsz, like most others in the period, had assumed that the twenty-four hours of sunlight meant that beyond the ice there would be a summer warmth that would make the long passage to China possible. His journeys did much to undermine the belief that the High North might ever be "friendly." One of his crew, Gerrit de Veer, kept a journal of the extreme hardships the sailors faced, and his account of capturing polar bears and killing arctic foxes, building a wooden house from the scraps to survive the winter, and then escaping on two open boats to be rescued by a Dutch ship established the Arctic as a place for heroes and for experiences beyond the imagination of those at home.

Although Frobisher's voyages ended in scandal and controversy and Barentsz's explorations in his own death, both inspired others to follow them. In assessing their significance, one sees three broad and persistent characteristics of the European encounters with the Arctic.

The first is the economic impulse. Frobisher attracted royal

patronage and enormous resources for his fruitless search for the
Northwest Passage and gold. His last expedition of fifteen ships,
approximately one-tenth of the English naval fleet, with an accompanying plan to set up a permanent colony to exploit the "gold,"
indicated how much the hope of finding an Eldorado spurred on
northern exploration. As noted above, Frobisher's initial support came
from the Muscovy Company, the first of the chartered joint stock
companies that were at the heart of the imperial expansion of England.
Created in 1555 by Sebastian Cabot, Richard Chancellor, and Sir Hugh
Willoughby, its initial purpose was to reach China by the Northeast
Passage and, as the name indicates, to establish contact with Russia,
which was then cut off from links with England. When Chancellor and
Willoughby both died on a Northeast expedition, the company, which
possessed exclusive rights to northern exploration, granted Frobisher
the right to sail to the Northwest.

Clement Adams set out the motivations of the Muscovy Company in
the 1550s in a contemporaneous account:

> At what time our marchants perceived the commodities and wares of
> England to bee in small request with the countreys and people about
> vs and neere vnto vs, and that those marchandizes which strangers
> in the time and memorie of our auncesters did earnestly seeke and
> desire, were nowe neglected and the price thereof abated, although by
> vs carried to their owne portes, and all forreine marchandises in great
> accompt and their prises wonderfully raised: certaine gi'aue citizens of
> London, and men of great wisedome, and carefull for the good of their
> countrey, began to thinke with themselves howe this mischiefe might
> be remedied.

Writing at the dawn of the Elizabethan age, Adams captured the spirit
that fuelled the explorers. In the North, the powerful Swedes and the
Lithuanians cut off the English from Russia, and English goods could
find no markets in Moscow, while in southern Europe the powerful
Spanish fleet controlled the coasts and assured that throughout Europe

the "commodities and wares of England" were "in small request." New markets, lands, and fortunes needed to be found.[19]

From Adams's laments in the mid-sixteenth century through the later voyages of Frobisher to the West and Barentsz to the East, to the twenty-first-century diamond and iron mines of the Canadian North, Russian president Vladimir Putin's vast plans for the development of oil and gas, and renewed enthusiasm for Northwest and Northeast passages to China, economic dreams and needs have driven southerners northwards. That these hopes have been so rarely fulfilled does not dampen them. For so many later generations of "Merchant Adventurers," as the Muscovy Company was first named, the allure of the North has rested upon the hope for profit. We will see that when those hopes diminish, so does the imprint of the Arctic in courts, political councils, and even the popular imagination.

The second characteristic of European interaction with the Arctic was the linkage between commercial interests and those of the emerging national state with its claim to monopolize force and its subordination of individual needs to reasons of state. Queen Elizabeth I herself took a deep interest not only in Frobisher's voyage but in Sir Humphrey Gilbert, who tirelessly argued the cause of the Northwest Passage after he returned from brutal attacks on the Irish in the English imperial cause. In Ireland, Gilbert used terror to subdue rebels, famously ordering the heads of Irish victims—men, women, and children—to be cut off and placed upon a road leading up to his tent so that, when the Irish came to meet him, they passed between the severed heads of their brothers, sisters, mothers, fathers, and friends.[20] Gilbert's bloody Irish triumphs won him favour in the English court where he was an enthusiastic promoter of the three voyages of John Davis (1585, 1586, and 1587), which continued the search for the Northwest Passage. On his first voyage, he rounded the tip of Greenland and found the site of the old Norse settlement and named the waters Gilbert Sound. As he carried on towards the Arctic Archipelago, he named features of the coast in honour of towns and persons who had financed his expedition: Mount Raleigh for Gilbert's famous half-brother, Sir Walter [Raleigh]; Totnes Road after the town in Devon where the Gilbert family and Davis were born; Exeter Sound in honour of the wealthy Devon town of Exeter; and Cape Walsingham to recognize the support of Secretary of State Francis Walsingham for the voyage. Of course, today we remember best Davis Strait, the major body of water separating Greenland from Canada.[21]

The explorers, like the merchants who supported them, worked, in Clement Adams's words, "for the good of their countrey." Frobisher, Gilbert, Davis, and others carried with them the swagger and billowing pride of England in their times and doubted not for a moment that new lands were theirs to shape and exploit. But they deeply resented others who did the same in the name of their nations. In his account of Sir Humphrey Gilbert's 1583 voyage to Newfoundland, Gilbert's rear-admiral Edward Haies complains that the French had cavalierly gone about "imposing names upon countries, rivers, bays, capes or headlands as if they had been the first finders of those coasts." They were not: John Cabot and Sebastian Cabot had long before claimed for England the lands north of the "Cape of Florida." And thus Sir Humphrey, in August 1583 in St. John's Harbour, made it clear that Newfoundland was English. Speaking before his own sailors and fishers of other lands, he declared that all lands within 200 leagues would forever appertain to the Queen of England. Literally taking up island turf in his hand, he proclaimed three laws: the first established the Church of England for all public services, the second proclaimed any activities against England as acts of high treason, and the third declared that anyone who uttered words "sounding to the dishonour of Her Majesty" would have his ears lopped off and his ship and goods confiscated. The Spanish possessed the South, the English the North. While Gilbert plotted throughout his life at ways to capture Spanish possessions, he recognized that, in their realms, others owed obeisance. He and his English counterparts expected the same from others.

The third characteristic was the deeply rooted belief that European law as it applied to property and persons prevailed over the new realms and the peoples who dwelt within them. The concept of *terra nullius* appeared immediately after Columbus's first voyage when Pope Alexander VI issued the historic papal *Inter Caetera*, which decreed that Christians had a right to rule over heathen savages. Even if the Europeans encountered other peoples, they had the "right to discovery" because there was no political structure. Alexander VI's bull drew upon earlier papal bulls that provided the Portuguese explorers of the mid-fifteenth century with the right to "subdue" the pagans they found on the newly discovered lands.[22] In truth, the concept of *terra nullius* was contested and remains controversial. Moreover, it did not mean that the initial encounters between Europeans and North American aboriginals were invariably hostile.[23] Frobisher's plans for an Arctic mining colony included a statement indicating that the colony should and would establish good relations with the peoples living in the Canadian Arctic. Similarly, despite his actions in Ireland, the plans for Gilbert's English colony on Newfoundland envisaged peaceful trading relations with aboriginals. Between this ideal and the reality of native-European encounters fell the shadow of the belief of European superiority. Fortified by a certainty that Christianity would benefit pagans and the sense that their boats, weapons, food, and practices were technically advanced, the early Arctic explorers possessed a confidence that normally dismissed the knowledge, experience, and trustworthiness of the Inuit they encountered. Frobisher, interestingly, had first considered using Inuit guides to lead him through dangerous waters, but the loss of five men, not surprisingly, caused him to distrust the Inuit. Those he took to England were treated in circus style. Their quick deaths confirmed their weakness and, after the curiosity was sated, their irrelevance. Their kayaks, whose speed and agility had stunned Frobisher's sailors, were unwisely dismissed as bizarre contraptions, and their obvious advantages were ignored. The Inuit became a pesky distraction to larger purposes, whether it was the search for resources, the Northwest Passage, or the North Pole.

This attitude persisted for centuries. Robert Peary, the American explorer who claimed to be the first to reach the North Pole in 1909, cared "for the local people's well-being only to the extent that it might affect their usefulness to him." Accordingly, he dug up native graves in Greenland and sold the remains to the American Museum of Natural History. He even sent five living natives to the museum, where they quickly died from diseases to which they had no immunity.[24] While the cultural blindness of the imperialistic explorers is now deplored, their fears had some actual roots. In a study of Inuit contact in the eastern Arctic with Europeans, between Frobisher in 1576 and Danish explorer Jens Munk in 1619, Renée Fossett found that only three encounters were without violence or threats of violence, and in each such case the Inuit were outnumbered. Moreover, of ten violent encounters, at least six were "apparently unprovoked attacks of local people against strangers, fuelled principally by Inuit desire for metal." Although little is known of eastern Arctic Inuit violence against Inuit, in the western Arctic "societies met more frequently in war than in trade." On the one hand, the European adventurers were a rough lot, schooled in war and vicious in battle. On the other hand, the Arctic natives did not shrink from violence among themselves and were quick to use it against outnumbered strangers. For both, the other was alien and threatening.[25]

The end of that first period of modern High Arctic exploration came gradually, not from the resistance of the Inuit but from the fierceness of Arctic weather, the impenetrability of Arctic ice, and, most of all, from the recognition that there was no easy Northwest Passage to the fabled riches of China. The experience left a profound mark on what the South knew of the North. Among the British adventurers, there were two great explorers in the early seventeenth century whose efforts remade the Arctic map. Henry Hudson, having failed to find a Northeast Passage in 1608, turned to the Western Hemisphere, where he first discovered the great river that now bears his name in New York State. Then, at the prodding of British merchants, he turned to the Northwest. Frobisher and Davis had both reported a strong current to the southwest of Davis Strait but it remained elusive. Hudson pushed a querulous crew beyond Hudson Strait, which divides Baffin Island from Labrador today, and entered a vast sea. Believing that he would soon reach the Pacific, he sailed on into the dead end of James Bay, where he was forced to winter. The crew could not sail again until June, and some of them mutinied. They forced Hudson to join "poor, sick and lame" sailors in a small boat that they cast adrift.

Hudson's bones rest somewhere near the great bay that bears his name. Many of the mutineers later died when Inuit attacked them on Digges Island, which Hudson had named for one of his backers. Those who survived escaped prosecution, partly because they had destroyed Hudson's own journal and had kept an undoubtedly prejudiced one by mutineer Abacuk Pricket. They also brought forward a chart revealing the extent of the great sea Hudson had discovered. It was enough to spur yet more voyages to seek the Pacific through the North.[26]

William Baffin was, a biographer writes, "certainly the most proficient navigator and observer of all the Arctic explorers of his period." Sailing with Robert Bylot, a surviving Hudson mutineer, Baffin served as pilot on a 1615 voyage in which he carefully charted Hudson Strait and Hudson Bay. He concluded that there was no passage out of the bay to the west. The following year he tested his thesis that the Northwest Passage, if one existed, would be through Davis Strait or northwards. In a historic voyage, Baffin sailed farther north than ever before (almost 78°N), and left behind the names of his English backers on the coastline he travelled. It was a historic voyage because of the great technical and astronomical abilities of the largely self-educated Baffin. He concluded that there was no passage north of Davis Strait, and the ice he encountered in the summer made him conclude that ships could not pass beyond to the fabled open waters of the Arctic sea. He wrote an epitaph for his own and many other efforts in his report to a sponsor of the voyage: "When I consider how vaine the best and chiefest hopes of men are in thinges uncertain; and to speake of no other than of the hopeful passage to the North-West ... Yea, what great summes of money haue been spent about that action, as your worship hath costly experience of." But to no avail. No other explorer would reach as far north as Baffin for 236 years. He turned from the east to the south and, fighting for the East India Company, died when a cannon shot tore apart his stomach in 1622 at Hormuz in the Persian Gulf.[27]

Despite Baffin's pessimism, a few persisted in the search for a passage, but the energies of Europeans were diverted by the savagery of the English Civil War and the Thirty Years' War that ravaged much of the Continent in the first half of the seventeenth century. By 1648 when the Treaty of Westphalia, which ended the war, was signed, Semen Dezhnev, a Russian Cossack, had sailed through the Bering Strait. He did not seem to be aware that Alaska was near and, not surprisingly, his accomplishment was largely unrecognized. The Dane Vitus Bering, who carried out two major voyages for Russia, in 1728 and 1740, finally proved that a strait separated America and Russia.[28]

As with the Norse in Greenland, the great Arctic explorations of the sixteenth and early seventeenth centuries became a faint memory in Europe when attention was diverted southwards where the settler colonies were becoming firmly established. The Inuit, ironically, had sharper memories, and almost three centuries after their contacts with Frobisher they still told tales of Frobisher's lost sailors to returning Europeans. Contacts did not end: whalers and fur traders followed the explorers' paths into the north of America and Russia, but their business lacked the excitement and attention that the heroic explorers had attracted. On eighteenth-century maps, most of the Arctic was a wide swath of white, though a few charts and people retained the notion that beyond the impenetrable ice lay Mercator's open sea, where, in the famous words of Mary Shelley's 1816 *Frankenstein,* one would find "a land surpassing in wonders and in beauty every region hitherto discovered."[29]

Interestingly, the Russians were the most tenacious in maintaining interest in the North after Peter the Great, the powerful early eighteenth-century ruler, looked northwards to find maritime passages to Europe. Using the charts of Russian adventurers, Russia's rulers in the following century sent expeditions to map the northern Russian coastline and the Siberian rivers and to find furs and greater empire. These maps often also drew upon the mainly English explorers who had charted the eastern Arctic of North America and Hudson Bay. After Bering's discovery of the strait that bears his name, the Russians crossed it often, and their traders and officials spread through Alaska and along the northern Pacific coast. The Danes were also active as the Lutheran pastor Hans Egede and Norwegian–Danish merchants established settlements in Greenland, where they struggled with British and Dutch whalers and vestiges of the Little Ice Age that made agriculture perilous. Although Vitus Bering was a Dane, he sailed for the Russians, and the North on eighteenth-century maps bore overwhelmingly Russian and British names, a lasting testimony to the fact that their nationals were the predominant Europeans in the North.[30]

The Arctic slipped to the side in the eighteenth century, whose final decades changed the world dramatically. At mid-century the British, Spanish, and French empires clashed from the Indian subcontinent and the Philippines through the slave-rich west coast of Africa, to the Caribbean islands and Quebec's Plains of Abraham. When the warring powers signed the Treaty of Paris in 1763, the British had become dominant beyond Europe. The clash between empires left the Russians as the sole power with continuing aims of Arctic expansion throughout most of the century. The French presence in North America was an entrapped Quebec whose trading lifelines to the Northwest were threatened by British presence above and below. But of more lasting significance was the revolution that began in British workplaces, where the way things were produced changed fundamentally and forever. The Industrial Revolution with its machine-based production would make Britain, and later much of the rest of Europe, wealthier than humans had ever dreamed before. But British dominance received a blow when a civil war broke out in its American colonies in 1775. Already wealthy by historic standards and as innovative as their kin in the motherland, the Thirteen Colonies became the United States of America, linked by blood and language with Britain, but separated by political institutions and the suspicions that are invariably the residue of civil conflict. The French stormed back in revolutionary fury at the end of the eighteenth century, reaching the gates of Moscow while their American allies made a final attempt to drive the British out of North America. Both attempts failed by 1815. By that time, the Russians maintained their sway over nearly all of the Eurasian Arctic. A much-diminished Sweden absorbed Norway and its Arctic lands, although the Peace of Kiel allowed Denmark to retain Iceland, Greenland, and the Faroe Islands. The British retained northern North America with the important exception of the Russian spillover into Alaska.

The Napoleonic Wars confirmed the grandeur of the British Navy, but its energies and reputation far outweighed its activities in the aftermath of the peace. Nevertheless, the spirit of adventure that had inspired the Elizabethans stirred thoughts of the Arctic once more in the British admiralty and among the British public. Moreover, the British whalers now dominated the trade that inevitably took them northwards, and the Hudson's Bay Company, swollen by its merger with its great competitor the North West Company in 1821, now extended its range far above and beyond its original posts. But the decision by the British Admiralty to search once more for the Northwest Passage and the North Pole arose, as adventure often does, from the imagination and talent of a leader. Sir John Barrow, the influential Second Secretary of the British Admiralty, fully accepted the praise of one of the voyagers he sent out when, in 1846, he wrote a history of the remarkable Arctic explorations:

It most opportunely occurred in the year 1817, that accounts of a change in the Polar ice particularly favourable to the undertaking were brought to England by our whale ships' and as it has been generally happened in this country that some individual, more sanguine than the rest of the community, has, by his superior knowledge, greater exertions, or more constant perseverance, succeeded in bringing a project to bear, which, in less vigorous or pertinacious hands, would have suffered to die away ...[31]

Barrow had no idea that his early efforts to persuade the Admiralty to explore the Arctic would endure for four decades. Indeed, he clearly expected the first voyages to bring scientific rewards and for the whole business and the discovery of the Northwest Passage to be accomplished quickly. "The image of the polar explorer as a romantic, knightly hero, noble yet modest and unpretending" had not yet been formed.[32] Yet Barrow soon caught the spirit of a new Britain emerging after the Napoleonic Wars. Thoroughly a self-confident Englishman of his times— enthralled with the possibility of science, confident of the superiority of his ships and sailors, and pertinacious in his curiosity about the planet and its peoples—Barrow was the individual who drove the extraordinary series of explorations that remade the Arctic map by mid-century.

Before entering the Admiralty in 1804, Barrow had worked and lived in China and South Africa, and his earlier experiences had convinced him of the value of finding a shorter passage to China. The "change" in the polar ice referred to reports from whalers and others in the area of Spitsbergen and Greenland that massive ice packs had blocked sailors. Barrow concluded that this meant that warmer temperatures near the Pole had caused the ice to break loose, thus affording a path to the North Pole from Spitsbergen and finally making possible the discovery of the passage to China. Some have also suggested that the massive unemployment of British sailors and ships after the Napoleonic Wars was the principal incentive for Barrow and his colleagues. There were no wars for the navy to fight: "Its new enemy would be the elements themselves."[33] But this interpretation diminishes the complex motives too much. The aims of the British and Barrow reflected the tremendous energies unleashed by the industrial and scientific revolutions and the sense that British imagination had boundless limits. Moreover, there was a challenge: the Russians, allies in the Napoleonic Wars but rivals in the North, had begun to move beyond Bering Strait and to seek an Arctic passage from the west.

Today scholars and others often mock the manner in which nineteenth-century British Arctic exploration was, in the words of an eminent anthropologist, a "mixture of class-bound imperial assumption and juvenile homophilic fantasy."[34] There were, as Barrow indicated, other important factors such as scientific curiosity, the need for a job, and the search for resources. And many explorers were not bound by upper-class backgrounds and prone to fantasize. Nevertheless, the failure to recognize that the indigenous peoples had lived for centuries in the North; the refusal to abandon military ways and prejudices unsuited to the Arctic; and the attachment to new technologies, which were often remarkable but not yet ready for the harsh cold, made the Arctic more impenetrable than it should have been.

One famous image conveys splendidly how present-minded and culturally bound the British were when they first began their voyages. On August 10, 1818, about 250 years after Martin Frobisher had sought out the Northwest Passage in the Elizabethan age and after numerous encounters with the indigenous peoples and the Arctic cold, two British officers, Commander John Ross and Lieutenant Edward Parry, had their first encounter with what they called "the natives" at what they named Prince Regent's Bay on Greenland. John Sacheuse, a Greenland Inuk, had a few years earlier stowed away in a whaling ship and arrived in England where he studied drawing. With this background he sketched his own people dressed in furs and skins appropriate for the climate. One wonders what he thought when he drew Ross and Parry. In Pierre Berton's caustic words, "The two men ... are attired exactly as they would be had they been envoys to some palm-fringed island in the South Pacific or off the coast of Africa," in their cocked hats, white gloves, and elegant buckled silk shoes.[35]

Ross was a brave explorer and a heroic soldier who endured thirteen wounds, two broken legs, and a bayonet thrust through his body during the Napoleonic Wars, but Sacheuse's image left a devastating impression. Moreover, Ross's contemporaries quickly condemned his published report that there was a chain of mountains blocking the passages to the west. His claim that the Inuit he had met and Sacheuse had sketched were "Arctic Highlanders" quickly became the satirist's delight. The many skeptics were fortified when reports emerged that Ross's decision to return to England and his eagerness to see mountains and describe them in scientific fashion where others did not had baffled Parry and others on the ship. Ross also made the mistake of boasting about his accomplishments, but luck was not with him. Barrow anonymously condemned him in a scathing article, and Parry whispered his criticisms to those whose opinions mattered. Ross, a wealthy man, turned away from the Navy and retired on half-pay in disgrace.

These early years were difficult for Barrow because a highly publicized expedition to the North Pole passing by Spitsbergen had also failed. He badly needed good news. Accordingly, he put his faith in Parry, who shared his belief that Ross had bungled and that a Northwest Passage was to be found beyond the mountains Ross had imagined. In 1819 Parry, the oldest of the crew at twenty-eight, set out on the first of his three voyages in search of the passage. Although his first voyage did not find the passage, it was enormously successful in stirring interest in the Arctic and whetting the fabled curiosity of Victorian Britons about the world. Parry's ships, the *Hecla* and the *Griper*, were specially fitted for Arctic conditions, and he carried sufficient provisions, including food in tin cans, to winter in the Arctic. They sailed to Lancaster Sound where Parry proved that Ross's mountains were an illusion. They sailed on and, in the words of the ship's purser, "arrived in a sea which had never before been navigated, [and] were gazing on land that European eyes had never held before." In five weeks in the summer of 1819, Parry sailed through the Arctic Archipelago, naming the islands and inlets for his patrons with pride of place reserved for Viscount Melville, whose name remains on the immense sound and vast island on which he and his crew became the first Europeans to winter in the Arctic Archipelago. He reached 110°W, enough to win a prize of £5,000 offered by the British Parliament. There he stayed for a long winter, where unimaginable cold and darkness did not destroy the sailors' spirits. But the dream of finding the passage the next summer ended when the ice did not let the ships free until August 1, too late for another thrust forward, and he returned home, reaching Scotland on October 30 with only one of his ninety men lost.[36]

Parry's historic journey had proven it was possible to winter in the Arctic, and had ventured far enough to keep the quest for the passage alive. His two remaining voyages were less successful, but each left a rich legacy of knowledge of the North and charts invaluable to others. He made his final Arctic voyage in an 1827 attempt to reach the North Pole by sailing north of Spitsbergen. Again he failed, but he attained 82° 45'N, a mark unsurpassed for forty-nine years. Although health and other preoccupations prevented Parry from returning to the North, he would join the group of British Admiralty officers whose northern ambitions endured into the 1850s and who were commemorated in a historic painting entitled "The Arctic Council." Parry's voyages, unsuccessful in their aim to find a passage to Asia, nevertheless stirred the public imagination and maintained the Admiralty's ambitions. Parry was a quintessential Victorian whose self-deprecating and understated demeanour concealed a romantic spirit that expressed itself in an infinite curiosity about the natural world and a thirst for the unknown.

The first encounter with aboriginals that Parry had, dressed in the finery of British naval garb, misleads. He and his crew did not sail and live oblivious to their surroundings, but rather recorded constantly, making observations that were of great importance to cartographers, natural scientists, astronomers, and future explorers. On his second voyage, he wintered near a large group of Inuit and drew upon their knowledge to survive the harsh winter and to gain knowledge of the waters, relying particularly on a talented female named Iligliuk who drew maps that guided him towards open waters once the winter ended. He experimented with dogsleds, which offered great advantage over the human sledges traditionally and foolishly favoured by the British, although he did not follow the lead of George Francis Lyon, commander of the consort vessel, the *Hecla*, in eating native food and even sleeping naked overnight with an Inuit family.[37]

Parry and, most notably, Lyon wrote long accounts of their voyages and experiences, which contain glimmerings of later anthropological studies of Inuit people. But for the moment they satisfied the thirst of the burgeoning British middle class for tales of heroic adventure and exotic peoples. Lyon, who had previously explored and written about Africa, was especially detailed and even provocative in his descriptions. Imagine the impact on increasingly moralistic Britain when he described how some drenched and cold sailors had their garments removed by extremely hospitable Inuit women and replaced by skins. Then the women danced before them and laid garments on their bare bodies: "At length the endeavors of our female attendants were successful, and these kind attentions which the tender sex has ever paid to men in distress, were sufficient to warm the whole of our parts." Indeed.[38]

Parry's voyages were complemented by overland voyages to the Arctic coast undertaken by Rear-Admiral John Franklin, the first of which resulted in the loss of the majority of his men amidst horrible conditions. Franklin became known as the "man who ate his shoes," which he understandably did in extreme desperation. Nevertheless, the British persisted in mapping the coastline and the Arctic Archipelago and naming the sounds, inlets, and islands after British notables and the explorers themselves. And yet, despite enormous resources devoted to the task of finding the Northwest Passage, the Admiralty had failed. In the mid-1840s it was decided that a final major attempt would be made. Several turned down the commission because they believed, rightly, that any serious attempt would be dangerous and life-imperilling. Finally, Franklin, who was fifty-nine, accepted the commission and set out on the *Erebus* and the *Terror* on May 19, 1845. The celebrated departure was followed by diminishing news of the venture; eventually one heard nothing.

The search for Franklin, which preoccupied the British literate public for over a decade after his disappearance and was formally acknowledged in 1848, eventually framed the Arctic in the minds of the British as a cruel, savage beast. It also became a major political controversy that critics of the government of the day used to prove its incompetence. Never had the Empire's power so formidably confronted the Arctic as with Franklin's exceptionally strong ships, the *Erebus* and *Terror*. But all was for naught, as Franklin died in 1847 and his crew members followed in an awful procession of death. It was, to use a modern term, the tipping point.

The crucial moment was the report to the Admiralty by Hudson's Bay Company employee and explorer John Rae in 1854. He had met Inuit who possessed items incontrovertibly from the Franklin expedition. They told him that the last survivors had sawn off arms and boiled flesh before they died. Charles Dickens, the Victorian giant who had made the search for Franklin a personal crusade, railed against the report, but he did not punish the messenger Rae, who bore "manly, conscientious, and modest personal character." He rather blamed the Inuit, who were "covetous, treacherous and cruel." The chatter of the "uncivilized ... with a domesticity of blood and blubber" should not be heeded. Rae defended the truthfulness of the Inuit reporters on the basis of his own experience, but Dickens and many others firmly rejected Rae's outrageous tales. Historian Janice Cavell convincingly argues that the incident "hardened" attitudes about race in England.[39]

John Rae told his stories of Franklin's relics in 1854, the same year in which Robert McClure, one of the many searchers for Franklin, finally proved that a Northwest Passage did exist but that it was impossible to use. Worst of all from the government's position, the fate of Franklin was discovered in 1859 by Francis Leopold McClintock, who had been personally commissioned by Lady Franklin herself in the face of an Admiralty's refusal to undertake further expeditions. He found records, several skeletons in Royal Navy uniforms, as well as silk handkerchiefs, sponges, slippers, and Goldsmith's *The Vicar of Wakefield*. The tales the Inuit told Rae were basically true: Franklin and his men had died horrible deaths of scurvy, starvation, and freezing, and cuts on some survivors' bones betray last-moment cannibalism. The often melo-dramatic Franklin search had a bad ending, one that stifled the appetite for similar adventures. The search for the Northwest Passage ceased, and the British, both the Admiralty and the public, averted their gaze from the Arctic for several generations.[40]

Sir John Barrow, who had originated Franklin's and many other voyages, had never considered the Arctic as a place for settlement. Indeed, he scorned its intrinsic worth and declared that it was "silly" to plant the flag "when the object is worthless, ... a barren, uninhab-ited country, covered in ice and snow, the only subjects of His Majesty in this newly-acquired dominion consisting of half-starved bears, deer, foxes, white hares and such other creatures as are commonly met with in these regions of the globe." There were other great purposes to serve. As geologist Sir Roderick Murchison told Benjamin Disraeli, the Arctic "in times of peace [was] the best school for testing, by the severest trials, the skill and endurance of many a brave seaman." Some failed the trial, but others passed with heroic colours.[41] In the process they helped to fit the Arctic into the Western consciousness. The Arctic itself was mainly a means to an end—for a proud navy that had few chances to fight in the long years of peace, for a political elite courting popular support, for an increasingly literate public searching for heroes and publishers seeking markets, and, not least, for a nation constructing a compelling imperial vision. For the future, there was a legacy unimagined at the time. Despite Barrow's scorn for planting the flag, the British explorations through their mapping, their naming of straits, seas, and islands, and their acts of discovery, had laid the foundations for later Canadian sovereignty over the Arctic Archipelago.

It is noteworthy and ironic that the great British explorations of the post-Napoleonic era had almost no Canadians involved. Indeed, the Franklin land expedition of 1819 was notable for the antagonism between Franklin and the Canadian voyageurs. This earlier pattern held. The Canada of its founding prime minister John A. Macdonald looked towards the Northwest, whose turmoil and promise captured popular and political attention. In contrast to the northern British colonies, it was the United States that took up the search for Franklin, and its popular press celebrated American explorers who, after the civil war, enthusiastically set out upon a search for the North Pole. In 1867 the United States itself became an Arctic nation with the purchase of Alaska from the Russians. For their part, the British in the late Victorian age turned towards Africa as the new place for adventure, rivalry, and imperial possession.

As Africa replaced the Arctic as the test for British manliness and a field for British imperial ambitions, the British, with barely a glance towards the past, transferred the vast Arctic Archipelago to Canada in 1880. The past remained in the brilliant imperial crimson colouring the new Canadian North and in the many English names dotting the maps. No longer *terra nullius,* the Arctic finally found its place on modern maps with the British and then the Canadians and Russians dominating, but with the Americans and Danes having a significant presence. Still, the Arctic remained a place like no other.

TWO

Owning the Arctic

During the Victorian heyday of British northern exploration, Sir John Barrow disdained those who dreamed of owning the Arctic. Although British names, including Barrow's, predominated on the Arctic Archipelago, they were, for him, mere markers for adventurous wayfarers passing near and through Arctic waters. But as British power perceived challenges to its worldwide sway towards the end of the Victorian era and in the early twentieth century, sovereignty became defined as the state's right to command and be obeyed, which in turn required the power to enforce those rights.[1] The so-called "scramble for Africa" illustrated the late-nineteenth-century enthusiasm to grab lands that were unclaimed. Arctic lands, which had long been *terra nullius*—no one's land—became caught up in the movement to make clear who owned what. Like motorcars and winged flight, new approaches appeared suddenly in the new century.

On September 6, 1909, American Arctic explorer Robert Peary rushed to a telegraph office in Indian Harbour in Labrador to tell the world, "Stars and Stripes nailed to the pole." Two days later the exuberant Peary informed American President William Howard Taft that he had the honour to "place North Pole at your disposal." Taft replied much less effusively: "Thanks for your interesting and generous offer. I do not know exactly what I could do with it."[2] His answer betrayed not only a fine sense of humour but also the spirit of earlier days when the quest for the North Pole or the Northwest Passage was, like the race to the moon for later presidents, primarily a test of mettle, a way to find the "right stuff" in America and its people. It was a clever rejection of Peary's implicit assertion that he had claimed a spot on the high seas for the United States. Heroism was the justification; establishing a claim to the Arctic or to the moon was not the ambition.

The fierce nationalism of Peary, who probably did not reach the Pole despite his much-heralded claim, was paralleled in northern Europe where the brilliance and daring of the great Norwegian explorers Fridtjof Nansen and Roald Amundsen served as national-istic inspirations for the Norwegians as they separated peacefully from Sweden in 1905. Prior to independence, Otto Sverdrup, a Norwegian who had participated in earlier Arctic expeditions with Nansen, spent three years in the High Arctic where he drew deeply on Inuit practices and knowledge. He was able to chart an astonishing 260,000 square kilometres and named three newly discovered islands—Axel Heiberg, Ellef Ringnes, and Amund Ringnes—after three brewers who had backed him financially. He claimed the territory for the Swedish crown, which responded in the fashion of President Taft and ignored Sverdrup's claim. The successor Norwegian government seemed equally confused about what to do. Freshly divorced from Sweden, Norway was under-standably more concerned with sorting out conflicting claims for nearby Spitsbergen, the largest island of the Svalbard archipelago. It was also making claims against Denmark for part of Greenland where the Norse had settled centuries before. The new Norwegian state celebrated remarkable feats by its explorers. In 1906 Amundsen led the first expedition to traverse the Northwest Passage successfully, which he immediately declared was "a great achievement for Norway." Amundsen soon moved on to challenge the British in the race to the South Pole. The Norwegian accomplishments left their mark on their new nation and on the Canadian Arctic.

The new century became an age for possession, for planting flags, and for staking claims. Canada, of course, had been the direct beneficiary of the great British Arctic expeditions described above. In 1880 the British government had transferred the Arctic Archipelago to Canada as a result of British concern about the many American whalers wintering there, American miners planning to stake claims, and American army captain Henry Howgate's proposal of a polar colonization colony on, of all places, Lady Franklin Bay on northern Ellesmere Island. Already a map presented to Congress proclaimed "Grant Land," in honour of President Ulysses S. Grant, Washington Land, and "Hall Land," after the American explorer Charles Hall. The latter surrounded, most inappropriately and embarrassingly, Lady Franklin Bay. In fact, the area around Franklin Bay, which was long believed to be a separate island from Ellesmere Island, was discovered by Isaac Hayes, an American, in the 1850. Perhaps fearing controversy, the Canadians requested through Governor General Lord Dufferin that the Imperial Parliament approve the transfer in an act specifying the boundaries. This the British refused to do, perhaps because of a desire not to draw attention to Hayes's discovery; nevertheless, after some delay the transfer occurred. As Shelagh Grant commented, Canada suddenly became the largest country in the world, but "the rationale and motivation directing the terms and process of the transfer remain an enigma."[3]

An enigma creates doubts. Peary's nationalistic flourish in 1909, therefore, had its Canadian counterpart. On July 1, 1909, Captain Joseph-Elzéar Bernier erected a remarkable memorial on Melville Island at Parry's Rock in Winter Harbour that proclaimed Canadian ownership of no less than "the whole ARCTIC ARCHIPELAGO."

A sea captain forced by circumstances to become the governor of a Quebec prison, Bernier had developed a fascination with the Arctic, and he worried about the state of Canada's Arctic claims. He was not alone. Prime Minister Sir Wilfrid Laurier had commissioned a confidential report on the legitimacy of the Canadian claims. It was not reassuring: it recommended that Canada immediately establish its sovereignty, particularly where the Americans had a presence. Moreover, Canada's famous loss in the Alaska Boundary Tribunal triggered a strong nationalist response. Canada therefore bought the *Gauss*, a German ship, renamed it CGS *Arctic*, and appointed Bernier its captain. He made three voyages in consecutive years beginning in 1906 with explicit instructions to raise the flag, which in those days was the Union Jack, wherever it seemed appropriate.[4]

Bernier's efforts were widely reported in the popular press in the South, and his popular speeches explicitly raised the threats to Canadian sovereignty over the Arctic Archipelago presented by the polar exploits of the Norwegians and the Americans. Never one to miss an opportunity and hoping to rival Peary and other Arctic explorers, Bernier constantly tried to secure "a little more latitude" in his instructions.[5] In a 1909 speech, Bernier displayed a map that divided the Arctic, following the so-called sector principle enunciated by Canadian Senator Pascal Poirier in 1907. It was the beginning of a long-lasting attempt to bring order to Arctic ownership claims through a simple extension of boundary lines to embrace ice and water between them. The Arctic Archipelago made an unexpected entry into Canadian politics in the 1911 Canadian general election. When Laurier concluded a reciprocal trade agreement with the United States and called an election on the issue, the Speaker of the American House of Representatives, Champ Clark, celebrated the agreement because he believed it would lead to the day when the Stars and Stripes would "float" over all of British North America, even to the North Pole. Laurier lost the election, and the new Conservative prime minister, Robert Borden, decided he too should look at what was happening in the High Arctic. Clark's bluster notwithstanding, Borden, a lawyer, was wary about the Canadian case for owning the Arctic. For his sharp legal mind, there were too many troubling ambiguities.

The Admiralty itself had acknowledged that the transfer of jurisdiction to Canada in 1880 left "the question of what is or what is not British undecided." When the Borden government checked with the British Colonial Office in 1913 about a possible Canadian Arctic expedition, it was clear that the situation required acts of occupation to establish full sovereignty. The colonial secretary advised that it was "not desirable that any stress should be laid on the fact that a portion of the territory may not already be British." While granting "authority for annexation" to the Canadian government, he added that he did "not consider it advisable that this should be published."[6] Quite apart from questions involving the emerging and evolving area of international law, the Arctic was to become a new national adventure for Canadians in the twentieth century. Some had ruminated about Canada's "northern" character in the earliest decades of Confederation, but Canadians themselves paid little attention to the High Arctic in those times. There was additional ambiguity because Canada in the late nineteenth and early twentieth centuries did not possess control of its external relations, which remained with London. The British in the Alaska dispute and on other occasions demonstrated their fear of offending the United States, which in the aftermath of the Civil War had become the wealthiest nation in the world, a growing international military power, and an enthusiast of Arctic adventure and exploration.

Thus, the Americans, with their tremendous energy and thriving popular press, took up the challenge of Arctic exploration with zest and considerable success, not least because some American adventurers were more open to different cultures than the British had been. Charles Hall, for example, is a particular favourite of Canadian nationalist Pierre Berton because Hall in his explorations was, in Berton's words, "the first white man to travel in the Arctic with only Eskimos as his companions."

Hall was the first to use the term Inuit in his writings, and "Joe" (Ebierbing) and "Hannah" (Tookolito) became his constant and legendary companions in his expeditions.[7] American popular interests and tastes have often deeply influenced Canadians who have sought to ape them. The Arctic was not an exception, and the interest of Bernier, Laurier, and Borden in the North reflected the stirrings south of the border as well as the actual presence of Americans and other foreigners in the High Arctic.

Quite apart from questions about the state of legal claims and the rise of nationalistic visions of the Arctic, the seeds of twentieth-century internationalism also sprouted in the late nineteenth century. The 1880 transfer to Canada of the Arctic Archipelago occurred simultaneously with the first International Polar Year (IPY). The IPY was the brain-child of Karl Weyprecht, an Austrian naval officer who had carried out Arctic experiments in 1872–1874 and had come to the correct conclusion that there were too many Arctic scientists and explorers with very different instruments and diverse purposes. Far better, he argued, to have a coordinated international effort that took "synchronous" observations. In terms of international politics, the moment was propitious to create international humanitarian or scientific efforts on the model of the Red Cross or the Universal Postal Union. Weyprecht died in 1881, but his idea took concrete form. The IPY actually extended over four years, 1881–1884, and was a remarkable success, with eleven participating nations and fourteen principal research stations.[8] Canada took part in the International Polar Year, but was a rather insignificant participant. Arctic science, as the leading authority Professor Trevor Levere has written, deeply reflected political and economic circumstances. Building upon Arctic scientific work by the British Admiralty, American universities, and German researchers, Weyprecht made the case for internationalism in science: the Earth, he declared, "should be studied as a planet. National boundaries, and the North Pole itself, have no more or less significance than any other part of the planet, according to the opportunity they offer for the phenomena to be observed." As Levere observes, imperialism, colonialism, nationalism, and internationalism were contending forces, and all would have enormous influence in the twentieth century. They would create the peculiar international science legacy bequeathed to the Arctic Council when it took form at the twentieth-century's end.[9] The IPY concentrated on geophysical observation, and its important contribution was the appearance of meteorological stations in the Arctic, but the practical applications of science and its human dimension were to influence the Arctic profoundly. Amundsen's success came partly because he borrowed eagerly from the knowledge and practices of the indigenous peoples and partly because he added an internal combustion engine to his ship. Just after Amundsen began his historic voyage in 1903, the Wright brothers took flight at Kitty Hawk and the dreams of air travel fastened tightly upon the popular imagination. As the promise of technology swelled, the possibilities of closer integration of the Arctic into the world economy and polity seemed much greater. Wireless communication and radio meant that the isolation of the Arctic explorer, which had created great suspense to Franklin and other Arctic sagas, was no longer complete. In the astonishing technological revolutions in the first three decades of the twentieth century, the Arctic, like so much else, would find its place. But what of its people?

By the twentieth century, Arctic explorers recognized that those who had dwelt there for centuries had much to teach southerners, even if some, like Robert Peary, were poor learners. Modern anthropology was emerging as an academic field and was contributing to a different understanding of non-Western cultures and, in some quarters, a recognition of the enormous harm caused to indigenous peoples through contact with Western guns, disease, and beliefs.[10] The pressure to plant flags, the opportunities of new technology, the search for glory and its magnification through a chauvinistic popular press, and an emerging social scientific community intrigued by traditional cultures threatened by modernity were combined in the person of Vilhjalmur Stefansson.

Stefansson was born in 1879 in Gimli, Manitoba, to parents of Icelandic descent. They moved to the United States soon after his birth, where, as a young man, Stefansson studied theology. He moved from religious studies to anthropology at Harvard, where he became excited about the possibility of discovering primitive tribes untouched by modernity. Their appeal was their communitarian values and apparent freedom from the constraints of Western society. He first considered Africa for his research work, but became a part of an American Arctic expedition in 1906 and developed a fascination with the Arctic that he never lost. Striking in appearance, with a thick thatch upon a strong face and wiry body, Stefansson immediately attracted the attention of others with his brio, commitment, and confidence. As part of an American Arctic expedition, he learned Inuktitut, lived with the Inuit, wore their clothing, ate their food, and even fathered a child, Alex, with Fanny Pannigabluk, who, in the fashion of many explorers, travelled with and counselled Stefansson.[11] Most controversially, he claimed in 1912 to have discovered "blond Eskimos," who he claimed were possible descendants of the missing Norse Greenlanders. His announcement caused a sensation and many critics ridiculed it, charging that Stefansson was a mere publicity seeker. He was, but he was more.

When Prime Minister Robert Borden considered a Canadian Arctic expedition to complete the mapping of the Canadian North and find new lands, Stefansson's rich Arctic experience qualified him immediately to lead the expedition. He had a faint tinge of Canadian background mingled with the apparent eminence of a Harvard connection, and his Arctic experience gave him the contacts to pull an expedition together. The expedition was expanded to include a strong scientific component under the direction of American-born zoologist R.M. Anderson. Although a future giant of Canadian anthropology, Diamond Jenness, was part of the expedition, he was a New Zealander arriving via Oxford's Balliol College. His research work had been in the South Pacific, and he did not yet know the Arctic. Indeed, Canadians born south of 60° were few in number and insignificant in the planning of the operation. Americans and Scandinavians far exceeded southern Canadians on the expedition, a testimony to their greater activity as whalers, scientists, and explorers in the North. Even the Fiji Islands had greater representation than Canada's western provinces. Northern Canadians, however, were well-represented. They were the "local assistants," the indigenous people who served as the seamstresses, guides, interpreters, and workers guiding the southern outsiders in the lands they knew so well. Among them was Pannigabluk, who is mentioned in many of the diaries as a highly accomplished seamstress and, according to the diary of one of the southerners, an "old friend" of all. Canadian Museum of Civilization researchers reported in 2011 that her granddaughter, Rosie Albert of Inuvik, recalled her grandmother warning that "You are going to be good for nothing like your grandfather! Always reading and writing while [Pannigabluk] hunted and did all the work!"[12]

R.M. Anderson, who was the leader of the "southern party" devoted to scientific work, would likely have agreed. He came to detest Stefansson, considering him irresponsible and willing to place scientific observation as a secondary goal to front-page news. In his 1961 obituary of Anderson, Diamond Jenness called him "a splendid companion, who cheerfully carried his share of the load." "He was," Jenness continued, "a reserved man, rather diffident, he was never more happy than when he was sitting at the door of a tent, legs outstretched, skinning a mixed bag of shrews, marmots, sandpipers, and perhaps one or two eiders, the while keeping both ears attuned to the murmur of wind and water, and the twittering of the birds."[13] With such different personalities and ambitions, the expedition was plagued by dissent and disaster: of the thirty-two men who gathered in Nome, Alaska in July 1913 to begin the expedition, seventeen would never return. Most died when the *Karluk*, the lead ship, became trapped in ice, drifting westwards and sinking in January 1914 near Wrangel Island off the Siberian coast.

Stefansson had left the ship with five others in September, supposedly to hunt caribou, but the ship drifted off. Thanks to the extraordinary bravery and skill of Captain Bob Bartlett, who travelled almost 700 miles across the Russian mainland to Alaska to organize a rescue party for the survivors on Wrangel Island, eleven survivors were picked up in September 1914 after enduring unimaginable hardship. The *Karluk* tragedy has stained the reputation of the expedition and of Stefansson, and the bitterness between Anderson and Stefansson endured and influenced later historians. The eminent Arctic anthropologist Robert McGhee, for example, scornfully describes Stefansson as "an explorer who thought of himself as an anthropologist," while historians Janice Cavell and Jeff Noakes accuse him of "relentless self-aggrandizement and publicity-seeking" while never admitting to mistakes.[14]

Stefansson's flaws were many, the expedition's direction uncertain, and the human tragedies enormous. Canadians, some suggest, have been particularly harsh on Stefansson.[15] Nevertheless, the impact of the Canadian Arctic Expedition upon the western Arctic was profound for its people and for Canada and Canadians more generally. When Stefansson first approached Borden for additional funding for an expedition for which he had already raised $50,000 from American institutions, the prime minister surprised him by telling him that Canada must fund it completely and that "any lands yet undiscovered in those northern regions should be added to Canadian territory." Borden, as mentioned above, was a lawyer who was concerned about the weight of the Canadian legal case. He wanted to strengthen it, and Stefansson, for all his flaws, had the profile to draw attention to Canada's northern presence.

That Borden did not share the disgruntlement of Stefansson's colleagues and many of Ottawa's public servants with the explorer is clear in the preface he wrote for Stefansson's *The Friendly Arctic*, which appeared in 1921. He pointed, correctly, to the "many thousands of square miles" that had been added to Canadian territory and to the abundance of "scientific observations." He did not note that the four large Arctic islands discovered by Stefansson's party in 1915–1916 were the only ones claimed by an explicitly Canadian expedition. In the fashion begun by Frobisher when he named lands in honour of English authorities, the Canadian islands took the names of politicians Arthur Meighen, James Lougheed, and, of course, Robert Borden. In 1947, the Liberals finally got their island when Prime Minister William Lyon Mackenzie King bestowed his name upon the last.

Borden was even more explicit in 1921, shortly after he retired as prime minister, than he had been when he met Stefansson in 1912 about how much ownership or sovereignty mattered. In the fashion of earlier prime ministers who extolled the opening of the Canadian West, where riches would abound as the railways extended their way, Borden accepted Stefansson's argument that the Arctic presented endless opportunity and potential riches. In a strange introduction to *The Friendly Arctic*, Borden wrote:

> The gayest social season among the Eskimos is in the winter months. During the war there was scarcely fuel both in Europe and on this continent. In a leading London hotel so uncomfortable did I find my sitting-room in December 1918, that I was constrained to seek a supply of firewood from the Canadian Corps, then working near Windsor. About that time Stefansson and his party, possessing an abundance of fuel, which the country supplied, were sitting in their short-sleeves, hundreds of miles within the Arctic Circle, comfortably housed in an edifice which was constructed of snow blocks in less than three hours, ... while we shivered in this temperate zone, there was vast comfort in the vicinity of the North Pole ...

Borden even suggested that life in the North would bring better health to "European races" that "last for no more than three generations" in tropical climes. The North would be the new Canadian West, fertile land to breed a hardy, long-lived race.[16]

Borden knew the doubts about Stefansson on the part of his own officials, but he placed Stefansson's efforts in the broader perspective of creating a distinctive Canadian identity in the aftermath of the horrors of World War I. Canada had got nothing out of war, Borden wrote in his diary, except "recognition." Postwar Canadian nationalism incorporated a strong northern and Arctic dimension that was reflected in literature and art. Stefansson's gift for publicity and his undoubted bravery and bravado meant that Canada received recognition and a sharper identity as a nation, and part of that was with a new, invigorating northern frontier. As noted in the preface, literary scholar Sherrill Grace, like Borden, has celebrated Stefansson's *The Friendly Arctic* as a brilliant marshalling of "materials—his language and other modes of representation—to argue the case for a *friendly* Arctic that will serve precise political, social, economic, and national ends." He does so, in Grace's words, "with fists flying," breaking his way "into the system, forcing a rupture, creating a discontinuity, resisting and challenging," while still relying on the "very discursive formation within which he must operate, by which he is himself ruled and appropriated." Two Americans led the Canadian Arctic Expedition and only five of the fifteen scientists were Canadian because of the absence of Arctic-oriented scientists in Canadian universities, and there were few Canadians among the whalers, sailors, and roustabouts who knew the Arctic.[17] Yet the expedition and its interpretation fitted the times well. Stefansson's *Friendly Arctic* was published the year when the census first indicated that more Canadians lived in towns and cities than on farms. In Toronto's Rosedale ravine, far from the Beaufort Sea, the Group of Seven landscape artists marshalled their materials to construct images of Canada as a northern nation. In the construction of a national identity that incorporated the North to the pole, the Canadian Arctic Expedition and Stefansson joined others in laying many bricks. The architecture was romantic, far from functional, and the place for people—those who had long dwelt in the North and those of the South—was not well-defined. But the bricks remained. Canada's rethinking of its own place in the world and its geography took place in a period of great fluidity in the international order.

The Arctic between the Wars

In the last years of World War I and the first years of peace, empires dissolved, new nations appeared, and a different world political order took form. The impact on the Arctic was profound. The force of nationalism, however, was undiminished in the new states that clamoured for their place on the international stage. Among them was Finland, which had long been part of the Russian Empire and whose nationalism possessed a strong northern sense. Russia itself, which had the largest and most developed Arctic presence before World War I, made peace with Germany and endured a bitter civil war in which the Bolsheviks triumphed. The allies reacted to the Russian disorder and sent an expeditionary force including Americans, French, British, Canadians, and Japanese to support the White Russian forces fighting the Bolsheviks. The anti-Bolsheviks occupied the key Arctic cities of Murmansk and Arkhangelsk in 1918. There were thoughts of occupying Siberia, but by the early 1920s, it was clear the effort was futile and only the Japanese kept their forces in former Russian territory.

While the Russians were preoccupied with their internal struggles, the protracted negotiations of the Treaty of Versailles had created the League of Nations and a new hope that international law could have substance it had previously lacked. But the most remarkable innovation in the postwar period as far as the Arctic was concerned involved the Svalbard archipelago in the Arctic north of Norway. First discovered by Barentsz, settled by the Dutch, quarrelled over by several nations in support of their whalers and later their miners, Spitsbergen (the name for the largest island and previously usually that of the entire peninsula) was without nationality, an impossible situation in the postwar national world. The result was the Svalbard Treaty of 1920, which gave Norway sovereignty over the archipelago, but a limited one. Others could freely engage in mining, scientific, and economic activities. Alone among the many experiments of the time—free cities such as Danzig, transfers such as the Saarland, and mandates such as Palestine—the Svalbard compromise has endured.

Today Norwegians and Russians have mining operations, and Poles, Indians, and Chinese are among the researchers on Spitsbergen. Now, as then, it stands out as a triumph for common sense over conflict.

Svalbard was an exception. The early twenties, more generally, were marked by the extension of exclusive national sovereignty, which had implications for the Arctic. There was much jousting as claims were sorted out in an Arctic world where legal uncertainties abounded and boundaries were unclear. During World War I the Danes sold the Danish Antilles to the United States for $25 million and assurances that the Americans would not contest Danish sovereignty over Greenland. Iceland, which possessed "home rule" in its relationship with Denmark, declared its sovereignty in December 1918, although it continued its link with the Danish crown. In the peacemaking process, the Danes sought similar assurances about Greenland from other major powers and their Scandinavian neighbours. After initially agreeing, the Norwegians, facing internal political pressure from nationalists, pulled back and occupied Greenland's eastern shore, which it dubbed "Eric the Red Land." The case went to the Permanent Court of International Justice after negotiations failed. The decision was finally rendered on September 5, 1933, in favour of Denmark. It was a landmark case that would have a lasting impact on international law.[18]

For the Canadians, the period from 1918 to 1925 was marked by "acts of occupation" by which Ottawa decided to try to clear up ambiguities in Canadian Arctic claims.* There was a dash of imperialism

---

*The appearance of Stefansson's *The Friendly Arctic* in 1921 was followed in 1922 by the more influential *Nanook of the North*, the first full-length documentary film. Nanook, a Northern Quebec Inuk whose actual name was Allakariallak, hunts walruses with spears, builds igloos, and meets the challenges of the world's harshest climate. The silent film was an immediate success although some later critics pointed out correctly that by the 1920s, hunters used rifles, not spears, and that Nanook's "wife" was actually Flaherty's companion. The film idealizes Nanook and the Inuit more generally as, in Flaherty's words, "kindly, brave, [and] simple." The film, nevertheless, is a great achievement. In 2005, prominent American film critic Roger Ebert said that "Nanook is one of the most vital and unforgettable human beings ever recorded in film." It endures in its entirety on YouTube: www.youtube.com/watch?v=yW6d6B_R2nM.

and, frankly, absurdity when in 1921, the year when *The Friendly Arctic* appeared, Stefansson connived to have the Canadian government send an expedition to claim Wrangel Island, which is located directly above Siberia, to establish a presence and a Canadian claim. The "wrangle over Wrangel Island" was a tragicomedy that ended with the death of most of the occupiers, including its leader Allan Crawford, as well as the rejection of Crawford's claim to possession of the island for the British Empire and Canada. After this debacle, the support for Stefansson in Ottawa vanished. He was blamed for Crawford's death by the young man's family, who released a statement indicating that Stefansson had deceived Crawford and that "Stefansson, who had no other British subject available to lead his expedition, appealed to our son's patriotism in such a way that the boy felt it his duty to go and raise the flag on Wrangel, and he died in the belief that he was dying for the empire."

Spurred on by patriotic zeal, the House of Commons unanimously paid tribute to Crawford's heroism and nationalism and implicitly condemned Stefansson and bade him go away. He did.[19] This humiliation, however, was counterbalanced by genuine success in the Eastern Arctic where the Canadians managed to work with the Danes to sort out conflicting claims and also with the Americans to establish Canadian sovereignty. Moreover, the civil-servant geographer James White, who had developed the sector principle put forth by Bernier in the first decade of the century, applied the concept to the Canadian claim to the Arctic lands (not waters) between the sectors. The Soviet Union followed suit for the ocean above Siberia in 1926 and thereby indirectly solidified the Canadian claim. Naturally, others objected since they lacked the elongated coasts of Canada and the Soviet Union. The sector principle would linger long as a foundation for Canadian claims in the Arctic, reappearing whenever other powers seemed threatening.[20]

Ambiguity still remained in the case of the islands claimed by Otto Sverdrup in the High Arctic. As noted above, neither the Swedes nor the successor Norwegian government had pressed the claim, but Sverdrup, who was rightly hailed as one of the greatest Arctic explorers in Norway and Europe, was still alive and a reminder of the claim. The Norwegians had occasionally raised the question of the islands Sverdrup had found, and their questions annoyed the Canadians. In October 1929, Lester Pearson, a young Canadian diplomat recently hired by the fledgling Department of External Affairs, wrote a memorandum urging Canada to settle the claim to strengthen the sector principle, which he thought a "practical solution of the Arctic question." Sverdrup had hinted that he would personally sign off the claims and provide his maps if the Canadians compensated him for the cost of the claim. With the Depression beginning, the Canadians proved tough negotiators, denying Sverdrup a pension and rejecting his $200,000 request. In 1930, the Norwegians gave up their claim while rejecting the sector principle in their statement, and Sverdrup settled for $67,000. He died fifteen days after the agreement was announced. The Canadians got a good bargain.[21]

In his memorandum on the Sverdrup claims, Lester Pearson made a case for Arctic exceptionalism, an assertion that the Arctic did not fit neatly within existing international law. The settlement of the Danish–Norwegian dispute over Greenland by the Permanent Court of International Justice reflected the evolution of the notion of law within the West that had developed from the rise of the national state in the previous three centuries. But, as scholars have noted, the very successful assertion of Canadian and Danish sovereignty in the Arctic created the foundations for state authority in the North, allowing the instruments of the state—its officials, its military, and its legal concepts and procedures—"to exert control over almost every aspect of Native people's lives."[22] It reflected habits of authority, ownership and, not least, superiority that had marked the expansion of Europe for over four centuries. The Inuit and others of the Arctic did not possess a sense of property rights and of ownership of land, as Europeans and southern North Americans did. Moreover, their traditions of community jarred against the individualism that had marked European society since the

Renaissance. Stefansson's *The Friendly Arctic,* as we have seen, bore the enthusiasm of technological modernism. As a recent historian has said of Stefansson, "No Muir or Thoreau, he longed to see oil wells, natural gas fields, deep-water ports and airstrips sprawling across the Arctic landscape, from Hudson Bay's northern shores to the mouth of the Mackenzie." His intellectual heirs remain plentiful.[23] Gradually the web of Canadian justice and sovereignty was spun over the North, and those who dwelt there became ensnared within its filaments. The Royal Canadian Mounted Police were the principal performers in the various "acts of occupation" of the High North. They enforced justice, registered births, and even doled out medicines when needed, but most of all they were there to turn *terra nullius* into *terra Canadensis.*

The establishment of a detachment at the Bache Peninsula on the east coast of Ellesmere Island illustrates the extent to which the Canadians would go to establish their presence. There were no humans within hundreds of kilometres of the post. It was almost impossible to supply, and conditions were extreme for the police. Yet Bache had a post office, which stamped letters that were eventually posted in Halifax. Even customs forms were available in the extremely unlikely event they were needed. Eventually common sense prevailed and the post closed, but, as a recent historical study remarks, "the police were the entire face of government in the region" in the 1930s. Elsewhere, the Hudson's Bay Company continued to conduct its business, while the Canadian government assumed greater authority over the Inuit as a result of a Canadian Supreme Court case *Re Eskimos*, which held that the Inuit should be considered "Indians" in a legal sense. Although this decision was not followed up in legislation, in practice the federal government had assumed educational responsibility and had given Canadian churches the right to establish residential schools for both Inuit and Indians. For the first time, children left their families, came under the authority of their teachers, and endured far too often psychological, physical, and sexual abuse. The consequences were enormous. On the one hand, the indigenous people of the North learned the languages, skills, and traditions of the South in these deliberately assimilationist institutions. On the other hand, the experience produced alienation and anger and eventually legal cases.[24]

But however strange and difficult it was for indigenous peoples in the Canadian North, it was not as menacing as the situation in the Soviet Arctic. Joseph Stalin, alas, knew the Russian North well. It had captured the vicious revolutionary's imagination when he was imprisoned just south of the Arctic Circle from 1914 to 1917. When he became the Soviet's supreme ruler, he located many islands of his infamous prison network, the "gulag archipelago" in Siberia and the North. The North for Stalin contained "colossal wealth" that, through "Soviet organization," could create the foundations for a dominant world power. The traditions of indigenous peoples and, indeed, nearly all others, were pushed aside. Eager to realize an old Tsarist dream and to fulfill the promise of his first Five Year Plan, Stalin decreed that a White Sea–Baltic Sea canal be built to link the Arctic with the historic commerce centres on the Baltic.

Over 100,000 prisoners worked with primitive tools in dreadful conditions to build a 227-kilometre canal in only twenty months. The North became a place of horrors and lies—the canal was too shallow to be of any use—but the Soviet North became central to the command economy and military might of the Soviet Union. In population and development, the Soviet and later the Russian North would be the dominant presence in the Arctic world.[25]

Despite the great differences between the Canada's northern Mounties and Stalin's gulag thugs, the two nations with the largest Arctic geography after 1930 shared many characteristics. Both extended the state's presence in the North and carried out "acts of occupation" that asserted ownership of the Arctic. While Soviet justice was brutal, summary, and indifferent to traditional customs, the Canadian government similarly imposed "British justice" upon indigenous peoples to establish that the North was Canadian and subject to its control. There was, in Canada as with the Danes in Greenland, a paternalistic flavour to justice, but its purpose was clear. In the 1924 trial of two Inuit, Alikomiak and Tatamigana, the judge was blunt in his charge to the jury: "... although you may feel that you should have some consideration for the simple mentality of these primitive people, yet you also feel that you owe a duty to your country, who extends to them its generous protection in every way." He made the trial's purpose and the jury's duty clear: "Make these tribes understand that the stern but at the same time just hand of British justice extends also to these northern shores." Their fate was not in doubt. The hangman had brought a portable gallows on which Alikomiak and Tatamigana died when its trap door sprung open on February 1, 1924.[26]

Hanging was ancient. The airplane was modern, and both of the major Arctic powers became enthralled with it and, for a period, dirigibles or Zeppelins, as the Germans named them. The Arctic, with its exotic blend of romance, danger, and "newness," fitted the spirit of the interwar years well. Stefansson's "friendly Arctic," as we have seen, was strongly based upon the modernist premise that technology would overcome the barriers of climate and the limitations of human beings. His enthusiasm for the promise of a new age unlike any other was of course widely shared, and it animated not only Stalin's statist and authoritarian plans to develop the Arctic but also, more happily, the individual daring of pilots and adventurers who sought to tame the Arctic through modern technology. Stalin glorified pilots as the personification of the "New Soviet Man" and led the celebrations of the remarkable feats of Valery Chkalov, who flew from Moscow over the North Pole before landing in Vancouver in the State of Washington.[27] The great Arctic explorer Roald Amundsen also became fascinated with the possibilities of flight and, in 1925, with the support of an American millionaire adventurer, flew farther north than any plane had ever reached. He passed over the North Pole in an airship the following year and may have been the first to do so. Later research has created profound doubts that the celebrated American polar explorer Richard Byrd actually reached the North Pole in an airplane on May 9, 1926, a few days before Amundsen in the airship *Norge* definitely passed over the Pole. In 1928, however, Amundsen died when his plane disappeared on a mission to rescue a missing Arctic airship. Great dangers still lurked, but there was a widespread belief that there were stunning opportunities and that the extraordinary isolation characteristic of Arctic exploration from Frobisher through Franklin to the twentieth century had ended with the discovery of flight and radio communications.[28]

The interwar years were exciting ones for polar scientists and explorers and their promoters in the South. Richard Byrd became a celebrity in the fashion of Charles Lindbergh. Moreover, scientists came together in a second International Polar Year (IPY) in 1932–1933, which marked the fiftieth anniversary of the first IPY. The difference between the nineteenth- and the twentieth-century polar years was striking, particularly in its emphasis upon how radio and air transport could open the Arctic; and the cooperation was exceptional among Soviets, Americans, Germans, British, Scandinavians, Canadians, and others. Indeed, the Soviets were remarkably enthusiastic, and their polar scientists, who wrote largely in German because of their German education, made significant contributions to the science of meteorology. Because of Stalin's personal interest in Arctic development, Soviet scientists continued to have support that other nations withdrew during the first years of the Depression, although some of these same scientists were to become the victims of the mindless violence of the Stalinist purges of the late 1930s. Nevertheless, genuine scientific advances occurred in a spirit of enthusiastic cooperation. Unfortunately, that spirit was lost as the decade moved towards its dreadful end in September 1939.[29]

The Arctic War

The German and Soviet assaults on Poland in September 1939, followed by the Soviet war on Finland and the German attack on Norway, began a new chapter in the history of the Arctic, one with unexpected turns, the major one being Hitler's decision to attack the Soviet Union in June 1941. With German dominance of the Western European heartland, the beleaguered Soviet Union had only the Arctic ports for a lifeline to their new allies as the German armies swept towards Leningrad and Moscow. During the war Murmansk and Archangel (Arkhangelsk) received seventy-eight convoys with approximately 1,400 merchant ships escorted by the American, British, and Canadian navies, with the first arriving as early as September 1941. The conditions were extreme and losses were great, but the Arctic became a major theatre for the European war. When the Japanese attacked Pearl Harbor on December 7, 1941, the western North American Arctic also became a major military focus. On the west coast of Canada and the United States, fears of Japanese raids billowed, and the Aleutian Islands of Alaska seemed a tempting target for Japanese to hop along to the mainland. In June 1942, the Japanese captured Kiska and Attu, and the Japanese success had considerable psychological import for North Americans. Suddenly Alaska became a potential target, and the Americans shifted enormous resources to reinforce the region, while the Canadians moved troops to the Pacific to reassure a fearful British Columbia. The American military had already convinced Congress that a highway through Canada to Alaska was essential. Construction of the road began in March 1942 and was completed on October 28, 1942. Canadians gave permission to the Americans to build the route on the condition that its ownership revert to Canada when the war ended. The impact of the war upon Alaska was monumental, and the presence of the military during the war fundamentally shaped the territory and future state.[30]

Tens of thousands of Americans encountered the Arctic during the war in Alaska, Canada, and Greenland, which the United States occupied on April 8, 1941, one year after Denmark fell to the Nazis. The British had invaded Iceland in May 1940 but transferred its defence to the still-neutral but sympathetic Americans in July 1941. There were three principal consequences: first, the recognition that the Arctic and its waters had great strategic significance in modern warfare; second, a growing nervousness among Canadian officials about the Americans swarming over the Canadian northwest, and a resulting search by Canada for a counterbalance; and third, a broader knowledge of the Arctic on the part of Arctic nations, particularly the United States and the Soviet Union. The Arctic lifeline to the West inevitably and ineluctably enhanced the position of the Arctic in the minds of Soviet leaders. In the United States, where normally persuasion was preferred over the compulsion that Stalinism favoured, the Arctic's charms were emphasized. Stefansson's "friendly Arctic" reappeared in public debate. In August 1944, Lt. Col. Charles Hubbard of the United States Army reflected upon his wartime experience in a lead article in the popular and influential *Saturday Evening Post* entitled "The Arctic Isn't So Tough."[31]

Hubbard's personal ambition was to establish weather stations throughout the North. His case seemed strong: the Atlantic and Murmansk convoys had established the importance of weather observation for naval operations, and the air war had also shown that meteorology was an essential science for aviation. Hubbard avowed: "The air seems likely to become even more important than the oceans as a medium of transportation ... If we are planning either a trans-ocean flight or a Sunday-School picnic, forecasts control our normal activities in a thousand different ways. They help the farmer protect his crops and the builder choose auspicious days to dig foundations for a new house." Hubbard proposed weather stations throughout the Arctic islands and Greenland, where the United States had a large wartime presence. The stations would be prefabricated and include the most up-to-date equipment, notably radio transmitters that would link the "Arctic denizens to civilization down south." Each week the "denizens" could chat with their families as with the "family telephone." There would be no problem of recruitment, for the war had exposed the real North and it was "friendly." "We must stop thinking of it as a white hell," Hubbard advised. "A measure of courage, perhaps, is required to appreciate the beauty of the arctic, but to those who are not afraid of solitude, nor of themselves, it is very beautiful indeed." Radio and air travel had changed the Arctic utterly: "arctic travel has become simply a technical specialty—a trade rather than an art."

Soon there would be flights over the Pole, which was "almost exactly halfway on the Great-Circle route between the centers of America and Russia [sic]." And the Soviets had shown the way towards these closer links with "well over 100 observation points above the Arctic Circle, strung along the Siberian coast and on all the outlying islands, even the most northerly Crown Prince Rudolf Island in Franz Josef Land, 1,000 miles north of the Circle." The Soviet "business of arctic development" was a model for Canadians and Americans to emulate.[32]

Hubbard wrote his essay the year after *Time* magazine declared Stalin its "man of the year." Portraits of "Uncle Joe" adorned many public places, and even Canadian diplomats complained privately that the Americans were not giving the Soviets the credit they deserved.[33] The Soviets had turned the tide in the East before the Allies landed on Normandy beaches just as Hubbard's article appeared. But the grand alliance against Fascism crumbled soon after the Soviets met the Americans on the River Elbe on April 25, 1945. The Iron Curtain soon descended upon Central Europe, and the Arctic became a major front in the new Cold War between the West and the Soviet Union. Suddenly the geopolitical place of the Arctic changed dramatically.

However, some parts of Hubbard's dream of multilateral cooperation across the Arctic were realized, although the fear of war rather than the dividends of peace provided the motivation. By 1950 the Canadians, Americans, and Danes had agreed upon weather stations stretching from Alaska to Thule in northern Greenland. Hubbard himself supervised the creation of the northernmost station, Alert, on the tip of Canada's Ellesmere Island in the spring and early summer of 1950. The conditions were extreme, with temperatures approaching –40 degrees Celsius. On

July 31, 1950, Hubbard flew in from Thule to assist in the work. His RCAF Lancaster crashed into the sea and all aboard died. Snow fences were placed around their corpses to keep away the foxes.[34] At his family's request, his body was interred at Alert, where his dream endured.

THREE

The Cold War
Chills the Arctic

In July 1946, when the Cold War was still young, Canadian Ambassador
to the United States Lester Pearson wrote "Canada Looks 'Down
North'" in the prestigious American journal *Foreign Affairs*. "Not long
ago," he claimed, "this vast [Canadian Arctic] territory was considered
to be little more than a frozen northern desert without any economic
value or any political or strategic importance." The article contained
many intimations of the impending Cold War. Reflecting fear and hope,
Pearson claimed Canada would work with the Soviet Union and others
in "exploiting to the full the peaceful possibilities of the Northern
Hemisphere," but he made clear that Canada's wartime alliance with
the United States mattered most. Although he did not mention the Soviet
Union, Pearson warned that "a policy of exclusive and isolated Arctic
development by any one country" in "this age of atom bombs and
jet-propelled planes" would "create suspicion in the minds of others."
Although Canada had a vast northern realm, Pearson concluded that

the "Great Powers," the Soviet Union and the United States, would decide whether the development of the North would take place in an atmosphere of "friendly" cooperation or one of "national rivalries, fear, and ambitions." To his great regret, the latter triumphed.[1]

The Bomb and the Bomber: 1946–1957

As noted in Chapter 2, Charles Hubbard's vision of weather stations linked together through a peaceful, modernizing Arctic was shattered by the confrontation between the West and the Soviet Union. Weather stations were of fundamental importance to air and naval operations during the Cold War, but for them, as for so much else, there was a sharp line dividing East and West. The Soviet explosion of an atomic bomb in 1949 and the subsequent tests of thermonuclear bombs by the United States and the USSR in 1952 and 1953 respectively brought new focus on the Arctic, the shortest route to the heartlands of America and the USSR. The first radar stations in North America were a string along the fiftieth parallel called appropriately the Pinetree Line. A Mid-Canada Line followed and then a Distant Early Warning (DEW) Line above the Arctic Circle. Construction began in December 1954 and was completed on July 31, 1957. Stretching across just over 8,000 kilometres of the High Arctic, the construction of the DEW Line had an enormous impact on the people who built it, those who ran the stations, and, not least, the indigenous people who faced a transformation of the land where they had long been almost alone. But the builders barely noticed they were there.[2]

"The Arctic, desolate, sage, remote," *The Dew Line Story* begins. This fifties documentary, sponsored by Western Electric with the cooperation of the United States Air Force, celebrates the building of the line in the "wilderness," which was "not too bad for caribou and polar bears" but "no place for human beings," a statement obviously contradicted by centuries of human occupation in the Arctic.[3] The film captured the fears of the moment. The Arctic had become a major focus of North

American military interests. It involved a delicate blend of cooperation forged by the perception of a common threat and a continuing concern on the part of Canada for sovereignty. There was an inherent paradox, because Canadian northern efforts in the Arctic were not only a deterrent to Soviet attack but also a counterbalance to the overwhelming American presence. The Canadian military, represented in the presence of the radar stations, occasional operations, and bases, replaced the RCMP as the "primary uniformed symbols of Canadian authority to safeguard the North—from friend and foe."[4]

Fear in the West of a common enemy compelled cooperation in the Arctic in the postwar era that would have been unthinkable in the 1930s. In Europe, Norway and Denmark broke their historic tradition of neutrality and joined the North Atlantic Treaty Organization (NATO) at its creation in 1949, thus linking their militaries with the West. As its contribution to NATO, Denmark agreed to allow the United States to build a massive airbase at Thule on the northwest tip of Greenland, 1,200 kilometres north of the Arctic Circle. However, Denmark, like Norway, refused foreign bases and nuclear weapons in continental Europe, even though Norway shared a border with the Soviet Union. Both countries had discussed a Baltic defence pact with Sweden in the early Cold War years, but the Swedes decided to remain neutral. History, present ideologies, and future fears combined to undermine Scandinavian unity during the Cold War.[5] In a sense, however, the closer collaboration of Denmark and Norway with the capitalist West meant that Sweden, a socialist state, could maintain a balance. Finland's position was much more difficult. After the war, unlike the Baltic states and Eastern Europe, Soviet troops did not occupy their soil and they maintained a precarious freedom, whose price was permitting a Soviet naval base near their capital and a Moscow-inclining neutrality. "Finlandization" was the scornful West German word for Finland's kowtowing to Moscow, but Finland did survive the war and the long difficult peace that followed.[6]

"The entire ring of the Arctic," historian John McCannon writes, "was strung by the Soviets and NATO alike with military facilities like a necklace beaded with pearls." The necklace thickened when the Soviets came closest to the West, notably on opposite sides of the Bering Strait and in the Kola Peninsula and the White Sea coast where the Soviets housed their massive Northern Fleet with its hundreds of submarines. Alaska's population swelled as its proximity to the Soviets brought hundreds of thousands of American military personnel to the North. The North bristled with nuclear weapons at the great air bases such as Eielson near Fairbanks in Alaska, Keflavik near Reykjavik in NATO-member Iceland, and, of course, throughout the Soviet North. The Soviets moved off the indigenous population, established a nuclear test facility, and exploded an estimated 224 nuclear weapons on Novaya Zemlya that spread radiation rapidly throughout the Siberian Arctic with unknown but certainly deadly consequences for human and animal life. These tests were the worst example of the despoliation of the Arctic during the Cold War, but other installations in the East and the West also left a black mark. With reason, McCannon entitles his chapter on the Arctic in the Cold War "Contaminations."[7]

The impact of these military installations upon the indigenous peoples of the North was profound, forever altering their ways of life as Cold War security trumped all other considerations. The Western approach was less brutal than that of the Soviets: at Thule the Americans, with Danish consent, simply moved off the local Inuit, but in justifying displacing the small local population, the Americans also referred to the negative impact a sudden exposure to modernity could have on what they viewed as a Stone-Age people. Though not for the same security reasons, Canada showed a similarly cavalier attitude to indigenous peoples when it moved seventeen Inuit families from Port Harrison (Inukjuak) in northern Quebec and Pond Inlet on Baffin Island to Resolute Bay and Grise Fiord in the High Arctic. The move was, in the words of a 2010 Canadian government apology, "due to

deteriorating traditional harvesting, health, and social conditions."
But life for the Inuit was initially much worse in the High North,
where flimsy tents and little support made for a miserable existence.
It was a deep wound to the proud Inuit who remained suspicious that
sovereignty and security concerns, not their welfare, had been the true
motivation of the Canadian government.[8] The motivations remain a
deeply contested subject. *Exile,* the extraordinary film by the Inuk
filmmaker Zacharias Kunuk, captures the agony of the exile and the
habits of authority of the Canadian state in the 1950s. Although it
does not directly dispute the analysis of the apology, the testimony of
the relocated is an eloquent indictment of the carelessness and abuse
of power.[9]

When the Canadian government made its apology in 2010, which
was based on a Royal Commission report, the indigenous presence and
voice was infinitely stronger than it was in the early Cold War years.
Considered by many in the interwar years as a dying people, the indigenous people of the North began to grow in numbers in the postwar
period. Although the Cold War brought militarization, it also meant
that hundreds of thousands of Canadian and American southerners
encountered the Arctic. Despite the early fears of "contact" between
the southerners and the Inuit, the barriers tumbled down quickly as the
former found they needed the knowledge of the northerners and the
latter discovered employment at a time when traditional ways of life
were increasingly difficult to maintain. As early as 1947, the Canadian
military turned to the Inuit and Dene to assist them in defending the
North. The Canadian Rangers became the "eyes and ears" of the North,
and the Norwegians and Danes also used indigenous peoples as a type of
local militia. Given a war-surplus Lee Enfield rifle and a badge for their
arm, the Canadian Rangers guided southern soldiers, translated their
words, and occasionally took a shot when a dark object broke through
the ice, no matter whether it was a Soviet or an American submarine
rising from beneath Arctic waters.[10]

The transformation of northern indigenous peoples in these times was complex and occurred in different ways. A study of the Inuit of the Central Arctic, for example, traces how the Aivilingmiut were "at the top" of a hierarchy that took form when government initiatives created more communities with a greater number of people. "They were more deeply involved with white men, at an earlier date, than any other group. They formed the first Inuit home guard and were the first to become employees of white men on a large scale, the first to live in wooden houses, the first to learn English, and the first to produce a mixed-blood generation." The differences between the Aivilingmiut and the "low-ranking Ahiarmiut were their relative economic positions and the degree to which they had instituted or accepted change." Even though the Aivilingmiut's adaptation attracted complaint and derision from other west Hudson Bay Inuit who largely continued traditional hunting, fishing, and nomadic ways, they occupied the "highest rung" while those who were "the last to give up dependence on the land, the last to move into government communities ... came to occupy the lowest rung on the Inuit social ladder."[11]

As the face of the Arctic changed on the ground and in the waters, a new presence in the heaven above would have profound long-term consequences for the North. In October 1957 the Soviet Union launched Sputnik, the first satellite to circle the Earth. The stunning news was accompanied by the successful Soviet test of an intercontinental ballistic missile. The Americans produced the first nuclear submarine in 1954, and by 1960 they carried nuclear-tipped Polaris missiles. The manned bomber remained part of the superpowers' arsenals but was no longer the dominant strategic weapon. By the early 1960s, the DEW Line was becoming obsolete and the military was turning away from the Arctic while still retaining a large presence, especially in Alaska. But life for northern peoples could not return to what it had been. While the North receded from the thoughts of North American military planners, its significance rose in the South, particularly in the imagination. Alaska, whose population rose from 72,524 in 1940 to 226,167 in 1960, attained statehood on January 3, 1959. Hollywood quickly responded in 1960 with *North to Alaska*, featuring John Wayne and a number one "hit" in its title song, "North to Alaska," whose lyrics repeated that the "rush" was on.[12]

Resources, Sovereignty, and Northern Peoples: 1958–1980

A new enthusiasm for the Canadian North appeared after Progressive Conservative John Diefenbaker became prime minister in 1957. He was a feisty defence lawyer from Prince Albert, Saskatchewan, which dubbed itself the "gateway to the North." His family had moved to a small prairie cabin when Diefenbaker was a child, and he would forever bear the romance of the opening of the West in his bones. With a courtroom lawyer's sense of the dramatic and a politician's shrewd sense of the moment, Diefenbaker grasped upon a "northern vision" for Canada. In his opening campaign speech in 1958, Diefenbaker called for a national development policy to create a new "sense of National Purpose and National Destiny." Canada's first prime minister, Sir John A. Macdonald, "opened the West. He saw Canada from East to West." "I," Diefenbaker proclaimed, "see a new Canada—a Canada of the North." His government would "open" the North, build roads to resources and riches, and bring a bounty to Canadians akin to the glorious days when the West first boomed. With patriotic flourishes and assertions of "Canada First," Diefenbaker exclaimed, "There is a new imagination now. The Arctic." Writing over four decades later on Canada and the idea of North, literary scholar Sherrill Grace calls Diefenbaker's address "a classic."[13]

Perhaps it was, in the category of rhetoric. Historians, however, give Diefenbaker poor marks for accomplishing his vision, particularly the ambitious plans to extract resources from the North. Most resources remained too far from markets and too difficult to extract in the harsh conditions of the Arctic, and the lack of environmental controls made some mines lasting scars upon the North. Nevertheless, Grace is surely correct in her argument that Diefenbaker seized upon a particular moment in the Canadian idea of the Arctic and gained political success from his action. There were three particular reasons for the new importance of the Arctic, and they are significant in understanding its future.

First, Diefenbaker responded to what he rightly called "a new imagination," one building on the earlier work by artists such as Lawren Harris, whose mystical, sculptural northern landscapes became ubiquitous, and administrator-novelist James Houston who encouraged Inuit sculptors in the early 1950s to organize a cooperative to market "Eskimo art," which quickly gained an international audience. Kenojuak Ashevak's 1960 stonecut, *The Enchanted Owl,* became iconic, and the artist, who remained in the North, became a representative of an enduring, imaginative, and intriguing people. In this transformation of attitude, novelist Farley Mowat was very influential. His 1952 *People of the Deer* is an emotional description of famine among the Ahalmiut (or Ahiarmiut) and a searing indictment of Canadian government indifference. Mowat, often derided by critics in the North and the South as "Hardly Know It," later admitted that his story was second-hand and that people and events were invented. But the book garnered international acclaim and appeared quickly on southern school curriculums. The effect was remarkable: "A cause was born: Save the Inuit. The government jumped. By 1960 the surviving Ahalmiut were relocated to the coast of Hudson Bay. Whole towns were erected, and emergency food was shipped." Mowat remains controversial, but critic Tim Querengesser in *Up Here,* a northern publication, rightly concludes: "No other writer, even today [2009], attracts to the north the audience and enthusiasm that Mowat does."[14]

Diefenbaker had probably not read Mowat. But in general terms he was correct: a new imagination had been born, one that was far more sensitive to northern peoples, and one that saw the impact of the South upon them through a different lens. In booming postwar Canada, government indifference or harshness had become increasingly unacceptable, and whatever the fantasies in Mowat's work, it bore an indisputable truth: the traditional institutions—the Mounties, the Hudson's Bay Company, the government agents, and even the military—had failed. They now seemed as outdated and inappropriate as the colonial structures tumbling down in Africa or, closer to home, the separate washrooms in the American South. The residential schools, which the government had entrusted to the churches and which had provided, in historian Jim Miller's words, the "minimum of schools that was politically acceptable to non-Native voters at the lowest possible cost," had produced young people who learned the basics of Western education, but at a horrible price revealed later in tales of extensive sexual and physical abuse of students by teachers.[15] From the broken debris of the past, new institutions would emerge that reflected a different imagination, one in which the North and its peoples possessed their own identity.

The second reason why the northern vision of Diefenbaker possessed an appeal was the enormous appetite for natural resources in the developed world. Diefenbaker's 1958 speech promised that his government would build "roads to resources" in the North. Diefenbaker's speechwriter, economist Merril Menzies, realized that Canada's North possessed great riches, which held a particular allure for Canadians in the South who celebrated the raucous spirit of the Klondike gold rush of 1898 and, more recently, the saga of speculator-prospector Gilbert LaBine's fabulous discovery of uranium at Great Bear Lake in the Northwest Territories in the early 1930s.* Gold continued to be mined in the Yukon, and mines clustered around Great Bear and Great Slave

---

*LaBine initially thought the mine's prize was radium, then the world's most expensive mineral at about $70 per gram. It was used medically to treat cancer and for "glow-in-the-dark" watch dials. Uranium at the time was an unwanted by-product. The market for radium was disappointing, and the mine closed in 1940 but reopened again in 1942 to mine uranium, which it began to ship to the United States' Manhattan Project that produced the atomic bomb. Hundreds of thousands of Canadians first encountered the LaBine story in a public school reader in the fifties. Robert Bothwell, *Eldorado: Canada's National Uranium Company* (Toronto: University of Toronto Press, 1984), 18–27, 95–120.

lakes, but the promise of a resource bonanza far exceeded the relatively meagre returns from mines in a harsh climate distant from the industrial heartland. In truth, Canadians knew little of what Arctic lands held, for geological exploration was rudimentary and largely by "canoe and foot until 1952." Then, the Geological Survey of Canada took advantage of new technological advances and aerial mapping, carrying out two major surveys, Operation Keewatin and Operation Franklin, in 1952 and 1954 respectively. These surveys identified vast potential oil, gas, and mineral resources in the North. Although new gold, silver, nickel, copper, zinc, and lead mines opened, they did so slowly, with the first being gold mines around existing settlements such as Yellowknife. For example, Cominco discovered vast reserves on Little Cornwallis Island in 1960, but only in 1970 did Polaris, the world's northernmost zinc mine, open. Moreover, the flood of cheap Middle Eastern oil in the later 1950s depressed the price and halted exploration. Marked by confusion and economic woes, the northern vision failed. The roads were never built and Arctic resources remained overwhelmingly in the ground.[16]

The race for resources also influenced the Scandinavians and the Soviets as new and old mines operated in northern Europe and Greenland. The Swedes had controversially shipped large quantities of iron to Nazi Germany from their mine at Kiruna above the Arctic Circle, and the lode continued to produce ore for postwar reconstruction. There were also northern mining operations in Norway and in Spitsbergen whose economic lifeblood was coal. But the Soviet Arctic development was the most striking. Taking advantage of its many rivers and, in the Murmansk area, a milder climate, the Soviet Union used its command economy to open the North. In the 1950s the Soviet Arctic produced three-quarters of the nation's gold, an amount second only to South Africa. Norilsk between the West Siberian Plain and the Central Siberian Plateau became one of the great mining centres of the world. Constructed by Stalin's prisoners in the thirties, the giant nickel, copper, cobalt, and platinum mines produced critical materials for the Communist bloc.

The Cambridge University journal *Polar Record* reported in 1960 that Norilsk produced most of the nickel for the Soviets through "a nice blend of compulsion ... and [an] appeal to patriotism." Directly comparing Norilsk and other Arctic enterprises, the article suggested that "the Soviet social and economic system has conferred decided advantages" over Canada in the development of the Arctic. For his part, Soviet admirer Vilhjalmur Stefansson speculated that, had Franklin Roosevelt or Mackenzie King been exiled to the Arctic as Stalin had been, Canada and the United States would have similarly had a "northward surge of development." Only when the Soviet Union fell was the human and environmental destruction of that surge apparent.[17]

Alaska shared the excitement and some of the wealth of the Klondike gold rush, but the twentieth century was marked more by military than mining operations, although the land was thought to contain great riches. The United States Navy had sufficient faith in energy prospects that it created a naval reserve on Alaska's north coast. Similarly intrigued by the geological promise, major oil companies followed John Wayne's advice to go "north to Alaska" after statehood was officially declared in January 1959 and received a huge bounty in 1968 with the discovery of oil and natural gas on the North Slope of Alaska. The Prudhoe Bay field was to make Alaska second only to Texas as a producer, and the find was to change fundamentally the political, economic, and social life of the Arctic. There was no doubt that the riches discovered were American, but what did these discoveries mean for other fields that lay beneath the vast Arctic Ocean or in areas of contested sovereignty, like the nearby Beaufort Sea where the boundary between Canada and the United States was unclear and where the Canadian Geological Survey had identified potential riches?[18] Similarly Norway and the Soviets jousted about their boundaries where radical improvements in offshore resource exploitation promised great rewards.

There was an additional factor that was important in considering the resources issue. Many of the resources that appeared, for example, on the

1954 Canadian Geological Survey study of oil and gas were offshore in the Beaufort Sea and off Melville Island. In the fifties, the limit of national jurisdiction under customary international law was three nautical miles. Were the riches beyond three miles a part of the "common heritage" like the world's great oceans? Within the bureaucracies of many Western countries—notably the United States, France, and the United Kingdom—Arctic issues were handled within offices that also bore responsibility for Antarctica.[19] In the 1950s many nations had made claims to Antarctica, although these claims remained unrecognized by international organizations. Antarctica, far more than the Arctic, became a focus of attention for international lawyers and scientists, even the Soviets. To the surprise of many, they agreed to participate in the International Geophysical Year (IGY) in 1957–1958, which the Americans had initially proposed. The IGY was based upon the earlier International Polar Years, although its scope was wider. Despite its broad ambit, the 1957–1958 IGY gave "special attention" to the Antarctic where its work provided new conclusions about the greater total ice content of the Earth.[20] The success had a sudden influence upon international politics and resulted in the Antarctic Treaty of 1959, the first arms control treaty of the Cold War and a significant statement that the resources of the Antarctic were not owned by any nation. The Treaty was initially signed by twelve nations, including the USSR, the United States, and others who had made claims to sovereignty over part of the region.[21]

What that meant specifically for the Arctic was, and is, unclear. Since the 1950s there have been many proponents of an "Arctic Treaty," and the allure of the demilitarization of the North, where nuclear weapons, submarines, and other military hardware were so abundant, was strong in certain quarters—but never in the Pentagon or Red Square, at least until Gorbachev called for a "zone of peace" in 1987.[22] Moreover, conditions in Antarctica made resource exploitation unlikely, if not impossible, in 1959. By the sixties, however, resource development was proceeding quickly in the Arctic. More troubling was the prospect of quarrels about resources in an area that bristled with weapons. And there was another fundamental difference between the polar regions: the Arctic had people, many of whom had lived on its lands and navigated its waters for centuries; Antarctica had none.

The international legal experimentation of Antarctica and uncertainties of the Arctic created problems and opportunities for Canadian politicians in the later sixties and early 1970s. Canadian nationalism roiled Canadian politics, and the new Canadian prime minister, Pierre Elliott Trudeau, called for a foreign and defence policy review. With justification, the military believed that Trudeau wanted to pull out Canadian troops from Europe and focus on Canadian "national interests." The military, which had been "unified" under the previous Liberal government of Lester Pearson, was asked to seek new roles. The Arctic beckoned, particularly since activity there obviously served "national interests" and "Canadian sovereignty," words that rolled quickly off the lips of many politicians and leading journalists of the day.

Authors with Arctic experience, such as Jim Lotz and Farley Mowat, and *Maclean's*, Canada's major newsmagazine, then edited by nationalist Peter Newman, railed against Canada's cavalier disregard for its "sovereignty" in the Arctic. The political impact of these writings was magnified in 1969 when Humble Oil announced that it would use a reinforced giant oil tanker, the S.S. *Manhattan*, to test whether Prudhoe Bay oil could be transported easily to the highly populated American East Coast. The Liberal backbench, then crammed with nationalists; the New Democrats moving quickly to the anti-capitalist and anti-American left; and even a few Conservatives, like the influential Dalton Camp and his bitter enemy former prime minister John Diefenbaker, rose in one voice to challenge the pretension of an American company passing through Canadian Arctic waters without the United States government asking permission. The United States government, deeply concerned about the precedent for international straits, adamantly refused to seek such consent.[23] How arrogant that seemed and how dangerous the oil tanker traffic would be in the pristine Arctic, Canadian politicians and the press declaimed.

Trudeau, who was deeply suspicious of celebrations of "sovereignty," whether in Quebec or Canada, moved gingerly over the nationalist terrain. His closest advisor on foreign policy was Ivan Head, a former Canadian diplomat and law dean. Coincidentally, in 1963 Head had written a relevant article, "Canadian Claims to Territorial Sovereignty in the Arctic Regions." It began, "These remote [polar] lands—for centuries unattractive to either colonizer or invader—present to the international lawyer a laboratory case."[24] The *Manhattan* voyage thus provided a laboratory for Canada's few international lawyers who proceeded to test arguments for Canadian sovereignty that would satisfy, on the one hand, Trudeau, who disdained nationalist rhetoric, and on the other, the backbench nationalists who proposed to parachute dramatically onto the *Manhattan* itself. As a former law professor, Trudeau was susceptible to ingenious legal arguments, and Head was perpetually ingenious. His 1963 article had concentrated on the need to define where the Arctic boundaries were—note the use of "regions" in the title—and on the importance of "occupation" in the determination of sovereignty in the modern period. Head knew that Trudeau, who had canoed through Canada's North and who was deeply curious about the emerging environmentalist movement, would respond to an initiative that neither rattled swords nor repeated clichés about sovereignty. Distrustful of the departments of External Affairs and Defence, Head worked with a few officials and drew up a plan whereby Canada responded to the *Manhattan* voyage in the summer of 1969 by asserting a twelve-nautical-mile territorial limit and a special responsibility to protect the fragile Arctic environment from "pollution" beyond the territorial limit. It was a brilliant stroke.[25]

The S.S. *Manhattan* passed successfully through the Arctic although its voyage needed Canadian ice breaking assistance, but the difficult passage raised doubts about the financial and logistical arguments for shipping oil across the Arctic. However, it had created a convenient opening for the Canadians. In the House of Commons on October 24, 1969, Trudeau announced grandiloquently that "Canada regards herself as responsible to all mankind for the peculiar ecological balance that now exists so precariously in the water, ice and land areas of the Arctic Archipelago. We do not doubt for a moment that the rest of the world would find us at fault, and hold us liable, should we fail to ensure adequate protection of that environment from pollution or artificial deterioration." The United States government, evidently, was not part of the "rest of the world," for it vigorously protested against the Canadian decisions.[26] In the Canadian House of Commons, it did not put an end to nationalist bluster with John Diefenbaker exclaiming, "What price Canadian sovereignty? Heaven help us!" and New Democratic Party leader Tommy Douglas demanding that the House make clear to the Americans "that we will not tolerate anyone pushing [the Canadian] government around."[27]

The plan for a second S.S. *Manhattan* voyage in 1970 compelled the Canadians to act quickly and forced the Americans to react strongly. Secretary of State William Rogers telephoned Trudeau to warn that the United States would defy the Canadian regulations. To Rogers's suggestion that the Americans would use a submarine to enforce their rights, Trudeau angrily responded that Canada was regulating oil tankers, not submarines. Moreover, "if you send up a tin can with a paper-thin hull filled with oil, we will not only stop you, we'll board you and turn you around," and "we'll have the world on our side."[28] Obviously, the United States was left out of the world again. The Arctic Waters Pollution Prevention Act (AWPPA) of 1970 went forward in Parliament and asserted Canada's right to establish tight environmental safety standards upon tankers or other ships within one hundred miles of the Arctic coast. With a separate act, Canada followed several countries in declaring a twelve-nautical-mile territorial limit. The AWPPA passed the Cabinet with angry dissent from a few ministers, notably Senator

Paul Martin, who warned that it clearly violated international law for which he and so many other Canadians had worked so ambitiously in the postwar era. And it probably did. The proof lay in Canada's refusal to refer the AWPPA to the International Court of Justice as the United States and other countries suggested. Instead, Trudeau instructed Head and other officials to work to make the legislation a basis for a new international law regime in the Arctic. In short, international law would be changed to fit Canada's own laws.

The work began at once. J. Alan Beesley, an exceptionally able foreign service officer, came to the foreground as the chief negotiator. He was the Canadian representative on the legal committee for the historic Stockholm environmental conference of 1972, of which Canadian Maurice Strong was the secretary-general. At the conference's end, the Canadian minister of the environment paid tribute to Beesley, who, he claimed, "more than anyone else at the conference, helped us to take a giant step forward in the development of international environmental law."[29] The efforts of the small-statured, soft-spoken but determined diplomat helped the field make a giant leap with the negotiation of the United Nations Conference on the Law of the Sea (UNCLOS), where he was the lead negotiator from the beginning of the negotiations in 1973 until 1982, when they finally concluded. He brilliantly advanced Canada's national interest while convincing others, as Trudeau had hoped, that Canada's environmental interest in the North coincided with, to use Trudeau's words, its "responsibility" to "mankind."

The United Nations Convention on the Law of the Sea had one central clause specific to the Arctic: Article 234. It provided that

> Coastal States have the right to adopt and enforce non-discriminatory laws and regulations for the prevention, reduction and control of marine pollution from vessels in ice-covered areas within the limits of the exclusive economic zone, where particularly severe climatic conditions and the presence of ice covering such areas for most of the year create obstructions or exceptional hazards to navigation, and pollution

of the marine environment could cause major harm to or irreversible disturbance of the ecological balance.

Despite this clause and many others obtained by Canadian and American negotiators, both countries hesitated to ratify the treaty because of strong pressure from mining interests against the International Seabed Authority, which American delegate Donald Rumsfeld denounced as a threat to American economic and security interests. These hesitations arose even though both countries, especially Canada with its long coastline, benefited from many of the other clauses, including acceptance of the 12-nautical-mile limit, the creation of a 200-nautical-mile Exclusive Economic Zone, and the recognition of the exclusive right to harvest minerals in the prolongation of the continental shelf. Despite the Reagan administration's objections, the Americans accepted the non-objectionable parts of the treaty in 1983, and American policy adjusted accordingly. Canada proceeded in similar fashion until its belated ratification of the treaty in 2003, the hundred and forty-fourth nation to do so.* For Canada, UNCLOS brought enormous benefits immediately. The protests against the AWPPA faded and, as states ratified UNCLOS, Article 234 became the basis for a customary rule of international law and the foundation upon which cooperation among Arctic states has proceeded. The centrality of the environment was clear not only for the indigenous peoples who had raised their voices against irresponsible drilling, transport, and polluting activities in their lands but also for the Arctic coastal states who had gained a new responsibility and legitimacy in the Arctic region. Moreover, there was now a developing sense of an

---

*In 2003 Canadian foreign minister Bill Graham approached Prime Minister Jean Chrétien and said he believed that Canada's failure to ratify was embarrassing. Chrétien responded that he could never get it past the "Newfoundlanders" and others in the Cabinet. However, he agreed to bury the item in an annex and hope that the dissenters would not notice. They did not and Canada ratified. – Discussion with Hon. William C. Graham, February 13, 2013

"Arctic region," one that drove collaboration, cooperation, and inter-action across the northern parts of the globe.[30]

This discussion of the international context leads to the third reason why the North commanded more attention after 1960. There was an inherent and persistent conflict between the desire to exploit resources and the growing recognition of the rights of indigenous peoples. The tension had two sources: on the one hand, there was the question of the ownership of land and how the rewards from its exploitation should be shared; on the other hand, there were the pollutants and environmental threats arising from development in the fragile North. The Prudhoe Bay discovery brought the question to the foreground in Alaska. The easiest way to get the oil to the South was through a pipeline, but such a pipeline would pass through environmentally sensitive lands where native rights had not been extinguished. Faced with pressure from the oil companies, the American government signed the Alaska Native Claims Settlement Act of 1971, which provided $462.5 million from the federal government over an eleven-year period, and $500 million from the resource companies. A "native" was one who was at least 25 percent Indian, Eskimo, or Aleutian. There was also a transfer of the surface rights to about one-tenth of Alaska and provision for corpora-tions through which most revenue would flow. The scheme had current and later critics—not least because it was a legislative imposition, not a negotiated settlement—but no one denies its fundamental importance in establishing a precedent for the settlement of land claims and the recog-nition of the rights of indigenous peoples.[31]

Resources, indigenous peoples, and the "new imagination" were linked collectively to a new understanding of the relationship among human beings, other organisms, and the Earth. The publication of Rachel Carson's *Silent Spring* in 1962 is often taken as the moment when the modern environmental movement was born, although concern for the preservation of species and wilderness on the one hand and fear of the impact of industrialization on the natural world on the other hand had been strong currents in modern thought since Blake wrote of "satanic mills" and Thoreau retreated to Walden Pond. But the 1960s broadened and intensified the concern for the planet's future as the movement blended with popular culture and political agitation. Carson had inspired a successful campaign against DDT, the widely used pesticide that she argued persisted in the food and water chain and caused profound harm to birds, fish, animals, and humans; hence, the silent spring. The powerful image inspired Canada's new prime minister Pierre Trudeau, who told the speechwriter for his government's initial Speech from the Throne in 1968 to use the word "pollution" as often as he could. Similarly motivated, the new American president Richard Nixon established the United States Environmental Protection Agency on January 1, 1970.[32]

Environmentalists, however, had doubts about Nixon. Among the causes of suspicion of the Nixon administration were its plans for an underground test of an atomic bomb at Amchitka in the Aleutian Islands in 1971. A strong protest movement erupted on the west coast, particularly in Vancouver, where concerns about American plans to ship Alaskan oil from the port of Valdez to the south were already high. A group of environmental activists determined to stop the test, if necessary by sailing a ship to the site and refusing to leave. On October 16, 1970, three of the greatest performer–singers of the age came to Vancouver's Pacific Coliseum and performed a benefit concert to support the protest. The funds raised by James Taylor, Joni Mitchell, and Phil Ochs paid for the voyage to the test area and inspired the creation of the famed environmental group Greenpeace (the name of the boat), whose strenuous efforts to preserve a pristine Arctic ran afoul of its inhabitants who charged that their campaign to "save" seals, whales, and other Arctic fauna undermined the way of life of indigenous peoples. By the seventies, northern peoples had developed their own understanding of the impact of technology, transportation, and industrial waste upon their lives, and they had their own voices to express their concern.[33]

The Emergence of Northern Voices

In the sixties and seventies, the voices of the North were heard more loudly in the South from Alaska, through Canada and Greenland, to Scandinavia. Although the indigenous peoples of the Soviet Union remained muffled, there was recognition of the common problems that peoples of the North faced. In the summer of 1971, a Canadian delegation headed by Jean Chrétien, the minister of Indian affairs and northern development, travelled to the Soviet North. According to John Hannigan and Walter Slipchenko, public servants and participants in Soviet exchanges, "the overriding purpose of the trip was to meet with senior Soviet federal, regional, and local officials to discuss the social and economic development of Native people and resource development in the Russian North."[34] The times were not yet right: Valery Tishkov, a former Russian minister and academician, now admits that Soviet officials of the time remained too wary and "did not allow practical steps to be taken."[35] Yet interchange occurred, with Slipchenko at the centre of continuing contact with Soviet scientists. Within the Canadian government, especially the Department of Indian Affairs and Northern Development, there was an increasing tendency to think in circumpolar terms where science and people were concerned.

Across the Arctic, indigenous people began to look beyond their homes, their region, and their national borders. The historic Alaskan land settlement had arisen from the demands first expressed by the Alaska Federation of Natives who organized in 1966 to seek a just settlement to land claims. Their example inspired the Canadian Inuit. By the 1970s, a generation of young Inuit had emerged from local and residential schools with English language skills and a new awareness of other aboriginal movements in the South. As a twenty-two-year-old Inuk, Tagak Curley had begun work as a "development officer" for the Canadian Department of Indian Affairs and Northern Development in 1966. Struck by the disappearance of traditional languages and ways, he became the editor of the *Keewatin Echo,* the first English–Inuktitut newspaper and in 1971 organized the Inuit Tapirisat (brotherhood) of Canada, which was the first major Inuit national organization that was based, significantly, in Ottawa. A young niece of Curley from Eskimo Point (now Arviat) on the western shore of Hudson Bay joined him in Ottawa in 1973 to attend school. Much later, the young girl, Nancy Karetak-Lindell, recalled that "as a young child growing up in Eskimo Point, where I was born in 1957, with an Inuk midwife attending to my mother, this was the only world I knew. Gradually, I became aware of other events happening outside of this comfortable environment and being impacted by 'the government's actions,' realizing we were part of a bigger picture." In 1997 Karetak-Lindell was elected to the House of Commons and became the first MP for Nunavut when it separated officially from the Northwest Territories on April 1, 1999.[36]

Karetak-Lindell, the daughter of an RCMP officer, reflected a new generation of aboriginal Canadians that was prepared to counter, and when necessary confront, "the government's actions." As aboriginal land claims became a major issue in Canadian and especially Quebec politics in the 1970s, these new and stronger voices were soon heard. Similarly, the Inuit of Greenland and the Saami of Scandinavia began to interact with the North Americans and to understand their common northern interests and experiences, particularly in their relationship to the land. The seeds of an international movement of indigenous people to protect their rights, their lands, and their ways were planted.

It was within this wider global context that the inhabitants of the Canadian North began to mobilize themselves, a process also spurred on by the growing pressure from the South to develop the Arctic. The result, an aboriginal leader later wrote, was the emergence during the seventies of "an energetic cadre of Indigenous activists, young men and women in their early twenties who after forming social networks at residential schools, and through their education in elite high school programs and university, were inspired by human rights and Indian rights movements sweeping North America to challenge the oppressive treatment that wrought poverty and misery in their communities."[37] For them land was not "a patch of ground legally surveyed, registered, and paid for," but a fundamental part of their being and history.[38]

Two giant Canadian projects of the seventies provoked extraordinary responses where the environment linked with native rights: the James Bay power project of Quebec, and the plan to build a Mackenzie Valley Pipeline. In both cases the voices of the North became louder and more eloquent. In the case of the James Bay project, the settlement created an economic and political base that permitted the emergence of leaders. Both linked environment and native claims in a compelling narrative that deeply influenced northern development and law.

The James Bay project was the dream of Hydro-Quebec and Quebec premier Robert Bourassa, and it was the last massive dam project in the Western world. Its ambition was to harness the powerful rivers of Northern Quebec to create hydro-electricity that would be used for Quebec industries and homes, with the surplus exported to the United States. The Cree and Inuit who dwelt beside the rivers and whose way of life would be forever changed were initially ignored and then brusquely pushed aside as the development began in the early 1970s. Then, in a pattern replicated many times, an ad hoc Quebec Association of Indians sued to stop the development, and in November 1973 a lower court agreed. It was a stunning defeat for the government, one that the Quebec Court of Appeal soon overturned, but the Court of Appeal did not reject the requirement that the government come to terms with the Cree and the Inuit.[39]

Eventually the Quebec government agreed to grant ownership of almost 14,000 square kilometres and extensive hunting and fishing rights over surrounding areas to the Cree and Inuit. There was a significant financial settlement of $225 million, but the real importance lay in the responsibilities that were given to the people for their own welfare and education. It bred leaders. Among the Crees, Billy Diamond, Ted Moses, and Matthew Coon Come took major positions among Canadian aboriginals with Coon Come, educated as a lawyer at McGill University, eventually becoming president of the Assembly of First Nations. With the Inuit, the influence on Arctic events of the James Bay settlement was extraordinary. The Inuit of Northern Quebec established the Makivik Corporation, which played an enormous role not only in the social, economic, and political life of the region but also in developing remarkable people. Charlie Watt, the founding president of the Makivik Corporation, became a member of the Canadian Senate, a founder of the Inuit Circumpolar Conference, and an outspoken advocate of Inuit points of view. Sheila Watt-Cloutier also emerged from the Makivik Corporation to become the president of the Inuit Circumpolar Conference and a leading international environmentalist who was nominated for the Nobel Prize for her outstanding work on persistent organic pollutants. Finally, Mary Simon was a broadcaster and journalist in the seventies who became a senior executive of the Makivik Corporation in the later seventies, president of the Inuit Circumpolar Conference in the eighties, and Canada's first Ambassador for Circumpolar Affairs in 1994. She is, in the view of former Canadian foreign minister Lloyd Axworthy, the individual who deserves the most credit for the creation of the Arctic Council.[40]

There is a clear conclusion: when these Inuit leaders from northern Quebec were young, the Canadian state moved several families from their community thousands of kilometres to the High Arctic. They had no choice; they lacked a voice. But voices that were silenced in the fifties became audible in the sixties, eloquent in the seventies, and powerful and influential later. The colonized now came to the colonial capitals no longer as subjects but as actors shaping their times and the lives of their people.

The inquiry into the building of a Mackenzie Valley Pipeline became the theatre where aboriginal eloquence reached its heights. After the Prudhoe Bay discovery, the idea of building a pipeline along the Mackenzie Valley to bring oil from the Beaufort Sea, where oil firms believed great potential lay, gained strength. The success of the Organization of the Petroleum Exporting Countries (OPEC) in raising oil prices in 1973 made the request for permission for a pipeline into a clamour. Prime Minister Pierre Trudeau wanted to protect Canadians from the soaring oil prices while increasing Canadian supply, and frontier energy exploration was alluring in a period of energy shortage and economic uncertainty. But Trudeau knew that the road to these new resources faced many obstacles. First, he lacked a majority government and needed the support of the nationalist and socialist New Democratic Party (NDP), which was wary of the designs of oil barons, particularly foreign ones. Second, he had been politically damaged by the reaction to the revolutionary White Paper his government had presented in 1969, in which it had proposed to deal with the inequality, poverty, social problems, and growing protests of Canada's aboriginal population through its integration within the broader Canadian population. The proposed abolition of the Indian Act failed in the face of angry protests that captured media attention. Trudeau, therefore, was cautious.[41]

In March 1974, with an election looming and very conscious of the failure of his White Paper, Trudeau appointed Thomas Berger, a British Columbia Supreme Court justice, to head an inquiry to investigate the "social, environmental, and economic" impact of a gas pipeline through the Yukon and another through the Mackenzie River Valley. It was a fateful choice. The appointment of Berger, a controversial former leader of the British Columbia NDP, annoyed some of Trudeau's colleagues, surprised others, and guaranteed that the voices of the aboriginal people most affected by the building of the pipelines would be heard. The Berger inquiry lasted three years, attracted international attention to indigenous rights, spurred indigenous organization, profoundly influenced northern politics, and, in the end, brought close scrutiny to all future pipeline projects. Berger's report appeared in 1977 in two volumes and was an immediate sensation. There were two fundamental arguments that affected future northern development: first, the rights of the native population, particularly land claims issues, had to be dealt with before development could occur; and second, the northern environment was especially fragile and required different processes in evaluating economic benefits. For the local population, Berger concluded, the social consequences of building the Mackenzie Valley Pipeline "will not only be serious—they will be devastating." The report, entitled *Northern Frontier, Northern Homeland,* with many striking cover photographs of the people of the North and only one uninspiring image of oil company drillers, became a publishing rarity—a government-produced bestseller.[42]

Berger had held meetings along the pipeline route, in small communities where the promoters and their consultants made their formal presentations and then locals talked. The contrast was striking, especially when promoters extolled the economic benefits of a pipeline and local residents eloquently explained how their ways of life, their hunting practices and trapping lines, would be altered forever by the changes a pipeline would bring. For the broader understanding of the emergence of an Arctic Council where indigenous participation on scientific panels is accepted, the Berger Inquiry is important. A creation of a national state, the Berger Inquiry gave legitimacy to local knowledge as an important component of judgment, to be credited along with the evidence of academically trained scientists and economists in analysis and policy-making. And it was Indian Affairs and Northern Development, the department that had relocated families and ignored their voices a quarter century earlier, that released *Northern Frontier, Northern Homeland* with its powerful record of indigenous voices.

The world seemed utterly changed; something new in the North was certainly born in the form of the emergence of strong northern indigenous voices, and the recognition that, in Berger's opening words, "we are now at our last frontier." Being the last made it precious, requiring special rules for protection. As well as emphasizing the rights of the indigenous peoples, Berger joined many other contemporary writers in pointing to the damage that earlier helter-skelter development had done to the environment. In

Amchitka protester Joni Mitchell's memorable phrase, "you don't know what you've got till it's gone," the balance tilted strongly against large mega-projects in sensitive environments. Even the Soviets, who too often dismissed environmental concerns for supposed economic development, began to cooperate in the 1970s in collective efforts to preserve and protect northern wildlife. By the end of the seventies, the environmental movement of the sixties had established deep roots in national and local governments throughout North America and much of Europe.[43]

The seventies were marked by détente, a thaw in the Cold War that brought progress in arms control, a lessening of tension, and, in Helsinki, an important agreement on exchange between East and West. The so-called Helsinki Accords culminating in the Conference on Security and Co-operation in Europe Accords of 1975, upheld sovereign inviolability of frontiers, peaceful mediation of differences, the right of national self-determination, and acceptance of the force of international law. All of the Arctic states were signatories, although the region itself was unmentioned in the final declaration. This moment was the high point of East–West collaboration.[44]

From Alaska through Finland, indigenous organizations became stronger and often received state support. Land claim settlements in Quebec and, after Berger, in the Canadian North greatly boosted indigenous organizational capacity. Private foundations also played a major role. In Canada, the Donner Canadian Foundation offered support for northern researchers. Even more influential was the Walter and Duncan Gordon Foundation, which gave grants directly to Inuit organizations and individuals. Its interest reflected and drew upon the knowledge of several board members with extensive Arctic experience, notably Jane Gordon Glassco and Kyra Gordon. The Foundation's mandate has been to enhance "Northern peoples' ability to participate and help shape public policy at any level." In short, it sought, in its own words, to have them "punch above their weight."[45] And they did.

Not only were indigenous peoples cooperating with each other within national borders, their international contacts created lasting bonds. In the early 1970s a young Greenlander, Aqqaluk Lynge,* became aware of the concept of a common indigenous interest being developed by academics and activists in Copenhagen where he was a student. He later recalled: "In May 1973 we came back from a meeting on Arctic oil and gas development in Le Havre, France. In Le Havre we had met the National Indian Brotherhood including James Wah-Shee from the Northwest Territories who had joined us back in Copenhagen where we discussed the possibility of organizing an Arctic Peoples' Conference." The conference took place in the Danish parliament; it brought together Inuit with the Saami and developed threads that would strengthen as common interests were discovered.[46]

The Copenhagen conference inspired North American Inuit to organize a similar gathering, one that took permanent form. The Inuit Circumpolar Conference, which became the principal non-governmental organization in the creation of the Arctic Council, had modest beginnings in mid-June 1977 at Barrow on Alaska's North Slope. The meeting occurred just after the first volume of Berger's report was published and just before the first barrel of Prudhoe Bay oil passed through the Trans-Alaska Pipeline to Valdez. Eben Hopson, the mayor of the North Slope Borough created in the aftermath of the Alaska land claim settlement, took the lead. The descendant of an English whaler and his Inupiat wife, Hopson possessed a shrewd political sense and, even more importantly, resources to manage an international conference. His 1975 application to the American Lilly Foundation explained the purpose clearly:

---

*A poet, politician, filmmaker, and Inuit leader, Aqqaluk Lynge was born in Greenland in 1947. In 1966 he went to high school in Copenhagen where he graduated in 1969. He returned to Greenland where he taught, but then returned to Copenhagen for university in 1973. Between 1970 and 1976 he was a leading member of the Young Greenlanders Council, and in 1976 founded Greenland's socialist Inuit Ataqatigiit Party. He was elected in 1983 and became minister for social affairs, housing, techniques and environment, a post he held until 1988. A true polymath, Lynge has twice served as president of the Inuit Circumpolar Council, longer than anyone else.

The North Slope Borough is seeking financial support from the Lilly Endowment for a three-phase program of international Eskimo community organization through which we Eskimo people of Alaska, Canada, Greenland, and eventually the Soviet Union, can join together to meet common problems posed by industrialized society encroaching upon our land, our communities, and our traditions. Toward that end, the North Slope Borough wishes to sponsor a major international Inuit community conference in Barrow in the early Spring of 1976 to discuss common problems and opportunities in the areas of language, communications, education, transportation, village health care and sanitation, housing, environmental protection, energy resource planning and community organization. This conference will follow-up, for the circumpolar community, the Arctic Peoples' Conference that was sponsored by the Inuit Tapirisat of Canada and held in Copenhagen in 1973, and will involve the cooperation of Eskimo leaders from Alaska, Canada and Greenland.[47]

Hopson pushed others to accept the need for a conference with a clear circumpolar focus, including the Inuk Charlie Watt, a Canadian government official who had helped to organize the 1973 Arctic Peoples' Conference in Copenhagen, but who was reluctant to come to Barrow. Truly a "one off" but superbly experienced for the task, Hopson was the first baby born in the Barrow mission hospital, a conscript in the American Army for which he facilitated Soviet lend-lease from Alaska, a construction worker on the DEW Line, the organizer of the North Slope borough, the executive director of the Alaska Federation of Natives during the land claims fight, a candidate for the Democratic nomination for governor in 1974, a witness before the Berger Inquiry, a state senator and, needless to add, a skilled political operator. Using his contacts and experience, Hopson brought eighteen delegates from Greenland, eighteen from Canada, and twenty from Alaska to his gathering in Barrow. He had rounded up most of the funds to pay for the participants and the conference itself from the proceeds of the land claims settlement. Hopson had a specific interest: a fight he was leading against the International Whaling Commission and Greenpeace, which were seeking to impose a ban on the hunting of bowhead whales.[48] But the platter he served in Barrow contained an abundance of goodies to tempt others: aboriginal land claims, the challenge of oil and gas companies, the importance of local knowledge, and the relationship with national states. In his opening speech he looked towards Greenland where the issue of Home Rule was strong, and wondered if it would be a model for northern peoples. He rallied the Inuit, declaring, "We are only 100,000 but, working together, we can be strong beyond our numbers."

Hopson's address was brief; he was suffering from advanced cancer. He did not use the word "Inuit" in his opening speech, probably because some from Alaska and elsewhere preferred the traditional "Eskimo" in preference to "Inuit," which had become the clear choice in Canada. Nevertheless, the message of circumpolarity found fertile ground among the mostly young representatives gathered in Barrow, through which, Hopson pointed out, their ancestors had passed long ago on their passage east. Hopson was too ill to participate in drafting the charter, a task that passed to a young Mary Simon and Alaskan Ralph Anderson, but the conference, which brought together government officials, scientists, and other aboriginals along with the delegates, gave birth to the most powerful northern non-governmental organization. The second Inuit Circumpolar Conference took place on June 28, 1980, in Greenland, which had obtained Home Rule in 1979. On the day it opened, Hopson died in faraway Alaska. Bishop Jens Christian Chemnitz, who had been in Barrow three years earlier, paid an emotional memorial tribute to Hopson, comparing him to Moses leading his people but never reaching the Promised Land himself. An Inuk played a saw sadly in the background while the conference attendees wept.[49]

The Cold War Returns

The conferences were marked by a large degree of consensus, although Hopson notably dissented on attempts to restrict the military in the

Arctic. He had been a soldier, of course, but his arguments expressed a broader viewpoint that emphasized the vulnerability of the Arctic and the need for vigilance. Arguments about demilitarizing or denuclearizing the Arctic had developed early in the nuclear age, but they had intermittent and unpredictable appeal, generally depending on the state of the Cold War. And its state turned suddenly worse in the later 1970s as the Soviets invaded Afghanistan and Ronald Reagan became president of the United States.

As the Cold War became ever more frigid in the eighties, differences were reflected in Arctic policies. While there could be no return to the 1950s when security had trumped all other interests, the Reagan administration's 1983 Arctic Policy Statement stressed "protecting essential security interests" as its first point, while failing to list the human presence as a "major element."[50] In the so-called Second Cold War of the early eighties, 1983 was a dreadful year. A recent American official history recalls the tension: "In March 1983, President Reagan denounced the Soviet Union as the 'focus of evil in the world' and as an 'evil empire.' Soviet General Secretary Yuri Andropov [the former KGB head who succeeded Brezhnev] responded by calling the U.S. President insane and a liar. Then things got nasty." On September 1, a Soviet interceptor coldly shot down a Korean airliner; rhetoric escalated and allies divided. In the G-7 meetings of 1983 and 1984, Ronald Reagan and Margaret Thatcher brushed aside the pleas for restraint from Pierre Trudeau and French President Mitterand. Peace movements crowded central squares in Western capitals; Trudeau launched a personal peace initiative, which Thatcher and the American and Canadian right despised. Military spending soared.[51]

The Arctic seemed once more in peril. The Soviet Northern Fleet swelled, and Soviet submarines were sighted everywhere. Incidents with Soviet submarines in Swedish waters forced leftist Prime Minister Olof Palme to chill Soviet–Swedish relations. Finnish president Mauno Koivisto, frightened by the worsening Cold War, warned Palme that it was actually Western submarines that were provoking the Soviets. Whatever the truth about the submarines, the northern world seemed much more dangerous. The Finnish policy of "active neutrality" became hyperactive as Koivisto urged a naval agreement to slow down the burgeoning activity in the North. With the long Norwegian coast and the Barents Sea above, Norway became more strategically important for East and West. Along the northern border with the USSR, Norway's troops directly faced the Soviet army. Because Norway had agreed when it joined NATO that it would not have foreign bases, NATO was pledged to reinforce the Norwegians in the event of an attack, with the Canadians agreeing to send approximately 5,500 soldiers within thirty days during a crisis. Faced with criticism that Canada was not ready to fulfill the commitment, the Canadian defence minister ordered in 1984 that the Canadian Air–Sea Transportable Brigade Group be made operational for the first time. In the election of 1984, Progressive Conservative leader Brian Mulroney excoriated the feeble Canadian defence efforts against Soviet domination. Once in office, he immediately ordered a Canadian defence review, which echoed the Cold War hard line of Washington.

Ironically, one of the major recommendations in the new review when it appeared in 1987 responded not only to the "Soviet threat" but also to American challenges to "Canadian sovereignty." The review urged the building of up to twelve nuclear submarines to patrol the Arctic, where the 1985 voyage from Greenland to Alaska of a United States Coast Guard vessel, *Polar Sea*, provoked public demonstrations in the South and strong Inuit opposition in the North. Although the American and Canadian governments tried to cooperate to minimize opposition—Mulroney had proclaimed a new era of friendship with the Americans—they failed. In radio and television talk shows and editorial pages, fury reigned. In a precursor of later peculiar alliances, the Soviet Union supported the Canadian position, saying that the Northwest Passage like their Northern Sea Route required consent before passage. The support pleased neither Ottawa nor Washington.[52]

But it was all theatre; the Canadian defence review was an anach-
ronism at its birth. The major drama was elsewhere. Yuri Andropov
died suddenly in February 1984. His decrepit successor, Konstantin
Chernenko, soon died of heart failure on March 10, 1985. Mikhail
Gorbachev succeeded him, full of doubts about the past and determination to make a new future. By spring 1987 the "Second Cold War" was
quickly thawing as Gorbachev prepared for the seventieth anniversary of
the Bolshevik Revolution. On June 12, 1987, Reagan went to Berlin and
challenged Gorbachev to "take down this wall." A furious Gorbachev
told his speechwriter and advisor Anatoly Chernyaev that Reagan's
performance was a cheap theatrical trick designed to provoke him to
bring back the "Soviet threat." But it wouldn't happen: he had fired his
generals that spring and had proven the power of civilian control in the
Kremlin. "The world," he told Chernyaev, "has shifted. Society feels
the realities and is interested in our policies." Polls in Western Europe
indicated that Gorbachev was more popular than Reagan and his policies
more trusted. The world was watching Moscow. That August, after
meeting a flood of foreign visitors, Gorbachev went with Chernyaev to a
dacha in the Crimea, where he worked on a book to tell the world about
how things were shifting. He worked furiously, away from the public
glare. On August 31, 1987, he told Chernyaev that "we have created the
carcass of a new building ... We will see what turns out." One month
later he arrived in Murmansk and began to poke the Arctic carcass. And
no one then knew how it would turn out, not even Gorbachev.

FOUR

The Finns
Make a Move

"Either I brought wonderful weather or you prepared for it," Mikhail Gorbachev remarked as he and his wife Raisa stepped from the plane in Murmansk where he would present the Order of Lenin and the Gold Star to the Arctic's largest city. In truth, no one had prepared for Gorbachev. He had not been seen for fifty-one days, but his influence was still deeply felt. There was a new climate in international relations in the early fall of 1987, with the United States and the Soviet Union agreeing in September that they would, in principle, forsake short-range and medium-range nuclear missiles. In Gorbachev's opinion, this decision and others related to it had created a "chain reaction" that would create a different world, one without the terror that had marked the worst moments of the Cold War.[1] To that end, he proposed to give a major speech in Murmansk that would counter the increasing militarization of the North and open the Soviet North to closer collaboration with its prosperous and democratic neighbours.[2]

The following day, before a large gathering of Communist officials, Murmansk dock workers, and sailors, Gorbachev presented his plans for the region's future in an address broadcast live on Soviet television. By traditional Soviet standards, the speech was brief, but its content was rich in detail. He began by deploring American congressional attacks on the trustworthiness of the Soviet Union and doubts about recent changes. "One can feel here [in Murmansk] the freezing breath of the 'Arctic strategy' of the Pentagon. An immense potential of nuclear destruction concentrated aboard submarines and surface ships affects the political climate of the entire world and can be detonated by an accidental political–military conflict in any other region of the world." A one-sided analysis to be sure, but Gorbachev indicated in his Murmansk speech that he was ready to end the chill that the Cold War imposed upon the Arctic.

While praising Norwegian prime minister Gro Harlem Brundtland for her notable work on the World Commission on Environment and Development and Finnish president Mauno Koivisto for his efforts on disarmament in the North, Gorbachev strongly and specifically criticized Canada for its testing of American cruise missiles in its North and its "vast build-up of forces in the Arctic." These remarks were unsurprising and, in the case of the "vast" Canadian "build-up," amusingly erroneous, but he then shifted dramatically, making six proposals. Conveniently, he listed them:

1. He called for a nuclear-free zone in Europe. The form could be through bilateral or multilateral agreements. He offered to remove submarines with ballistic missiles from the Soviet Baltic Fleet.

2. He supported Finnish president Koivisto's proposals to restrict naval activity in "the seas washing the shores of northern Europe." He further proposed a progress meeting in Leningrad and raised the possibility of a nuclear-free zone in the Arctic.

3. He urged joint efforts to develop northern resources and explicitly suggested that Canada and Norway could assist in the opening up of Soviet energy resources.

4. He noted expanding cooperation with Canada on scientific matters and urged expansion of such efforts more generally. He proposed the establishment of an Arctic Research Council and suggested that Murmansk could host the initial meeting. In this context he urged recognition of the "interests of the indigenous population."

5. Noting the growing concern for the environment, Gorbachev called for "an integrated comprehensive plan for protecting the natural environment of the north."

6. The Northern Sea Route could be opened to "foreign" traffic with Soviet icebreakers clearing the path for the vessels. There could be cooperation on transportation and communication in the north more generally.

The program, Gorbachev warned, faced many shoals and determined opponents, but he called for it to move forward guided by the "warm Gulfstream of the European process and not by the Polar chill of accumulated suspicions and prejudices."[3]

Reaction was swift. The Polar chill was still present in Washington, Ottawa, and at the NATO headquarters in Brussels. In Washington, State Department spokesperson Phyllis Oakley dismissed the speech, declaring that other areas of Soviet–American negotiation had a higher priority than the Arctic. In Ottawa, Joe Clark, the minister of external affairs, admitted that Gorbachev had made an "interesting" proposal but suggested it would have been much more interesting "if the Soviet Union made it clear they were prepared to act as they were talking." Defence Minister Perrin Beatty, whose defence review had proposed the "vast build-up" Gorbachev directly attacked, was dismissive. At NATO, there was little interest in the proposal of demilitarization of the northern

Arctic straits because, NATO officials averred, they were "crucial to the United States' naval strategy in the event of superpower conflict, which is to block the Soviet Northern Fleet from surging out through the Bering, Davis and Denmark Straits and the gap between Iceland and Scotland." Beneath the skeptical bluster, diplomats, the *New York Times* reported, privately conceded that their cautious reaction "reflected extreme sensitivity in NATO to new Soviet arms proposals that [had] caught the allies off balance that year."[4]

The Scandinavians, who escaped the criticisms Gorbachev directed at the North American Arctic nations, responded more warmly, particularly the Finns. Worried about environmental pollution from the industrial plants on the Kola Peninsula and evidence that the Soviets had been dumping radionuclides in the Kara and White seas, fearful of the nearby nuclear installations, and eager to engage the Soviets in a multilateral rather than a bilateral relationship, the Finns pored over Gorbachev's words to find opportunities to act. During the Cold War, the Finns had to maintain a neutrality that required careful and continuous reassurance to the superpower beside them. By the later 1980s, they were eager to move towards Europe, whose integration had produced remarkable economic and cultural strength, and away from a stagnant Soviet Union. President Koivisto, who was meeting soon with Gorbachev, enthusiastically welcomed talk of a zone of peace and, especially, the warm references to his own proposals for naval confidence-building measures to improve stability in the North.[5]

The zone of peace and the discussion about a nuclear-free zone in the Arctic may have not attracted defence and foreign offices in North America, but it astonished and excited many North American peace activists, environmentalists, and others who despaired at the militarization of the North in the "Second Cold War" of the eighties. Tom Axworthy, for example, had been Pierre Trudeau's principal secretary when Trudeau launched his peace initiative in 1983 and, after Trudeau's resignation in 1984, worked closely with Walter and Duncan Gordon on their foundation and its Arctic and disarmament interests. He recalls that Gorbachev's proposals stunned him and others; they determined quickly that the opportunity Gorbachev offered must not be lost. Trudeau's peace initiative left no trace on Brian Mulroney's Progressive Conservative government, but there were two Ottawa institutes that continued the initiative's support for arms control and disarmament: the Canadian Centre for Arms Control and Disarmament (CCACD), which was privately organized but mainly government-funded, and the Canadian Institute for International Peace and Security (CIIPS), which was completely funded by government and gave grants to scholars and to non-governmental organizations (NGO) such as the CCACD.[6]

Non-governmental organizations in which citizens came together to influence public policy outside of traditional party organizations were hardly new. Since the earliest days of democratic politics, movements such as anti-slavery leagues, temperance associations, and suffragist groups had profoundly affected legislation and democracy itself. But, in the words of Harvard historian Akira Iriye, the twentieth century was "a century of NGOs," particularly in its last decade. Despite its origins in the United Nations Charter, the term "NGO" was virtually unknown before the 1970s but ubiquitous by the 1990s when international organizations gave "NGOs" formal recognition and governments often funded them generously. For example, in the case of Canadian NGOs working internationally, more than half of their funding in the early nineties came from government, in many cases over 90 percent of total income.[7] The process of introducing a charter of rights and freedom and patriating the Canadian constitution during the early 1980s created a demand by many sectors, notably women and aboriginals, for a voice and formal recognition within the constitution. For aboriginals, who were largely ignored in the first constitutional efforts, the final resolution in 1982 and a special amendment on land claims in 1983 were major victories. The greater legitimacy for aboriginal rights provided by the Charter and the Constitutional Act and the many rallies, protests, and consultations that took place to obtain that victory spurred the creation of new aboriginal NGOs and strengthened existing ones.* At Canada's future constitutional tables, its indigenous people would never again lack a strong voice.[8]

Those who have studied the remarkable efflorescence of NGOs in the second half of the twentieth century have noted two important characteristics. In tracing political activism against the atomic bomb, historian Paul Boyer demonstrated how protest movements shift to related issues, from, for example, an anti-nuclear focus to opposition to the Vietnam War. Later analyses by others have confirmed these insights and further reveal how local and domestic activism is a catalyst for the establishment of linkages beyond national boundaries. These linkages tend to be intermittent and often concentrated on specific issues, but they have become far more frequent as communication costs have dropped dramatically. The study of such linkages has been fashionably dubbed as "transnational," but even enthusiasts recognize that many exaggerate "transnational activism," which, social movement analyst Sidney Tarrow writes, "does not resemble a swelling tide of history but is more like a series of waves that lap on an international beach, retreating repeatedly into domestic seas but leaving incremental changes on the shore."[9] In our case, on the Arctic shore.

Gorbachev's speech left four principal openings: security, with the proposal for a zone of peace; the environment, with the offer of closer cooperation; science, with the prospect of collaboration on northern research; and the most vaguely defined, the linkage of Soviet indigenous peoples with their counterparts elsewhere in the North. Those

---

*The Charter of Rights and Freedoms (Section 25) stated that the Charter would not "abrogate or derogate from any Aboriginal, treaty or other rights or freedoms." Section 35 of the Constitution Act (1982) was more significant in that it stated that "Aboriginal Peoples of Canada" includes Indian, Inuit, and Métis, and "affirmed and recognized aboriginal and treaty rights." Canadian courts have interpreted this section as creating a "duty to consult" on decisions affecting aboriginal lands, development on those lands, and changes in the Canadian constitution.

who moved quickly to grasp the opportunities did not always focus on a single opening. The Finns, for example, grasped at all four immediately. Moreover, individuals and NGOs had multiple Arctic personalities. Canadian diplomat J. Alan Beesley, who greatly influenced the Arctic future through his work on the law of the sea and, in particular, clause 234 (the Arctic clause), switched effortlessly from work on disarmament as Canada's representative at the Conference on Disarmament to environmental negotiations later in the decade.* Interestingly, his obituary summarized his life's work as "protecting the environment and promoting peace."[10] There was a close synergy between the two, not only for him but also for many northern indigenous leaders, who had long been wary of the impact of militarization upon the Arctic. But sometimes there were complications: Greenpeace explicitly linked "peace" with the environment, as its name suggests, but by the later 1980s, the group was anathema to indigenous leaders because of what leaders believed was complete indifference to Inuit cultural traditions and economic needs. The Inuit Circumpolar Council's first meeting was inspired, among other things, by the strong opposition of Greenpeace to the hunting of the bowhead whale, which was important for the traditional "country food" of the Inuit of Alaska's North Shore. Greenpeace's advocacy became a threat to the traditional way of life of northern peoples at a time when many other forces were shattering those ways. There was not only collaboration and linkages among NGOs in the North, but also, in some cases, suspicion and rivalry. And it sometimes seemed that alliances and issues shifted as often as the Arctic ice.

---

*A lawyer, Beesley joined the Department of External Affairs in 1959 and became one of the most respected diplomats of his generation. His major achievement was his central role in the drafting of the United Nations Convention on the Law of the Sea. Soft-spoken, shrewd but steely when needed, Beesley was central in law of the sea negotiations for over fifteen years and skilfully shaped the final draft. Although recognized as a supporter of indigenous rights, Beesley possessed a diplomat-lawyer's hesitations about innovations such as indigenous presence at negotiation tables. He served as a special advisor on marine conservation and the environment to the minister in 1989–1991 and, according to Inuit leader Mary Simon, clashed with her on the question of participation.

Although the North Americans hesitated when Gorbachev mentioned security, the Canadians and Americans did embrace the offers of scientific collaboration. As Gorbachev noted at Murmansk, there had been growing collaboration in the 1980s. In 1984, for example, the Canadian government through its Department of Indian Affairs and Northern Development (DIAND) had signed a protocol with the Soviets that provided for scientific exchanges. The result was immediate, with scientists, indigenous leaders, and DIAND minister David Crombie visiting the Soviet Union, and in particular Siberia and its people. DIAND had an effective circumpolar group, whose purpose was to press forward the exchange agreement. They did so with vigour. In February 1987 the protocol was renewed. One of the notable projects in 1988 was "Polar Bridge." A team of thirteen Canadian and Soviet scientists skied from Severnaya Zemlya across the North Pole to Ellesmere Island during which they "conducted scientific experiments related to physiological adaptation to the cold," an easy task to be sure. Then, in the words of a Canadian history of Soviet–Canadian Arctic collaboration, the "favourable climate" created by Gorbachev at Murmansk led the Soviets to turn the protocol into a formal agreement, which was signed when Prime Minister Brian Mulroney visited the Soviet Union in November 1989.[11]

Shortly before the Canadians signed their agreement, twenty-nine scientists from the Arctic states created the International Arctic Science Committee in Stockholm on March 24–26, 1988. Arctic science was not, of course, restricted to Arctic states. Many of the major institutes carrying out Arctic research were in West Germany, France, and the United Kingdom, and many scientists in the southern hemisphere emphasized the relevance of Antarctic research to Arctic conditions. The organization soon expanded to include others with its secretariat eventually being located in Potsdam, Germany. Although many of the Canadian scientific initiatives of the mid-eighties emphasized research on and the involvement of indigenous peoples, many scientists saw this focus as a distraction from the pure scientific investigation of a region with broad geophysical importance. Indigenous leaders in the 1980s began to criticize "scientists" for focusing on Arctic subjects relevant to southern interests, as geological surveys of resources or Arctic flora and fauna intrigued Europeans who then campaigned for their preservation with negative results for Arctic hunters and trappers. Where, indigenous leaders asked, was the "human dimension" of research in and on the Arctic? How did the scientists use the "traditional" or "local" knowledge to reach their conclusions?[12]

Concern for the environment crossed many divisions, particularly in 1987 as the radioactive clouds from the Chernobyl disaster in the Soviet Ukraine spread menacingly over Eurasia. Chernobyl itself had fuelled *glasnost* and *perestroika* in its clear illustration of the environmental carelessness of the Soviet system and its implicit warning of future catastrophes. Moreover, scientists were confirming the concerns of northerners that their waters, and in some cases lands, were subject to pollutants from far distant sources. Gorbachev had talked about exploitation of the rich resources of the North, but evidence was accumulating of the costs of development, not only for the polar regions but for the remainder of the planet. On the day Gorbachev spoke in Murmansk, the United Nations Environment Programme reported that the ozone layer depletion in the Antarctic was the greatest ever, and scientific research had shown that human-made chlorofluorocarbons were the cause. Gorbachev had commended the work of Norwegian prime minister Brundtland and her efforts to develop a concept of "sustainable development" through which the need for growth was balanced by respect for the planet's health. Indeed, the famous report of the Brundtland-chaired World Commission on Environment and Development, *Our Common Future,* appeared in October 1987, shortly after Gorbachev's Murmansk speech. Its central concept of sustainable development would profoundly influence debates about the Arctic future and, specifically, the emergence of the Arctic Council as a collaborative forum in the later 1990s.

While Norway, a NATO member with an armed border with the Soviets, was still wary of the Soviets, it was intrigued by the environmental component of the Russian speech. The traditionally neutral Swedes shied away from disarmament discussions, but scientific and environmental collaboration were always of great interest to them. But it was the Finns who took the lead in Northern Europe in responding to Gorbachev. Despite the generous reference in Gorbachev's speech to President Koivisto's efforts at northern naval disarmament, the Finns quickly abandoned the issue. Finland knew that the two superpowers reserved to themselves the right to sort out and limit their vast arsenals. Gorbachev's security proposals, a senior Finn official remarked in July 1988, "were directed to [the] other side," not to Finland, which was self-declared as being on neither side. And yet the Finns, more than any other nation, had reason to grasp at the Gorbachev proposals for the Arctic even though, lacking a port and an evocative "Arctic" vision, they had not found it a significant concern. While conceiving of Finland as a "northern" nation, their history taught them that their eastern border, so often violated and changed within the lifetime of many Finns, needed freer passage and the flow of commerce and people. It was important to strengthen bilateral ties and to embrace the Soviets within broader, multilateral organizations. Gorbachev, Koivisto declared, had extended "an outstretched hand" to the Arctic countries, and it had to be grasped firmly.[13]

If the zone of peace was to be built by others, if at all, the Finns leapt forward in other areas of potential collaboration. The Finnish–Soviet Scientific and Technical Cooperation Committee, for example, moved beyond traditional scientific subjects and attempted "to promote contacts between the Finnish and the Soviet researchers in Lappish culture," much like the Canadians with their scientific collaboration. But it was the environment that offered the greatest possibilities in Finnish eyes. Here the Gorbachev proposal represented a "promising new opening" where Arctic countries, despite their different alliances, could work together well.[14] But, with the fury of an American presidential year, the multiple challenges to Gorbachev's plans from defence establishment, and the chaos of a world whose bindings were coming undone, little actual progress was made in 1988.[15]

In spring 1989, an academic analysis by a British scholar of the Murmansk initiative concluded that "The response from the West has, on the whole, been reserved and in some cases critical." The fact that the Arctic was "traditionally the fiefdom of the military" made major initiatives tentative and change-halting. Only in the area of science and environment had there been clear "enthusiasm."[16]

The enthusiasm was, as we have seen, greatest in Finland, particularly in the Finnish Ministry of the Environment, which correctly regarded the Gorbachev Arctic proposal as an opening to establish a highly desirable multilateral forum that was badly needed. For the Finns, the International Arctic Science Committee (IASC) provided an interesting precedent in that its founding conference at Stockholm included delegates from the five Arctic coastal states (United States, Canada, Denmark, Norway, and the Soviet Union) and the three other states whose boundaries stretched above the Arctic Circle—Sweden, Finland, and (just barely) Iceland. IASC initially excluded West Germany and the United Kingdom despite the significant scientific work done in those countries on Arctic matters. The exclusion was a precedent, and precedents matter, particularly for smaller nations.

Discussions began between the Finnish ministries of foreign affairs and environment about how to proceed with what both agreed was an immense opportunity. The documentary evidence suggests that in Finland, unlike Canada, the relationship between the two responsible departments, the traditional foreign office and the young activists of the environment department, was marked by trust and cooperation. The Gorbachev speech, in the words of a senior Finnish official, "awakened" all of them: it was "a shock that even today seems strange in terms of its motivation." There were also important domestic political considerations

shaping their decision to act. The first was the criticism of the government for its failure to confront the Soviets over serious pollution from the
Kola Peninsula that affected the northern Finns. Finns knew that bilateral
negotiations on difficult issues with the Soviets were less satisfactory than
embracing the issue within a multilateral bosom. The second was the sense
that Finland, because of its historic "active neutrality," needed to take the
initiative in a period when Cold War divisions were breaking down. The
third was a new challenge, one mounted by indigenous peoples for recognition of their rights within international organizations. In 1989, the
International Labour Organization put forward Convention 169, which
rejected earlier assimilationist approaches and accepted—some would
say, asserted—that indigenous peoples had the right to control their
own institutions, economic development, and way of life. Scandinavian
social democrats, and in particular Norwegian Saami representative Leif
Dunfjeld, played a major part in developing the convention, and Norway
was the first nation to accept it, in 1990. The Nordic Saami Council,* not
surprisingly, accepted its premises, and the issue inflamed Finnish politics
when, most surprisingly, a doctoral thesis at the University of Lapland
asserted that the Saami claim to ancestral lands was legitimate. A major
public controversy ensued.[17]

The Finns, therefore, had powerful domestic incentives to take a
lead on the Arctic environment issue, which combined with considerable interest within its foreign policy community. Environment and
Foreign Affairs both had powerful ministers: the former, Kaj Bärlund,
who would later become the director of the environment and human

---

*Saami in Norway, Sweden, and Finland created the Nordic Saami Council in August 1956. Its
purpose was the "promotion of Saami rights and interest" in Fennoscandia, which includes the
Scandinavian Peninsula, the Kola Peninsula, Karelia, and Finland. Originally, Russian Saami
did not participate, but they joined in 1992 and the adjective "Nordic" was dropped. It was
instrumental in establishing Saami Parliaments, first in Norway in 1989 and later in Sweden
and Finland, and also in promoting the World Council of Indigenous Peoples. The Saami
outside of Russia have living standards approximately equal to the general population, unlike
Canadian Inuit who have much lower life expectancy and general well-being.

settlements division of the United Nations Economic Commission for Europe (UNECE); and the latter, Kalevi Sorsa, a former prime minister and one of the major figures in Finnish postwar history. With the environment ministry providing the leadership and a young scientist, Satu Nurmi, given enormous responsibility to coordinate a campaign, the foreign ministry approached its Nordic colleagues with proposals to collaborate more closely on the Arctic environment. The environment department, like most in those times, was "crammed with activists," and Nurmi recalls that she had only four employees working on the initiative, but they possessed an infectious enthusiasm—which she no doubt inspired. The foreign ministry gave senior career diplomat and northerner Esko Rajakoski, who combined earnestness with unending energy and responsibility for the environment and polar regions within the ministry, the task of persuading other foreign ministries. Sorsa, of course, brought his considerable political skills—he was prime minister four times—to all diplomatic tables. It was an impressive team.

What they sold was a simple, clear statement that did not fill a page. Sent to the foreign ministries of other Arctic countries on January 12, 1989, the document began with the comment that Finland had observed "the rapid deterioration of the environment in various parts of the Arctic region in recent years. The alarm caused by this development has been underlined by the extremely fragile ecosystems prevailing in that cold region." It then noted that the Arctic needed "multilateral cooperation" on environmental issues, as had occurred elsewhere. It continued: "We believe that the eight Arctic countries have the primary responsibility for solving the problem of protecting the Arctic environment. This is so even of other countries outside this circle of eight, which also contribute to the pollution of air and sea. Coordinated action should therefore be taken by the Governments of the eight Arctic countries. Before taking this initiative, Finland has carried out preliminary consultations with other Arctic countries. The response received has been extremely encouraging."

The letter concluded with a proposal for "a Conference on the Protection of the Environment of the Arctic [to] be convened in Helsinki in the near future." A working paper was attached to the letter pointing out the various agreements and conventions covering the Arctic, but adding that "there exists no comprehensive regime concerning the conduct of human activities having an adverse impact on the Arctic environment or its resources."[18]

The Finns were both quick and persistent. Odd Rogne of the Norwegian Polar Institute recalls Rajakoski "pulling his sheet of paper" out of his pockets or briefcase whenever he encountered other diplomats. Reactions to the proposal were mixed. The Swedes, who shared neutrality, the absence of an Arctic coast, and social democratic leaders, readily agreed to participate and thought the idea of sorting out existing agreements a good idea. Denmark and Iceland also gave assent. The Norwegians, however, were more hesitant—perhaps, the Finns suggest, because they thought an Arctic coastal state should act first, or because they would like to have taken the lead themselves.

The Finns knew the Scandinavians well and the Soviets all too well. The Canadians, however, were largely unknown, a fact that is clear in Finnish diplomatic cables. While the Canadians had extensive dealings with the Norwegians and the Danes through NATO and close ties with Sweden because of many joint diplomatic initiatives during the Cold War, their contact with the Finns had been limited. A 1997 Canadian parliamentary report on the Arctic described Finland as "locked into the Soviet orbit during the Cold War" and suggested that its greatest value was the "inner ear" it had for "obscure and conflicting signals that emanate from the East"—not the Arctic, it should be noted.[19]

Ambassador Rajakoski knew the Canadians with their vast Arctic expanse were critical to the success of the Finnish Initiative. He not only met with Canadian officials but also agreed to attend a conference on the Arctic in Edmonton in March 1989, which would be attended by indigenous rights advocate Thomas Berger and the Soviet ambassador to Canada. In February, Rajakoski had publicly presented the Finnish proposal to an Arctic conference in Paris, where he had stressed the environmental dangers facing the Arctic.[20] In Edmonton, he sounded the same theme: "I think it's prudent to start from that very urgent point, the protection of the environment." He warned against complicating the issue with other issues "that would have a political connotation or would deal with the differences—disputes actually—that exist in the area [that] could only hamper this very important initiative." It was time "to do something about the Arctic."

The Canadians were immediately supportive, so much so that some observers believed that they wanted to hijack the process. The Finns welcomed the support but wanted to maintain their imprint upon the initiative. Canadian government officials, mostly from DIAND, were enthusiastic about his message and the proposed initiative, although Rajakoski's references to the solution of the "equally fragile Antarctic environment" through an international treaty conflicted with existing Canadian policy, which was to avoid comparisons with Antarctica and the Antarctica treaty process.[21] Within DIAND, the Finnish Initiative was most timely. In the last half of the 1980s, Canadian government scientists had discovered high levels of organic pollutants, such as DDT, in the blood and fatty tissue of northerners who ate so-called traditional or country foods. This evidence demonstrated that the Arctic Ocean was a "sink" that drew in pollutants produced far away. DIAND officials and indigenous leaders combined to argue within government that the only solution was international. DIAND official Garth Bangay, who was constructing a northern contaminants program, recalls that when the "Finns came knocking" with an international environmental proposal, he immediately jumped at the opportunity and encouraged Canadian support.[22] The Canadian reactions were encouraging for the Finns, but the Americans and the Soviets of course were the most significant.

The Americans were ambiguous and hesitant. The influential State Department official Ray Arnaudo did convey to the Finns his agreement that greater cooperation on the Arctic environment was welcome. While accepting that the Arctic environment was a matter of concern, the State Department pointed out "that there are already several bilateral and multilateral agreements already in force." It would be worthwhile to study these first. The Americans added that "any study or discussion of environmental pollution or sources of such pollution should be open to all interested or affected parties, including those from non-Arctic countries." In making this point, the Americans echoed the views of non-Arctic nations and continued to do so for the next decade. On January 25, 1989, just as the Finns were making clear progress with their initiative, Bertrand Lavezzari of the French Embassy in Helsinki expressed French anxiety about the Finnish Initiative. What did it all mean? Would it go beyond environmental protection? Risto Rautiainen of the Finnish Foreign Office replied that it would not go beyond environmental issues and that only the eight Arctic states would sit at the table. Lavezzari questioned what the "Arctic" meant. Would not the French islands of St. Pierre and Miquelon qualify under the rather vague definition of the Arctic's limits used by the Council? No, they were too far south. But why, Lavezzari asked, would not other countries, which also have environmental concerns related to the Arctic and a history of significant scientific research in the Arctic, not be participants? There was no clear answer, and these questions have never gone away.[23]

The Soviets did not raise such questions, but replied at much greater length than the Americans to the brief Finn proposal. The initial pages of their long response blamed the capitalist system of production for pollution but then proceeded sensibly to admit that the Soviet Union also had serious problems and welcomed help. It pointed to the extensive industrial and mining development in the Soviet North in which 50 percent of Soviet gas and vast quantities of coal, nickel, and copper were produced. Unlike the hesitant Americans and cautious Norwegians, the Soviets thought "the time so kindly offered by the Finnish colleagues for this consultative meeting will hardly be sufficient" to do the work that was so badly needed. There should be "a high level conference" very soon to issue a "general political direction" and a "concrete program or plan."[24]

The Finns had enough to move forward. They invited the "Arctic eight," as they now dubbed themselves, to Rovaniemi for September 20–26, 1989. Exactly on the Arctic Circle, it was the European home of Santa Claus. It had been destroyed during the war by the Germans and rebuilt according to the designs of the great Finnish architect Alvar Aalto in an ambitious urban design called the Reindeer Antler Plan because of the hidden antler shape that he deliberately incorporated in the plans. His modernist town hall was finally completed in 1988, twelve years after his death, and just in time to receive the conference: delegates marvelled at its exterior whiteness faced with rich blond wood and its remarkable integration with the northern environment.

In the cool of an approaching winter, the delegates thanked the Finns, the official report notes, for a "timely and warmly appreciated initiative." Rajakoski chaired the meeting, which the minister of the environment opened. Diplomat J. Alan Beesley of Canada, and Désirée Edmar, a major cultural figure from Sweden, were the co-chairs. The Swedes and the Canadians were well represented, but Iceland sent only one representative, Norway only a director general from the Foreign Office who left on the conference's third day, and the United States, as it had indicated before the conference, saw fit to dispatch only two representatives from their Helsinki embassy.[25]

The dynamics of international conferences require a flow towards consensus to be successful, and the Rovaniemi conference found common ground on the subject of "pollutants." In moving towards this common ground, the Canadian delegation was particularly forceful, with Garth Bangay taking the lead. Initially, Bangay, a practical and informal official who had worked closely with indigenous peoples, was wary of the diplomat Beesley who was initially "prickly and snooty."

When Bangay arrived five minutes late for an initial meeting, he felt like he had "walked into the room naked." But both came to respect each other as Bangay demonstrated that the work he and his colleagues had done on organic pollutants was precisely what was needed to define the program for the Finnish Initiative. Equipped with a pile of slides and panels with Velcro coverings that lifted to reveal the foundations of an environmental policy, Bangay quickly provided "science" to support the argument for action.[26]

Delegates readily agreed that the Arctic was "special": "The Polar basin seems to function as the final depository of a number of air- and sea-born pollutants." Edmar's working group focused on the marine environment, particularly the evidence of "contaminants in the Arctic terrestrial and aquatic food chains." Interestingly, climate change was mentioned, but the conference minutes point out that there were already international forums where those topics were being considered. "Living resources"—flora and fauna—were frequent topics, and "it was felt that a strategy for the integrity of living resources would be needed." The Edmar working group concluded that the Arctic states should produce a "series of reports" concentrating on main pollutants in different parts of the ecosystem." The "leading idea" of this strategy would be "the integration of economic and environmental concerns of the Arctic according to the principles put forward in the World Conservation Strategy and the report of the World Commission on Environment and Development."

Beesley's working group concentrated on "existing legal instruments" for the protection of the Arctic environment. Prior to the meeting, scientist Satu Nurmi had organized a Finnish effort to discover what international treaties, conventions, agreements, and other instruments dealt with the Arctic environment. She discovered that only the 1973 Agreement on Polar Bears directly addressed the Arctic region, its existence testimony both to the impact of détente in the seventies and to the deleterious impact the Cold War had

had more generally. Other agreements, such as those dealing with maritime regulation, touched upon the Arctic, but, the working group concluded, "particular Arctic conditions of life and features of ecology should be more distinctly reflected." Moreover, agreements were often badly, partly, or not at all implemented. The Arctic, very simply, seemed an afterthought.

The Beesley group then raised two critical topics: the participation of "indigenous peoples of the Arctic" and the role of non-Arctic states "in the future co-operation on the Arctic environment." The Rovaniemi meeting was a gathering of states and their officials from the "Arctic eight." Indigenous peoples, non-Arctic states, and the many NGOs such as the World Wildlife Federation and Greenpeace, which had Arctic interests, were not at the table. In the case of indigenous peoples, the "importance of involving" them was recognized, but "different situations in the Arctic countries may call for different ways of achieving this ..." The other question was "the issue of the participation of the representatives of non-Arctic states in future co-operation on the Arctic." Many non-participants had significant scientific programs and were, in some cases, "sources of some kind of Arctic pollution." The report noted, however, that Beesley, while agreeing that their participation was desirable, suggested "they should be invited to participate as observers or in other appropriate ways." While Canadian officials from the Indian affairs department favoured broader indigenous participation, Canadian diplomats were wary of introducing new, non-official voices at diplomatic negotiating tables. And they were not alone.

The meeting ended on September 26 with agreement that Satu Nurmi would coordinate a task force to draw up a list of "international instruments" relevant to the Arctic and assess their contents. "State of the Arctic Environment Reports" were also commissioned on six "issues of concern" with lead countries appointed to coordinate:

Issue	Lead
1. Acids	Finland
2. Heavy metals	Soviet Union
3. Noise	Denmark
4. Oil	Norway
5. Organic contaminants	Canada
6. Radioactivity	Finland

Norway and the Soviet Union agreed to coordinate "Arctic Monitoring," while Sweden and Canada took on the responsibility for the "Arctic Sustainable Development Strategy," with the former concentrating on "early actions" and the latter on "common objectives and principles."[27] The delegates planned to meet again in the spring of 1990 and to send the Finns the results of the promised research.[28]

The Rovaniemi meeting took place as the postwar world was rapidly coming apart. The Soviet leadership had decided it could no longer maintain its domination of east-central Europe, and the Soviet Union stood back as the Communist governments of Poland, Hungary, East Germany, Czechoslovakia, Romania, and Bulgaria collapsed in the autumn of 1989, spectacularly symbolized by the fall of the Berlin Wall on November 9. The influential *New Scientist* reported on October 28, 1989, that the United States was "dragging its feet" as the Finns pushed forward their initiative for greater cooperation in the Arctic. The analysis was true, but the Americans certainly had an excuse as the political shape of the world changed fundamentally in the final months of 1989.[29] The changes in Eastern Europe and the turmoil in Moscow would also profoundly affect the Finns, whose largest trading partner was the Soviet Union. The Swedes, who shared neutrality and non-membership in the European Union with the Finns, were on the precipice of an economic crisis. The Norwegians replaced the social democrat Brundtland with a conservative government, which was understandably less enthusiastic about Brundtland's cherished notion of "sustainable development."

Given the crowded international agenda, it is unsurprising that the United States sent token representation from its embassy in Helsinki to the Rovaniemi meeting and took little part in planning for the future. But it was a clear statement of lack of interest that most other states interpreted as outright opposition.[30]

Apart from the Finns themselves, the Canadians had been the most active at the conference, a mark of the intense activity in Canadian government circles on Arctic and aboriginal issues in the late eighties. Prime Minister Brian Mulroney saw the Arctic as important for his domestic political success and his international standing. By late 1989, Mulroney was caught up in the excitement of change in Eastern Europe and eager to demonstrate a Canadian presence. In November 1989 he visited the Soviet Union, and in Leningrad on November 24 he spoke to the Arctic and Antarctic Institute about the need for Soviet–Canadian cooperation. "Eventually," he told the audience, "we would like to see the nascent multilateral environmental and scientific cooperation become more broadly based to cover the full range of economic and social issues, just as Canada and the U.S.S.R. are doing bilaterally." Then, he asked: "Why not a council of Arctic countries eventually coming into existence to co-ordinate and promote co-operation among them?" In the tumult of historic change, the speech attracted little international attention— except in Helsinki.[31]

It might have been useful if Mulroney had travelled the sixty miles from Leningrad to Helsinki, but he did not. The Finns were puzzled, but not irritated, by his proposal. After all, Gorbachev had spoken about the need for a broader Arctic forum, and it was to be expected that other states would react. The Canadians reassured the Finns that Mulroney's comments were not meant to disparage the Finnish Initiative begun at Rovaniemi; his proposal should be seen as complementary and supportive. The Canadians and Finns shared one important approach: they expanded the "Arctic" far below the Arctic Circle, the Canadians traditionally favouring 60° latitude, which includes, for example, northern Quebec where the Makivik Corporation, so important to Inuit leadership, had taken form. The Finns, through their invitations to the Rovaniemi meeting, had established that the "Arctic" was comprised of eight nations, not the five states bordering the Arctic Ocean who, during the Cold War when military issues dominated, were normally regarded as the Arctic states. This was, for the Finns and the Canadians, an important distinction, even a victory.[32]

Although the Rovaniemi meeting had produced some clear tasks and an agreement to meet again, problems appeared soon after the meeting. Non-Arctic states, notably West Germany, the United Kingdom, and France, had pointedly asked why they had not been invited to Rovaniemi, particularly since the focus of the Finnish Initiative was scientific. And, they asked, why was the European Economic Community, the forerunner of the European Union, absent? As a small state, wary of the tremendous changes occurring around it, Finland sensed trouble.[33] It soon got more.

Mary Simon had become a major actor on the Arctic indigenous stage in the 1980s. Present at the creation of the Inuit Circumpolar Conference (ICC), and a principal drafter of its founding document, she became the ICC's president in 1986. She immediately grasped the significance of Gorbachev's 1987 speech in Murmansk. The following year, she and her executive council travelled to Moscow to meet Gorbachev to request that Soviet Inuit be allowed to attend the next year's annual meeting of the ICC. They then took an extraordinary journey across the vastness of Siberia to Chukotka on the northeast tip of the Soviet Union. In the last days of the Soviet empire, the KGB eyed Simon and her delegation warily, and an agent stood outside her hotel room door every night. On the delegation were Alaskans who had been separated from the Chukotka Inuit by the Cold War. In some cases, family members had not seen each other for over a generation. When they met after the long separation, the emotions ran high. As Simon and others literally wept with joy, the KGB anxiously fussed about the strange language they heard which none of them could understand. Apparently no negative reports went back to headquarters. In 1989 the first Soviet indigenous representatives attended the ICC General Assembly in Sisimiut, Greenland. Mary Simon had made her international mark, and Gorbachev had kept his Murmansk promise that Soviet indigenous people would no longer be shut off from the world.[34]

Fresh from these successes, Simon wrote on December 5, 1989, to the Finnish foreign minister Pertti Paasio commending the Finnish Initiative but objecting strongly to the failure to involve the ICC and indigenous leaders in the process. She reminded Paasio that the ICC had been working "on a strategy for sustainable and equitable development and the protection of the Arctic environment" since 1985. Its work had been "recognized and honoured" by the United Nations Environment Programme, which had named it to the Global 500 Roll of Honour. The ICC had recently been concentrating on "toxic contaminants," a topic discussed extensively at Rovaniemi. Why, Simon asked, had "no direct and specific participatory role for the ICC" been found? She concluded bluntly: "We therefore formally request that urgent consideration be given by your government to appropriate inclusion of the ICC in the process which your government has initiated." Paasio took over three months to reply to Simon's letter, and did so briefly, although not without extensive discussion within the Finnish government. He knew that indigenous participation was a sensitive domestic issue because of the Saami claims, but nation states carefully guarded their diplomatic exclusivity. His answer was direct: he said that Finland was in favour of the ICC as an "observer" but it was a matter for "all the Arctic countries to consider." He copied his answer to the other Arctic capitals. Simon received the letter just before the next meeting of the "Rovaniemi Process," as it was already called. The meeting would be held not in Rovaniemi, but in Yellowknife, Canada. It had become the Canadian problem.[35]

Simon herself was not a problem for the Canadians. With a broadcaster's penchant for directness and a spunky character, she had

impressed officials in DIAND with her articulate and thoughtful leadership of the ICC. The Department's leadership worked well with Simon,
and the deputy minister, the highly capable Harry Swain, "always
had time for the Arctic."[36] The government encouraged her visit to
the Soviet Union, and officials from several departments had worked
closely with her at several conferences in the mid-1980s, exploring
pollutants in the Arctic. The Canadian government shared the ICC's
views on the dangers they posed for Arctic flora, fauna, and humans.
Moreover, Simon and many other aboriginal leaders were familiar faces
in Ottawa in the 1980s as the Canadian government dealt with land
claims, a process spurred on by the Constitution Act (1982) and by the
continuous attempts to revise the Constitution Act by the Mulroney
government after 1985, known as the Meech Lake and Charlottetown
Process. DIAND knew about Simon's letter, although it is not clear
whether External Affairs was informed.

With their considerable skill in finding solutions and their awareness
of the traditional exclusivity of diplomatic table, the Finns wanted to
avoid an incident that could undermine their initiative. They did understand the argument that Simon and the ICC were making about the
impact of a future environmental forum upon the Inuit way of life. The
existence of "toxic contamination" and its impact on the Saami and
their North was a principal reason for taking the Rovaniemi initiative.
But, as Paasio correctly noted, there were other Arctic countries and
other views.

The Yellowknife conference on "Protecting the Arctic Environment"
began on April 18, 1990, with Germany, the United Kingdom, Poland,
and the ICC (but not France) present as observers. J. Alan Beesley of
External Affairs chaired the meeting, the purpose of which was to report
on the activities of the two working groups established at Rovaniemi.
The vice-chairs were Désirée Edmar of Sweden and Tom Grönberg of
Finland. Again the American presence was weak, although they had
created some stir with their comments on the Rovaniemi Process. The

Scandinavians and Canadians produced the major working papers. But there was tension in the air. Representing the ICC, Simon entered the room as an "observer," along with West Germany and the United Kingdom. She saw the Arctic state government representatives at the central table and realized she would be sitting at the side and only able to speak when called upon. It was a closed meeting, as diplomatic negotiations normally are. Simon understood the rules and had told a Canadian Broadcasting Corporation (CBC) journalist standing outside the meeting room that she could not tell him what was said. Then she saw her place in the room. She listened for a while, but then decided to interrupt the discussions. She asked to speak because, as she later said, "they needed to hear me." She told the officials that the indigenous voice was missing at the table, but that it was her people who ate the toxic food and had increasing poisons in their bodies. It was their lives that were at stake. She then left the room, called over the journalist she had seen earlier, and said, "Now, I'm willing to talk." Beesley quickly emerged from the meeting, took her aside, and asked for a chat. Simon said she would not attend a meeting where the ICC's voice was silenced. Simon told her story to the CBC, and Beesley pulled rank and asked Bangay to speak to the CBC to explain the government's stand, which he recalls he did badly. From that moment, the ICC moved closer to the diplomatic table. The heads of delegation agreed that they could sit at the table with the diplomats except at heads of delegation meetings. It was a historic moment.[37]

After the opening day formalities and remarks, an ad hoc group took form to consider an "environmental strategy." Garth Bangay chaired the group, and on the twentieth he reported they had a document for the meeting to consider: a draft "Arctic Environmental Protection Strategy (AEPS)." The document built upon the discussions at Rovaniemi but drew mainly from a submission made by the Canadians with the same title, which was based upon a domestic Arctic Environmental Strategy produced to deal with contaminants. It reflected the earlier discussions, particularly in its emphasis upon the need for collaboration "to address the threats of transboundary pollution in the Arctic," but it more strongly stated the need for indigenous participation. The objectives of the AEPS were to

1. Ensure the health and well-being of Arctic ecosystems;
2. Provide for the protection and enhancement of environmental quality and the sustainable utilization of resources, including their use by Arctic peoples;
3. Provide that indigenous perspectives, values, and practices be fully accommodated;
4. Enable countries to fulfill their national and international responsibilities in a sustainable and equitable manner.

The list of principles that followed constantly emphasized the term "ecosystem," which had become prevalent among Canadian policy-makers in the 1980s. Growing out of negotiations between Canada and the United States on "acid rain" and water quality in the Great Lakes, the Canadian negotiators and scientists had developed the concept of "ecosystem" because they believed that the term "environment" was "too flat," that it didn't capture the complexity necessary to deal with questions like acid rain or transnational pollutants. The Canadian influence upon the document was marked. Canadian academic Rob Huebert has pointed out, for example, that almost every example of pollution given was Canadian in nature. The Canadian imprint was also present in the statement that, "developments in, or affecting, the Arctic shall be compatible with the sustainable utilization of results of scientific investigations and the traditional knowledge of Arctic peoples." At the end of the Yellowknife meeting, Beesley asked Bangay to become the head of the delegation. After their difficult beginning, the two had developed mutual respect and a sense of accomplishment.[38]

Had Canada hijacked the Finnish Initiative? Certainly it had shifted its direction, and the Bangay draft was essentially the final document. Nevertheless, as the Finns acknowledged then, the initiative needed stronger foundations than Finland, a small state profoundly troubled by the historic changes taking place in its own neighbourhood. They were aware that a multilateral approach to its challenges was much to be preferred to sorting out problems with the Russians bilaterally or even within a Barents Sea grouping, which the Norwegians were then championing. Where the Canadians made an impact at Yellowknife, and in consultations prior to the meeting, was in the place accorded to indigenous voices in the Rovaniemi Process and in shaping the draft AEPS document around the concept of the "ecosystem." But 1990 was tumultuous, and external events played a major part in shaping discussions. The Soviet Union crumbled, the Baltic states struggled free, the two Germanies had united, and the first Gulf War began in the months around the Yellowknife conference. The Americans had good reasons to have other priorities, the Finns to seek strong partners. But somehow in the fury and flurry of historic change, the Rovaniemi Process moved ahead with plans for a ministerial conference in Rovaniemi in June to create a new Arctic partnership in a greatly altered world.

As the conference organizers, the Finns realized much had changed since the first gathering at Rovaniemi in 1989. They scrambled to adjust to new circumstances, which was extraordinarily difficult. Fortunately, there were individuals who maintained continuity, the heads of delegations at the earlier meetings, notably Beesley of Canada, Edmar of Sweden, Grönberg of Sweden, and Sergei Zhuravlev of the Soviet Union, who, in Oran Young's words, "developed a sense of common purpose and worked together effectively to hammer out the terms of agreement." Their role in heads of delegation meetings was critical because the international system received so many shocks.[39] They developed a good personal rapport over lunches, in bars, and at the negotiating table itself. On the evening of June 12, 1991, just as the Rovaniemi ministerial opened, delegates learned that Boris

Yeltsin had been elected president of the Russian Federation and that voters in Leningrad had approved the renaming of their city as Saint Petersburg. Who would speak for the Soviet Union, which was rapidly disintegrating? Increasingly, the answer was, different voices and ones sometimes unfamiliar with Arctic issues or with English, which was the lingua franca of the Rovaniemi Process. Translators would be needed. And what to do about indigenous representation? As Russia pointed out to the Finns, most of the Arctic's indigenous people dwelt within its borders, but they were not organized and had only recently associated themselves with the Inuit Circumpolar Conference. How could they choose among the various groups, of which only some were Inuit? The Americans were similarly troublesome about the issue since the Inuit represented only part of the indigenous of Alaska. To confuse matters more, the new Russian Parliament declared its sovereignty, effectively ending the Soviet Union from which other new states were now emerging and whose boundaries were uncertain. The Finns, of course, knew the Nordic Saami Council well and believed that Inuit representation would require Saami voices too. But what form would participation take in the future Arctic environmental organization? There were many dissonant voices heard.

The Finns had asked the United Nations Economic Commission for Europe to the first Rovaniemi meeting, but its presence spurred others to seek a place in the conference room. More troubling were the NGOs who asked to attend. It seemed impossible not to invite the newly organized International Arctic Science Committee, particularly since the linkage between science and the environment was strong and reflected within national government structures. But there were problems. The scientists tended to push away the demand that indigenous traditional knowledge be represented in their work and deliberations, and the indigenous populations were wary of the emphasis on pure sciences and flora and fauna rather than on the human presence and problems in the Arctic. Finally, there were the many NGOs with a specific focus on the Arctic.

Greenpeace had become a pariah due to its refusal to consider how bans on sealing, trapping, and whaling would affect indigenous lives. Other NGOs, such as the World Wildlife Federation, worked diligently to gain the confidence of indigenous leaders, but their broader purposes still raised doubts among some Arctic indigenous leaders because of statements that some indigenous leaders believed threatened their traditional hunting and trapping life. The Finns, whose very existence depended upon the conciliation of the strong and recognition of the weak, managed the diverse challenges remarkably well.

It was perhaps appropriate that Finland's foreign minister, Paavo Väyrynen, a controversial politician who had once predicted in his doctoral thesis that the Soviet Union would triumph over the West, opened the conference. A Centre Party leader, he placed the conference clearly within the contemporary international environment and the need for a "concerted environmental plan for the Arctic." He thanked the Canadians and the Swedes for holding preparatory meetings, and noted that his government had "welcomed" the "Canadian initiative," which looked forward to future cooperation beyond the environment. He did so even though he knew that the Americans, as we shall see in the next chapter, were strongly opposed to the "Canadian initiative." Leif Halonen, the president of the Nordic Saami Council, followed him and immediately paid tribute to the "Finnish Initiative" for its role in furthering the cooperation among governments and "indigenous cultures." He proposed that the next ministerial meeting of Arctic states "include the issues regarding Arctic indigenous peoples." The ICC was also present along with the newly formed and awkwardly named "USSR Association of Small Peoples of the North."[40]

The ministers representing the Arctic states reflected the different approaches of their governments to the Arctic. Väyrynen was the sole foreign minister. Canada sent Tom Siddon, minister of Indian affairs and northern development, who unsurprisingly reflected his department's strong emphasis on indigenous participation. Finland, Iceland,

and Sweden sent their ministers of the environment, Norway its deputy environment minister, while the Soviet Union sent a deputy prime minister who was the chair of its Arctic and Antarctic Commission. The United States sent John Giffen Weinmann, a Louisiana oil company executive and member of George Bush's 1988 finance committee who, in the fashion common in American diplomacy, had become ambassador to Finland in 1989.[41]

Weinmann was fresh to the issues and, ironically, as an oil executive he had to reflect the strong influence of American environmental NGOs upon the process. Leading up to the June 1991 Rovaniemi meeting, the State Department had to consult with other relevant agencies, the two most significant being the Office of Management and Budget—which indicated that no new resources should be allocated—and the environmental bodies, which triggered the interest of the environmental lobbyists. The United States became the strongest advocate of a place at the observers' table for the large environmental groups, which created tensions with indigenous groups and states that defended their traditional ways of hunting. The Americans, with their "relatively low level of ... interest in the Arctic," had allowed these forces to remain dormant until the last minute. Not surprisingly, the other states were extremely annoyed with such last-minute interventions. It was a pattern that would endure in Arctic negotiations throughout the decade.[42]

Canada's Tom Siddon was the first to speak, and began, significantly, by welcoming the indigenous "representatives" to the ministerial conference. He then invited participants to a conference in Canada on Arctic flora and fauna in 1992 and called attention to a Canadian Arctic environmental strategy announced on April 19, pointedly noting the generous funding of $100 million that the Canadian government had promised for the strategy. Then he explained how the "Finnish Initiative" should lead to the "creation of a council of the Arctic Countries as a means for our nations to pursue other common objectives in respect of the Arctic." Prime Minister Mulroney, he added, would be writing to other leaders of Arctic nations proposing a meeting in Canada in the fall to discuss such a council.

Bertel Haarder of Denmark invited the next ministerial conference to meet in Greenland, but said little before making a curious/challenging remark: "At our little gathering before lunch I was introduced as not being indigenous. I think in a way we are *all* indigenous but in different places. We all want to influence our fate and protect our homelands just as the indigenous peoples of the North want." He then gave the platform to Ove Rosing Olsen, Greenland Home Rule minister for health and environment, who pointed out that Home Rule did not mean that Greenland could solve the problem of "pollution" alone. Olsen had worked with the Inuit Circumpolar Conference to develop an Arctic regional environmental strategy over the past eight years, but argued that an NGO "can merely point to the problems." Nation states must become engaged, and he hailed the Finnish Initiative as a model "not only by establishing our position through the principles and objectives, but also by incorporating our organizations in the preparatory work and by securing our continuing participation in the future work."

Iceland's Eidur Gudnason was brief and generous, praising the Finns, supporting the "Canadian proposal," and singling out Norway for establishing an Arctic Monitoring and Assessment Programme (AMAP). He also pointed to the importance of the United Nations Law of the Sea Convention but regretted that, among Arctic nations, only Iceland had yet ratified it. It was an important point that others passed over quickly.

Norwegian Thorvald Stoltenberg linked the environment and disarmament more directly than other speakers, pointing out the need for an atomic-test-ban treaty and demilitarization in the North. He was vague on the question of indigenous participation but not opposed to it, and emphasized the importance of the creation of the Arctic Monitoring and Assessment Programme, whose secretariat would be in Oslo.

A prominent international environmentalist, Birgitta Dahl of Sweden had supported the Finnish Initiative strongly from the beginning, and now sought to integrate it with the major UN environmental conference planned for Rio de Janeiro in 1992. She also welcomed the "Canadian proposal" as "an inspiring idea." Dahl, an outspoken politician of the Left, enthusiastically supported the participation of indigenous organizations but also called for the presence in the room of "non-Arctic countries and international bodies" and "environmental NGOs, with particular interest or expertise in Arctic matters ..."

The two superpowers then took the floor. The Soviet representative spoke in Russian and few understood what he said, although a translation was available. Befitting the confusion in Moscow, his comments were vague and not reflective of the major role the Soviet/Russians had played in the development of the AEPS. Indeed, Oran Young argues that "while Finland remained an advocate of the AEPS, Canada and the Soviet Union emerged as the most enthusiastic boosters of the project during the negotiation stage," an unsurprising outcome because of the vastness of their Arctic expanse and their common fear of pollution, which Gorbachev had eloquently expressed in Murmansk in 1987.[43]

American ambassador Weinmann extolled the value of AMAP and said it must become the cornerstone of a future Arctic strategy. He welcomed "indigenous participation" and the presence of Alaskans in Rovaniemi. It was important they assist in future planning. Unlike other delegates, he made no reference to the "Canadian proposal," while he did praise the Finnish Initiative. It was a significant omission. After Weinmann's relatively brief and obviously prepared remarks, Finnish minister of the environment Sirpa Pietikäinen concluded by returning to where the Rovaniemi Process had begun: the "major threat to the Arctic environment" of long-range transportation of various pollutants. She welcomed the presence of the International Arctic Science Committee (IASC) but did not mention indigenous participation.

The 1989 Rovaniemi meeting had filled the halls; the 1991 gathering swelled far beyond them. Three non-Arctic states spoke: Germany, the United Kingdom, and the now-democratic Poland. They argued for the importance of non-Arctic states in future scientific work, and the Poles were especially sharp in their argument that non-Arctic states had interests that should be reflected in negotiations affecting the Arctic future. Fred Roots, a Canadian long-involved with northern science as a public servant and consultant, spoke on behalf of the newly organized IASC. The relationship of IASC to an Arctic Environmental Protection Strategy was yet unclear, but Roots asserted that the IASC would complement, not conflict, with AEPS efforts. His point was strengthened by his admission that the IASC did not yet have a budget. While indicating the importance of science to indigenous people in the North, he significantly did not mention their participation in scientific projects, a controversial subject among scientists. Roots touched a subject that was and would remain sensitive. Indigenous leaders such as Mary Simon often complained that southern scientists ignored the problems of the residents of the North. Their research agendas, these leaders claimed, reflected the interests of mining companies seeking resources, the use of the "Arctic" to test abstract theories, or the ambitions of militaries to advance particular interests. Roots, who was well aware of the controversies, ended with the 1875 International Polar Commission statement: "Science in the Arctic is not a territory for national possession."[44]

There was unintended irony when Roots's evocation of the nineteenth century was followed by the ICC's statement, which was presented by the Inuk poet-politician Aqqaluk Lynge of Greenland. An eloquent critic of southern "imperialism" and an advocate of indigenous cooperation, he did not disappoint. After beginning with a description of ICC environmental work, Lynge said that "our work is made more difficult by having to withstand challenges from well-intentioned but often ill-informed groups from outside the Arctic who would prevent us from continued use of the living resources critical to the survival of our people." He strongly supported the "Finnish Initiative," adding that where "indigenous peoples have been displaced" or have lost control of their lands, environmental destruction quickly follows. The new AEPS promised a break with that past, and he expressed appreciation for the role given to indigenous peoples in its development. Then, his poetic spirit appeared with the telling of an Inuit legend:

> In the beginning the Arctic was a beautiful tropical paradise and human beings were created there, sharing a common spirit. Then the climate became cold and many of the people left the Arctic. While they were away, they changed in many ways. Some became very dark and some became very pale. Now they are beginning to return to the Arctic, and although we Inuit sometimes find them very strange, we are getting used to them. This legend says that it is in the Arctic that we will find that the importance of our common humanity and concerns outweigh our differences.

He concluded: "In the interests of human survival and protection of our beautiful homeland, I hope it is so."[45] The conference ended with a Declaration on the Protection of Arctic Environment.[46]

The Finnish Initiative had given birth to the Arctic Environmental Protection Strategy. Its adult shape was yet unknown, but important limbs had already appeared. The major one was AMAP, the monitoring program to which the Norwegians committed substantial resources and provided a secretariat. Its purpose, initially and importantly, was scientific study of persistent organic pollutants, oil, heavy metals, radioactivity, and acidification. The three other limbs were less developed. The Conservation of Arctic Flora and Fauna (CAFF) had the advantage of the conference on its subject matter in 1992 to which Tom Siddon had invited the Rovaniemi delegates, but the programs on Protection of the Marine Environment in the Arctic (PAME) and Emergency Prevention, Preparedness and Response (EPPR) were embryonic. Participating states agreed to produce reports, consult, and take appropriate actions, but there was no central direction. The declaration indicated that the three indigenous groups would be observers at future meetings and participate fully in their work. Other organizations would be invited if it was thought they could contribute to the meetings.

The declaration built upon the one Canada had presented at Yellowknife, but was more detailed and had some significant differences. Specifically, there was less use of the term "ecosystem" favoured by Canadians and no reference to "sustainable development," a term that the United States government found vague. There was grumbling about missing words, lack of funding, and ambiguous commitments and ambivalent language. Those at the table and others beyond it worried about whether AEPS might undermine Norwegian plans to strengthen cooperation in the Barents Sea region, the new Northern Forum, an Alaskan initiative to link sub-national governments, or the Canadian proposal for an Arctic Council. But the Finnish Initiative was historic. The Rovaniemi meeting was the first gathering of ministers of the Arctic states that had ever occurred. It assured there would be more. Equally important, it defined for future international meetings who the "Arctic states" would be: eight, not five. Moreover, indigenous leaders rightly saw Rovaniemi as a triumph because, for the first time, they had participated in an international ministerial meeting, and the process assured them they would do so in the future. Few had reached to grasp the hand Gorbachev had extended at Murmansk in 1987, but the Finns did when others hesitated. The Finnish Initiative—the Rovaniemi Process—was, without doubt, a success.

Success, as always, has many authors, and several stepped forward to claim a role, ranging from Greenland's Aqqaluk Lynge, who saw the roots of the AEPS in the ICC environmental strategy developed in the 1980s, to Canadian minister of Indian affairs and northern development Tom Siddon, who claimed in a letter to Bob Cameron, the president of the Ottawa branch of the Canadian Institute of International Affairs, that his ministry "has been responsible for the preparation" of the AEPS.[47] The Canadians had contributed greatly in the design of the strategy, to be sure, but in the end, Gorbachev had provided the inspiration and the Finns had ignited the spark. While rapidly being shoved off the Russian political stage, the last Soviet leader could take some pride in the bold act he performed in Murmansk in a very different setting. It had left its mark.

FIVE

The Canadian
Initiative:
The Arctic Council

The Finnish Initiative to create an Arctic forum on the environment coincided with a budding Canadian movement inside and outside government to create a broader "council" of Arctic states. In their approach to a new Arctic body, the Canadians took different approaches, a reflection of Canada's history and recent Canadian politics. First, the bureaucratic centre of Canadian Arctic policy was not the environment or foreign affairs department, but the department responsible for "Indian affairs" and "northern development." The Department of Indian Affairs and Northern Development (DIAND) had, since the 1970s, participated in international gatherings dealing with Arctic issues, and they took pride in their expertise. Second, Canadian constitutional reform and, even more, land claims negotiations had moved Canadian indigenous leaders out of the political shadows and even into the limelight. Several agreements on indigenous land claims recognized that the government of Canada must consult indigenous populations when international agreements affected their lands and interests. Moreover, the Canadian government after 1985 began to use "Inuit use and occupancy" as a foundation for Canadian "sovereignty" in the Arctic. When Inuit leader Mary Simon came forward to rebuke startled diplomats and others for excluding the Inuit voice at the Arctic Environmental Protection Strategy (AEPS) negotiating table in Yellowknife in 1990, her arguments and words gained force from recent moral and legal commitments of the Canadian government. Third, even though indigenous groups did gain special status at the AEPS table, the AEPS was principally the work of officials, mostly from foreign affairs and environment departments of the Arctic states, although the Canadians were an important exception with the strong presence of Indian and Northern Affairs. The push to create an Arctic council gained force from powerful groups lobbying the Canadian and other governments to respond to the startling changes in the north of the Northern Hemisphere.[1]

Long before the Finns began their initiative and the Cold War ended, the notion of some type of Arctic council had appeared with the first gusts of détente in 1970. Maxwell Cohen, the most prominent Canadian international lawyer of the age, proposed what he called an Arctic Basin Treaty. His proposal arose from the development of Canadian Arctic policy in response to the SS *Manhattan* controversy and the ongoing law of the sea negotiations. The time was not yet ripe however, and the proposal went nowhere. But the idea survived, and as the Cold War wound down it took on new life. In the mid-1980s, Cohen revived the idea as a member of the Ottawa branch of the Canadian Institute of International Affairs, where a special group was formed to advise on Canadian Arctic policy. But the "Arctic Basin" of Cohen's day had expanded significantly to become the "Arctic Region," with eight states rather than the five coastal states, and it now embraced all lands and waters north of 60° latitude. After discussion in the working group, Donat Pharand of the University of Ottawa School of Law developed a proposal for an Arctic treaty that he presented to a seminar in Trømso, Norway, in December 1987, shortly after the Gorbachev Murmansk speech. But the Finns were about to seize the moment while the Canadians hesitated.[2]

The Polar Sea Incident

The Canadians lost a step when the Finns put forward their proposal for an environmental forum. In the early 1970s, the Canadian government had ingeniously used the environment to advance Canada's claims through the Arctic Waters Pollution Prevention Act, which claimed, in Prime Minister Pierre Trudeau's words, a 100-nautical-mile limit "to ensure that any danger to the delicate ecological balance of the Arctic is prevented or preserved."[3] But the environmental aspects of Gorbachev's Murmansk speech were not the focus of initial Canadian interest, although, as we have seen in the previous chapter, Canadian negotiators did play a major part in shaping the Finnish environmental initiative. However, it was the Gorbachev proposals for Arctic disarmament that initially found greatest resonance in Canada. There, a coalition developed that took up Gorbachev's rather vague ideas and shaped them into a concrete proposal for an Arctic Council that would extend beyond environmental topics to encompass the security questions that had been so critical in shaping Arctic history since the beginning of World War II. The Canadian initiative had the advantage of the strong support of the Walter and Duncan Gordon Foundation, which had generously funded Arctic conferences and projects. After Gorbachev spoke, Kyra Montagu, the daughter of Liberal politician and business leader Walter Gordon who died in 1987, called upon the foundation "to encourage the development of a Canadian security and demilitarization policy for the Arctic which is successfully integrated with related social, scientific, environmental, developmental, legal and other Canadian Arctic Policy goals, and which complements and supports International Circumpolar cooperation." The proposal was a heaping plate. In response to her proposal, the foundation set up a committee chaired by former Trudeau aide Tom Axworthy* to steer this initiative and quickly gave support to existing organizations, notably the Canadian Arctic Resources Committee (CARC), the Canadian Centre for Arms Control and Disarmament (CCACD), and Science for Peace.[4]

At first glance the proponents, many with close political and personal ties to the previous Liberal Trudeau government, would seem to have had little influence upon the Progressive Conservative government of Brian Mulroney. But Mulroney was not averse to new ideas, whatever their provenance: indeed, soon after entering office he had taken up the cause of free trade with the United States, which two years earlier he had publicly deemed unthinkable. The Americans had even furnished a politically sensitive issue to call Canadian attention to the Arctic, in the voyage of the American Coast Guard vessel the *Polar Sea* through the Northwest Passage in 1985. The contretemps disrupted Mulroney's approach to international affairs, which was based on working closely with the United States and the Ronald Reagan administration in particular.[5]

Canadian nationalists worried about Mulroney's apparent willingness to take the American point of view on international issues, and even Mulroney's supporters worried that he had embraced American neo-conservatism too tightly. When, therefore, the *Polar Sea* made its summer voyage through the Northwest Passage shortly after the Mulroney–Reagan Shamrock Summit, there was a strong reaction in Canada, and not only in traditionally nationalist circles. Although the United States and Canada negotiated an agreement in May whereby the voyage would meet the requirements of the Arctic Waters Pollution

---

*As a young Liberal activist Tom Axworthy worked with Walter Gordon in the 1960s, wrote his M.A. thesis on Gordon in 1972, and became president of the Walter and Duncan Gordon Foundation in 2009. He served as principal secretary to Prime Minister Trudeau from 1981–1984 and was deeply involved in constitutional negotiations that profoundly influenced aboriginal status. He served as the volunteer chair of the Gordon Foundation's Arctic Steering Committee between 1988 and 1996 while teaching at Harvard University. His brother Lloyd was Canadian foreign minister when the Arctic Council was created in 1996.

Prevention Act and would be accompanied by a Canadian icebreaker, the Canadian Coast Guard's *John A. Macdonald*, and Canadian observers, the fact that the United States would not bend on its insistence that the Northwest Passage did not lie within Canada's internal waters was the catalyst for the voyage's foes. Very quickly editorials and opinion pages declared the *Polar Sea* an "uninvited" intruder and a "threat" to Canadian sovereignty. The *Toronto Star*, with its close ties to the Gordon family, was particularly fierce in its criticism of government inaction:

> So far, Ottawa has done little but babble ineffectually about what it can do. It failed to launch a diplomatic protest over the *Polar Sea* fiasco. It isn't willing to go to fight things out at The Hague. And now [external affairs minister Joe] Clark talks about passing unspecified laws in Parliament that have the "incidental impact" of helping the sovereignty cause. Incidental impacts won't do it. What we need is a government that's prepared to get started—and very soon—on some or all of these projects vital to Canada's interests.

With the government's popularity dropping and with Canadians overwhelmingly indicating that they believed that the Northwest Passage lay in "Canadian waters," the *Polar Sea*'s voyage roiled Canadian political waters in the summer of 1985.[6]

The *Star* could be dismissed as partisan, but others could not be ignored. On June 13, 1985, in the usually Conservative *Globe and Mail*, University of Toronto political scientist Franklyn Griffiths* warned that the *Polar Sea* presented serious dangers for the Mulroney government:

---

*Franklyn Griffiths emerged as Canada's leading scholar on the Arctic and its place in international politics in the 1970s with the publication of *A Northern Foreign Policy*, in 1979. As a professor of political science at the University of Toronto whose father had attended the Royal Military College with Walter Gordon, he had earlier gained prominence as a scholar with his work on the Soviet Union. His knowledge of Russian greatly enhanced his value as a commentator, and Canadian officials turned to him for guidance, particularly in the mid-1980s. A quiet, thoughtful, sometimes earnest man, Griffiths is a Canadian nationalist deeply influenced by his extended contacts with indigenous Canadians whose "civility" has become for him a model for relationships among northern states and peoples.

Ottawa's current options are also limited by a growing public perception that sovereignty is already being compromised in Canada's economic and defence relations with the United States. Where military matters are concerned, cruise missile testing and uncertainty about Star Wars and prospective continental defence arrangements raise difficult questions about the future of our northern occupancy. The voyage of the *Polar Sea* is likely to affect Canadian–American defence relations.

Griffith's balanced tone in the *Globe* article was not reflected when he participated in a panel discussion just before the *Polar Sea* sailed: "We've got to get up there. We've got to put up or shut up." In a phrase that would become a Canadian cliché, he warned that Canada must "use it or lose it."* Others on the panel, including a former Canadian naval officer who had monitored the SS *Manhattan* voyage in 1969, agreed that the government must greatly augment its Arctic presence and immediately begin construction of a new icebreaker.[7]

The *Polar Sea* planned to embark at the beginning of August 1985. The Mulroney government announced a review of its policy on Arctic sovereignty and declared on August 1, 1985, that it considered the passage to be within Canadian internal waters and that, accordingly, the United States should ask permission for a ship's passage, which the Americans promptly refused to do. The Canadian government followed by granting the permission that the Americans had refused to request. The *Polar Sea* then sailed into the Arctic seas and political storms.

The Inuit Tapirisat, the leading Canadian Inuit organization, joined in the protests, pointing out that there had been no consultation with those who dwelt near the passage who would ultimately pay the price

---

*Griffiths, a supporter of "civility" and an opponent of "militarism" in the Arctic, was surely horrified when he heard Prime Minister Stephen Harper declare in 2007 that Canada must "use it or lose it," in support of greater military spending in the North. He was probably gratified when the Canadian Broadcasting Corporation began to credit Stephen Harper with the invention of the phrase: www.cbc.ca/news/canada/story/2009/08/19/harper-nanook-arctic-north-sovereignty414.htm (accessed February 2, 2013).

when oil spilled and pollutants spread in Arctic waters. In the eighties, Inuit and other northerners had identified increasing "pollution" in those waters, and scientific evidence was supportive of local observation. Canadian foreign minister Joe Clark eloquently embraced their cause and used Inuit use of sea ice for snowmobiles as an argument for sovereignty. The Arctic islands, he claimed, "are joined and not divided by the waters between them. From time immemorial Canada's Inuit peoples have used and occupied the ice as they have used and occupied the land."[8] The newly created nationalist Council for Canadians captured the international attention it craved when, on August 7, 1985, it chartered a Twin Otter plane on which it placed two University of Alberta students and two Inuit protesters. The plane flew over the *Polar Sea* as it passed near the southwestern tip of Melville Island and dropped a canister with a document proclaiming Canadian sovereignty over the Northwest Passage on the ship's deck. The plane then landed directly in the ship's path, and the protesters emerged to plant Canadian flags and build snow huts on a nearby island. The exuberant president of the Council, Edmonton publisher Mel Hurtig, proclaimed that the snow huts would "symbolize traditional Inuit hunting and fishing rights." The Council, he declared with disgust, took the action because of the "weak and wimpy" Canadian government response.[9]

The uproar and the protests stirred Ottawa to action. Clark, a former prime minister who was eager to make his mark in foreign policy, was quick to counter Hurtig's jabs. Within a month of the *Polar Sea's* departure from Canadian waters, Clark announced a major policy shift. Echoing Franklyn Griffith's warning in May, he said that, with the Arctic, "we obviously have to use it or lose it." He soon brought Griffiths to Ottawa to act as a special advisor on Arctic policy. On September 10, 1985, he responded to critics with an assertive program. First, he announced that Canada would commit to building a sophisticated icebreaker capable of breaking through ice 2.4 metres thick and operating year-round. It would be the world's largest icebreaker, twice the size of any existing Canadian icebreaker. Second, he indicated that Canada had accepted the jurisdiction of the World Court, thus exposing Canada's Arctic Waters Pollution Prevention Act to international challenge and opening the possibility that Canada itself would ask the Court to rule on Canada's Arctic sovereignty. Third, he promised a greater Canadian military, political, and civilian presence in the High Arctic. Fourth, in an echo of the past, he declared that Canada would use "straight baselines" to define its Arctic Archipelago outer limit and used recent studies of Inuit presence in the High Arctic to solidify Canada's case. Finally, he announced a commitment to negotiate an agreement with the United States on Canada's Arctic sovereignty.[10]

The *Polar Sea* had stirred Canadian political waters. A recent study of the affair has concluded that neither the Canadian government nor the American State Department wanted a diplomatic incident, but the "chattering classes," which are described as "academics, aboriginal spokespeople, national interest groups, [and] politicians in opposition parties," raised a clamour that made the *Polar Sea* voyage a major issue within Canada and between Canada and the United States. A Gallup Poll taken in October 1985, shortly after the voyage and the Clark announcement, largely confirms this view: 46 percent of those polled had never heard of the *Polar Sea*. Nevertheless, over two-thirds of those who knew of it supported the Canadian view that the ship had intruded into Canadian waters. A Toronto gathering of members of the "chattering classes" organized by the Canadian Arctic Resources Committee in early November 1985 was clamorous, with lawyers strongly disagreeing about the wisdom of placing Canada's claims before the World Court, and aboriginal leaders and others pointing out that it was "hypocritical of Canada to tout the historical Inuit occupation of the area" as the grounds for Canadian sovereignty while "foot-dragging" in allowing the Inuit "to set up their own institutions." Others decried the emphasis on the armed forces in the enhanced Arctic presence while others said that Soviet and American submarine traffic under the Arctic ice was a greater danger to Canadian sovereignty than the benign voyage of the *Polar Sea*. Controversy, of course, always breeds chatter—and, not infrequently, confusion.[11]

With his poll numbers tumbling just as he embarked upon negotiations for a major constitutional revision and for free trade with the United States, Mulroney was deeply annoyed. He told visiting American vice-president George Bush in January 1987 that "the *Polar Sea* incident was a great embarrassment to us," scarcely the kind of treatment one expects from a close friend. In Mulroney's view, the United States was behaving bizarrely at a time when Soviet nuclear submarines with atomic missiles were lurking menacingly beneath the surface of the Arctic ice. Mulroney had a point, although in terms of American politics, it was not the first or last time that one segment of the U.S. government—in this case the military—had acted to contradict a policy of another part of the government—in this case the president and his diplomatic advisors. Worse still, the Americans were establishing a precedent that they did not really want. After all, if the Northwest Passage was an international strait, surely the Soviets had the right to passage as much as did the Americans.

It is in this context that the 1987 Canadian defence review, with its strong Cold War rhetoric, can be best understood. Canada would do its part for continental defence, Defence Minister Perrin Beatty proclaimed in late spring 1987, by strengthening the northern flank and by building ten to twelve nuclear attack submarines to patrol the Arctic waters at a cost of $370 million each. While appealing to the Pentagon, the proposals infuriated many Canadians. Inuit leaders immediately attacked the new Canadian nuclear presence in the Arctic: Inuit Circumpolar Conference president Mary Simon drew upon international examples to point to examples of the ill effects of "militarization" upon indigenous peoples, whether nuclear testing in the South Pacific, the Soviet Arctic, or Amchitka in the Aleutian Islands. Soviet and NATO "military activities" often "serve to promote Inuit insecurity and may threaten the unique and delicate polar environment." Nuclear disarmament in the North was imperative because "any radioactive pollution, arising by accident or out of conflict, could easily devastate the Arctic environment and the traditional Inuit way of life."[12] Canadian peace groups shared Simon's outrage at the expenditure on arms when human needs in the North were so great. There was worse to come. While publicly welcoming the hawkish new Canadian defence policy, the U.S. Navy did not really want neighbour Canada to have its own nuclear submarines. Though both sides tried to conceal this embarrassing fact, the controversy had an impact in Washington and in Moscow. Mikhail Gorbachev joined in and, as we have seen, denounced the Canadians' Arctic military plans, specifically in his Murmansk address in the early fall. The U.S. Navy on this point, at least, agreed with Gorbachev, not Canadian defence minister Perrin Beatty.[13]

Mulroney was angry, and understandably so. The Republican *Chicago Tribune* warned President Reagan on the eve of a Canadian visit in April 1987 that Mulroney "had made a career of being reasonable about the United States" and had made no secret of his admiration for Reagan, but he had nothing to show for it: the trade agenda was stalled, acid rain continued to fall in southern Canada, and there was a "painful dispute" about the Northwest Passage. Mulroney later recalled confronting Reagan: "When President Reagan visited Ottawa in 1987, I showed him the Northwest Passage on an antique globe in my office and told him bluntly, 'Ron, that's ours.' Later, after a working lunch at 24 Sussex, he raised it with his own officials, and as I noted earlier, instructed them to make reference to our position in his speech to Parliament." But the problem persisted and so did Mulroney. American secretary of state Colin Powell recalls that whenever the two leaders relaxed together, there would be a round of Irish banter, and then, after the president had had a drink or two, Mulroney would pull out a map of the Arctic from his suit pocket and point to the narrow Northwest Passage. Powell recalls that, after every visit, it would take a couple of weeks to convince the president that where Mulroney pointed to land, Americans saw ice, and ice melts. And it did so more often with the growing evidence in the later 1980s of global warming.[14]

The persistent Mulroney eventually obtained an Arctic sovereignty agreement from Reagan, who explicitly told his aides that Mulroney's aims were also America's goals. But, as we have seen, they weren't entirely. The Canadian–American Arctic agreement announced on January 11, 1988, meant that, in the future, the United States would seek permission from Canada before American icebreakers on *scientific* missions could navigate through the Northwest Passage, but it further pointed out that the American and Canadian legal positions on the passage remained the same. The Canadians did not win the war, but they did obtain a minor victory. In the words of Canadian legal advisor Len Legault, "Brian had a political problem." An election was looming, the polls were bad, the relationship with the United States was an issue, and thus "Ron" helped. And help he certainly did: just before the November 21, 1988, Canadian general election, the *Polar Sea*'s sister ship, the *Polar Star,* sailed through the Northwest Passage in October with Canadian permission, and there was not a whiff of protest. The Americans gave up more than they had anticipated or desired, but they—particularly Reagan—concluded that a practical solution had to be found because of other pressing issues. Christopher Kirkey, the major analyst of the negotiations, points out that the experience demonstrated that "mutually satisfactory solutions can be achieved, even in the face of long-standing jurisdictional disputes, through the use of co-operative, problem-solving methods." The Arctic moved to the sidelines in one of the bitterest elections in Canadian history, which was fought almost exclusively on the issue of free trade in the fall of 1988. The Arctic agreement made a minor but real contribution to Mulroney's decisive victory. It made the Americans seem less threatening.[15]

The *Polar Sea* controversy had affected the Arctic policy community and had greatly expanded its members. As noted often in previous chapters, attention upon the Arctic is intermittent and unpredictable, although, in the Canadian case, sovereignty concerns are usually the catalyst for greater activity. As Mulroney complained, the *Polar Sea* controversy was profoundly embarrassing and required him and his officials to concentrate on an issue that threatened to undermine the government's broader political direction. It muddled his government's principal foreign and domestic policy initiative: the negotiation of free trade with the United States. Beginning in the summer of 1985, senior Canadian officials in several departments, including the office of the prime minister, were compelled to focus on Arctic issues, engage with Arctic actors, pore over old and new maps of the Northwest Passage, and jostle with journalists eager to discover insults and injuries to Canadian sovereignty and dignity. As noted above, external affairs minister Joe Clark, often caricatured as fumbling and indecisive when he served as Progressive Conservative Party leader, was anxious to conduct a foreign policy that was not, in the Canadian nationalist Mel Hurtig's nasty words, "weak and wimpy." The Department of Indian Affairs and Northern Development, very much engaged with aboriginals on the land claims issue and linked with the Soviet Union through the recent joint scientific program, maintained close relationships with the emerging aboriginal leadership to prevent unexpected disruptions. Its ministers in the period—David Crombie, the former Toronto mayor, and Bill McKnight, a respected Saskatchewan businessman—possessed considerable weight in Cabinet, and Jack Stagg* gave leadership within

---

*John Ewart "Jack" Stagg was born in Galt, Ontario, the son of two war veterans. After studying for a history doctorate at Cambridge and developing a special interest in aboriginal–British relations and the Royal Proclamation of 1763, Stagg joined the Department of Indian Affairs and Northern Development in 1974. Remembered for a booming voice that attracted immediate attention, he became a leading negotiator of land claims and a frequent participant in international indigenous gatherings. Mary Simon calls him "a model bureaucrat," and Rosemarie Kuptana refers to him as a true friend, who was lost when he died prematurely in 2006. Deeply respectful of indigenous ways, Stagg despaired at the desperate poverty and social problems in Canadian aboriginal communities and worried deeply about the future of the indigenous governments whose existence he created in land claims negotiations.

the departmental bureaucracy in negotiating land claims and advancing circumpolar cooperation. The Department of Environment became increasingly important within the Mulroney government, partly because of the *Polar Sea* affair but mainly after the 1988 election with the appointment of Mulroney's Quebec lieutenant Lucien Bouchard as its minister. In the prime minister's office, Derek Burney, an able and blunt foreign service officer, brought order to chaos after his 1987 chief of staff appointment and assured careful attention to the Arctic file among the various departments. Burney brought his considerable diplomatic experience to the centre of the final negotiations of the Arctic accord with the Americans.

Those negotiations showed that "mutually satisfactory solutions" could be obtained through "co-operative, problem-solving methods."[16] The broader experience of interaction with land claims negotiation, aboriginal leadership, non-governmental organizations, foreign policy and defence interests, and the political aims of Canada's Progressive Conservative Party filtered through its ambitious prime minister, was an education by the current event for Canadians. Simply put, a lot of Canadian bureaucrats and politicians learned a lot about the Arctic quickly.

The Arctic Attracts Attention

For different reasons, the Arctic also attracted new attention in the United States, where there was a revival of the romantic, nineteenth-century vision of the Arctic as an Arctic sublime, a place to teach us what we once were before humans despoiled the Earth. Barry Lopez's elegiac *Arctic Dreams* won the 1986 National Book Award and brilliantly evoked images of a land "that one searches out and eventually finds what is beautiful." "Eskimos," he wrote, "are trapped in a long slow detonation. What they know about a good way to live is disintegrating." Civilization may deem their insights trivial but they are not. Their acceptance of the land as it is, contrasting so strikingly with the West's will to alter it, contained profound lessons, linking Arctic ways with those of the Sahara, the Mohave, and Antarctica where a similar spirit dwelt. Lopez's elegy reflected the growing international sense of indigenous solidarity, one that was influencing indigenous leaders in the Arctic.[17]

This extraordinary concatenation of dreams, political designs, strategic shifts, and personalities shifted the Arctic's place. As American political scientist and Arctic activist Oran Young later wrote, "Starting with Gorbachev's 'Arctic zone of peace' speech in October 1987, the region became a target of opportunity for those interested in promoting various forms of international and transnational cooperation." The Finns, as we have seen, took immediate advantage. The Americans and Canadians were both embroiled in elections in 1988, although because of the *Polar Sea* controversy and the greater salience of northern issues in the political arena, Canadians continued to focus upon the "target of opportunity" more closely. Moreover, while the events of the mid-1980s had brought Canadian agencies and departments closer together, their American counterparts were, at the same time, plagued by internal dissension that prevented an effective response to changing Arctic circumstances. While the powerful MacArthur and Ford foundations supported important research and conferences in the United States, they had less influence upon the policy process than the less-affluent Gordon Foundation, the venerable but under-funded Canadian Institute of International Affairs (CIIA), and the government-supported Canadian Institute of International Peace and Security had in Canada. As contemporary critics noted, the American government was not prepared to direct its aim at the "target of opportunity." They thereby created a vacuum, which the Finns, the Canadians, and many NGOs rushed to fill.[18]

The Gordon Foundation board followed these events and became excited about the possibilities. It convened a group in Toronto on April 8, 1988, to discuss what might be done. Participants in the meeting included the Toronto-based Science for Peace, the Canadian Centre for

Arms Control and Disarmament (CCACD), CARC, and the CIIA, which was represented by Franklyn Griffiths, a CIIA board member. William Kincade of the Carnegie Endowment for International Peace brought an American perspective. After the meeting, Gordon board member Kyra Montagu wrote to John Lamb of the CCACD:

> I found the day fascinating. I hope you found it interesting too. You did a wonderful job leading the discussions and your knowledge of the field and the status of all the weapons and agreements was an invaluable contribution. It was intriguing how everyone's quite distinct viewpoints still meshed at a fundamental level; for instance matching strategy for arms limitation with Franklyn's [Griffiths] environmental survival standards and even with Professor [Anatol] Rapoport's belief in negotiating conflict resolution to achieve 0 weapons and with [Carnegie Endowment Senior Associate] Bill Kincade's view that political realism requires support of the right wing!

She concluded with a tempting offer: "Let me know if you think we can be helpful." Not surprisingly, Lamb responded promptly, promising continued support and asking politely whether there was the "possibility of the Centre receiving a grant."[19]

There was—but not just now. First, the Gordon Foundation and the Canadian Institute of International Peace and Security supported a Science for Peace conference on October 26–28, 1988, which involved Rapoport, Nobel laureate Toronto physics professor John Polanyi, and approximately eighty others, including Soviet scientists and even some Soviet indigenous representatives. Having departed from his post as an advisor to the Department of External Affairs, Griffiths chaired the conference at which the official Science for Peace report declared the most "ubiquitous commentator" to be Arkady Cherkasov of Moscow's Institute for the U.S.A. and Canada. Oran Young wrote a joint paper with Cherkasov, while Inuit Circumpolar Conference president Mary Simon indicated in her paper that northern peoples solidly endorsed the aims of Science for Peace for the North. The overall impression left by the conference was, in the words of Norwegian Arctic researcher Willy Østreng, that "the pursuit of 'national self-sufficiency' is to be supplemented by an international research" movement. This direction was strengthened at a December 1989 conference in Moscow, which gave further impetus to the fledgling International Arctic Science Committee and to the spirit of cooperation and openness that marked those most unusual times.[20]

The Toronto conference illustrated how much the Canadian academics, aboriginal leaders, and political activists were concentrating on the "zone of peace" comment in the Gorbachev speech. Publication of the conference proceedings was delayed until 1990 because of the turmoil within the Soviet Union; it was then republished in 1992 because the world had changed so much. Its title bluntly expressed the mood in Toronto in late 1988: *Arctic Alternatives: Civility or Militarism in the Circumpolar North*. Although there was discussion of environmental, health, and economic development, the Cold War's militarization of the North dominated the conference debates and discussions.

At the time, it seemed that the zone of peace was a possibility. Indeed, even a representative of Canada's Department of External Affairs spoke in explicit detail at the conference about the state of Arctic demilitarization proposals. In the early months of 1989, Ottawa began to monitor carefully the various proposals relating to the Arctic in a post–Cold War age. Following the advice of American foundation executive Bill Kincade, the Gordon Foundation and even Science for Peace involved leading Progressive Conservatives. Tory MP Walter McLean, a former minister, was active in creating Parliamentarians for Global Action (PGA), an international group devoted to collaboration and demilitarization, and he took up the challenge presented by the Toronto Science for Peace conference at PGA meetings and within the Progressive Conservative caucus in Ottawa. The Gordon Foundation funded a November 1, 1989, "Parliamentary Seminar on Security and Cooperation in the Arctic," which was held in Montreal and attended by parliamentarians from the seven Arctic democratic countries. The group considered a report by the Canadian Centre on Arms Control and Disarmament on the Murmansk initiative and declared that they were "disappointed by the lack of response of other Arctic nations." The parliamentarians called for their national governments "to include an Arctic perspective in bilateral and multilateral meetings dealing with arms control and security issues." This meeting planted the seed for a future association of parliamentarians of Arctic countries. And the participants also promised to pester their own leaders until they paid more attention to the Arctic.[21]

Lobbying was the key. Two Progressive Conservatives, approached by Tom Axworthy after the Gorbachev Murmansk speech, were to play a central role in pushing the Mulroney government to take an Arctic initiative. Charles McMillan, a York University economist, had been senior policy adviser to Mulroney until 1987, and according to former Mulroney aide and journalist Ian MacDonald, "there was no aspect of the Mulroney agenda that was not substantially influenced by Charley McMillan." Bill Fox, another Mulroney communications aide, also indicated to Axworthy that he was willing to lend his skilful hand to advance the cause.[22]

With the Finns promoting their environmental initiative, the negotiations over land claims and the future Nunavut with its Inuit majority continuing, and the Soviet bloc rapidly disintegrating, the Arctic took on greater importance for many Canadian politicians, officials, and NGOs in 1990. The moment seemed propitious. The Defence Department was reeling from the shock of the unravelling of the Cold War. The April 1989 federal budget, which responded to a swelling budgetary deficit, ripped apart the 1987 defence proposals. The plan to build nuclear submarines was cancelled, as were projected purchases of Arctic surveillance aircraft. Canada's soldiers seemed adrift.[23]

The Ottawa Canadian Institute of International Affairs Arctic working group included many retired foreign service officers who had ready access to their former colleagues, and they used their influence to promote the notion of the Arctic council the working group had first presented in 1987. Similarly, the Gordon Foundation built upon its earlier initiatives and in March 1989 decided upon a three-stage plan in which they would, first, try to influence the Conservative government; second, develop a "rationale and plan for a new Arctic governance organization"; and third, sketch out the role and functions of the new organization. To that end, the Foundation formed a steering group whose initial members were Tom Axworthy as chair, John Lamb, Franklyn Griffiths, Bill Fox, Charles McMillan, Fred Roots of International Arctic Science Committee, John Merritt of Canadian Arctic Resources Committee (CARC), Mary Simon, and lawyer Paul Joffe who was advising the Inuit Circumpolar Conference (ICC). On behalf of the Gordon Foundation, Axworthy had insisted that Simon and Joffe be invited to join the group.[24] Among these individuals and groups, responsibilities were divided. CARC took the lead in the development of Arctic governance along with the ICC, while Franklyn Griffiths, with his recent Ottawa experience, respectful demeanour, and academic expertise, was immediately identified as the future chair of the group to chart the design of the Arctic Council. Axworthy would help to raise funds, while McMillan and Fox would prod the government and keep others informed about the government's mood. To boost the effort, John Lamb's CCACD finally received a grant, which would support further research on the security question, try to involve the Department of National Defence, and develop interaction with the Soviets and northern Europeans.

With Mulroney planning to visit the Soviet Union in the late fall of 1989 and with the momentous changes in the international system, Ottawa's doors were unusually open to new ideas. Although Ottawa, and indeed the world, buzzed with excitement as the Iron Curtain lifted and new possibilities emerged, there were reservations and doubts among defence officials, conservative journalists, military lobbyists, East European immigrants, intelligence officers, and pockets of the foreign affairs establishment whose experience with the Soviets had left deep distrust. In negotiating a grant with John Lamb, Kyra Montagu privately outlined the ambitious aims of the Gordon Foundation and the emerging Arctic steering group. They wanted to move "toward an institutionalized Arctic Basin conference (equivalent perhaps to the Conference on Security and Cooperation in Europe) and to an Arctic accord which incorporates arms control proposals acceptable to as many people in the region as possible." These goals were ambitious, but too grand even for a prime minister with a new majority government and a healthy dose of hubris.[25]

Mulroney in Leningrad on November 24, 1989, was cautious, avoiding all reference to security questions. His caution reflected his government's "categorically negative" response to an October 1989 Canada–Soviet conference organized by John Lamb's CCACD, which had called for dramatic arms cuts and a Canadian circumpolar ambassador to promote such plans. On the "institutionalized Arctic Basin conference," Mulroney made no specific proposal, simply musing, "And why not a conference of Arctic eventually coming into existence to coordinate and promote cooperation among them?" Coming so soon after Gorbachev's Murmansk speech and the first Rovaniemi meeting, Mulroney's remarks did signal that the Canadians had an item for the crowded Arctic agenda, and others noticed. The Finns, as we have seen, wondered what it meant for their efforts; the Americans were curious as to what the unpredictable Canadians were up to; the Soviets asked for more details; and in Canada, critics complained that Mulroney had tiptoed around the opportunities to advance arms control in the Arctic.[26]

Despite its emphasis on arms control issues, the Arctic Project Steering Committee was not at all critical of Mulroney when it met on January 18, 1990, at the Four Seasons Hotel just below Parliament Hill in Ottawa. Conservative Bill Fox told the group, "You've done very well": in just a few months, the committee had made an international mark with Mulroney's Leningrad speech. John Lamb had briefed Mulroney speechwriter Larry Hagen before the speech, and the Steering Committee's imprint was present in the prime minister's words. But Kyra Montagu rightly wondered what had happened to the arms control issue, which Mulroney had not mentioned. Lamb did not answer directly, but rather reported on meetings in Europe on an "open skies" proposal and broader discussions with Norway. He further indicated that the October conference he had organized in Moscow with Gordon support had attracted interest in some parts of the government—although, very obviously, it had not influenced the prime minister's speech. Bill Fox thought that the Arctic Basin Council proposition should move forward, and in time, security could become a part of the discussions. Although Franklyn Griffiths was a leading Canadian authority on Soviet politics and the Cold War—the obvious choice to lead the effort—it was clear he had had other matters on his mind. He told the group that he was willing to move forward quickly with the Arctic Basin Council but could only do so if he had a northerner to co-chair the Panel with him. Griffiths was deeply troubled by a meeting of the Arctic Basin Council working group on January 4, 1990. It was, he later said, "a disaster," and with "all southerners present, there was no indigenous representation despite many invitations." Without northern voices, the Council would have no legitimacy. In response to Griffiths's request for a northern co-chair, Kyra Montagu suggested Rosemarie Kuptana, the vice-president of the Inuit Circumpolar Council (ICC) who had the direct personal charm of an experienced broadcaster.* It was an inspired choice, one that greatly strengthened the indigenous voice in future discussions.[27]

---

*Rosemarie Kuptana was born in 1954 at Sachs Harbour on the Beaufort Sea in the Northwest Territories. Raised in a traditional home speaking only the Western Arctic traditional dialect, Kuptana was sent away to a residential school where she spoke only English. Later, she went to Ottawa to live with the family of a civil servant, and became involved in aboriginal politics in the early 1970s. By then articulate in English and passionate in defence of her people, Kuptana quickly gained notice as a broadcaster for the Canadian Broadcasting Corporation in 1979. She quit that position when she discovered that news on the Inuit broadcasts were mostly simple translations of the standard English language news. She later served as vice-president of the Inuit Circumpolar Council (1986–1989) and as president (1995–1996) when the Arctic Council was created.

The Arctic Basin Council group soon became the Arctic Council Panel (ACP), with its first meeting on April 4, 1990. Griffiths had undertaken to write the final report by June, and CARC, ICC, and CCACD were the sponsoring agencies. Gordon largely footed the bill. Griffiths opened the meeting by stating that the target audience for the final report would be "those southerners who do not know much about the Arctic and are indifferent to what happens there." With Kuptana and Griffiths as co-chairs, the Arctic Council Panel was transformed; the majority of members were now aboriginal, and Griffiths himself had become deeply sympathetic to their arguments. The co-chairs were very different in their origins, but, Kuptana recalls, Griffiths was profoundly open to the different voices of her people. In the 1980s he began to see the "strengthening of the aboriginal voice" and the importance of making southerners listen to these voices as his major priorities. His experience in 1990–1991 travelling through the North and meeting with Inuit, Innu, and Dene in their small communities, deeply affected him. He encountered in those gatherings "a civility I'd not encountered before" and began to see his "own behaviour and assumptions in a new light." He "began to question and discount received Western ways" but, sophisticated scholar that he was, he never disowned them.[28]

Griffiths knew Western ways prevailed in Ottawa, and his panel's success depended on responding and even reflecting them. John Hannigan, a former foreign service officer who chose to work with aboriginals, acted as the rapporteur for the Arctic Council Panel and kept the focus on its purposes, while Stephen Hazell, the executive director of the Canadian Arctic Resources Committee (CARC), provided indispensable administrative guidance. Griffiths's paper passed through many drafts and was affected by the continuous consultations, particularly in northern Canada where, in Griffiths's view, fresh insights abounded. For example, at a meeting in Iqaluit, the indigenous participants expressed concern "regarding [the] possible duplication of an international institution that would be set up to deal with international issues as Inuit already have the Inuit Circumpolar Conference to promote their rights." The proposed new institution's vague character with its NGO and indigenous representation along with government officials was, frankly, confusing. At a meeting in Iqaluit on August 22, 1990, participants asked pointed questions about whether the proposed Arctic Council would sign treaties, be recognized by the United Nations, have a place for third parties such as the United Kingdom, define the Arctic as a region, or mediate international disputes. At Rankin Inlet six days later, the questions focused on what "special role" indigenous peoples would have on the Council and whether it would be a governmental institution or simply another NGO. In truth, there were as yet no answers. And, in Ottawa, still too few listeners.[29]

The political agenda had become overcrowded with the collapse of the Meech Lake Constitutional Accord in June 1990, the choice of Jean Chrétien as Liberal leader the same month, Saddam Hussein's invasion of Kuwait on August 2, the declaration of independence from the Soviet Union by the Baltic states, the collapse of the Mulroney Progressive Conservatives in public opinion polls, and the stunning victory of Bob Rae's socialists in the October Ontario election. Suddenly the existence of Canada in its present form was up for negotiation; understandably, other problems could wait.

Into this melee in early November 1990 arrived Griffiths's seventy-nine-page paper, entitled "To Establish a Council on Arctic Security and Co-operation: A Proposal for Action." Beginning with Mulroney's November 1989 question—"And why not a council of Arctic countries?"—the paper asserted: "The need is real. The time is right ... Canada is well positioned to lead and has good reason to take the lead." Deliberately echoing the Conference on Security and Co-operation in Europe, whose emphasis on human rights, economic intercourse, and institutional linkages many credited with hastening the end of the Cold War, the paper stressed the "intimate inter-relationship between international and domestic affairs in the life of the Arctic countries." The paper drew attention "to the awkward reality that northerners at present have more in common with one another than they do with fellow nationals to the south who have yet to come alive to the value of a circumpolar perspective." This reality was present not only in the continuous collaboration of aboriginal peoples across the North but also in the "extraordinary outburst of collaboration" between regional governments across the North, which occurred in Anchorage in September 1990, inspired by Alaskan politicians who believed that southern capitals lacked understanding of the problems of the North.

The meeting in Anchorage created a Northern Forum of sub-national Arctic governments, and with the Finnish Initiative and the creation of the International Arctic Science Committee in August 1990, the "ice states [had] clearly crossed a threshold in Arctic institution-building." But the Arctic Council Panel (ACP) had reservations about the process by which these new institutions were taking form. Their primary worry was the absence of indigenous peoples and NGOs at the Council tables. There was also the continuing question of military cooperation in the region, which remained home to significant naval and nuclear assets. None of the AEPS, the Northern Forum, or the International Arctic Science Committee (IASC) dealt with the huge military presence in the Arctic. The ACP found this silence unacceptable: "International and national inclinations to employ the Arctic as a dump for sustained military activity are no more acceptable than those that lead to the use of the arctic as a sink for pollutants." There was a clear choice between civility and continuing military and strategic obsessions, between an institution to build a shared Arctic future and continued fragmentation and distrust. There was a need to "jump-start," to commit "an act of political leadership that produces the will to follow through." The new institution would be a "unique and lively plenary" between North and South, and must feature "active participation by Arctic non-state entities" that would "acknowledge that the outstanding resource of the Arctic is not its oil and gas, hard minerals or space for military operations." No, "the principal resource of the Arctic is its people." As the ACP's focus narrowed, the insistence on the need for indigenous voice in Arctic decision-making became more intense.[30]

In the Arctic Council Panel's view, the IASC and the Finnish Initiative might provide some useful "knowledge-gathering services" and could act on their limited mandate, but they were no substitute for a Council on Arctic Security and Co-operation (CASC). Moreover, they would "require some degree of guidance from a superordinate body with wider responsibilities." They would also allow the proposed CASC, unlike the Finnish Initiative, to give "closer attention to issues that are not primarily environmental and scientific in nature," problems "with a *socio-economic* and *military* character [italics in original]." Unlike the IASC and the proposed Finnish environmental body, CASC would have "baskets" and layered working groups that would permit northerners to "achieve local effects without delay, without waiting first for the Arctic Eight to act." CASC would be an intergovernmental body, although it would "embrace" non-state actors. There would be three categories: First, the states as "founding parties"; second, associated parties such as the ICC, the governor of Svalbard, the state of Alaska, and Germany— these "observers" could "make a contribution, material or otherwise" although, unlike the states, they would not be required to fund the CASC or to fulfill "significant joint undertakings," which remained the preserve of member states. Finally, there would be observers who would participate by invitation and present written presentations. These observers would not have a voice at CASC meetings. If this model was unacceptable, an international non-governmental body that concentrated on exchange of information, experience, and solutions among northerners was a possible alternative.[31]

The timing was perfect. From his days in Ottawa, Griffiths knew Larry Hagen, a speechwriter in External Affairs Minister Joe Clark's office. With his strong Tory ties, Charles McMillan simultaneously lobbied the prime minister's office to follow up on Mulroney's November

1989 rhetorical question about an Arctic Council. External affairs minister Clark had promised to speak to a Canada–Soviet conference in Ottawa. Hagen told Clark that the department would probably hold the minister "back from saying much." Griffiths told Hagen about the Arctic Council paper, sent on the presentation on the proposed council that he was delivering at the Canada–Soviet conference, and urged Hagen to incorporate its idea into Clark's speech. As Clark's office ruminated about what to say, Mulroney decided he would give the speech himself. In the end, Mulroney had to attend a conference in Europe and it was Clark who finally delivered the speech, which Hagen wrote, on November 28, 1990. From the audience, Griffiths looked on as Clark announced that Canada would propose an Arctic Council at Rovaniemi when the Arctic Environmental Protection Strategy ministerial occurred in the spring of 1991. "The moment," Griffiths later recalled, "was a great one. Looking back on it, I say we performed an act of political ventriloquy."[32]

Clark's reference in his speech to the Arctic Council was brief but substantial and reflected his personal views. Canada would propose a council of eight nations at Rovaniemi, would offer to host a small secretariat, and, crucially, would also provide funding. The Council should, Clark argued in words reflecting CASC rhetoric, "allow the voice of Northern People to be heard so that they may contribute to decisions affecting their lives and interest." Non-member countries should also have a voice. While pointing to the environmental challenges of the Arctic that required immediate attention, Clark was oblique in his reference to the changing military situation there. He was not hesitant, though, in declaring that Canada with its vast Arctic presence had a special responsibility to make certain that "the Arctic must cease to be a frontier and become a bridge."[33] The Arctic Project Steering Committee met on November 30, 1990, and toasted their work. The Arctic Council Panel was praised for their work in "fleshing out the concept" of an Arctic Council, and McMillan's influence on the prime minister's office was generously acknowledged. But so much remained to be done. Fred Roots, who had long experience as a government scientist, worried that the idea did not yet have bureaucratic "ownership," while Stephen Hazell of the Canadian Arctic Resources Committee* scribbled a note indicating that there was a possibility for potential conflict between the departments of External Affairs and Indian Affairs and Northern Development over that ownership. It was a prescient comment, as External was casting a dubious eye at the extensive international travel by Indian and Northern officials, and its lawyers were worrying about the mixing of NGOs and indigenous leaders with government officials in official gatherings.[34] John Lamb expressed some concern lest the security issues be moved to the side, while Inuit Circumpolar Conference lawyer Paul Joffe worried that the organization would not have a strong "northern" character. Clark's speech had not addressed either issue specifically. With much Ottawa seasoning and a close relationship with the government, McMillan knew that things could get lost quickly. Now, "everything is on the table," he said, pointing to the stunning changes in international affairs. The Arctic Council idea had filled an "intellectual vacuum" in Ottawa, and there was now a "window of opportunity" of, perhaps, three or four months.[35] He was, alas, an excellent prophet.

Clark's personal leadership and ties as a respected foreign minister were critical to the success of the Arctic Council. Immediately after his major speech advocating the creation of an Arctic Council, he sent out envoys to test his proposal. The Finns were consulted immediately after the Clark speech and were reassured that the Canadian initiative would not undermine or conflict with the Rovaniemi initiative. The Finns accepted the Canadian interpretation and were told on January 10, 1991, by a Canadian envoy that the Canadian proposal would cover

---

*The Canadian Arctic Resources Committee was an early proponent of circumpolar cooperation and land claims negotiation since its creation in 1971. It published many reports including the influential Canadian Institute of International Affairs 1988 report, "The Arctic Environment and Canada's International Relations." Because it was not an environmental NGO, CARC was more acceptable to indigenous groups.

a broad range of topics including transportation, communication, science, technology, Arctic marine life, and hydrocarbon development. Peter Burnet, the envoy from External Affairs, explicitly told the Finns that "Canada's initiative is more modest than the proposal of Professor Franklyn Griffith [sic]. Canada's proposal does not include cooperation in the field of security policy." He added that the United States was very supportive. The Finns, however, knew that Burnet's statement was untrue.[36]

Just after the Clark speech, Norwegian and American officials contacted a Finnish official to express "their concern about Canada's initiative." The Finns were warned not to associate their initiative with the Canadian proposal. The Finns reassured the Norwegians and the Americans that their plan did not include any proposal for a permanent secretariat or any relationship with another institution. Acting upon the conversations with the Americans, Finnish diplomat Kai Granholm told a Canadian official that he feared the "whole Arctic environmental proposal" could come apart if a new "institution" were to be created. According to Granholm, the Canadian proposal had "astounded" the Norwegians and the Americans, and the latter simply did not want the Arctic nations meddling in security matters, particularly with the Soviet Union disintegrating. They feared that "they have fallen into some kind of trap: they have committed themselves to discussions about Arctic environmental cooperation and now it suddenly seems that there is going to be a parcel of other matters on the agenda."[37]

The hesitations in Europe were complemented by changes in Ottawa. Clark left External Affairs in April 1991 when Mulroney called upon him to deal with the emerging constitutional crisis that had resulted from the failure of Mulroney's Meech Lake constitutional scheme. Clark departed just as the Americans advanced a new complication. On June 7, 1991, just before the Rovaniemi ministerial meeting creating the AEPS, the Americans told the Finns that they would "stay away" from the conference "if the Canadian plan is on the table in Rovaniemi."

The Finns, with their long experience of navigating around nasty, international whirlpools, restrained the Canadians from "presenting the issue officially in Rovaniemi" and conveyed the news to the Americans, who apparently could not get independent confirmation from Ottawa of the Canadian government's intentions. As noted in Chapter 4, the American opposition reflected concerns about costs, the association of the Canadian plan with "security," and not least, the impact the Canadian schemes might have on Alaska and its politics. The Finns knew that it was not only the Americans who opposed the Canadian proposal but also the Norwegians. The Soviets had been supporters, but Soviet policy had become terribly muddled by the political whirlwind in Moscow. In the end, lacking Canadian confirmation that they would not present their Arctic Council proposal, the Americans failed to send the senior official from Washington they had promised. But they did "show up."

The hostility to the "Canadian proposal" did not relent after the Rovaniemi meeting. An American embassy official told Asko Numminen of the Finnish Ministry of Foreign Affairs that an "interagency" meeting in Washington had given a discouraging reaction to the proposal. There was much doubt "whether there is a need for the establishment of a new organ."[38] News of the strong American opposition to the Canadian initiative travelled slowly to Canada. Flushed with their success in lobbying for the Arctic Council and vaguely aware of the opposition from others, the Arctic Council proponents pushed their case forward. They set out ambitious lobbying targets and sent the Griffiths/Kuptana Arctic Council proposal to various political actors, notably indigenous leaders. In late February, Griffiths, Kuptana, Mary Simon as president of the ICC, Lamb for CCACD, and Hazell for CARC wrote a draft letter to Mulroney, praising him for the Arctic Council initiative and explaining how their work concentrated on how a council "could best serve the interests of northern Canadians, especially Canada's aboriginal people." But they had learned that "Canadian officials now working on plans for the Council seem prepared to limit the aboriginal presence to observer status," a status that would deny "effective participation." Unless this situation was rectified, aboriginals would "withhold their support and may even actively oppose the council." The coalition had also learned that "Canadian officials are already suggesting that certain matters, notably security, might be expressly excluded." This exclusion, they argued, was "unnecessary, and would likely attract avoidable criticism of the Council." Finally, they asked for the government to "initiate discussions with aboriginal and other northern Canadians" just as they would with business leaders on "industrial competitiveness." In the end, a milder letter was sent by Hazell himself, which praised Mulroney but emphasized that External Affairs—increasingly the target of criticism from the Arctic Council Panel after Clark's departure—should consult with aboriginals and receive their support before going forward.[39]

Brian Mulroney probably did not see this letter in which a small dollop of praise is submerged in successive layers of criticism. However, he would not have missed the op-ed that Franklyn Griffiths and Rosemarie Kuptana published in the *Globe and Mail* on April 8, 1991, which strongly criticized the government. Joe Clark, they charged, had indicated a preference for an open agenda arrived at by consensus. But Washington and Moscow had interpreted these comments as a friendly wink, suggesting that "Canada is prepared to see certain matters, notably security, expressly excluded from the council's mandate." The Canadian approach was "timorous and outdated." It was time, they added, to make the future Arctic Council "a tangible symbol of a shared sense of northernness, capable of bringing Canadians together." But the officials drafting Canada's position seemed prepared "to confine native participation to representation on national delegations and to some form of observer status for international aboriginal organizations." In their view, "this would submerge and drown the northern voice." Given the circumstances and the risks he had already taken, Mulroney could be forgiven for wanting to submerge the authors.

As Griffiths and Kuptana observed in the opening paragraph of their article, Mulroney was facing the first Gulf War, a nasty recession, and a constitutional debate in which aboriginal participation was essential for the legitimacy of the constitutional process he was proposing. Mulroney also knew how strongly the Canadians had fought to have indigenous representation on the Arctic Environmental Protection Strategy, how opposed the United States was to the proposal for an Arctic Council, and how his government had persisted with the initiative despite strong pressures against it from the Americans and some Canadian officials, especially in the Department of External Affairs. The Americans and Scandinavians believed that domestic pressures were pushing the Canadians forward. After the collapse of the Meech Lake constitutional accord, Mulroney tried to put the broken pieces together through a process of public consultation, one that began with extensive consultation and effective presentations that appealed to Canadian nationalism. In their *Globe* op-ed, Griffiths and Kuptana used this mood and moment to advance their arguments, claiming that "Canada's northernness needs to be drafted into the search for a renewed national identity." An Arctic Council could be "a tangible symbol of a shared sense of northernness, capable of bringing Canadians together." In their view, they were giving Mulroney a trump. But he had good reason to fear it might become a joker.

With the Americans privately damning the Canadian initiative, and Canadian journalists, aboriginals, and opinion leaders calling for immediate action, the vise tightened upon the government in the turbulent summer of 1991. On May 14, 1991, the Arctic Council Panel released its "framework report" entitled "To Establish an Arctic Council." Simultaneously with its release, Kuptana said that "aboriginal people should have a direct participatory role" in the new council, while Griffiths charged that the Department of External Affairs was "still in low gear" in moving the Council initiative forward and had not yet consulted properly with "aboriginal people of the north." The report strongly emphasized the need for a circumpolar ambassador with special responsibilities for Arctic cooperation and institutions. The report's opening page had quotations from Mulroney's November 1989 Leningrad speech, Clark's November 1990 declaration that "now" was the time to create an Arctic Council, and Inuit Circumpolar Conference President Mary Simon's 1987 declaration that the Inuit supported an "international forum" where they could "contribute to the integrity of the world environment and world peace." That was precisely what Washington and some others were coming to fear—a forum of non-state actors and motley governments dealing with war and peace as the Soviet Union, with its thousands of nuclear weapons, fell apart. The framework report incensed the State Department, who told others that while they did not like the "Canadian Proposal," they loathed the "Griffiths" document. They freely expressed their view to other Arctic nations.[40]

In Helsinki in late August, an American official told the Ministry of Foreign Affairs that the United States had considered the Canadian proposal once again and that the reaction was "not encouraging." The Canadians, he charged, had not clarified their objective, and it was not clear how the proposed council would operate. Above all, the Americans failed to see the need for a new "organ." An interagency meeting in Washington had also pointed out that "in the last year or two, new Arctic fora have been created [AEPS and IASC]" and "these should perhaps be allowed time to develop before countries consider an umbrella organization on Arctic issues." More critically, before responding directly to Canadian officials, they pointed out that some "agencies" of the American government "also expressed the view that while there may be bilateral or trilateral Arctic issues (e.g., with Canada and/or the Soviet Union), the number of arctic-wide issues outside of science and environment are limited." They added that "other Arctic countries," a clear reference to Norway, shared their profound doubts. The author of the memorandum was Lawrence Eagleburger, the deputy secretary of state, who had little patience for Canadian meddling. In the 1980s he had gained notoriety when he denounced Pierre Trudeau's peace initiative as making sense only to pot-smoking leftists.[41]

This time Eagleburger did not publicly vent his concerns since the Mulroney government was much admired by the president, George H.W. Bush. Nevertheless, the American campaign against the Canadian proposal was intense, not least because of irritation with the increasing Canadian insistence on direct aboriginal participation. Mary Simon carried the message about direct participation in a future council to various conferences and meetings throughout the Arctic region and managed to irritate the Americans greatly. At a dinner, Ray Arnaudo, a senior American official, sat beside Whit Fraser, Simon's husband and the head of the recently created Canadian Polar Commission. He told his dinner companion that the obnoxious Simon was driving him crazy. Fraser ignored the comment about his wife and quickly changed the subject.[42]

Despite their nervousness, Canadian diplomats continued to press others for an official meeting to create an Arctic Council. In early October, diplomat Paul Heinbecker, seconded to Mulroney's office, told the Finns that they hoped to have the meeting early in 1992 and mentioned the "internal pressures" from Canadian indigenous peoples as a factor to sort out first. On November 22, 1991, Kathryn McCallion, a foreign service officer noted for her bluntness and vivacity, indicated that Canada's hesitation came because some "western countries" were still having problems with the Council's proposed character, especially Canada's insistence on aboriginal participation on the panel itself. On December 19, 1991, Jack Stagg of Indian Affairs and Northern Development took a break from the intense negotiations on the creation of Nunavut and visited European capitals to brief them on the Arctic Council initiative. He told the Finns that the Russians were now "extremely positive" and willing to go beyond Canada in terms of the Council's mandate. The Americans, he admitted, were "not interested." They had told Ottawa that a new body was unnecessary in light of "existing cooperation." Moreover, the United States believed that too much cooperation would inevitably have an impact on their military activities in the area. The creation of the Northern Forum, with its members being sub-national governments, had further complicated matters. The Canadians were willing to consider sub-national representation on the proposed council but the form of that representation should be left to individual states. For its part, the United States did not want the role of Alaska, a sub-national state, "to be emphasized." While Stagg indicated that Canada accepted that military matters could be excluded, a Finn official asked, sensibly, how they could be excluded when they often had an environmental impact. This question would linger.[43]

Stagg's hopes that a solution to indigenous representation could be found in the Rovaniemi precedent were quickly dashed. Another Canadian official, Gilles Breton, said that the question of representation was becoming "crucial" and was unresolved. Moreover, he feared that insistence by indigenous leaders like Simon that the proposed council should have the capacity to consider risks caused by nuclear-powered submarines could "endanger the whole proposal." In Canada the new external affairs minister, Barbara McDougall, who had no experience with Arctic issues, got off to a bad start in the department when she blamed officials for not telling her about the grant of a special visa to Iraqi diplomat Mohammed Al-Mashat. Bill Fox of the Arctic Council steering committee warned the Arctic Council in May that her position had been weakened, although he added that his committee colleague Charles McMillan had close ties that should be advantageous in dealing with External Affairs. The Council advocates and especially the indigenous advocates were increasingly turning towards Indian Affairs and Northern Development, whose new minister, Tom Siddon, was taking a particular interest in the international aspects of his portfolio and giving Jack Stagg major responsibilities. The result was that DIAND produced a discussion paper in December 1991 that did not specifically mention indigenous representation.* It spoke of "representatives of international arctic non-governmental organisations," being present as permanent observers, whereas other "non-arctic national and sub-national governments" should be allowed to attend meetings "on demand."[44]

This wording, not surprisingly, satisfied no one. Indigenous leaders objected to its vagueness, and international lawyers in External Affairs to the admission of private individuals to exclusive diplomatic circles. It reflected, of course, the strong opposition of Washington and to a lesser extent Norway and Russia. (The Soviet Union officially disappeared on December 31, 1991.) But there was another important factor—what came to be called the "Norwegian Initiative." After the end of the Cold War, a divisive debate emerged in the Norwegian Foreign Office between those tied to traditional Cold War alignments and others who responded to the tremendous economic and political changes in Europe's north by seeking a new regional focus for policy, one that would take form in the creation of a Barents Euro-Arctic Council. On March 5–6, 1992, the foreign ministers of the Baltic States met in Copenhagen and agreed to go forward with a regional body to consider relevant problems. There was no provision for indigenous representation in the founding document, a point noticed by the Americans, the indigenous leaders, and the Arctic Council Panel. In Griffiths's papers is a copy of the terms of reference for the newly established Council of the Baltic Sea States. The only marking is beside term 16, which provides that the Council may invite "special participants, guests, or observers" but makes no reference to aboriginal peoples. The Norwegian Initiative was driven by its

---

*DIAND official Garth Bangay, who played the major role in drafting the Arctic Environmental Protection Strategy proposal, recalls being "called on the carpet" by senior DIAND official Richard Van Loon and Stagg and told that he had been accused of being too close to the indigenous leaders and interests. Although his superiors were not specific, it was clear the accusers were Americans. Senior American Arctic official Ray Arnaudo became a friend of Bangay and later apologized to him, saying "I put you through a lot." Bangay recognized that Arnaudo "did what he had to do" and did it with exceptional skill.

powerful foreign minister, Thorvald Stoltenberg, who had earlier been decisive in overcoming Norwegian doubts about the AEPS.[45]

The Arctic international agenda had become crowded, the United States was in a presidential election year, the Western economies were in recession, the remnants of the Soviet Union in economic collapse, and Canada was in the turmoil of a major constitutional crisis. A desperate Prime Minister Mulroney was wooing aboriginal leaders to support his Charlottetown Accord, a major constitutional revision to be approved by a national referendum in October 1992. He received their support, not least because the historic Nunavut Land Claims agreement had finally been achieved in principle in April 1990. There was, then, a powerful domestic dynamic—the constitutional crisis, Mulroney's sense that his time as prime minister was coming to an end, and the wide consultation on the Arctic Council that had stirred much interest—driving the "Canadian Initiative" forward.

When the federal document on the proposed council finally came forward, there was an important change: it declared that "such a Council must provide an opportunity for Northern residents and aboriginal peoples most immediately affected by national strategies bearing upon the Arctic to have direct voice in the inception and proceedings of the Council." Its final wording reflected Indian Affairs and Northern Development rather than External Affairs. On March 5–6, 1992, aboriginal leaders met in Yellowknife with government officials present to develop a joint strategy to advance their interests. The aboriginal leaders stated strongly that they would regard the Arctic Council as just another layer of bureaucracy if they were not recognized as full participants. Simultaneously, the Arctic Council Panel pressed forward with meetings with officials and ministers, particularly with Tom Siddon, who was emerging as the champion of the aboriginal interests. On April 30, Kathryn McCallion told Mary Simon that there would be an experts' meeting on the Arctic Council proposal and asked if she would attend as the Inuit Circumpolar Conference representative. Another Canadian aboriginal could be part of the Canadian delegation. It was a last-minute affair, but the Arctic Council group managed to organize a reception for the evening of May 4. The experts' meeting began the next day.[46]

The lobbying and pressure had a clear impact. When the Ottawa experts' meeting began on May 5, Martha Greig of the Inuit Women's Association was a member of the Canadian delegation, and the ICC was independently represented by Mary Simon, its president, and Patricia Hayward. It was the sole non-state delegation at the table. The United States sent two officials from the embassy; the Swedes sent three delegates, including the respected Désirée Edmar; the Norwegians six, including one Saami Parliament member; the Finns three, including a Saami Parliament member; the Danes five, including a Greenland Home Rule representative and an indigenous official working for the Greenland premier; the Canadians six; the Russians two; and Iceland, one. McCallion, who was the director general of External Affairs' Western European bureau, headed the Canadian delegation, but Jack Stagg of DIAND was the dominant government presence. In his opening remarks he promised the Canadian government's strong support for an aboriginal presence on the Council. Simon, not surprisingly, endorsed his position, since her memorable intervention at the Yellowknife negotiation on the Finnish Initiative had established that precedent. But the American delegate, Thomas Wajda, soon dashed hopes for consensus, stating that "the United States opposes the formation of another northern body and ... in the view of the United States, existing bodies should be allowed to grow and develop and an additional body is not required." Then, to the relief of all, he added, "however, the United States is prepared to listen to those who are in favour of an Arctic Council."

By the end of the conference, after considerable redrafting of the document, the experts' group presented a text in which it was stated that, in addition to the eight Arctic states, "the Inuit Circumpolar Conference and the Nordic Saami Council will participate in the work of the Council as permanent observers." Other observers "may be invited to attend ... as appropriate" and may be NGOs or non-Arctic national governments. The Canadians agreed that they would sponsor and host a small secretariat. At the end of the meeting, the Arctic Council Panel issued a press release celebrating the meeting, particularly the changed wording on aboriginal participation. Nevertheless, Franklyn Griffiths cautioned that "the level of direct and meaningful participation by international aboriginal organizations remains a critical issue and will have to be discussed further in the talks to come."[47]

There would be no "talks to come." The presidential campaign absorbed American energies and attention during the summer of 1992, as Democrat Bill Clinton assailed George Bush with increasing success. In Canada, the constitutional crisis and a weak economy caused Brian Mulroney to become the most unpopular prime minister in Canadian history, with only 8.4 percent of Canadians telling the pollsters that they would vote for him in May 1992 when the Arctic experts' meeting occurred. In September, Ray Arnaudo of the State Department told the Canadians directly that the United States would not support "the establishment of an Arctic council." The value of the body was not apparent to the United States, and there was no assurance that it would refrain from dealing with security issues, despite Canadian pledges it would.[48]

In October 1992 the defeat of the Charlottetown Accord doomed the Progressive Conservative Party in Canada, and the victory of Bill Clinton in the American presidential election in November meant that the fate of the Arctic Council would await a new president and another prime minister. The Arctic Council initiative lingered in a state of limbo.

SIX

A Worthwhile Canadian Initiative

In the July 28, 2010, issue of *The Atlantic Wire*, Michael Kinsley wrote of a contest he'd held among readers several years ago at another publication to identify the most boring headline published in a newspaper. "There were many excellent submissions, but none beat the headline that had inspired the contest. It was over a *New York Times* column by Flora Lewis—the Tom Friedman of her day—and it was three simple words: 'Worthwhile Canadian Initiative.' To this day, I think, it has not been topped."

Worthwhile Canadian initiatives not only bore; they sometimes irritate. Unlike the "Finnish Initiative" to create an Arctic environmental council, and the "Norwegian Initiative" to link the European northern periphery more closely together, the "Canadian Initiative" had lingered for over three years since Prime Minister Brian Mulroney had proposed an Arctic Council in Leningrad in November 1989.

Mulroney's proposal was a particular Canadian response to the startling changes in international politics in the later 1980s. It also reflected Canadian domestic political circumstances, notably the emergence of aboriginal and especially Inuit leaders in the previous decade, their deep involvement in the Canadian constitutional debates of the period, and the obligation, which arose from the constitutional process, to inform and consult aboriginals on international actions that would have an impact upon them. Land claims negotiations had also brought officials and aboriginals to the table together in a way that had never occurred before, shattering the paternalistic models that had dominated for generations. But things had stalled internationally. An Arctic experts' meeting in Ottawa in May 1992 reflected the deadening impact of domestic politics upon the Canadian initiative and made little progress. The summer and fall of 1992 in Canada were consumed by the debate about the Charlottetown Accord on the constitution, which was finally defeated in a referendum on October 26, and by the controversial expansion of the free trade agreement with the United States into the North American Free Trade Agreement. In a reflection of Ottawa's distraction, Prime Minister Brian Mulroney had not made a recent public statement calling for an Arctic Council, although Mulroney and Russian president Boris Yeltsin, euphemistically described as "pale and tired," had signed a declaration supporting "an international Arctic Council" during a brief stopover in Ottawa in February.[1]

When the Canadian government took up the idea of an Arctic Council in 1989, it had drawn upon intellectual concepts developed during the Cold War and, in particular, the framing of a Canadian Arctic policy that responded to the paradox that the fundamental Canadian national interest resided in alliance with the United States in its confrontation with Soviet Communism. However, the political interest of Canadian governments, whether Liberal as in the controversy around the SS *Manhattan* or Progressive Conservative with the *Polar Sea*, was to assert Canadian sovereignty in the Arctic against incursions by the United States. Small wonder, then, that many Canadians drew a deep breath when Gorbachev proposed to take the Arctic off the Cold War points of confrontation. The Gordon Foundation reflected this excitement when it eagerly took up the challenge to promote Gorbachev's call for an Arctic zone of peace. Its choice of early allies—Science for Peace, the Canadian Centre for Arms Control and Disarmament, and the Canadian Institute for International Peace and Security—reflects its focus.

By the time Yeltsin landed in Ottawa, the situation had changed dramatically. Russia was quickly going bankrupt, and its North was witnessing a rapid depletion of its professional classes as, freed from Soviet restrictions, they moved to southern climes. The remaining super-power, the United States, had moved beyond boredom to irritation with the Canadian Arctic Council initiative, whose possible impact on Alaska was an annoyance in their presidential election year. Alaskan issues were significant beyond the state itself, not least because of the influence of their powerful and controversial senators Frank Murkowski and Ted Stevens.* There would be no more meetings until the Canadians decided their constitutional future by voting on the Charlottetown Accord and the Americans chose their president on November 3, 1992.[2]

Just before the two votes, Kathryn McCallion, the lead official in External Affairs, told the Finns that she had hopes that a future Clinton administration would be more positive towards an Arctic Council than the Bush administration had been. Unfortunately, she added, she was "a bit worried because Canadian indigenous people were dissatisfied with the government's proposals about the new constitution." She feared that

---

*Stevens, who was first elected in 1968, was the longest serving Republican Senator in American history. His long service gave him exceptional power within the Senate until he lost in 2008 after serious corruption charges against him. He had been deeply involved in the Alaska Native Claims Settlement and resource politics. Murkowski was elected in 1981 and served until 2002 when he successfully won a race to become governor. He appointed his daughter Lisa to replace him. The controversy of her appointment affected his popularity and he finished third behind Republican reformer Sarah Palin in the 2006 gubernatorial race. As chair of the powerful Energy and Natural Resources Committee, he promoted mining and resource interests but was unsuccessful in his attempt to open up the Arctic National Wildlife Refuge to oil drilling.

this discontent might be reflected in their attitude on "Arctic cooperation at the government level." With Clinton victorious, McCallion
called a meeting to clarify "Canadian Objectives" and to prepare for the
resumption of experts' meetings in the new year.[3]

McCallion's concern about the "indigenous" attitude after the
constitutional drama ended was short-lived because aboriginal leaders
maintained their strong commitment to a council, not least because of
the active support of the Arctic Council Panel on which they were well
represented. After the May meeting, Walter Slipchenko, the veteran
official who had worked on circumpolar issues for over a generation,
wrote an invaluable summary of where matters stood in the summer of
1992. According to Slipchenko, the Panel with its northern majority was
generally satisfied with the course of events. Mary Simon told Slipchenko
that the result of the Panel's work was positive, even if the Americans
were resistant. There was recognition that many External Affairs
officials and some in the Department of Indian Affairs and Northern
Affairs (DIAND) were annoyed with the publicity and lobbying the
Panel had carried out. There were also concerns that the Norwegians
and the Russians might abandon the idea if the Americans pulled out,
but DIAND's Jack Stagg's words were "most gratifying" in their clear
support for the "voice of northern people" in any future Arctic council.
Seven of the Arctic countries had agreed to provide "special status to the
ICC and the Saami Council as 'permanent observers.'" Slipchenko then
wrote: "The use of 'permanent participants' would have been better, but
as a first step demonstrates that most of the arctic countries are serious
in having meaningful participation by northerners ..."[4]

Between an "observer" and a "participant" fall many shadows.
What Slipchenko suggested would be historic: the presence of indigenous
representatives, not as members of delegations or as observers of the
actions of state officials, but as participants at the table, with full access
to discussions and documents. Slipchenko's document is the first to use
the term, and it became central to future discussions.[5] While External

Affairs was fending off international and particularly American doubts about the Council, DIAND was supporting an indigenous presence, a stance that did not escape the attention of Rosemarie Kuptana, Mary Simon, and other indigenous leaders. Gilles Breton, an official in the Circumpolar Affairs Division of DIAND, told a University of Alaska audience on August 14, 1992 that it was "our view that people in the region must be given a *full* [italics added] opportunity to speak in the Arctic Council." They should have meaningful participation. It may be, he subtly warned, that they "decide that they do not wish to partici- pate, but the opportunity to do so must be there." After Breton spoke, American academic Oran Young spoke up in apparent support, claiming that "We have entered a period in which opportunity is knocking." It was time to open the new door.[6]

The Canadian government gave the door a firm shove. External Affairs and DIAND invited the Arctic Council Panel to meet with them on December 15, 1992. The mood was festive. McCallion told Rosemarie Kuptana, Mary Simon, John Lamb, Terry Fenge, and Walter Slipchenko that the government was moving from "neutral" to an active "marketing" role. Even better, the Panel would now have a role itself. It would be formally asked to comment upon the proposed "Declaration on the Establishment of an Arctic Council." Simon, who had jousted effectively with American and Canadian officials, was asked to join External Affairs officials on their journey to Scandinavia to market the Council plan. Rosemarie Kuptana would participate in choosing the aboriginal representative for the Canadian delegation for the next meeting. The term "open agenda," which protests from other states had pushed off the draft declaration of May, would be reinserted as the Panel had requested. Henceforth, there would be "an open door policy" at government offices for Panel members. Slipchenko concluded: "All in all a very good meeting and finally we seem to be moving in step and in the same direction." "Best wishes for the New Year," he scrawled at the end of his note.[7]

It was too soon to break out the champagne. The highly articulate and feisty British-born Terry Fenge had joined the Canadian Arctic Resources Committee (CARC) in 1992 after serving as Director of Research for the Inuit organization negotiating the Nunavut Land Claims Agreement. In 1996 he joined the Inuit Circumpolar Conference and worked closely with its chair, Sheila Watt-Cloutier. He was a central player throughout the creation of the Arctic Council. Just before New Year's Eve, he sent the Arctic Council Panel an assessment of some recent meetings he'd had in Alaska, a state that was critical to the formation and understanding of American Arctic policy. He found that the environmental and aboriginal groups were suspicious of each other and had little positive interaction. But the environmentalists recognized that the Arctic Environmental Protection Strategy (AEPS) working groups were now coming to life with a Conservation of Flora and Fauna (CAFF) meeting in Alaska in May. The American government, Fenge reported, was accused of buckling under to "industrial interests." This apparent subservience was responsible for what David Cline of the National Audubon Society called an "embarrassing" performance by the Americans in Finland during the AEPS negotiations. Fenge told one Alaskan meeting about Canada's Arctic Council proposal and found that Alaskans appeared to know little about it. He then made the core argument against the Americans' insistence on "letting the Rovaniemi process" work itself out: "I stressed the political nature of the proposed Arctic council as a means to bring together ministers of foreign affairs and, perhaps, heads of state, and contrasted this with the essentially technical nature of the Rovaniemi process." They received his argument sympathetically but did not immediately support "the idea of an Arctic Council."[8] There was still much work to do.

With the Canadian government in a marketing mood, they knew that Mary Simon would be a splendid salesperson to Canadian groups. With government encouragement, Simon as president of the Inuit Circumpolar Council (ICC) organized a meeting in Yellowknife with

Canadian aboriginal leaders for March 5–6, 1993. The government would fund the travel, and the ICC would use the occasion to develop a unified position before the Arctic states next met in a formal setting. Simon had already met with Saami leaders in Scandinavia to ensure that they would develop joint positions with the ICC on the role of indigenous peoples on the Arctic Council. It is a mark of the new relationship that the records of invitations sent on ICC stationery are found in the papers of the Department of External Affairs. Even more telling is the presence in the papers of the draft declaration on the establishment of the Arctic Council, which was produced after consultations between McCallion and other government officials and the Arctic Council Panel. In the January 14 draft, there was a fundamental change. After stating in the terms of reference that the "council will operate on the basis of consensus among the eight Arctic governments," it continues: "In addition to the Arctic governments, aboriginal northern international organizations, such as the Inuit Circumpolar Conference and the Sami Council, will participate in the work of the Council as Permanent Participants."

"Permanent Participants" was double-underlined in the original preserved in the External Affairs papers. Significant it surely was, as was the following statement: "observers may be invited to attend meetings of the Council, as appropriate." The revisions thereby elevated the role of indigenous peoples while diminishing greatly—"may be invited" and "as appropriate"—the place for non-Arctic states such as the United Kingdom and Germany and NGOs such as Greenpeace, the World Wildlife Fund, and others who had earlier sought a place at the table. The non-Arctic states were the major concerns of the Finns when they first embarked on their successful initiative; for the Canadians the major concern had become indigenous peoples. Now, the revolution was complete—at least on paper. And at this point it was purely Canadian paper.[9]

With full government support, the ICC hosted the meeting in Yellowknife, NWT, on March 2–3, 1993, to rally aboriginal support for the Canadian Arctic Council draft. The attendance was poorer than hoped, but the mood was positive, even celebratory. Jack Stagg, who had been recently promoted to the post of assistant deputy minister in DIAND, told the aboriginal leaders, who included highly respected John Amagoalik of the Tunngavik Federation, Chief Bill Erasmus of the Dene Nation, Senator Charlie Watt, and two others from the Quebec Inuit's Makivik Corporation that emerged from the James Bay settlement, that "aboriginal peoples' participation in the Arctic council process is Canada's position." He further assured them that "if an Arctic Council did not respond to the needs of those in the north, it would not be useful for Canada to be part of such a Council." In answer to a question, he spoke of American reluctance to permit the Council to handle security matters, but said that Canada "would be morally bound to look at such issues." In the end, the government accepted recommendations from the group to strengthen the draft's wording to make it clear that the Council reflect more strongly the "aspirations, concerns and objectives of the indigenous peoples and other arctic residents." The government representatives also accepted that the Association of Russian Aboriginal Peoples of the North and Indigenous Survival International, an international lobbying group for indigenous issues, should be added as permanent participants. Mary Simon would assist in the drafting of the letter the Canadian government would send to the other Arctic states inviting them to Ottawa to create the Council.[10]

The government also agreed to work with a committee chosen by aboriginal organizations to prepare for the formal Arctic Council negotiations that were to take place in Ottawa in mid-May. The committee members were Simon and Kuptana of the Arctic Council Panel, Gary Bohnet of the Métis Nation, and Bill Erasmus of the Dene Nation.[11]

On May 19–20, 1993, representatives of the eight Arctic countries came to Ottawa to consider the Canadian Arctic Council proposal. Some delegations included indigenous peoples (Denmark–Greenland, Finland, Sweden, and Canada) and had senior people. The ICC, the

Saami Council, and the Association of Aboriginal Peoples of Northern Russia were also participants. The United States, however, did not send a representative, but rather an "observer" from its embassy in Ottawa. Thomas Wajda, a science and technology specialist in the American diplomatic service who had attended earlier meetings, made it clear at the beginning of the meeting he was instructed only to observe and later report. McCallion's hopes that American policy would change under the new administration seemed forlorn. The other Arctic states generally supported the Council proposal, although the Norwegians clearly had trouble with the notion of aboriginal "permanent participants" who would possess powers equal to that of nation states at the table. Before the meeting, McCallion told Canadian aboriginals that the Norwegian Barents Sea initiative had "shifted the focus of [the Norwegians'] enthusiasm." The Norwegians did not plan to include indigenous peoples as "permanent participants" in the Barents Euro-Arctic Council and obviously worried about the precedent. The Danes were also no longer fully supportive because the Council process had tended to treat Greenland, which had secured Home Rule in 1979, as a separate entity. But, McCallion warned, it was the Americans who expressed greatest reluctance and were the greatest danger to the plan. If they did not change, others would pull out, including the Russians. Canada therefore had to avoid "putting them in the role of 'maker or breaker.'"[12]

The meeting accomplished little except to illustrate differences. The Russians were allies of the Canadians in arguing for a council that would be a broad umbrella, while the traditional Canadian allies in Scandinavia appeared to accept a more limited focus. The Norwegians had clear doubts about the substance, but were willing to go along if all others did. The ICC and the Arctic Council Panel gloomily summed up the outcome: "The Arctic Council negotiations have reached the final stage. Whether or not there will be an Arctic Council depends on the American Government becoming part of the process. If the U.S.A. decides for whatever reason that it will not join the process, then the initiative of an Arctic Council is likely to be put on hold ... It is evident that the Scandinavian countries together with Russia are not prepared to join Canada to form an Arctic Council [without the United States]."

With the meeting's failure and the impending Canadian election legally required for the fall of 1993, the Arctic Council was frozen once again in its political tracks.[13] As Simon later wrote, even though the Canadian government took a "pro-active position," the Arctic Council "was not to be."[14]

In retrospect, the Arctic Council lacked the powerful wings to fly in the cross-currents that swirled in the Arctic in the early 1990s. Oran Young pointed out in his 1998 study of the creation of the AEPS that the framing of the AEPS by Finland as "an initiative designed to deal with a collection of environmental concerns" was limiting, not least because it made linkages between Arctic systems and major global problems such as ozone depletion and climate change more difficult and complicated dealing with pollutants reaching the Arctic from non-AEPS states. Yet the tight focus of the AEPS and its various compromises, such as recognition of Norwegian priority in Arctic measurement and research, acceptance of the Mulroney Arctic Council initiative, and the admission of the ICC to the conference room, had made the AEPS possible. The politics of framing were exceedingly important.[15]

Until 1993 the "zone of peace" proposal, the initial focus of the Arctic Council initiative, had been the major factor delaying progress in creating an Arctic Council. By the May 1993 experts' meeting, the zone of peace had only a vestigial presence. It endured in the concept of the "umbrella" that the Arctic Council would become, one where all things Arctic could huddle under its protection. But the process and the major players had deeply influenced and changed the substance of what the Canadians were presenting to the other Arctic states. Because of the deep commitment of Franklyn Griffiths and the Gordon Foundation to the importance of indigenous peoples deciding their own fate, the Arctic Council Panel shifted away from security and international political concerns to emphasize the representation of indigenous voices on the proposed council. In a broader sense, the land claims process identified leaders within the aboriginal communities, brought new resources to the table in the form of advisors, and established a close relationship between federal negotiators like Jack Stagg and his indigenous counterparts. Of major government officials, Stagg was the strongest voice for indigenous participation and focus in the new Arctic Council. There was no mention of indigenous interests in Brian Mulroney's Leningrad speech, and indigenous leaders were initially indifferent to the proposal. By the spring of 1993, however, both Indian Affairs and Northern Development and External Affairs were funding, consulting with, and deferring to indigenous interests in the drafting of the terms of reference for the new council. It was a distinction that had become a substantial difference.

The American Dissent

We must pause here, as governments changed in Canada and the United States, and consider why the United States dissented so strongly from the proposal of its northern neighbour for an Arctic Council. The dissent came not only from the Republican Bush administration but from the Democratic Clinton administration that took office in January 1993. The Arctic, of course, had been marked by Canadian–American cooperation during World War II and the Cold War, but there had always been difficulties. Having brushed up against Canadian prickliness in the *Polar Sea* controversy, the Americans were wary of their neighbour's sensitivities. Indeed, they had hesitations about other nations seeking to create diplomatic tables for the Arctic, an area where they had complex relationships with particular interests in different government departments. The Finnish Initiative was troubling to the United States, but its narrow focus made it tolerable. The Canadian initiative had four fundamental problems for the Americans. The first was the increased emphasis upon indigenous participation. They worried about what it would mean for

Alaska, for resource development, and for diplomatic processes more generally. In the early 1990s, the controversy over indigenous rights and development reached a fever pitch with the historic United Nations Conference on Environment and Development (UNCED), the so-called Rio Earth Summit. At Rio, the United States was a frequent target for its objections to the protections contained within the Convention on Biological Diversity and, more broadly, for the cantankerous attitude it expressed towards traditional indigenous knowledge and its place in the recuperation of indigenous human and economic rights, and for its legal objections to the recognition of "peoples" in international organizations. At Rio, indigenous groups in the North and South linked together for the first time and gained strength from their contact and from their inter-action with international environmental NGOs. Mary Simon emerged as a major international figure at a Geneva preparatory meeting for UNCED where she said: "Our points of view, concerns and expertise should be integrated into all the work of UNCED and not limited to issues identified as 'indigenous.' Too often international policy and cooperation are perceived as the sole and sacred domain of national governments. Indigenous peoples are, however, very much aware of the existence in the world of various political philosophies, systems and governments." What did Simon's words mean? Very simply, what national states refuse, international organizations could insist. In their indigenous activist forums, Simon, Aqqaluk Lynge, and other Arctic voices could be sharp, and for American officials, annoying.[16]

Other Americans, notably in the resource industry and among its political allies, were understandably wary of the attitude of indigenous activists associated with the Arctic Council initiative towards develop-ment issues. On the one hand, the indigenous leaders wanted a share of resource riches. On the other hand, they were willing to use courts and diplomatic tables to halt developments they did not approve. Here Alaska was central. The historic Alaska settlement came early, and Canadian aboriginal latecomers were achieving better results in the eyes of some Alaskans. In 1983 the International Circumpolar Commission (ICC) commissioned Canadian Thomas Berger to evaluate the impact of the Alaska settlement. In his 1985 report published by a major New York publisher, the outspoken Berger was scathing in his criticism of the Alaska Native Claims Settlement Act. He charged that, in shaping the Act, Congress had the clear intent to assimilate and "to eradicate communal patterns of leadership and decision-making, customs of sharing, aboriginal rights to hunt and fish and traditional notions of land use and ownership." On October 28, 1985, the *New York Times* reported that existing rivalries between villages and the corporations, "based on geography and culture, have been intensified" by the publication of Berger's book, *Village Journey*. The book called for support for traditional village ways and the grant of local sovereignty to tribal governments. These comments, unsurprisingly, caused many Alaskan politicians to cast suspicious eyes upon the Canadian embrace of the ICC in its pursuit of an Arctic Council. Caught up in the dispute among Alaskan groups, American government officials sought to limit the damage while pushing forward Alaskan indigenous groups that were less "political" than the ICC leadership. After initially opposing indigenous participation at the table, the American effort shifted to making non-Inuit Alaskan voices a presence in the discussions.[17]

The second problem was the use of the concept of sustainable development. The Rio Summit had drawn upon the concept of sustainable development expressed in the Brundtland Commission report of 1987. At the 1993 AEPS ministerial in Nuuk, Greenland, the ministers declared their support for sustainable development and for the achievements of Rio. Moreover, they specifically stated "our belief that the principles of the Rio Declaration on Environment and Development have particular relevance with respect to sustainable development in the Arctic." Although the United States delegation at Nuuk supported the statement, the Reagan and Bush administrations consistently suspected that sustainable development would be inimical to American economic interests and complained that it was so vague that it could mean almost anything. It is a measure of the distance between Ottawa and Washington that the 1993 draft terms of reference for the Arctic Council explicitly used a quotation from the Brundtland Commission to define sustainable development and to appropriate it as a central organizing principle for work of the proposed Council. But, a senior American official later said, "the Canadians could never explain what it was." It was razzle-dazzle, hocus-pocus that could expand infinitely, dragging in all kinds of subjects that the United States had no intention even discussing, much less settling, at a table where NGOs and indigenous leaders were also present. It was not that sustainable development itself was objectionable—Vice President Al Gore proclaimed the concept to be central to the American approach to the environmental future. It was its specific use in the Arctic context that bothered the Clinton administration and senior American officials.[18]

The third problem, an enduring one, was security. Although the Canadian draft proposal omitted security, the Americans feared the "umbrella" approach the Canadians proposed would inevitably touch upon military and security issues. The belief was understandable. The initial impetus for an Arctic Council had come from Gorbachev's tempting reference to a "zone of peace." The Arctic Council Panel grew directly from Canadian concerns about the increasing militarization of the Arctic in the 1980s, including by Canada with its 1987 commitment to build about a dozen nuclear submarines. Even though the Finns in advance of Gorbachev's Murmansk speech had pressed for demilitarization of the Arctic waters, they quickly realized that protection of the Arctic environment rather than military topics would gain greater traction quickly. But the Canadians persisted, as indigenous leaders, political scientists, politicians, and some officials insisted that security not be swept off the table in any future multilateral Arctic organization. They often made the excellent point that the dominating military presence in the Arctic overlapped with environmental issues and human welfare more generally. But there was a Cold War hangover in Washington and a few other capitals, which meant that security issues stood above other concerns.

The fourth problem was the place of the Arctic in Washington. In truth, American politicians and officials, apart from Alaskans and some with a military focus, had traditionally paid little attention to the Arctic. As former State Department Arctic official Elizabeth Leighton noted, "Despite renewed interest in Arctic research and increased involvement and awareness of indigenous peoples and environmental groups, the Arctic tends to fall behind other major international initiatives and the pressing concerns of the 'lower 48.' Americans generally do not feel a historical or cultural attachment to the Arctic, and thus there is little domestic pressure to promote programs in the Arctic."

Moreover, powerful American environmental groups and agencies of government had concentrated their attention upon the negotiations leading up to the 1991 Protocol on Environmental Protection to the Antarctic Treaty. The campaign for the treaty had attracted celebrities such as Jacques Cousteau and the powerful Ted Turner of CNN, as well as the major international environmental NGOs, which correctly saw the Protocol with its ban on mineral exploitation and its preservation of the Antarctic continent as a preserve for science as a historic landmark. Many of these environmental groups had jousted with Arctic indigenous groups over hunting and trapping; the Antarctic was less complicating and more satisfying for them. Within the State Department—and many other foreign offices—the principal concern of "polar" officials had been the Antarctic process. In the Arctic Council negotiations, Ray Arnaudo of the State Department, who was respected by other diplomats, became a target because he stood on the front line. His task was difficult. Behind him was an array of American agencies that thought the Canadian initiative would bring too much new work, would cost scarce money, and was ill-conceived and distracting. They were well represented in the Interagency Arctic Policy Group that met most irregularly. Above

Arnaudo, under the Bush administration, was Lawrence Eagleburger, a powerful Washington voice, who had long distrusted Canadian initiatives cooked in the stew of domestic politics and spilling over into areas where they were, for him, thoroughly distasteful. Eagleburger departed with the Clinton election, but the legacy of his concern about the impact of the Canadian proposal upon American diplomatic and military interests endured.

Given the strength of opposition in Washington and beyond, it is remarkable that the Canadian Arctic Council initiative endured as long as it did. That it did is a tribute to the persistence of its advocates, the effectiveness of some Ottawa officials and non-governmental organizations, and the eloquence and determination of indigenous leaders in the North. The Arctic Council seemed a forlorn hope in early 1993.[19] Then the idea gained force again, and, with a sudden political stroke, it became inevitable.

Clinton and Chrétien Bless the Arctic Council

After the May meeting of experts failed to reach an agreement, the Canadians dropped plans for a ministerial gathering to form an Arctic Council. Uncertainty also marked Canadian politics after Mulroney's resignation on June 25, 1993. The Liberals had maintained a solid lead in public opinion polls, but many doubted leader Jean Chrétien's appeal to voters. After Mulroney's resignation, the Progressive Conservatives chose British-Columbian Kim Campbell as leader, and she became prime minister on June 23, 1993. She had served briefly as DIAND minister but had little time in that position to learn about her department and its priorities. She would have the same problem as prime minister. An election had to be held before winter as Parliament's term was expiring, giving Campbell all of two or three months to present a fresh face to the electorate. At first, the signs were good: Campbell's vivacity and youth caused the Conservatives to rise quickly in the polls. On Labour Day her fortunes seemed bright, but the electoral climate quickly changed.

On October 25, 1993, the Progressive Conservative Party, which had won 169 seats in 1988, was reduced to two. The Liberal Party under Chrétien, a former DIAND minister, won a majority government, whose MPs included Jack Anawak, an Inuk, and Ethel Blondin-Andrew, a Dene.

The Arctic Council idea survived the change of government. Though it had had the support of influential Conservatives like Bill Fox and Charles McMillan and Conservative MPs such as Walter McLean, its principal sponsor outside of Ottawa officialdom had been the Walter and Duncan Gordon Foundation with its impeccable Liberal pedigree, and former Trudeau aide Tom Axworthy, who chaired the Arctic Council Steering Committee. Thus, the tattered and dormant Arctic Council proposal immediately received a new breath of life.

The Liberals had been well lobbied, not surprisingly since the foreign policy critic for the Liberals while in opposition had been Lloyd Axworthy, Tom's brother, a former academic, and an influential and artic-ulate MP. In opposition, Axworthy had worked very closely with NGOs and valued their expertise and influence more than any senior Canadian politician of the age. With the help of the party's foreign policy research director Michael Pearson—the grandson of former prime minister Lester Pearson, the Liberal Party's revered Nobel Peace Prize laureate—Axworthy organized conferences, produced papers, and rallied the Liberal caucus behind various foreign policy initiatives. The Arctic was a favourite of his and the subject of a major 1992 report by the Caucus Committee on Foreign Affairs. The report, written largely by Pearson, closely reflected the interests and writings of Arctic Council advocates: the Ottawa CIIA working group; the Arctic Council Panel co-chaired by Pearson's former professor Franklyn Griffiths, whose collaboration with Joe Clark's Conservatives had long since been forgiven; and the Canadian Arctic Resources Committee (CARC), whose publications are lauded throughout the document. Although caucus matters are normally secret, a copy was faxed from Pearson's office to Terry Fenge of CARC, who surely read it with approval.[20]

Although Liberals of the day normally excoriated Mulroney and all his works, the caucus committee was generally supportive of his Arctic policies. Its dissents reflect very much the views expressed by the Arctic Council Steering Group, CARC, and especially aboriginal groups. Thus, the Liberals "strongly" supported the Arctic Council initiative and the enhanced role of aboriginal people in the shaping of the future Council. The criticisms were specific: Canada should have an Arctic Ambassador as the Gordon Foundation and the Arctic Council Panel had recommended; there were too many departments involved in the Arctic, and External Affairs was not sufficiently involved at senior levels; and there should be a national debate and public education on the Arctic to link the international initiatives to domestic discussion and debate. Arctic policy lacked coherence and failed to address the profound human problems of the Canadian North.

These promises became part of the Liberal Party's foreign policy handbook but not part of the party's so-called Red Book, the first attempt by a major Canadian political party to present its entire platform in point-by-point detail at the beginning of an election. The Red Book nevertheless emphasized the concept of sustainable development, which had become central to the Arctic debate. Chrétien, who was unfairly criticized as a lightweight, clung to the book throughout the campaign as a defence against personal attacks and against charges that his party had a secret agenda to bring back the reckless spending ways his Liberal predecessor, Pierre Trudeau, had allegedly followed. It was enormously successful but meant that the party had promises to keep, and for the Arctic they were significant ones.[21]

Axworthy, to the surprise of many, did not get an international ministry: the Department of External Affairs was renamed the Department of Foreign Affairs, and Quebec political veteran André Ouellet became the new minister. Ouellet had no background in the area, but he brought a quick mind and a valuable political assistant to his office: Michael Pearson moved from the Liberal research office, where he worked with Lloyd Axworthy, and became Ouellet's major advisor. Pearson soon gained a reputation as a hard-driving policy entrepreneur who was impatient with departmental roadblocks and hesitations. He proudly quoted the description of him by a senior departmental official as a "son of a bitch but a competent son of a bitch." However, the Arctic would have to wait. The Liberals had promised an extensive review of foreign and defence policy, a reflection of their general attack on Mulroney's foreign policy as too close to Washington and too oblivious to the end of the Cold War. But one Arctic-related promise could be quickly fulfilled.

In November 1994, the government appointed Mary Simon as Canada's ambassador for the Arctic and circumpolar affairs. The dual title emphasized the commitment to building circumpolar linkages, a point underlined in an interview Simon gave immediately after her appointment. She told Gordon Barthos of the *Toronto Star* that "northerners have been calling for a more coherent policy for a long time" and that her first job was to lobby for the creation of the Arctic Council and the second was to develop an Arctic foreign policy for Canada. She did not underestimate the challenge, domestically as well as internationally. "My role," she said, "is just part of that process, making a better future for our youth." The appointment received surprisingly little publicity—the national newspaper the *Globe and Mail* did not report it—but it raised eyebrows in some circles, including the Department of Foreign Affairs, who recalled Simon's biting attacks on Canadian policy and her close relationship with the Department of Indian Affairs and National Development, whose globetrotting activities were unpopular with some diplomats. No one, however, doubted Simon's determination.[22]

But doubts were abundant about how the Arctic Council process should proceed. The United States in opposing the Arctic Council proposal in 1991 had suggested that the Arctic Environmental Protection Strategy (AEPS) and other new Arctic innovations should be given time to develop before a new institution emerged. The Americans had a point. In creating an Arctic Council, the role of the AEPS had to be clarified immediately. The 1993 Nuuk ministerial meeting of the AEPS brought significant changes, most notably a shift towards the concept of sustainable development and away from a more exclusive concern with scientific study of the environment. It also advanced the position of the indigenous organizations within the AEPS. Now it was made clear that the three groups—the ICC, the Saami Council, and the Association of Indigenous Minorities of the Northern Siberia and the Far East of the Russian Federation—could participate in the meetings of the Senior Arctic Affairs Officials (SAAO) and in the working groups. The Rio Summit's recognition of the significance of "traditional knowledge" had influenced future approaches and discussions in the AEPS. These changes recognized or implemented at Nuuk had clear consequences. They worried some states, notably the United States, and placed a much greater burden upon the limited foundations of the AEPS. In retrospect, they made creation of a broader organization more necessary yet more difficult.[23]

The AEPS was essentially a scientific organization whose four working groups were comprised overwhelmingly of natural scientists. In truth, only one functioned well, the Norwegian-supported Arctic Monitoring and Assessment Programme (AMAP). The Canadian-supported Conservation of Arctic Flora and Fauna (CAFF) was active but lacked the institutional and financial support of AMAP. Emergency Prevention, Preparedness and Response (EPPR) was considerably weaker, not least because it clearly overlapped with military interests in the Arctic, which the AEPS had studiously avoided. Finally, the Protection of the Arctic Marine Environment (PAME) floundered because its subject matter was roiled in controversy, featuring pitched battles between primarily European environmentalists and indigenous peoples over the harvesting of seals, whales, and other aquatic life. Its budget was pitiful, its prospects dim. The lesson was clear for working group management: politics were dangerous, "pure science" was preferable.[24]

The working groups were unlike other components of the AEPS in that non-Arctic states, especially the European countries, took an active part in scientific work and often provided generous funding. The working groups also had interaction with some of the major environmental NGOs such as the World Wildlife Fund (WWF), which conducted its own scientific research on the Arctic region. The indigenous representatives had effectively put forward at the ministerial meetings the argument for incorporation of traditional environmental knowledge. Accomplishing this goal was difficult. Many scientists were suspicious of oral tradition, their discourse and methods were often highly specialized, and funding was unavailable for indigenous participation. Over time, AMAP found some valuable indigenous participants, but their number was limited and their funding ad hoc.[25]

As often occurs in scientific organizations within governments, there was a communications problem between the workers in the laboratories and senior officials who often lacked scientific or technical understanding. These difficulties were reflected in AEPS gatherings. As noted earlier, the founding meeting at Rovaniemi had some states send ministers and officials from environment ministries, while diplomats or foreign ministers represented other states. In the Canadian case, the Department of Indian Affairs and Northern Development was at the centre of the AEPS and Arctic Council negotiations. Simon reported to both the minister of foreign affairs and DIAND's minister as Canada's Arctic ambassador. It became clear early in the life of the AEPS that, like the horse built by a committee that turned out to be a camel, it had parts that didn't fit together easily. Lars-Otto Reiersen, the Norwegian scientist who has been central to AMAP's work since its foundation, argues that his major problem has been that the abundance of Arctic research AMAP has undertaken has often not penetrated to the political level where decisions are ultimately made.[26]

Finally, the increasing presence of indigenous representatives on the working groups was mirrored more generally within AEPS operations. The Russians were perpetually unable to participate because of funding and organizational problems; more surprisingly, the Saami faced similar difficulties. This meant that the ICC had a dominating presence in the early years of the AEPS. The ICC represented the Inuit population of the Arctic, which was concentrated in Canada and Greenland. With the important exception of Greenland, the Inuit were a minority of aboriginal peoples in the North. Because of the ICC's close ties with the Canadian government and the strong position of Greenland's Home Rule government in Danish policies, the Inuit voice in AEPS deliberations and operations was magnified.[27] The Americans did not hesitate to point out this fact; so did many Northern Europeans, including political scientist E.C.H. Keskitalo. In her detailed analysis of how the AEPS and the Arctic Council were negotiated in the 1990s, she asserts that the ICC in close collaboration with the Canadians chose the issues and created the boundaries and what she terms the "discourse" of the new Arctic at the expense of Scandinavia and Russia where the overwhelming majority of Arctic indigenous and non-indigenous peoples lived, as Chart 1, which was produced for a 1996–1997 Canadian Parliamentary committee, indicates. While Keskitalo's broader conclusion merits later consideration, the evidence that Canada and the ICC collaborated closely is, as we have seen, incontrovertible.[28]

Certainly Canada was more active, had a greater political prod from Canadian aboriginals, and took advantage of unusual circumstances to forward its agenda in the early 1990s. Indeed, the initial June 1990 draft statement from Franklyn Griffiths and Rosemarie Kuptana asking others to participate in the Arctic Council was far more blunt than Brian Mulroney had been in Leningrad in November 1989. Canada, it declared, was "well positioned to take a leadership role." Even though Canadian initiatives had been famously and recently mocked, the invitation concluded: "Canada should take the initiative." It did, but without success. Canada had, in political parlance, "punched above its weight,"

Comparative Profile of the Arctic Eight (1997)

Country	Percent Territory Above 60°N	Northern Indigenous Peoples (est.)
Canada	30	52,000/ 30,000,000
Denmark	100 (Greenland)	45,000/ 55,000 (Greenland)
Finland	99	4,000/ 5,120,000
Iceland	100	0/ 265,000
Norway	82	40,000/ 4,250,000
Russia	45	1,000,000/ 12,000,000 (Northern pop.)
Sweden	70	15,000/ 8,820,000
United States (Alaska)	15 (Alaska)	85,000/ 550,000 (Alaska)

SOURCE: House of Commons, Second Session of the Thirty-Fifth Parliament, 1997. *Canada and the Circumpolar World: Meeting the Challenges of Cooperation into the Twenty-First Century* (Ottawa: Public Works and Government Services Canada, 1997), 204.

but the punches often failed to land and, a few suggested, simply created hot air.[29]

Despite much frustration, the appointment of Simon, the commitment of Ouellet as minister, the incorporation of an "Arctic Council" within the Liberal Party program, and the continuing strong support for a council by the Gordon Foundation and the Arctic Council Panel kept the Canadian initiative alive. Terry Fenge, a member of the Panel, reported to the Arctic Council Panel that leading American NGOs, such as the National Audubon Society and the Sierra Club, fresh from their triumph on Antarctica, were finally beginning to focus on the Arctic after their concentration on Antarctic matters, and they were having an influence on the bureaucracy. On March 28, 1994, Fenge sent on to André Ouellet "the results of [the American Arctic policy] review" but cautioned that they "have yet to be made public." It was, he remarked, "good news for Canada. It focuses on sustainable development, environmental clean-up, and the involvement of aboriginal peoples in decision making ..."[30]

While the still-confidential document Fenge attached to his letter insisted that "environmentally sustainable development must occur" in the Arctic, it also listed as the first American objective "meeting post-Cold War national security and defense needs." This meant, the document continued, that the United States "must maintain the ability to protect against attack across the Arctic, to move ships and aircraft freely under Law of the Sea principles, to control our borders and areas under our jurisdiction, and to carry out military operations in the region." This principle rested most uneasily with the Liberal foreign policy handbook's pledge to bring "states and peoples into a cooperative arrangement designed to scale back militarization of the Arctic region, preserve the fragile ecosystem and protect the interests of indigenous peoples."[31]

There was also the muddle of acronyms that confused politicians and officials who turned to Arctic matters, and a rash of new actors such as a new Indigenous People's Secretariat in Copenhagen and a new Sustainable Development and Utilization Task Force attached to the AEPS. Who could be an AEPS observer? How could an indigenous group become a permanent observer at the AEPS table? The answers were unclear. And what of the AEPS whose 1996 ministerial was approaching and which Canada would chair? Mary Simon had made it clear that her first priority was the establishment of an Arctic Council. No other Arctic nation had that priority. What would be the new council's relationship to the AEPS? An optimist by nature, Simon was worried. Towards the end of 1994, she asked the Finns whether they would still support an Arctic Council if the United States did not "come in." The answer was a firm no. The Finns also told her that other Nordic countries probably shared that view; certainly Norway did. Knowing the challenge she faced, Simon travelled to Washington in late January 1995, met with officials, and spoke to the press. Her ebullience, indigenous background, and passionate commitment to improving life for young people in the North "who don't have much of a future" caught attention. Privately, Simon indicated to the Americans that the Canadians were willing to take "security" off the Arctic Council negotiating table. Her visit to Washington finally brought a breakthrough.[32]

Hillary and Bill Clinton came to Ottawa in February 22–24, 1995, his first official visit. Canada was once again facing a national unity crisis with fiery and unpredictable Quebec premier Jacques Parizeau promising an imminent referendum on separation. Clinton responded elegantly, telling the House of Commons that "in a world darkened by ethnic conflicts that tear nations apart, Canada has stood for all of us as a model of how people of different cultures can live and work together in peace, prosperity, and respect." Chrétien, who regularly mocked Brian Mulroney for golfing and fishing too often with former president George Bush, gave Clinton credit for the fact that polls now showed that twice as many Canadians as in the Bush years thought relations between the two countries were good. Clinton joked that he would lend Chrétien a fishing pole; Chrétien confessed that he now called the president "Bill." In private, however, Chrétien jostled and bantered the president into agreeing to a statement that the two leaders would "set up" an Arctic Council by the spring of 1996. They did not note that the Council would have six additional members, who presumably would simply assent to the Canadian–American decision to "set up" a council.[33]

This announcement, so significant for the Arctic, attracted little attention in the Canadian press and no mention in the *New York Times*. But for public servants who harken to all prime ministerial and presidential utterances and to the Arctic Council Panel and other promoters of the concept, it represented an enormous breakthrough. Ottawa quickened its step at once. Washington, however, is a behemoth that stirs slowly, and Clinton's agreement to an Arctic Council was a twitch—a large twitch—among many Washington stimuli. Nevertheless, a president's approval is a powerful currency, and the Canadians took immediate advantage, consulting with the Arctic states. Simultaneously, CARC energetically lobbied Washington environmental groups who had "tipped [them] off" that the American government's Interagency Arctic Policy Group was willing to reconsider the Arctic Council proposal because of Simon's January Washington visit.

Foreign Affairs and DIAND had produced a discussion paper prior to the Clinton visit, which argued that there was a "compelling" need for an "overall coordinated approach to Arctic issues" to promote circumpolar cooperation and "to meet the new challenge of sustainable development." Protection of the environment was important but there were other issues that required a broader focus. Examples given were economic development, trade and movement of peoples, development of transportation and communications, social welfare of "Northern residents, especially indigenous peoples," provision of educational and medical services, and promotion of tourism and cultural exchange. The Arctic Council would become "the sole international institution" to address the full range of Arctic concerns, and would support the current AEPS and IASC, which might become "functional bodies for the Council." Security was significant by its absence. The terms of reference, the discussion document declared, "should reflect the elements of the Declaration of May 1993 on the establishment of an Arctic Council (adopted by seven Arctic countries)." Obviously one country—the United States—had been missing.[34]

That country, as Simon had quickly learned, was essential, a term its foreign policy elite was employing regularly in its post–Cold War exuberance. With Clinton's agreement, the United States would come agree to an Arctic Council, but for the Americans, many questions remained. First, what should happen with the AEPS? Canada was scheduled to host an AEPS heads of delegation meeting in Iqaluit on March 14, 1995, and there had been talk of greater "institutionalization" of the AEPS, the possible creation of a permanent secretariat, and, more ambitiously, the formalization of AEPS declarations into a treaty. The Canadian talk about an Arctic Council had thrown these considerations into disarray. In any case, earlier Canadian consultations had revealed significant opposition to a formalization of the AEPS into an international legal instrument, despite arguments by Donald Rothwell, the leading international legal scholar of the period, that the protection of the environment in the North was inadequate in the absence of a "framework multilateral convention."[35] The Finns, incidentally, thought that there was no need for such a convention and that a permanent secretariat was unnecessary for the AEPS.

Immediately after the Clinton–Chrétien agreement, Mary Simon and Jack Stagg flew to Northern Europe bearing an American "non paper" on the situation, which had been written prior to the Clinton–Chrétien meeting. It was a fascinating example of bureaucratic legerdemain illustrating what can happen when political powers meddle in agendas. It is worth quoting at length:

> As part of a larger understanding on Arctic issues, the U.S. is willing to concur in the essence of the Canadian proposal on the Arctic Council as set forth in "Structure of the Proposed Arctic Council," Canada's discussion paper of January 16, 1995, with the following understandings:
> - An important understanding the U.S. requires is Canada's agreement to negotiate a maritime boundary in the Beaufort Sea with

recourse to binding dispute settlement if the negotiation does not succeed within a reasonable period of time.

- Further, the U.S. seeks Canada's understanding on the following points related specifically to the Council proposal:
  - The AEPS Ministerial should become the Council meeting; it should be regularized to take place every two years. Senior official meetings could occur more often.
  - The level of participation at Council meetings will depend on the agenda and the likelihood of substantial progress being made at the meeting.
  - The four original AEPS work groups would continue under the Council umbrella.
  - The Council could form other work groups by consensus; we would agree that the AEPS Task Force on Sustainable Development could become a work group under the Council umbrella.
  - Secretariat functions should be rotated among the countries akin to the present practice under the Antarctic Treaty system; the United States does not support the establishment of a permanent Secretariat; nor does the U.S. at this stage support the negotiation of an Arctic Treaty among the eight Arctic countries.
  - Representatives of indigenous groups that have participated in the Arctic Environmental Protection Strategy, as well as other indigenous groups with an interest in Arctic issues and sponsored by their national government, will receive permanent participant status to ensure meaningful involvement in the proceedings of the Council.
  - The United States and Canada agree that the Arctic Council is not the appropriate forum to discuss national security and defense issues.
  - With respect to the maritime boundary, in moving forward on Arctic issues and Arctic cooperation, the U.S. and Canada should resolve the longstanding maritime boundary dispute in the Beaufort Sea.

The United States had essentially provided a draft of what the Arctic Council would become. Overall, it wasn't what was hoped, but was probably much better than the Canadians had expected. It reflected the contemporary American emphasis on "informal cooperation" among states in preference to the creation of formal international organizations. On the attempted linkage with the Beaufort Sea dispute, Canada "took note" and "promised to provide a response." The dispute lingers still.[36]

Simon and Stagg consulted with Norway, Sweden, and Finland to sort out what was to happen to the Finn-inspired AEPS and how the fledgling Norwegian Euro–Arctic Barents Council would work alongside the new Arctic Council. Negotiations went well, not least because the four nations shared their grumpiness about the European Union's attitude towards their exports of fur. In any event, there was now wind behind the sails, even if its direction sometimes changed. After final consultations with the Danes, the Americans, and the Russians, Canada issued a thirteen-page document with five appendices, "The Arctic Council: Objectives, Structure and Program Priorities," which reflected the various consultations and the American "non paper." On June 6–7, the eight Arctic states and the three indigenous groups identified as "permanent participants" met at Ottawa's Westin Hotel to discuss the document.

In the Canadian document, the proposed Council was much pared down from the lofty hopes expressed by the Arctic Council Panel in the last hours of the Cold War. It described the rather vague objective of a future Council enhancing the "collective security of Arctic states and peoples," but this goal was melted down in the discussions to a bland commitment to work for peace and cooperation. The 1993 Terms of Reference had also called for annual ministerial meetings, but the 1995 document called for biennial ministerials. Plans for a permanent secretariat were also abandoned. Instead, the chair, which would rotate every two years among member nations, would assume the costs and responsibility for the secretariat. Based upon the experience of the AEPS, the

Canadians recommended that the Arctic Council founding document provide "a strong, unambiguous statement articulating the Members' readiness to provide national resources sufficient to ensure the effective implementation of activities agreed to by the Council." Because it was recognized that the agreement would be non-binding, this type of statement was considered essential.

The AEPS obviously had to become part of the new Arctic Council. Moreover, the new Copenhagen-based Indigenous Peoples' Secretariat (IPS), which operated under the AEPS, complicated the participation of indigenous peoples in the new council. After much discussion, the negotiators agreed in June that the AEPS, its four working groups, and the IPS would be incorporated within the Council. The 1993 AEPS Task Force on Sustainable Development, however, would become part of a sustainable development "pillar" within the new council. The Canadian proposal that there be a working group on social and cultural development died, and another on science and technology was deferred and disappeared later in the fall. The new Arctic Council would have two pillars: the AEPS and sustainable development. Finally, although there was no agreement about what the new entity should be called—organization and forum were two possibilities—all accepted that it would operate on a consensus basis with full participation by the three indigenous permanent participants except at certain heads of delegation meetings.[37]

The mood was good in Ottawa as negotiators sorted out drafts in glorious spring weather. The "Polar Affairs Chief," Bob Senseney of the State Department's Bureau of Oceans and International Environmental and Scientific Affairs, represented the Americans. With security shoved off the table, the only issues seeming to trouble his government were the role of non-Arctic states, the place of American aboriginal groups and Alaska more generally, and the role of non-state observers. The draft needed to be tidied, and the Ottawa meeting created a drafting group comprised of Canada, Denmark, Norway, the United States, and the

ICC to sort out the differences in Copenhagen in late August—if the group could not reach an earlier agreement. An indication of this era of good Arctic feelings was Senseney's telefax of August 2, 1995, to his colleagues indicating that he would not be travelling to Copenhagen if the meeting did occur. He might be able to send someone from the embassy, but even that was not certain. But not to worry. "You will note that most of the U.S. comments [on the draft] attempt to tighten the English usage and do not break new ground. Please know that my decision not to attend a Copenhagen meeting is reflective of our interest to minimize travel expenses in the absence of any major issues needing to be addressed." The summer drifted towards its end—and then the good times ended abruptly.[38]

The first troubles began in Alaska and Washington where the rapid movement towards the Arctic Council and its potential shape aroused sudden opposition. The ICC had been the dominant player among indigenous groups. Its former president, Mary Simon, was now Canada's ambassador for circumpolar affairs, and she joined with the ICC and three other governments to draft the final terms. Because of Simon's strong identification with the ICC, some other indigenous groups worried about excessive Inuit influence while diplomats suspected, often correctly, that she had little time for traditional diplomatic practices. The definition of the Arctic was the one set out by the Canadians in 1993, one that built upon the Arctic eight, as defined in the AEPS and by Inuit leadership. Although the ICC was born in Alaska and its president in 1995 was American, its dynamic came from Greenlanders, where the Inuit were a majority population and possessed home rule, and from Canada where Simon's charisma and achievements had brought the ICC within the corridors of government power. But the ICC was unique. The Russian NGOs were poorly organized and unfunded, and the Saami played a much less significant role with their own governments. The Inuit were a minority among aboriginal groups in the expanded definition of the Arctic Region created by the AEPS and the Arctic Council negotiations, and suddenly their dominance seemed unfair to some, including some NGOs with Arctic interests.

Two days after Senseney sent his letter indicating that there were no storms upon the horizon, the major American environmental NGOs sent out letters attacking the proposed council. The process was too closed, the participation too limited, the environmental terms too vague, and the speed too hurried. In a letter to Alaska's recently elected Democratic Governor Tony Knowles,* twelve major environmental groups, including Greenpeace, the U.S. Arctic Network, and the National Audubon Society, requested the "designation of all Arctic indigenous groups as 'Permanent Participants'" and urged new models for the Council, one that had broader participation by environmental NGOs. Suddenly, proposed changes in the draft document flooded in, and the focus was on the position of the Permanent Participants and observers with the Americans seeking to end the exclusivity of the three existing Permanent Participants and broaden the role of observers.[39]

New potholes emerged on the path to Washington where the final deal was supposedly to be sealed by officials in early September. The incidents began before the meeting, but continued when the United States unexpectedly invited two Alaskan aboriginal groups, the Aleuts and the Athabaskans (Dene), to the meeting and indicated that they would be proposed for permanent participant status. The current three indigenous groups immediately opposed the motion, claiming that a flood of applications would then come from Russia where the majority of indigenous peoples dwelt. There was already an agreement that the indigenous permanent participants would be less than the number of member

---

*The liberal Knowles became Alaska's governor on December 5, 1994, after he won a close election in which the conservative opposition was split between two candidates. Term limits required him to step down in 2002. He was close to environmental groups and was considered by President Obama for the posts of energy and the interior in his first administration. He lost to Sarah Palin in the 2006 gubernatorial election.

states. Angry words followed, but the United States would not budge. Influential American environmental NGOs, who were earlier courted with some success by Canadians such as the Canadian Arctic Resources Committee's (CARC) Terry Fenge, were also upset. With good reason, some Canadians believed. An internal CARC memorandum reflected the suddenly querulous mood:

> Sometimes I tap on my keyboard just to get rid of the frustration. Perhaps this is one of those times.
>
> I just received a call from Carol St. Laurent of WWF Canada. Carol had been in Washington for the public day of the Arctic Council talks. She told me the following:
>
> 1.   WWF Canada had made inquiries with Mary Simon's office about attending the public day of the talks. She was told in no uncertain terms that WWF was not invited and that WWF was not going to obtain a copy of the agenda.
> 2.   WWF Canada had to engineer an invitation to the public day through Bob Senseney, the head of the American delegation.
> 3.   [The International Union for the Conservation of Nature— Canada] was at the meeting—our representative was Tim Lash. Apparently IUCN also had to get an invitation from the Americans to attend the public day.
>
> So much for consensus building and inclusivity.

The consensus was breaking apart—not only between Canada and the United States but also between current permanent participants and future aspirants, whether aboriginal or environmental. The simmering distrust between northern indigenous groups protective of their hunting and trapping traditions and southern environmental NGOs came to a boil.[40] Within the Canadian government, things also came undone. During the Arctic Council negotiations, the AEPS and its working groups continued to be active, and an AEPS meeting had taken place in Iqaluit

Martin Frobisher (1539–94). The English adventurer set out to find a passage to Asia but left a lasting mark on the Arctic. (Glenbow Archives NA694-1)

Sir John Franklin (1786–1847). Franklin's fame derives from the extraordinary quest to find the remains of his ships and crew. Despite Franklin's many successes in charting the Canadian North, his death is the principal memory of his Arctic experience. (Glenbow Archives NA 1194-5)

Captain J.-E. Bernier lays claim to the Arctic on July 1, 1909, at Parry's Rock on Melville Island. *Report on the Dominion of Canada Government Expedition to the Arctic Islands and Hudson Strait on Board the D.G.S. 'Arctic.'* (Ottawa: Government Printing Bureau, 1910, 196)

North meets South. Inuit onboard the CGS *Arctic* during an expedition commanded by J.P. Craig and Capt. Joseph-Elzéar Bernier, 1922. (William Harold Grant, LAC/PA2099523)

Polar bear hanging from a rope on board the S.S. *Corwin* as the *Corwin* participates in the relief expedition on Vilhjalmur Stefansson's Canadian Arctic Expedition, 1914. (Glenbow Archives NC-1-410v)

Despite the considerable loss of life on the Canadian Arctic Expedition, Vilhjalmur Stefansson continued to promote "The Friendly Arctic" here on a Chautauqua tour in 1929. (Glenbow Archives NA3783-12)

The *St. Roch* was the Royal Canadian Mounted Police boat that patrolled the North. Here it is in Boothia Inlet in about 1940. (Glenbow Archives. NA 2821-8)

Frobisher Bay (now Iqaluit) from the air on May 14, 1961. The Canadian North was much less developed than the American, Soviet, and Scandinavian Arctic at the time when John Diefenbaker expounded his "northern vision."(Charles Gimpel Fonds, LAC 3002852360)

Mary Simon, the principal architect of the Arctic Council. (Courtesy of Walter and Duncan Gordon Foundation)

Charles (Charley) McMillan, member of the Arctic Council Panel and former principal secretary to Progressive Conservative Prime Minister Brian Mulroney, with Mulroney. (Courtesy of Charles McMillan)

Tom Axworthy, chair of the Arctic Council Panel and former principal secretary to Liberal Prime Minister Pierre Trudeau. (Courtesy of Walter and Duncan Gordon Foundation)

A powerful Inuit foursome: Kuupik Kleist, Eva Aariak, Leona Aglukkaq, and Aggaluk Lynge. (Courtesy of Harald Finklar)

Nuuk. (Courtesy of Harald Finklar)

Greenpeace protests the Canadian plan to open the Arctic to oil drilling. (Courtesy of Alexander Shestakov)

Carl Bildt of Sweden, the former Arctic chair, hands the chairmanship to Leona Aglukkaq. (Courtesy of Alexander Shestakov)

Michael Stickman and Chief Bill Erasmus of the Arctic Arthabaskan Council at Kiruna Arctic Council Ministerial, May 15, 2013. (Courtesy of Alexander Shestakov)

American Secretary of State John Kerry and Sergei Lavrov at the Kiruna Arctic Council ministerial meeting, May 15, 2013. (Courtesy of Alexander Shestakov)

in March 1995 with Canada as chair. There was departmental jockeying for positions among Environment, DIAND, and Foreign Affairs. To assist their work and link AEPS with the international indigenous agenda, Dr. Leslie Whitby, a scientist from Environment Canada, moved to DIAND and chaired the Iqaluit meeting and invited Mary Simon as Arctic ambassador to speak briefly at the meeting. As the Special Arctic Official for the AEPS, Whitby had become more prominent in Arctic Council activities as environmental groups became more active. In that capacity, she sent a letter to Bob Senseney on October 18, 1995, in which she commented on a letter to Senseney from American "conservation groups." She told Senseney that "accreditation of observers to the AEPS has been a delicate balancing act." She said that only one conservation group had actually applied for accreditation during the Canadian chair period (1993–1995) and, despite discussions that she had with several "conservation non-governmental organizations," none had applied for AEPS observer status. She congratulated the American government for its open consultation process and said Canada's was similar but "lower profile."[41]

The copy of this letter between government officials is found in the papers of CARC, a reflection of how closely Canadian NGOs and indigenous leaders were involved in the international lobbying for an Arctic Council and how a new approach to diplomacy was emerging in Canada and some other countries in which NGOs had become closely linked with state structures. As noted above, Canadian and American NGOs had collaborated in 1993 in advancing the stalled Arctic Council proposal. But Margie Gibson of the U.S. Arctic Network, based in Anchorage, was deeply annoyed by the substance and the provenance of the Whitby letter. On October 25, she faxed a memorandum to Terry Fenge of CARC and to others, which underlined the ambiguous character of the relationship between national NGOs and their national governments: "For future reference, please note that all documents from the Arctic Network regarding recommendations to the U.S. government (USG) are for your eyes only. If this puts any of you in an untenable position for some reason, please inform me and [I] will not send them to you."

It was "unfortunate," Gibson continued, that Whitby's letter indicated she had seen the conservation organizations' letter to Senseney. It was "a response to a request by the USG for comments on the USG position. *This is an internal domestic process.* [Italics in original.] Our department of state was not pleased." Moreover, Whitby was expressing "her views" and had not bothered to check her facts with the relevant American organizations. She concluded the biting note with a question as to whether the Canadians agreed "with Dr. Whitby's statement that Canada has a similar but lower profile open process and if you are included." She ended with a note to Senseney in which she said that AEPS accreditation rules were "excessively burdensome" and that Whitby had not consulted with them.[42]

The incident reflected the overlap and confusion that marked Canada's leadership of its initiative. Whitby had come to DIAND from an environmental background and chaired the AEPS meeting in Iqaluit in March 1995 where Foreign Affairs was seeking to incorporate AEPS within the Arctic Council. DIAND also had responsibility for the Arctic Environmental Protection Strategy, the largest single Canadian fund for Arctic innovation. Foreign Affairs had almost no funds but was responsible for Arctic Council negotiations. Mary Simon, who reported to the ministers of Indian affairs and northern development and of foreign affairs, became increasingly irritated with the dispersal of responsibility for the Arctic and the fact that she, as an indigenous representative and a Canadian ambassador, was not in the lead at a meeting of Arctic states. She also found the Department of Foreign Affairs difficult and distrustful of an outsider now among the highest rank of Canadian diplomats. Foreign affairs minister André Ouellet and his aide Michael Pearson remained strongly supportive in the minister's office, but the fall of 1995 was tumultuous in Canada with the Quebec referendum on separation. The country barely survived, but when it did, Simon asked her two ministers to make it clear that she spoke for Canada on Arctic issues. They agreed. Whitby was pushed aside.[43]

The Canadian government's internal troubles paralleled a sharp American reaction to the new draft of the Arctic Council declaration. Influential Alaskan consultant Bob Childers wrote to Fenge to warn him that the November 3, 1995, draft Arctic Council declaration "has had a very serious effect on U.S. government support for the council, and on the faith of [American] NGOs in Canada's good intentions." Things were being rushed, the language of the draft had not reflected earlier meetings, and the references to "opportunities for economic development" and "cooperation in trade and economic relations to raise the standard of living and ensure employment" were unacceptable. The Gwich'in people, who dwelt on both sides of the border, regarded those words as an argument "to open the coastal plain calving grounds of the Arctic National Wildlife Refuge to oil and gas exploitation." But their survival depended on caribou, and, for them, "caribou are more important than money." The Americans had made it clear that they would never agree "to include domestic issues such as employment and infrastructure" in the Arctic Council. The language on trade and economic relations was viewed "by many within the U.S. government as an assault on U.S. wildlife laws." The Norwegians were also unhappy with the clumsy transition plans for the AEPS. They had planned to chair in 1996, only to learn that Canada envisaged folding it into their Arctic Council of which they would be the founding chair. The new draft, Childers warned, "is a diplomatic blunder of high order that threatens all progress to date."

Successful initiatives require clear focus, strong coalitions, trust, and acquiescence of political leadership. They were lacking. As winter approached in 1996, a sudden chill entered the negotiations. While some now doubted that the Canadian initiative was worthwhile, it certainly was not boring.

The Swift
Wings of Truth

What went wrong? The Canadian initiative to create an Arctic Council had irritated the United States, which was certainly not the Canadian government's goal at a moment when a Quebec referendum on separation compelled good relations. The Scandinavians—whose enlightened internationalism had inspired Canadians from the fifties, when Dag Hammarskjöld was the United Nations secretary general, to the nineties, when various peace initiatives in the Middle East and the Balkans had Scandinavian leadership—were also unhappy with the bickering and delays that had marked Canada's attempts to create a new circumpolar organization to replace, complement, or build upon the Finn-sponsored Arctic Environmental Protection Strategy (AEPS). The Russians shared the Scandinavian discontent, particularly because of the demands upon their tottering bureaucracy and empty treasury. Within Canada, the many realists among Canadian diplomats and in the finance department had become exasperated with the frequent meetings, high travel costs, and open-ended financial commitments made to promote the Arctic Council proposal. Despite these problems and severe Canadian government cutbacks in 1995, the proposal still breathed life. But its shape had changed.

The original vision for an Arctic Council that would take the lead in the creation of a demilitarized and even nuclear-free Arctic had vanished. Moreover, the argument that the Arctic faced serious dangers from air and sea pollutants, which played such an important role in the Finnish Initiative, had become somewhat less compelling for governments by the mid-nineties. That argument, while based upon scientific studies tracing the spread of pollutants into the Arctic, sometimes derived from a romantic sense of the Arctic as peculiarly sensitive and unspoiled, a virgin environment despoiled by despicable outsiders. This presentation of the Arctic was unsurprising since so many government officials, scientists, and environmental NGOs were absorbed in the work of crafting an Antarctic agreement where similar concerns existed. But the Antarctic had no human presence; the Arctic did. NGO advocacy of conservation worried indigenous groups in the Arctic who believed that it represented an attack on their traditional hunting and trapping ways and on their hopes for economic development. Not surprisingly, Arctic indigenous groups were initially wary of the plans of the Finns and Canadians to create new Arctic institutions, seeing them as yet another in a long series of southern intrusions upon their homelands. They knew their lands best and wanted to make the decisions about their lives themselves. The Finnish and Canadian initiatives, therefore, both had to come to terms with two fundamental and dramatic changes affecting the Arctic: the movement for autonomy among indigenous peoples and the collapse of the Soviet Union. While there were no initial plans for direct indigenous participation in the Finnish Initiative, the issue arose quickly, not because of pressure from the Saami of Finland, but because of the Inuit Circumpolar Conference (ICC) and its effective leaders, whose case for participation was strongly supported by the Canadian government. The

ICC had developed an environmental strategy during the 1980s that emphasized the human presence in the Arctic. When the Brundtland Commission presented the concept of sustainable development, the ICC adapted its arguments to the emerging debate about the character of sustainable development. With Mary Simon as its articulate, globe-trotting president, the ICC reminded state officials that the Arctic was not Antarctica, that the impact of southern government decisions had historically had an enormous impact upon northern peoples, and, not least, that many northerners lived in deplorable conditions. Simon and other Inuit leaders believed that those who romanticized the North—such as environmentalists who conjured up images of a pristine, untouched land threatened by mining, trapping, and other human activities or southern politicians supposedly saving seals and whales—spoke from ignorance. The ICC, it will be recalled, had its origins in Alaskan Eben Hopson's annoyance with Greenpeace's and the International Whaling Commission's campaign against the hunting of the bowhead whale. By being consistent when so many were not, the ICC's position gained force.

Over time, the indigenous peoples warmed to the idea of an Arctic Council as its potential role broadened. The year 1992 had shifted the balance within the AEPS towards greater indigenous influence, and the Rio Earth Summit in June 1992 had been important in creating a linkage between Arctic indigenous peoples and those in developing countries. The importance of traditional indigenous knowledge gained currency in international discourse about the environment and economic issues. Northern leaders began to see other advantages in an Arctic Council. For example, Northwest Territories official Bob Overvold observed in 1992: "At the present time, multilateral organizations are beginning to spring up like mushrooms after a rain, e.g. the International Arctic Science Committee, the Northern Forum, etc. An International Arctic Council could be an effective umbrella organization to provide a forum for these organizations on issues of concern to the Arctic countries." It could, he suggested, come together quickly to handle a problem such as a "sunken nuclear

Soviet submarine in Arctic waters." He saw a further advantage: "With a pro-active Arctic Council solidly united against the anti-fur harvest protest, the reaction by the non-Arctic governments knowing that the eight Arctic countries had joined forces, could change significantly."[1]

In 1993 the Nuuk Declaration of the AEPS reflected Rio's statements relating to the "vital role" of indigenous peoples in "environmental management and development" and recognized the three indigenous groups as independent and permanent participants at the AEPS table. Denmark established an Indigenous Peoples' Secretariat, with its headquarters in Copenhagen, to coordinate work of indigenous peoples' organizations. The ICC, which received substantial Canadian funds for travel, remained the most active organization, although Russian indigenous peoples, with financial help from others, and the Saami did participate in meetings of officials. American Henry P. Huntington, a 1991 Cambridge Ph.D. in polar studies, served as the ICC environmental coordinator between 1994 and 1996. He described the efforts made when he served as a coordinator as "a means to an end ... to get more influence and control." He listed the benefits of indigenous knowledge as, first, "to make a real contribution;" second, "a nice, interesting new thing to attract funding," and, third, "a feel good project." For the ICC, the demand for respect for traditional indigenous knowledge raised the fundamental question: "Who can speak for somebody else?"[2]

By early 1996 the influence of the ICC upon the Arctic Council negotiations was remarkable and resented by some other non-Inuit northerners. Simon was the principal Canadian negotiator, and she was protective of her role. She warmly welcomed senior Indian Affairs and Northern Development official Jack Stagg with his long experience in working with northerners when he replaced environmental scientist Leslie Whitby as Canadian Senior Arctic Official (SAO).[3] From hesitation about a circumpolar environmental organization, the ICC had become its enthusiastic promoter and the protector of decisions made. With the support of some governments, notably Canada, it resisted an expansion of the role of state observers and especially of the European Union within the proposed Council, partly because additional players could dilute indigenous voices and partly because Germany, the United Kingdom, and the European Union were the principal advocates of fur bans. Their opposition to a greater role for environmental NGOs had similar roots. In her history of the early years of the AEPS and the rise of the Arctic Council, Finnish political scientist Monica Tennberg concluded that, in the Arctic Council negotiations, "the uniqueness of the indigenous peoples survived better than the environment in the end."[4]

Simon's resolve also survived, and it acquired new strength when Lloyd Axworthy finally became minister of foreign affairs on January 25, 1996. With a Princeton doctorate in political science and a deserved reputation for vigorous skepticism towards military adventures and strong support for multilateralism, Axworthy was intrigued with post–Cold War notions of "soft power" where states and organizations like the ICC could get what they wanted through respect for their values rather than coercion. The emerging concept of "human security," which extended the concept of security beyond the boundaries of the state to the protection of the individual, also caught his attention. Most famously, Axworthy applied these concepts in developing the campaign to ban anti-personnel landmines, in which several states cooperated with NGOs to break through institutional barriers and military establishments to achieve an almost universal ban on the use of such mines. He had a fondness for NGOs that most politicians lacked, including his predecessor André Ouellet, who was suspicious that NGOs in Quebec were cells harbouring separatist activists. (He cut their budgets mercilessly when Canada turned sharply to austerity in 1995.) Ouellet, however, had been a strong supporter of Simon, and Michael Pearson remained in the minister's office to establish an important continuity when Axworthy arrived.[5]

Despite Ouellet's support, the "Canadian Initiative" might have died in the face of severe budget cuts, American opposition, and doubts in the

North and the South. Axworthy, however, located the initiative within his broader approach to human security and his belief in the importance of collaboration with civil society. Curious by nature, he enjoyed debate with opponents, relished discussion of the latest articles in the *New York Review of Books* over a late-night Macallan single malt, and took delight in spinning out new ideas to stir up the dust he found on too many desks in Foreign Affairs' Pearson Building. When his emphasis on "human security" received strong criticism as "pulpit diplomacy" from Dean Oliver, a historian at the Canadian War Museum, and Fen Hampson of Carleton University's Norman Paterson School, he did not call the minister to whom the War Museum reported or threaten to withdraw the considerable support the Paterson School received from Foreign Affairs, tactics many other ministers employed before and later. Instead, he wanted to meet with the authors to challenge their point of view. With Axworthy, ideas ignited like sparks off a flint. Some, such as the landmine campaign and the move to establish an international criminal court, created a firestorm; others, such as the move to ban small arms and to end the use of child soldiers, finished as duds. In January 1996 it was not yet clear whether the idea for an Arctic Council would fully ignite.[6]

Despite the strong gusts that battered the Arctic Council initiative in the fall, there was still fuel for the flame. The principal support was the presidential–prime ministerial agreement that an Arctic Council should be formed. Admittedly, the Canadians had done nothing to satisfy the American condition that the dispute over the Beaufort Sea be ended.*

---

*The dispute over the boundary in the potentially resource-rich Beaufort Sea began in 1976 when the United States protested the boundary line used by Canada in the issue of oil and gas concessions. It involves 21,436 square kilometres northeast of the land border between Alaska and Canada where Canada argues for a straight line based upon the 1825 treaty between Russia and Great Britain. The United States rejects this claim, and the current mapping of the continental shelf has complicated the dispute. On May 16, 2010, Canadian foreign minister Lawrence Cannon noted the resolution of a long-standing Norwegian dispute and said that Canada and the United States much reach a similar agreement on the Beaufort. They have not. An excellent brief analysis is found in Michael Byers, *Who Owns the Arctic? Understanding Sovereignty Disputes in the North* (Vancouver: Douglas & McIntyre, 2009), 98–105.

That was always a possible breaking point. Second, there was the bureau-cratic momentum that came from the public declarations in support of the Arctic Council made by the eight Arctic states. Their officials had worked closely together over several years, and failure would be personal as well as national. Third, the initial hesitations of aboriginal groups had been replaced by significant support, particularly from the ICC and Inuit leaders. Simon's appointment as ambassador signalled the importance of the issue for indigenous peoples, and the failure to create a council would be a personal and institutional failure for Simon and indigenous organizations. At the Ottawa meeting in December 1995, there were six representatives of Permanent Participants, including Rosemarie Kuptana, the former co-chair of the Arctic Council Panel, and Kuupik Kleist of Greenland, a future Greenland premier. Other national delegations had substantial aboriginal representation, including the American, where three NGO representatives and three aboriginals flanked two officials.[7] Finally, whatever its complications, the proposed council could fulfill an important need to have coordination among the plethora of bodies that had sprung up after the Cold War's end, and it was an important linkage with Russia, the national state with the greatest Arctic presence.

But success was far from assured. The influential *WWF Arctic Bulletin* gave a harsh assessment of the situation in an article entitled "Arctic Council Fast Track Derails?" in early 1996: "Negotiations to establish an Arctic Council have lurched from meeting to meeting since 1989. Throughout, there have been significant differences in expecta-tions related to the Arctic Council's structure and mandate, its members, and its form: treaty versus forum. Despite numerous draft declarations, confusion remained. In the last year, a fast track attempt to complete negotiations has left important preparatory meetings of the AEPS minis-terial in disarray, damaging the cause of Arctic cooperation."

In the World Wildlife Federation's view, the problem was disagree-ment on the meaning of "sustainable development." "Some see [the Council] as an opportunity to promote development, employment and trade across the Arctic, while others believe this would interfere with domestic issues and instead prefer a 'forum' on sustainable development, consistent with the aims of the AEPS. Others believe the Council is unnecessary as it duplicates and even weakens ongoing regimes such as the AEPS and others which can address sustainable development." The influential WWF itself feared that the Arctic Council would weaken the AEPS for "short term economic gain."[8]

Amidst the doubts and delays, the Canadians pressed forward with their plans, inviting officials and other representatives to Ottawa to work on the final text of the declaration of an Arctic Council in late March 1996. The AEPS would meet at Inuvik on March 19–21, and the integration into the new body would be worked out. The Canadians were determined that the fast track was not derailed; others, however, thought it was time to slow down. The Swedish ambassador for circumpolar affairs Wanja Tornberg responded to the invitation by agreeing to come to Canada in March but said that no date should be given for the inaugural ministerial meeting to announce the creation of the Council: "There are still several questions that should be discussed and solved." It would be wise to wait before announcing a ministerial date. The Swedes, alone among the Arctic nations, politely suggested that it might be time for the Canadians, who had dominated the Arctic Council initiative for so long, to consider passing the leadership to another country. The Canadians ignored the gentle prod. While the Americans did not try to push the Canadians aside, they strongly agreed that the "train" should be slowed down, pointing to the need to sort out questions around Permanent Participants, observers, and sustainable development.[9]

The hesitations are understandable: the January draft of an Arctic Council agreement was replete with reservations and indications of "lack of consensus," principally—but not only—from the United States. The Russians no longer were capable of working effectively in English, and although translators were available, the Russians were at a disadvantage. Simon recalls that she was never sure which Russians would show up for the meetings in those troubled years in Russia. Indeed, the United States and Russia were both on the sidelines in the mid-nineties, the latter because of tremendous social and political disorder, and the former because of interagency bickering and lack of leadership. The Canadians were therefore heartened when Will Martin, the deputy assistant secretary of commerce for international affairs, was chosen to head the American delegation to the AEPS ministerial meeting in Inuvik in March. The enthusiasm for Martin might at first glance not seem obvious. Jack Stagg had known Martin from earlier negotiations on Atlantic swordfish and on the straddling stocks convention. He had been, Stagg reported, "one of [the] key people in admin to overcome resistance in State Dept ..." He could be valuable for Canada, Stagg thought: "His personality may appear low-keyed but he packs a lot of political punch in [Washington]. A lawyer specializing in corporate law, his perspective is probably a little more 'green' than we might wish." This background, including a stint as director of polar affairs for an environmental NGO, might mean that he would tilt too much towards the environment rather than development and reflect the environmental NGO criticism of the Canadian vision of sustainable development with its emphasis on traditional indigenous hunting rights and economic growth in the North. Nevertheless, Stagg, who had tussled often with Canada's diplomats, believed that "Canada is much better off with Martin" than with the State Department. Martin was "a member of VP [Al] Gore's network," and "whatever problems he has will be real and authoritative, not phony: and whatever he agrees to, will stick."

Despite Stagg's hopes, the meeting started off badly when Martin showed Stagg the draft of a letter he planned to send to Mary Simon with copies to other capitals. It criticized the conduct of the negotiations and the Canadian stand on sustainable development. Stagg thought such a letter would cast a pall over the next negotiation and asked Martin to reconsider the tone and wording. Then, the mood shifted. Martin said that the United States wanted an Arctic Council but the challenge was "to keep [an] eye on economics and avoid institutional proliferation." The Americans wanted to identify areas where cooperation really mattered. He did not like Canada's "institutional separation between [environmental] protection" and sustainable development. Economic development must respect environmental protection and be embraced within a single institution. But, Martin added, Canada surely cared about the environment and the right words could be found.

Stagg then gave an illuminating and frank description of where Canada stood in the winter of 1996, a few months after the dramatic Quebec referendum and in the first year of the severe 1995 federal budget cuts. In the abbreviated language often employed in dispatches to Ottawa, "Stagg recalled that the issue[s] of institutional proliferation and cost of bureaucrat's [sic] travel were raised and dealt with long ago. [Canada] was equally concerned with economical use of govt resources." He said that the fundamental problem governments faced was how to "build upon but go beyond the work of AEPS." Stagg then bluntly said that the AEPS had narrow environmental objectives and values. Its work was legitimate but it did little for the northerners who often lived in desperate conditions and who lacked the economic development needed to better their lot. The United States could talk about potential economic costs, but they should "look at tremendous financial transfers to native peoples and territorial govts" in Canada's North. These transfers "were [a] growing item in [government] accounts and illustrated fundamental problems" with economic development in the North. What northerners wanted to see, Stagg argued, was Northern governments that balanced environmental protection with an equal commitment "to wealth creation and jobs, native health, education, etc." The AEPS, in the view of Stagg and indigenous leaders, was an "institution of, by and for" environmental groups. Those were the groups whose protests against whaling, sealing, hunting, and trapping had deeply offended northerners. Sustainable development would have no "credibility in the north if it were undertaken as part of AEPS." The Arctic Council had to be different, had to recognize the way northerners lived, and had to involve them directly. The "Arctic Council had to offer something new and different or the whole enterprise would have no credibility. It would become exactly what U.S. said it didn't want: a waste of [government] resources."

Martin liked Stagg's candour and told him "wryly" that his legal background was in mergers and acquisitions and could be helpful in blending the AEPS into the Arctic Council. The Americans wanted a unified organization and did not want two pillars, one the science-oriented AEPS, the other sustainable development. In their view, the two could not be separated. Stagg said that governments needed to do more than "engage in preservationism" in the North. There was a "big gap" between what governments were doing collectively in the area of environmental protection and the little they were accomplishing in wealth creation. The AEPS task force on sustainable development should not be "exalted" into a working group like the other scientific working groups within the AEPS because it would skew the merger badly. The situation was complicated by Norway's plan to take over the task force and by Leslie Whitby's departure as the Canadian chair. Stagg emphasized the need to move forward quickly with an announcement without worrying about "every last 'i' to be dotted" before an inaugural meeting. Martin said he would reconsider the wording of the letter to Simon and concluded that Canadian–American "differences seemed largely in tactics rather than fundamentals ..." Unfortunately, they weren't.[10]

Stagg met later with some Alaskan state representatives in Washington, who told him that Alaska strongly supported the Arctic Council "along lines advocated" by Canada. However, they would act "behind scenes," and try to "offset pro-[environmental] predelictions [sic] of most U.S. participants." The Alaskans told Stagg that the circumstances in Alaska and the Canadian North were the same, with rising expenditures and "soaring birth rates" surpassing the ability of governments to manage with "traditional programmes and approaches." They hoped that Alaskan-based environmental groups would take a larger role since they were not merely "preservationists" and better understood the need to create wealth than those based in Washington. Encouraged by the response, Stagg blamed the failure to create an Arctic Council on "bureaucratic resistance from those engaged in AEPS, Nordic anxieties about future of AEPS, and suspicions of [economic] development among [environmental] NGOs." He admitted that Canada's stand on trade in marine mammal products had fed environmentalist doubts but said that Canada did not "intend to gut the U.S. Marine Mammal Protection Act." It was unfortunate that the issue had created "suspicion as to our motives." Environmental protection, he claimed, "had a huge head start," and the environmental NGOs so prominent in the South should not fear that there was finally attention to "the other side." The Alaskans told Stagg that it was too late to have Alaskan "natives" merely represented on the American delegation; the Aleuts and Athabaskans required the same status as the existing three indigenous groups. Stagg ended by saying that there was a need to find projects for the proposed Arctic Council that had meaning for northerners: "We don't need more business theoreticians. We need to hear from people who are actually doing things now."[11]

Stagg's remarkable comments illuminate the tensions and complexities underlying the creation of the Arctic Council. They also reflect his own pessimism about human conditions in the Arctic. Battles between Canadian northerners and governments, on the one hand, and international environmental groups, on the other, were well known, not least because international celebrities such as Brigitte Bardot took up the cause of seals, whales, and other mammals. The impact of these protests on Canada's relationship with the United States during the Clinton–Gore administration became much greater because of Gore's close ties with environmental NGOs and continuing controversies over whaling. Moreover, while Mary Simon persistently spoke of the difficult social conditions among northern indigenous peoples, her words did not resonate in other capitals except Copenhagen, which heavily subsidized Greenland, and Moscow, where the Russians faced increasingly desperate health and social problems in their Arctic. Simon, of course, was an Inuk; Stagg was a senior official whose career had concentrated upon northern indigenous issues. In their backgrounds, they were unlike nearly all others with whom they negotiated, many of whom came from environmentalist backgrounds while others were foreign service officers. Not surprisingly, in the Arctic Council negotiations, representatives often talked past each other, leaving a trail of unfinished documents and frustrated governments. In spring 1996, patience was near its end.

The United States and Russian governments were in political disarray, the former with the normal presidential-year disruption, the latter with a bitter struggle between Yeltsin and the oligarchs and a resurgent Communist Party. All Arctic states knew that the Russians and Americans mattered most; each had an implicit veto of the proposed council. Recovering from a near-disastrous Quebec referendum campaign, the Chrétien government had little tolerance for failures. Lloyd Axworthy finally had the foreign office he had craved, and he was determined to avoid taking on initiatives where he was unlikely to succeed. Prodded by Michael Pearson in his office and Mary Simon, whose spunk he admired, he pushed forward with the Arctic Council initiative, inviting Russian foreign minister Yevgeny Primakov and American secretary of state Warren Christopher to the Arctic Council ministerial meeting on his first encounter with them and even before formal invitations were sent. Canadian missions in Arctic states were told in mid-April to inform foreign offices that the inaugural ministerial meeting for the Arctic Council would take place in Iqaluit on July 10, 1996. There was, however, one major hurdle: the final negotiations for the document that the ministers would sign were far from complete.[12]

Mary Simon presided as chair when the negotiations opened in Ottawa on April 17, 1996, in the cavernous former railway station clumsily converted to a government conference centre. She began by admitting that there were still outstanding issues, notably the question of additional permanent participants. She noted, however, that the recent AEPS meeting in Inuvik and a March conference of Arctic parliamentarians in Yellowknife had expressed a "strong" commitment to the creation of an Arctic Council "as soon as possible" although she failed to note that the United States was not represented at the parliamentarians conference. She announced that a secretariat for the Arctic Council was already in existence in Ottawa and was actually providing secretarial services for the meeting. She thanked DIAND and Jack Stagg personally for funding "Aboriginal representatives from both Canada and Alaska" to attend the meeting in Yellowknife and the current meeting. Stagg then presented Canada's views on three central questions. On the mandate, Canada wanted "economic, social and cultural issues" included under the Arctic Sustainable Development Initiative (ASDI), a complementary pillar to the AEPS. Reflecting his discussion with Martin in Washington, Stagg indicated that, once the Arctic Council was formally announced, the Arctic states could then work out a "revised terms of reference" to deal with the different views on sustainable development. Finally, he indicated that his department had paid for meetings of aboriginal leaders in order that they could sort out among themselves how many Permanent Participants there should be.

The Canadians had nine delegates, more than any other state. Denmark and Norway had four, Finland three, Russia and Sweden two, and Iceland only one. The American delegation had seven members, two of them representing the Aleuts and Athabaskans who were linked with the Dene of Canada and were seeking Permanent Participant status. Together the delegates worked on the January 16, 1996, Canadian draft, and very quickly things bogged down. Norway and the United States made the most frequent comments, the former reflecting concern about the future of the Arctic Sustainable Development Initiative, while the latter concentrated on the use of "economic" and the distinction between indigenous and other peoples in the Arctic. The Americans also insisted that the Aleuts and Athabaskans should immediately become Permanent Participants. Their clear intent was to strengthen the Alaskan voice, but the Canadians and the ICC refused. The meeting ended with a commitment to move forward but, as Stagg had put it earlier, to leave several "i's undotted."[13]

Making the Agreement

At the earlier AEPS meeting in Inuvik, after too much talk about the Arctic Council, American delegation head Will Martin had declared bluntly: "Just do it."[14] It seemed there was finally an agreement to get it done. Mary Simon was upbeat when she sent on Canadian comments on the draft declaration in advance of a meeting of Senior Arctic Officials in Ottawa on June 8–9, 1996. "We are confident," Simon wrote on May 26, "that the few remaining areas to be discussed at the June 8–9 meeting will be settled at that time." She suggested, however, that delegates might consider staying an additional day or two in the event more discussion was needed. A confidential list of items of difference prepared at the same time suggested Simon's advice was good. There were many problems to sort out, including an ICC dissent on Canada's plan to assign arbitrary permanent participant seats by country, American objection to the use of the plural "indigenous peoples," serious reservations about the method of transfer of the AEPS into the Arctic Council (which meant that Norway would lose its chair position), uncertainty about what states and NGOs could be observers, and, most significantly, lack of consensus on what "sustainable development" meant.[15]

The Arctic states soon learned they would have more time. On May 22, 1996, Bob Senseney, the American delegate who had been the main American representative in previous meetings, sent a fax to Mary Simon indicating that the American secretary of state would not be available at any date in the summer to participate in an announcement of the Arctic Council. The hopes for a July announcement died.[16]

Simon recalls being optimistic on the eve of the June meetings, confident that the public expressions of support for an Arctic Council would compel private agreement on its creation. This mood similarly infused parliamentary committees charged with evaluating Canada's circumpolar environmental and foreign policy. The House of Commons Committee on the Environment attended the Arctic Parliamentarian Yellowknife and AEPS Inuvik meetings and strongly endorsed the creation of an Arctic Council. The House of Commons Standing Committee on Foreign Affairs and International Trade made the Arctic its major concern during 1996, beginning with hearings in Ottawa at which several experts castigated Canada's fragmented northern decision-making while others, including Oran Young, correctly described in the report as the "preeminent American [Arctic] scholar," emphasized that the Arctic had unexpectedly become a primary "region" of international relations. Enthusiastic Canadian officials briefed the committee on the negotiations to create the Arctic Council, although the many disagreements among them were not detailed. In May, committee members travelled to the Arctic and assumed, as did Simon, that the Arctic Council was on the brink of formal existence.[17]

The Arctic Council was a distant image, often invisible, to the eyes of the northerners whom the parliamentarians, the author among them, encountered. Their thoughts and soon those of the committee became preoccupied with the everyday challenges of Arctic life. The collapse of the fur trade brought anger in Iqaluit against faraway European capitals, but artists in Cape Dorset had just welcomed many Germans who enthusiastically collected their works. In all Arctic encounters, people complained that their priorities were lost in the bureaucratic clutter around their lives. There was a yearning for the hunting and trapping Arctic past, expressed in the social relations among the Inuit we met, but also an acceptance that that world was forever lost. In private homes dwelt grandparents who had lived as their people had centuries before and who spoke only Inuktitut, while their grandchildren sat nearby listening to Alanis Morissette's "Jagged Little Pill" on a Sony Walkman. At Resolute on Cornwallis Island, the relics of the Cold War abounded and great piles of unused pipes testified to the dashed hopes of an Arctic energy bonanza in the eighties. The Polar Continental Shelf Program at Resolute, the centre for Canadian science in the High Arctic, was shrivelling under the impact of budget cuts, and there had been more Americans than Canadians using the facility in recent years. Science to many northerners seemed far away from their lives. Although the Kyoto Accord was soon approaching, almost no one spoke of climate change. Pollution, however, was a constant theme of conversation and an abiding fear. Northerners knew about scientific research proving that wastes such as mercury and other damaging substances flowed into their waters and were entering their food chain and, literally, their blood. Here the work of an international circumpolar body might find a task that touched the lives of Arctic residents. But could an Arctic Council open closed markets for fur, as northerners bitterly demanded? Between kindling forlorn hopes and stirring positive support, the committee steered a difficult path. When committee members appealed to Inuit pride by invoking the appointment of Mary Simon as Canada's circumpolar ambassador and Nunavut's Jack Anawak as DIAND's parliamentary secretary, the usual response was "We don't see them here."

On June 3, 1996, just before final negotiations began, Bob Senseney told Ottawa that a more senior State Department official, Tucker Scully, would head the American delegation of five people, which would include the executive director of the Arctic Research Commission, a scientist; an Alaskan representative; a congressional staffer; and an officer of the World Conservation Union. Many American scientists were upset with the pushing aside of the International Arctic Science Committee from the Arctic Council negotiating table, and their voice would be heard on the American delegation. So too would the complaints of the environmental NGOs about their muted voice at the negotiating table. It was not a good omen.[18]

From Washington where the presidential election campaign captured attention, the Arctic Council was viewed mainly through the prism of Alaskan politics, which vividly projected energy and environment concerns. Clinton had vetoed the Republican-controlled Congress's election-year attempt to allow oil and gas drilling in the Alaska National Wildlife Refuge, an issue that divided Alaskans, aboriginals, and other Americans. The Americans were becoming increasingly exasperated as the ICC fussed about adding other permanent participants from Alaska. The American position paper, which was circulated before the meeting, makes it clear that there were several items that were, for the Americans, non-negotiable. First, national security and defence issues could not be within the purview of the Arctic Council. Second, the working group on sustainable development could not go forward unless there were clear terms of reference. Third, there could be no permanent secretariat. Fourth, the Athabaskan and Aleuts must be represented among the Permanent Participants. Fifth, environmental NGOs and non-Arctic states should be suitably represented as observers. Sixth, financing should be voluntary and the notion of "common costs" raised at Inuvik should be abandoned. In truth, the United States had hardened its position. The American position paper bluntly said that the Canadian draft declaration was "not consistent with the essential/basic/critical elements of the United States position." In essence, the American presentation for the final negotiations sharply criticized what the Canadians had done:

> The structure of the draft is both complicated and confusing. The first three sections—preamble, objectives and tasks, responsibilities and priorities—include elements that are repetitive, elements that are inconsistent and elements that seem inconsistent with the nature of the Council as envisaged by the United States.
>
> First, there are provisions that presume that the Council would be a formal international organization with an independent legal personality. This is inconsistent with the generally accepted concept of the Council as a regular high level forum and would be unacceptable to us.

Second, there are provisions that presume that the Council's mandate would extend to the domestic economic and social policies of Arctic Governments, as well as their international obligations pursuant to various treaties. The terms of reference of the Council must exclude competence that covers the international obligations of any of the arctic [sic] governments or their domestic legislative prerogatives;

Third, the manner in which references are made to indigenous groups raises significant political difficulties at least for the United States. Use of the term indigenous peoples (in the plural) is construed in the United Nations fora to reflect the right of self-determination. This is not the intended usage of the term in this context for the United States. In addition, references to indigenous inhabitants of the Arctic are made in such fashion as to imply that indigenous groups enjoy legal rights additional to those of "other" inhabitants. Although there are a number of special rights accorded to native groups in the United States, this is a domestic matter and not subject to agreement with and interpretation by other Governments. Additionally, the rights of other Arctic residents must be recognized.

Fourth, the terms used to refer to environment and development are confusing and unclear. There should be consistent usage of such terminology. The United States suggest not using ill-defined terms, such as "equitable use." We may support use of terms for which there is reasonable common understanding such as 'conservation' and 'sustainable development' as used in the Rio Declaration, and including the notion that sustainable use is maintained in the concept of conservation.

To make their points concrete, the Americans redrafted the declaration to reflect their fundamental objections just before the meeting. The United States's position reflected a fundamental difference between the place of the "North" in its politics and identity and its much greater significance in identity for Canadians and, in different ways, the Danes, Norwegians, and Russians. The remarkably large role of the Inuit in the Canadian imagination and in politics in vast Nunavut where they form a majority had no American counterpart, where Alaska is on the margins and aboriginal people are less than 15 percent of the population.* When policies are made in Ottawa and Washington, the filters are different.[19]

The Americans were not alone in their belief that the Canadian negoiators wanted an Arctic Council too much in their own image. The influential Pål Prestrud, the director of research for the Norwegian Polar Institute, openly worried that the Arctic Environmental Protection Strategy (AEPS) whose working groups had advanced "many concrete measures that improve Arctic environmental quality" would no longer thrive under an Arctic Council. There was "a worrisome possibility that the AEPS will be derailed and replaced by a badly structured Arctic Council." And there was trouble at home. Lloyd Axworthy and Mary Simon later recalled that officials in the legal division of Foreign Affairs shared the American reservation about the use of "peoples." These legal advisors warned that a Quebec separatist government could take advantage of the usage to advance their ambitions for independence. As the delegations arrived in Ottawa there was an increasing wariness and a growing sense that things could quickly come undone.[20]

All agreed that American State Department official Tucker Scully was immediately impressive—cool, deliberate, and direct. An experienced international negotiator with extensive polar experience who had previously expressed the view that American Arctic policy had been "sporadic," he bluntly put forward the American objections, expertly skewered the opposition, and abandoned the generalities, ambiguities, and congratulations that had sometimes marked earlier meetings.[21]

---

*When Jack Stagg came before the Foreign Affairs and International Trade Committee on April 30, 1996, he was passionate in his comments about the domestic and even local focus of the Arctic Council initiative. Committee members were struck by his vehemence when he asserted that "if the Arctic Council does anything initially, and I disagree with the [Reform Party MP] who said that it likely will talk and do nothing for a while ... my sense is that the real challenge is getting it up, getting it going, and getting it doing concrete things that quickly benefit those small communities. This is not to be some larger kind of international foreign policy forum. Those of us who worked towards it have seen it much more as a practical forum and a tool that will mean something to people in small communities in the various circumpolar regions."

There was a need for coordination, but the Arctic Council proposed by the Canadians would complicate cooperation and needlessly meddle in domestic concerns. Sustainable development was too vaguely defined, the role of non-state participants and observers ill-considered, and the loose use of the term "peoples" potentially dangerous. He "blew it all up," Mary Simon later recalled although she also remembers how impressive and courteous Scully was.[22]

The first day, June 8, ended with frustration and bitterness and a declaration by Stagg and Simon, the Canadian co-chairs, that if agreement was not reached by the end of the next day Canada would completely abandon its efforts to create an Arctic Council. The threat was Stagg's idea; a distressed Simon agreed it was necessary. As Arctic Council historian and former official Walter Slipchenko recalls, "some participants suggested they were prepared to meet that evening, but the Canadian Chairs declined to attend, leaving it to the delegates to resolve the remaining obstacles. The Chairs felt that they had gone as far as they could and it was, in effect, a 'do or die' moment."[23]

Simon, Stagg, and many others did not want the Council to die. But what to do? Through the evening into the early morning, telephones rang constantly in all Arctic capitals and in NGO offices. Emails, which were quickly replacing faxes, bore drafts and corrections of the Arctic Council document. Anger abounded in the corridors and, later, in bars in the evening and in delegates' hotel rooms into the early morning. The Arctic Council's fate depended upon a single thread, the public agreement between Chrétien and Clinton, but it was fraying rapidly. Canadian officials and Tom Axworthy of the Arctic Council Panel, who knew many administration officials through his teaching at Harvard, frantically sought out friends in Washington. Neither country really wanted the Arctic Council to "blow up" and, fortunately, the major press organs remained completely unaware of the bitter negotiations. Neither the *Globe and Mail* nor the *New York Times* made a single reference to the Ottawa diplomatic brouhaha. By the end of the second day, the exhausted delegates found a solution: they would create a council without deciding what it would be. Prodded by the Americans, the Norwegians, and, to a much lesser degree, the Russians, they did conclude what it was *not* to be.

Not surprisingly, the Arctic Council would have nothing to do with "security," an undertaking Chrétien had given to Clinton when he pressured him to go forward, which was reinforced at the Ottawa meeting. As recently as the March 1996 Parliamentarian conference, many still spoke of the need for a security focus. For example, Arto Nokkala of Finland, a former soldier, said the Arctic was still "a repository of Cold War weaponry" without a Cold War and suggested that the environmental approach could be linked with removing the weaponry. It was a stretch too far, and "security" maintained its substantial existence outside the Arctic Council framework. As a limited body, it would not have a permanent secretariat, and funding would be entirely on a voluntary basis. Nor would it have a legal framework in the form of a treaty similar to the Antarctic Treaty. The "Arctic region" would not be defined principally through an environmental focus without geographical boundaries. It could therefore be expanded when politically necessary, as in the case of the Alaskan Aleuts, aspiring Permanent Participants, who dwelt beyond the normal scope of definitions of "the Arctic." There were two other negative decisions. The Northern Forum, the organization of sub-national governments, had sought an enhanced place at the Arctic Council table, perhaps equal to the three permanent participants. Its request was denied. There would also be no "scientific" voice at the table; the International Arctic Science Committee would not be absorbed within the Council bosom but would be simply "advisory" to it.[24]

What, then, was left of this peculiar "forum" emerging from the bitter early spring debates in Ottawa? Unlike the earlier Finnish Initiative, the Arctic Council extended beyond environmental issues to social, political, and, more controversially, economic concerns in the

Arctic. Although the Arctic's boundaries lacked precise definition, the Arctic states were clearly identified and others with enormous historic Arctic interest and presence, such as the United Kingdom, or extensive scientific resources, such as Germany, were shoved firmly to the sidelines where they possessed a yet undefined "observer" status. It was less apparent where the major international environmental groups would find themselves on the Arctic Council. Vice President Al Gore and Tim Wirth, a former Democratic senator from Colorado who had become the senior State Department official responsible for the Arctic Council, had close ties with such groups, but the ICC and also some Alaskan aboriginals and Arctic governments were wary of their influence. Some might be observers, but they would never be at the table with the Arctic states and the Permanent Participants.

Whatever its weaknesses, however protracted its gestation, the Arctic Council was near birth. Progress had finally come because the eight states agreed to disagree while accepting that an announcement of the creation of an Arctic Council could be made. The real battle had been between the Canadians and the Americans. The Russians took little part in the debates, and their indigenous groups were not yet effectively organized. The Scandinavians watched the debate warily, accepting that an Arctic Council could be a useful body but unwilling to antagonize the Americans if Washington decided to scuttle the idea. The Danes, apart from the Canadians, were the strongest proponents, a reflection of the strong Inuit voice within their delegations. The Senior Arctic Officials of the Arctic states met on August 5–6, 1996, in Ottawa to dot the last "i's" and make final arrangements for the announcement. Disagreement remained on three issues: the terms of reference and rules of procedure for the Council, the admission of new Permanent Participants, and the place of sustainable development and the AEPS within the new structure. After the delegates returned to their capitals and homes, governments and the permanent participants approved the final wording of the "Declaration on the Establishment of the Arctic

Council." (See Appendix.) In striking contrast to the generalities of the text were two remarkable footnotes in the declaration. The first indicated that "the Arctic Council should not deal with matters related to military security," and the second read that the "use of the term 'peoples' in this Declaration shall not be construed as having any implications as regard the rights which may attach to the term under international law." The notes were clearly in an American hand.

On August 15, 1996, a slow summer news day, Lloyd Axworthy called in reporters to tell them the Arctic Council would be formally inaugurated "to coordinate environmental efforts in the Far North and deal with common aboriginal issues." He told reporters that the secretariat would have only four people drawn from Environment Canada, DIAND, and Foreign Affairs with a small budget of $1 million. Although no other countries were required to support the secretariat, the Norwegians offered to lend a staff member to augment council effectiveness. After some generalities, Axworthy, a Manitoba minister who often heeded the advice that "all politics are local," pointed out that the Russian experience with giant icebreakers might help keep the ports open at Churchill, Manitoba, later in the season. Before making the announcement, he had sent a private letter to Franklyn Griffiths, the co-chair of the Arctic Council Panel, and Kyra Montagu of the Gordon Foundation telling them that the work of the Foundation, and by implication the Arctic Council Panel it had funded, would be formally recognized at the launch. Under his leadership, he added, the department had "instituted a process by which Canadians from all walks of life can contribute to the formulation of foreign policy." The "Arctic Council initiative" of the Gordon Foundation was proof of a fundamental change in the making of foreign policy, one in which civil society found its place at the table. It was, Axworthy later wrote, a new way in a new world. But would it last?[25]

On September 19, the representatives of the Arctic states and aboriginal organizations gathered with Canadian parliamentarians, environmentalists, and various officials to witness the signing of the Arctic Council declaration. The setting in the West Block on Parliament Hill reflected the age of Franklin, not of the internet, and the South more than the North. Crystal chandeliers were reflected in giant mirrors with gold rims surrounding their wooden mouldings. A stuffed muskox in the centre of the room was the sole northern decoration. Although Canadian officials had predicted that Cabinet-level officials would attend from every country, they did not. Although the initial meeting had been postponed because of the unavailability of the American secretary of state Warren Christopher, the United States sent not the secretary but Tim Wirth, the under secretary of state for global affairs, as its representative. Still, the moment was memorable for all, especially participants such as Mary Simon, Franklyn Griffiths, Rosemarie Kuptana, Kuupik Kleist and Aqqaluk Lynge of Greenland, and Leif Halonen of the Saami Council, who had laboured so long to construct the Council. Axworthy, Minister Ron Irwin of Indian Affairs and Northern Development, and Minister Sergio Marchi of Environment Canada represented Canada and reflected the complicated Canadian management of its initiative. Past bureaucratic battles were forgotten as the three praised the handiwork, with Marchi eloquently calling for the message of the day to "move with the swift wings of truth." The mid-September diplomatic moment was "only the beginning, the first day of spring."[26]

Then, early in the late-summer evening, the group crossed over the Ottawa River to the Canadian Museum of Civilization, the largest single repository of Arctic aboriginal artifacts in the world, where they dined in the soaring great hall on five courses of northern specialties, such as caribou consommé and muskox stew while throat-singers Nellie Nungak and Alacie Tulaugak serenaded them. Surprisingly, the event captured little attention, although Jane George wrote an entertaining and detailed account for the *Nunatsiaq News*. As mentioned in the preface, the *Globe and Mail* sent no reporter and reprinted a brief Canadian Press account containing several errors, while the *New York Times* simply ignored the announcement. Bizarrely, the report in the *Tampa Tribune* was more substantial than a brief notice based on the Canadian Press story in the *Ottawa Citizen*. Interestingly, most American coverage was based on a Reuters report, which wrongly emphasized that the Arctic Council was an "environmental forum." The finest analysis, ironically, came in the British newsmagazine *The Economist,* which in Victorian times had memorably chronicled the Arctic explorers. It deftly summed up how the "Arctic had been no ocean of brotherly love," even between the normally amicable Canadians and Americans. After emphasizing the role of NGOs and the part the AEPS had played in the Arctic Council creation, it turned to Mary Simon and the central issue of dispute:

> Ms. Simon has long preached the gospel of sustainable development. She does not think development can or should be barred, but she foresees a difficult task of balancing oil, mining and industrial ventures with concern for the ecology. Discoveries of a huge diamond deposit in the Canadian Arctic and a fortune in nickel and cobalt in Labrador have pointed up the difficulty. She is also eager to build up trade between Arctic peoples. Cape Dorset, a hamlet on Canada's Baffin Island, boasts a higher proportion of working artists among its 1,200 people than anywhere else in the world. They are mostly stonecarvers. Could they also make traditional clothing for export to other northern peoples?

Among the litter of old arguments, sharp words, and unfinished tasks, there was still room for dreams.[27]

Finding the Council's Place

The Economist identified "contaminants" as a principal reason for the Council's formation, particularly since they were definitely affecting wildlife and northern people. Simultaneously with the work towards an Arctic Council, negotiations on the pollutants problem took place under the leadership of the United Nations Economic Commission for Europe. At the time, Canada and Sweden took the lead in promoting scientific research on what came to be termed "persistent organic pollutants" (POP). The Canadian effort joined together scientists from Environment Canada with officials in Indian Affairs and Northern Development and, importantly, linked the scientific work with information from Arctic residents. The Northern Contaminants Program of the Canadian government provided generous and consistent funding for these efforts. Moreover, traditional indigenous knowledge helped to guide scientific research that developed the list of pollutants. Canada chaired the ad hoc working group that carried out the preparatory work for a report to the United Nations Environmental Program and the World Health Assembly, which was due in 1997. Prior to the summer Arctic Council negotiations, Canada had prepared an extensive paper on POPs that emphasized how the Arctic fears inspired first a regional response and later an effort to extend restrictions globally. In the linkage between indigenous concern, scientific research, and regional and global action, the path towards a POP convention afforded a clear and important illustration of what the Arctic Council might and should do. This research and its dissemination would provide the foundation for the first success of the Arctic Council. But that triumph would come in the next century.[28]

In the aftermath of the Ottawa festivities, many were still wondering about what the Arctic Council might do. Jane George of the *Nunatsiaq News* reported that Leif Halonen of the Saami Council told her that the lack of voting rights for the Permanent Participants was disappointing and the Council, in his view, "has quite serious shortcomings." ICC president and Arctic Council Panel co-chair Rosemarie Kuptana was much more upbeat but said she supported both the Council and Halonen's views. "We are here with mixed feelings," she remarked. "The process was a difficult one for indigenous peoples, and it tells us that governments have to re-educate themselves about circumpolar cooperation." Aqqaluk Lynge of Greenland saw it as a historic moment despite the misgivings and gave Canada and Denmark credit for persevering against the odds. "We never get what we want," he said, "but this is the first time that non-governmental organizations have sat at the table with ministers."[29] Even though the Permanent Participants lacked voting rights, the Arctic Council represented a breakthrough for indigenous peoples of the North.

George concluded after listening to state officials that "what the newly-formed body is supposed to do depends on which country's leader is talking." Lars Emil Johansen, Greenland's premier, said the "great historical deal" would bring economic benefits to his island and could promote "industrial cooperation and mutual trade." Iceland's foreign minister, however, "seemed primarily worried about fish stocks and the sound use of other marine resources." The Russian deputy minister of foreign affairs said the Council could be a way of settling conflicts, but the American delegation "was quick to affirm that the council should steer clear of military conflicts." Norway and Sweden spoke about "social equality" and increasing the role of indigenous people while Finland's environment minister thought the Council could, in George's words, "strengthen this small nation's identity." But then came the topic of sustainable development for which terms of reference had to be developed within two years. Future Greenland premier Kuupik Kleist, an ICC representative in Ottawa, feared the task was too great and that the Council "will stall before starting." Canadian environment minister Sergio Marchi dismissed such concerns, saying that the Council could move quickly on sustainable development. "They know it when they see it," Marchi said.[30]

In truth, they tended to see different things. When the Canadian Parliamentary Committee sought reactions to the Council's formation, it got ambivalent reviews. Northern Canadians thought the Council should be located in the North, and Inuvik's Aurora Research Institute even prepared a formal proposal with the cooperation of local authorities. What Inuvik proposed, Iqaluit then wanted, and it received a "branch office" in response to its complaints. While troubling, this lobbying was less disturbing than comments by Oran Young, a rare American academic whose opinions mattered in Washington, who told the parliamentarians that the Arctic Council Declaration "contains very few, if any, substantive commitments on the part of the signatories to take concrete action." He was disappointed with the top-down nature of the organization, which compared poorly to the "functional flexibility of European regional bodies." He reported that there was skepticism about the Council in some foreign ministries and expressed the fear that inter-state rivalries rather than "Arctic realities" would drive and dominate the Council.

British academic David Scrivener, who, like Young, wrote an important early analysis of the Council, was even more critical. He said there was still much resentment, especially among the Nordics, who thought the process had been driven by Canadian domestic concerns. Norway, whose chairing of the AEPS was abruptly truncated by the creation of the Arctic Council, had given up its planned chairing of the Arctic Council in 1998 when the United States indicated it wanted the position. "Intensive care" was needed to make the Council work and to add value to the many other circumpolar bodies. Yet it was slow off the mark with no clear agreement on the working groups, on how the Finn-inspired Arctic Environmental Protection Strategy would be integrated, and on creating clear relationships with other bodies such as the Barents Euro-Arctic Council, which, in Scrivener's view, worked very well. The Council, he warned, risked not being the "one-stop shop" it promised, but a "one-more stop shop" with little impact.[31]

The "swift wings of truth," which Sergio Marchi hailed, carried the new Council at very low altitude in the months following the September launch. The new secretariat suffered from its location, which was distant from the relevant departments, especially Foreign Affairs. Foreign Affairs senior official Jim Wright, a Russian specialist who had taken an interest in the Arctic Council proposal after his return from London in 1996, asked veteran Arctic official Walter Slipchenko, who had been influential in drafting earlier proposals, to help set up the secretariat, which he did with the help of the employee seconded by the Norwegian government. Another departmental officer, who conflicted with the Ambassador's office, was gradually forced out. For her part, Mary Simon knew that power in Ottawa now resided more in the Pearson Building, which housed Foreign Affairs, than at DIAND and Environment Canada. There was much sorting out to do, and internal conciliation was needed to salve the wounds that came from shifting bureaucratic responsibilities and the loss of the glamour of international negotiation and travel. The small secretariat, Slipchenko recalls, confronted enormous tasks and a Foreign Affairs department that was generally unhelpful, preoccupied as it was with a crowded agenda that included the historic campaign to ban anti-personnel landmines that also began in the fall of 1996 and involved the same departmental chain of command.

Over the next eighteen months, the major task of the Canadian chair was to sort out how the AEPS and its working groups could be subsumed within the Arctic Council. She constantly found herself in need of assistance and received some valuable help from Bernie Funston who was lent by the Government of the Northwest Territories. The fundamental challenge was the satisfactory establishment of the meaning of sustainable development and integration of the concept within the mandate of the Arctic Council and its yet undefined working plan. On September 20, immediately following the inaugural celebrations, the ICC issued a press release on sustainable development that set forth its position that "the council's sustainability agenda must be issue and problem driven, and not subject to political caprice." Faced with these challenges, the ministries of the environment of the eight Arctic states requested a study of where things stood and what might be done. Håken Nilson of the Norwegian Polar Institute received the commission for the study and interviewed senior officials and others to identify problems. His conclusion in the spring of 1997 was that an undesirable "two-pillar" system was emerging: "The development towards such a two-pillar system has gained momentum due to the simplicity of keeping the AEPS intact while lumping all other activities together as a Sustainable Development Program." There was some advantage in that it could lead to a "safe" transfer of the AEPS and its working groups, but, he added, such "a two-pillar system may complicate effective integration of the environmental and development agendas.[32]

There were, in fact, more than two pillars described in the report, and they still were unmatched and uncoordinated. Part of the problem was the relationship of working groups to relevant government departments, which were organized around such topics as fisheries, natural resources, environment, and indigenous affairs while Arctic issues spanned all such topics. The Canadian government, which was charged with coordinating the integrative activities, was itself divided with the Arctic Council secretariat within Foreign Affairs, where Simon felt uncomfortable with many but not all officials, while most of Arctic Council activity occurred in Indian Affairs and Northern Development (DIAND), which modestly funded the secretariat. However, most government scientists treating environmental and resource issues were in departments such as Natural Resources, Environment, or Industry. Canada's delegation to the important meeting of the AEPS in Kautokeino, Norway, on March 11–12, 1997, which considered the questions of integration, working group activities, Permanent Participants, and observers, was comprised of Simon and two Foreign Affairs officials, three senior DIAND bureaucrats, and representatives of the Yukon government, the Council of Yukon First Nations, and the interim chair of the Arctic Council Sustainable Development Program, who happened to be Canadian Bernie Funston. Bill Erasmus of the Dene Nation and Mike Paulette of the Métis Nation were invited but not able to attend. Despite Marchi's embracing eloquence in Ottawa in September, no member of his environment department had a place on the delegation, and no major science ministry was represented.[33] Without a place at the table, departments become reluctant to contribute to the menu.

The meeting itself reflected the problems of the past while identifying troubling challenges for the future. Most attention concentrated on the report on "Arctic Pollution Issues," produced by the Arctic Monitoring and Assessment Programme (AMAP), chaired by scientist David Stone of DIAND. The report's focus on the extent of Arctic pollution reflected indigenous concerns, and it received general praise. However, it managed to irritate Nordic countries, notably AMAP host and leading funder Norway, because of comparisons between Northeastern Norway and the very "polluted" Kola Peninsula of Russia. Other working groups produced indifferent responses, with Conservation of Arctic Flora and Fauna (CAFF) being praised for its work on biodiversity, but its request for more funding was firmly rejected. It was told that its work plan was "still too ambitious." The Protection of the Arctic Marine Environment working group noted the absence of cooperation with other groups despite overlapping responsibilities while the Emergency Preparedness, Protection and Response working group failed even to produce a report. There was no agreement on how working groups should be financed. Russia and the United States insisted it must be on a voluntary basis except for secretarial work, but even that should be provided on an "in kind," not a cash, basis. Russian delegates, including Permanent Participants, had little or no knowledge of English, the lingua franca of the Arctic Council, and could not participate in the important corridor chatter. Canada and Denmark, the nations with the largest percentage of indigenous residents in the Arctic, pressed for funding for Permanent Participants, but again no agreement was reached.

Nilson's report on the AEPS came under attack from the ICC, which circulated three questions used by Nilson in interviews:

1. How representative are the three IPO Permanent Participants?
2. Have they squeezed out other Arctic stakeholders, have they taken over the agendas of other groups?

3. Were the three IPOs allowed to achieve their prominent positions for "political correctness" reasons, at the expense of participation for other stakeholders?

Canada and Denmark/Greenland immediately spoke up in support of
the ICC and the existing Permanent Participants, with Simon, the former
president of the ICC, saying that the questions had not been sent to
Canadian officials. The minutes reported that "the Chair concluded that
the meeting was unanimous on this issue and that the questions from the
consultant had been a mistake." Evidence of continuing tensions also
appeared when the World Wide Fund for Nature was granted "ad hoc
observer status," while Canada and Norway rejected the application of
the International Fund for Animal Welfare application brought forward
by the United States. Throughout the meeting the American delegates
disagreed with or contradicted Canadian delegates, particularly Bernie
Funston, the chair of the drafting group, who wondered whether the
Americans actually wanted the Council to function.[34]

The disappointing meeting of officials was preparatory for the final
AEPS ministerial in Alta, Norway. In advance of the ministerial, a draft
declaration was circulated. The American comment on the draft was
harsh from the first paragraph, which it criticized as "overly long." The
Americans called for deletion of the second paragraph's definition of
sustainable development and utilization: "This is a controversial matter
[that] has never been settled and doesn't need to be resolved here."
And so it continued, with stylistic swipes—"redundant," "exaggerated,"
"confused," "incomprehensible"—and substantive: "The U.S. has never
agreed to universal monitoring and assessment as part of AMAP or
AEPS"; "the stated definition of biodiversity has not been agreed
to"; and "the U.S. has not agreed to work on obtaining international
recognition of the Arctic as a sensitive seas area. Nor has it agreed
that protection of marine biodiversity requires legal instruments."
The ten-page critique bore the tone of a frustrated professor grading

an inept first-year undergraduate who had somehow stumbled into a graduate seminar.[35]

Others with much different perspectives thought the Arctic Council was failing. Arctic Council Panel co-chair Franklyn Griffiths, who had written to Lloyd Axworthy in the spring of 1996 calling for a broad celebration of the achievement of the Arctic Council, did not like the way the offspring was developing. In a March 1997 paper and a widely circulated May letter, Griffiths lamented that the Arctic Council had not had "the best start" and suggested that a remedy must be found immediately. Although Griffiths, in traditional Canadian fashion, blamed the "restrictive attitude of the United States" for most of the problems, he also pointed to Canadian inaction as Council chair. Given that Canada would pass the chair to the United States in 1998, the present situation was unacceptable, and Canada had "no choice but to act at the political level again." Lloyd Axworthy knew there were serious troubles and through the Canadian Centre for Foreign Policy Development, a controversial, ministerial-directed think tank within his government department, he commissioned consultant and Arctic Council Panel member Terry Fenge to write a report on what had gone wrong and what should be done.[36]

Fenge's report lamented that many of the initiatives of the kind urged by Griffiths in spring 1997 had stalled or had not been taken up, such as children in the Arctic, Arctic food contamination, climate change, and marine transportation. Griffiths had implored the government to develop an Arctic action plan, which had been promised by the Liberals in 1992 when they were in opposition. Fenge argued that there needed to be a national, Arctic, and international communications strategy to present what the Arctic Council could do and was doing. Later described as possessing a unique "historical memory" of the Arctic Council because of his extensive work as consultant to indigenous groups and advisor to government, Fenge was blunt in his criticism and unsparing in his analysis. He began his assessment with a quotation from the 1993 Liberal Party *Policy Handbook* that had promised an "Arctic Region Action Plan, encompassing both domestic policy and multilateral efforts," which would "involve a central role for aboriginal communities in policy formation and implementation."[37]

Fenge asked his interviewees two basic questions: Why has the Arctic Council made so little progress? and What should Canada do to improve things? The answers by myriad officials, aboriginals, environmentalists, and others were, in Fenge's words, "embarrassing." By January 1998 the Council had not yet addressed the fundamental problem of what it should and could do but had spent many rancorous months debating the rules of procedure. On the broadest level, the debate had substance because the Arctic states reflected their own different perceptions of the Council and the Arctic. The United States, for example, drew upon its experience with Antarctica, which had created close ties between officials and environmental groups, which were controversial with Arctic indigenous peoples and some other governments. The Arctic Council declaration also presented serious problems with its poor drafting and many ambiguities: "Because Canada pushed so hard for the council other nations acquiesced in its formation but did not embrace it with enthusiasm." Differences were "papered over" to emerge later as angry words and misunderstandings. The Canadians had "insisted" upon becoming the chair of the Council for its first two years, and this demand fitted poorly with the AEPS, which Norway then chaired, and with AMAP, which Norway hosted. The Scandinavians, increasingly the collaborators in Axworthy's human security initiatives, sometimes felt on Arctic matters like Canadians often did towards the United States.

Apart from these national differences and disputes, there were serious difficulties within Canada's overall approach. There was, as many other critics suggested, the inability of Canada to "articulate the sustainable development vision, approach, or agenda" to create a collective will to move forward. But the intellectual construct was secondary to the bureaucratic politics and personal animosities that vitiated attempts to fashion an effective Canadian policy. Mary Simon, Fenge wrote, "is a person of real moral authority in the Canadian and circumpolar Arctic, readily recognized from Barrow to Nuuk, with a wealth of political experience." Since her much-publicized appointment, she had found navigation of Ottawa's bureaucratic paths treacherous and had openly complained about the lack of funding and staff.[38] The dispute with Leslie Whitby, the Canadian Senior Arctic Official of the Arctic Environmental Protection Strategy and a respected environment scientist, had damaged her relationship with certain civil servants in DIAND and the Department of the Environment who "became immediately wary of [Simon] and, it appears, this wariness was reciprocated." The departments were crucial to the effective operation of the Arctic ambassador's office, especially when a major task was the sorting out of the relationship with the AEPS. The incident even affected other Nordic countries, who interpreted it "as a rejection by Canada of achievements under the AEPS and a clearing of the decks for the Arctic Council."

Faced with American hostility, bruised Nordic sensibilities, and a ravenous though understandable Russian appetite for more resources for its Arctic, Foreign Affairs was sometimes a reluctant host of the Arctic Council initiative. Ministers and their offices had been enthusiastic, but the department was "lukewarm" and saw limited foreign policy opportunities in the Arctic. Some interviewees described the department's attitude as one of "foggy resistance" and Council activities as not "career enhancing." Simon had been "parachuted" into the department and, as Fenge put it, did "not share the peculiar culture of those in the department who see themselves as the 'best and the brightest' that Ottawa has to offer." The department had few with knowledge of Arctic issues and was incapable of providing adequate staff for the ambassador and the Council. Simon reported to a Foreign Affairs director general rather than to a senior officer and "to status conscious civil servants this is an important point."[39]

Fenge echoed Griffiths in his criticism of the government's inability to develop the long-promised Arctic action plan and urged the government to link Arctic issues with broader international issues, notably climate change and transboundary contamination. The fact that many northern Canadians knew little about the Arctic Council testified to the government's failure to draw upon northern knowledge. Clearly, Fenge said, the distrust and disorganization that marked the operations of the Arctic Council secretariat and the office of the Arctic Council Ambassador must come to an end, and the public servants must learn that the ambassador "is a central figure in Canadian decision making, not to be ignored." To engage the United States, the Canadian federal governments and other bodies should work with Alaska to find common purposes and interests. Despite the woe and grumblings, the enhanced interaction among the Arctic states provoked by the Arctic Council initiative had produced some good results, such as the proposal to create a University of the Arctic and greater collaboration among Arctic parliamentarians. Moreover, as a later analysis recognized, the Arctic Council soon became the forum for defining the Arctic as a region, one whose boundaries encompassed "Alaska, Canada north of 60°N, all of Greenland, Iceland and the Faroes, the northern counties of Fennoscandia, and a large swath of northern Russian [sic] together with the Arctic Ocean and marginal seas." This vast region inevitably raised the question of what is shared. But the Arctic Council's creation and birth had demonstrated that there was more in common than many realized, not least "the fact that with the exception of Iceland, the region consists of northern peripheries or dependencies of countries whose economic and political centers of gravity lie well to the south." That situation defined the Arctic Council's challenges and problems but also, to a large extent, its fundamental and important raison d'être.[40]

Axworthy tussled constantly with his department as strong ministers often do, but his successful landmine initiative, which culminated in a December 1997 ceremony with international press, Kofi Annan, and a slew of celebrities, brought him enormous credibility. He got on well with the new American secretary of state Madeleine Albright despite some policy differences and shared liberal internationalist viewpoints with British foreign secretary Robin Cook and the Scandinavians. He had developed a good relationship with Russian foreign minister Yevgeny Primakov, "a tough veteran of the old Soviet system, but [with] a warm personal touch with just a touch of zaniness," which he expressed memorably in a take-off on *West Side Story* with Madeleine Albright. The spirited duo, Axworthy later reported, gave "the boffo performance of the diplomatic borscht circuit." With the intensity that marked Axworthy's political career, he lobbied ferociously for the Arctic Council when it seemed to be coming apart. With their wives, Primakov and Axworthy spent an evening at Ottawa's Pearson Building pondering how "history might have been different if the mapmakers of the sixteenth century had used a north–south axis instead of an east–west bias." After the ruminations, both promised to work together on the Arctic.[41]

There were other positive achievements, developing out of earlier AEPS work, notably the studies on transboundary pollution and the integration of the Arctic region with international collaboration on climate change. Nevertheless, with only months remaining before Canada handed the chair of the Arctic Council to the United States, Canada risked seeing the Council becoming yet another mostly ineffectual international forum, which diplomats attended with an eye on the clock and a more alert eye on nearby relatives, girlfriends, boyfriends, and bars. In early 1998 Fenge reported that Mary Simon, despite her "undoubted strengths," was being "left to flounder." Many told him that she was being "sandbagged" and would become "the scapegoat if the Arctic Council fails."[42]

EIGHT

Into the New Millennium

Britain had no place at the Arctic Council table, but its diplomat's analysis, as reported by the Finnish Embassy in London, was perceptive: "The meetings of the Arctic Council are going nowhere, which now hampers the work of AEPS working groups. All eight countries in the Arctic Council seem to have their own agenda and their own interest groups. In particular, the antagonism between the United States and Canada prevents breaking of the deadlock. Canadian activities in the Arctic Council are guided only by the interests of its indigenous people, whereas the real motives of the United States are more difficult to analyze—unless the ineffectiveness of the Council is in the interest of the United States."

Canadian persistence had kept the Arctic Council initiative alive in the face of indifference and opposition throughout the 1990s. Prime Minister Brian Mulroney's proposal for a council, which he made in Leningrad in November 1989, had been transformed by the historic changes that soon followed with the end of the Cold War and the end of the Soviet Union. Early hopes for Arctic disarmament failed. When the Finns grasped the opportunity to develop a scientifically oriented Arctic environmental forum, the Canadians made it clear that science was not enough. They consistently argued for a broader, comprehensive approach, one that reflected the new possibilities for the Arctic after the Cold War and the greater challenges Arctic nations and, importantly, Arctic peoples faced— ranging from southern pollutants, the shrinking of the polar ice cap, and the poor health and social conditions of many Arctic communities. The Americans did not dismiss this interpretation, but the Arctic occupied a minor place in their politics and a much smaller niche in their national identity. Their powerful military was not prepared to open the Arctic Ocean to multilateral meddling, and Washington politicians harkened to different voices such as conservation groups advocating bans on whaling and cruel hunting. While it is unfair to suggest that the American voices at the Arctic Council table after its creation in 1996 wanted an ineffective council, it is true that they feared what others, especially the Canadians, thought an effective council would be.

The Canadian initiative to create an Arctic Council and to have a sustainable development pillar within the Council very much reflected the "interests of its indigenous people." The deep commitment of Mary Simon, Rosemarie Kuptana, and many other indigenous leaders who pressed the case of the Council reflected their concern for their people. The situation in the nineties was dire. Blood tests revealed that northern peoples who ate traditional diets had high levels of contamination from pollutants produced thousands of kilometres to the south. The Arctic Ocean, scientists concluded, was a "sink," a drain for noxious materials from the South. When Nunavut was separated from the Northwest Territories on April 1, 1999, its Inuit majority and indigenous leaders faced striking human challenges. Fifty-seven percent of the population was under twenty-five, even though the rate of infant mortality was 20.9 per 1,000 live births, compared to the Canadian average of 5.8.

Its suicide rate was 135 per 100,000 compared with 24.5 for Canadian aboriginals and 11.8 for the general population. The life expectancy for Inuit compared to all Canadians was ten years less for males and twelve less for females. These figures were well-known to leaders like Simon and also to the Department of Indian Affairs and Northern Development, which took the lead in pressing for an Arctic Council in an attempt to deal with the enormous human and financial costs of the human tragedies in the North.[1]

The 1990s were very bad times for Russia and its northerners. The professional class took advantage of the new freedom to move south, while others, particularly former Communist officials, found great opportunities in the economic chaos to appropriate the resource riches of the north. The Arctic Council documents of the time reveal a Russia eager for Western help, but generally outside the central debates. Their participation was intermittent and largely concentrated on specifically Russian matters, often as a supplicant. There were successful initiatives, such as the ICC's humanitarian assistance to Inuit villages in Chukotka using Canadian development funds. But the challenge was staggering. Russia's north was an administrative area of twenty-nine regional entities, across twelve time zones with 12 million people, only 200,000 of them indigenous. Although Russia was preponderant in Arctic population and possessed enormous mineral and energy resources, its voice in the early Arctic Council was far weaker than it ought to have been. As the Soviet Union broke up, Arctic regions such as Chukotka and Yakutia began to break away and form separate administrations. But, as British historian John McCannon later wrote, "To its deep distress ... the region would soon discover that it had exchanged authoritarianism for a solid decade of anarchy." Life expectancies fell dramatically, and desperation marked northern life.[2]

Although the Russian voice on the Arctic Council was weak, Russia received far more attention in the 1997 Canadian Parliamentary Report on the Arctic than did the Nordic countries and Iceland. The Committee did not even visit Iceland, which had no indigenous population, and the sections on Finland and Sweden were brief. Norway garnered more attention, not least because Norway, which had the largest Saami population, and Canada were both tussling with the United States about the International Whaling Commission (IWC), of which Norway was a member and Canada was not. Norway, in a fashion familiar to sovereignty-minded Canadians, had announced in 1996 that it intended to harvest 425 minke whales of an estimated stock of 110,000. The IWC, the United States Congress, and the European Union strongly objected, with the United States threatening trade restrictions. Canada, too, was the target of American action and joined with Norway in arguing for sovereignty over fishing rights to assure the livelihood of remote northern communities. Here again was another fault line in the Arctic Council. Although Norway and Canada shared some common interests, David Scrivener, a British academic, and Richard Langlais of Göteborg University in Sweden told the Parliamentary Committee that Canada and Norway were "natural rivals for the leadership of the Arctic" because both had significant Arctic populations, expectations of resource development, and had made "northernness" part of their identity. Both warned, however, that Canada should not be "heavy-handed in its work in the Arctic Council and other areas of circumpolar cooperation."[3]

Carina Keskitalo of Umeå University in Sweden reflected these concerns about Canadian Arctic Council leadership in her major 2004 study of the Council's early years. Through discourse analysis, she argued that Canada and its partner, the Inuit Circumpolar Council, came to dominate in framing the issues, defining the Arctic as a region, and advancing their common point of view. She shares Scrivener's and Langlais's view that Canada could be "heavy-handed," particularly in shoving the Nordic states to the sidelines: "Canada was the only one for which the national identity and, thereby, substantial central state resources and discourse development were explicitly connected to the Arctic. The hegemony for the Canadian state context in Arctic cooperation derives from this fact of historical development and the multiple bodies, alliances and conflicts that came to exist domestically with regard to these issues." Canada, Keskitalo argued, gained its weight in Arctic power "not from its overall power," but from what she calls "its *discursive power* [italics in original] in matters 'Arctic'" and determining the issue agenda. In short, the Canadians had important domestic reasons and considerable resources to advance their interests in an area where others, for various reasons, lacked the interest or resources.

Keskitalo's vision of Canada's dominance contrasts strikingly with Terry Fenge's strong criticism of the under-resourced and often ineffectual promotion of the Arctic Council in the first year after its creation. It would surely surprise others, such as Gordon Foundation board member Janice Stein, who recalls lobbying Lloyd Axworthy furiously for more resources for the feebly funded Arctic Council initiative. Moreover, Mary Simon and other indigenous leaders complained constantly that the Liberal government was not keeping its promises to have a fully funded Arctic action plan. Knowing that Simon lacked resources from the federal government, the Northwest Territories provided the talented Bernie Funston to assist her and to play an important role in drafting the terms of reference for the Council. And it ignores the fact that Canada's strong indigenous focus was nearly always backed by Denmark, whose Arctic Council representation and votes reflected Greenland's indigenous population. Keskitalo's argument, nevertheless, reflects a common perception of Canada's actions and motivations and clarifies the issues that caused so much conflict within the Council during its early years.[4]

In the period after the September 1996 formal creation of the Arctic Council, the Canadian presence and the indigenous perspective was unquestionably dominant. For example, at the meeting of Senior Arctic Officials (SAO) in Kautokeino, Norway, on March 11–12, 1997, Environment Canada official John Karau chaired the working group on Protection of the Marine Environment; Peter Nielsen of Greenland (no Danish identification) chaired the Conservation of Arctic Flora and

Fauna (CAFF) working group; and scientist David Stone of Canada's Department of Indian Affairs and Northern Development chaired the most significant working group, the Arctic Monitoring and Assessment Programme (AMAP). In the case of AMAP, which was hosted by Norway, Keskitalo suggests that Stone's role was central in promoting an "indigenous" focus, which is scarcely surprising given Stone's departmental attachment. She also credits him with being a major force in the development of the idea of a University of the Arctic, which would possess a strong indigenous component. She further points out that the major report presented in 1997 under Stone's chairmanship was a "State of the Arctic Environment Report," whose section on "persistent organic pollutants" (POP) reflected indigenous concerns and emphasized the role of "traditional environmental knowledge" as well as traditional Western science in reaching its conclusions.[5]

While Stone took care to point out that the University of the Arctic proposal did not come from AMAP but was a personal suggestion, he did not hesitate to object when the United States at Kautokeino suggested that the meeting chair, Mary Simon, was chair *only* [my italics] of meetings themselves and did not "chair" the Arctic Council between meetings and, especially, in its dealings with other organizations. Identified in the minutes as AMAP chair, Stone disagreed, stating that Senior Arctic Officials were "moving into a very proactive role in the management of the Arctic Council and that it would be very difficult to operate without the executive being given some degree of confidence from this group to be able to make intersessional decisions between meetings of the SAOs." The comments, of course, reflect common sense, but the perception of Canada's dominance in setting the agenda was undoubtedly fortified. The World Wildlife Federation, which was now working with the Inuit Circumpolar Conference, formally received an invitation to the Kautokeino meetings. The American-sponsored application of the International Fund for Animal Welfare (IFAW), with whom the ICC had long quarrelled, was once again firmly rejected.[6]

The IFAW's activities had profoundly irritated Inuit leaders and the Canadian and Norwegian governments because of their strident opposition to whaling and traditional trapping and hunting practices. The IFAW, however, had strong supporters in Congress and the European parliament, and the American government had consistently supported its application to be an observer at Arctic Environmental Protection Strategy and Arctic Council meetings.* When Norway rejected the IFAW application to attend the AEPS meetings, which it chaired in the spring of 1997, Ambassador Mary Simon wrote on February 19, 1997, to other Arctic Council states that "Canada concurs with Norway that IFAW should not be granted accredited observer status to either the March or the June AEPS meetings. Nor should IFAW be given such status at any future SAAO or AEPS ministerial meetings." She then added that "under no circumstances, in Canada's view, should IFAW be granted observer status at any Arctic Council meetings," which, of course, Canada would chair. On February 21, 1997, Bob Senseney of the U.S. State Department wrote to the Norwegian official who had informed the United States of the decision to bar the IFAW and to Mary Vandenhoff, the Foreign Affairs official serving as the executive director of the Canadian Arctic Council secretariat. He was "deeply concerned" that the IFAW's request had not been sent to all Senior Arctic Officials. He further pointed out that the decision to bar the IFAW was made based upon "the informal responses received from several delegates and the formal response from Canada." The Arctic Council, he firmly reminded the Canadians and Norwegians, was a body that had agreed to act upon consensus, not simply a veto. An

---

*The International Fund for Animal Welfare and other Western environmental non-governmental organizations had been extremely active and successful in their lobbying for an Antarctic treaty. Because the same officials in Washington and many other capitals dealt with Arctic and Antarctic issues, they came to know these environmental lobbyists well. In some cases, friendships developed. The antagonism between many of these groups and indigenous peoples because of the traditional hunting practices complicated the negotiations for, and operation of, the Arctic Council.

IFAW representative took a place on the American Arctic Council delegation at several meetings.[7]

Differences over details irritated, but the broader disagreement—so evident in the minutes of meetings—concerned the nature of the Arctic Council itself and, in particular, the meaning of "sustainable development." Broadly stated, the Canadians, the Permanent Participants, Greenland/Denmark, and sometimes others conceived of sustainable development as an integrated program that emphasized the human, economic, and social aspects of the Arctic, a guide that was to pervade all aspects of Arctic Council work. The problems arose in one of the first meetings leading to the Arctic Environmental Protection Strategy when Mary Simon strode forward and demanded an indigenous presence at the table because the officials, scientists, and politicians did not live in the North, did not bear the outcomes of their decisions, and, crucially, did not understand the unique character of environment and development in the Arctic.

The United States did not reject "sustainable development." Vice President Al Gore embraced it immediately when the Clinton administration came to office, and it became a central part of the administration's 1994 Arctic policy statement. But his understanding of the concept—which was shared by his friend, the leading State Department official and former Colorado senator Tim Wirth—was different, with explicit emphasis on conservation, less on the Arctic as a particular region, and more on combined polar regions as part of a global environmental framework. Thus, the United States favoured an Arctic Council that featured individual research programs and collaborative operations, rather than an organization that had a distinct, overarching, and exclusively Arctic focus. Hence the Americans argued the case for observers like Britain and Germany with their powerful scientific establishments and for the involvement of international conservation NGOs and international organizations such as the International Whaling Commission. In February 1997, President Clinton issued a message to

Congress denouncing "Canada's unilateral decision" to authorize the hunting of two bowhead whales by Canadian Inuit. Canada's conduct, Clinton declared, "jeopardizes the international effort that has allowed whale stocks to recover." To reinforce his concern, he said that he had "instructed the Department of State to oppose Canadian efforts to address trade in marine mammal products within the Arctic Council." His statement signalled that the influence of conservation lobbyists was significant.[8]

These Washington opinions mingled with varied views in Alaska, a state that had voted consistently Republican in presidential elections since 1968, whose economy thrived on energy exploitation, whose indigenous groups differed with the Inuit on many questions, and whose politicians had given the lead in the creation of the Northern Forum, a group of political representatives who were naturally wary of an Arctic Council dominated by officials and Permanent Participants making decisions that had a political impact.

In normal circumstances, Canada's role would not have been dominant, but the most powerful Arctic nations were most often at the sidelines—Russia by necessity in the late 1990s, the United States largely by choice. The latter, as Oran Young frequently pointed out, was "dragging its feet," reacting to the initiatives of others and getting caught up in the often Byzantine world of congressional and domestic politics.[9] The second Clinton administration faced fierce opposition from Newt Gingrich's partisan Republicans, and Clinton himself stumbled as he sought to avoid impeachment because of the lies he told about his involvement with Monica Lewinsky. Other states sensed that the two most significant Arctic nations were preoccupied or disabled and recognized they must help because for the other Arctic states the collapse of the Arctic Council, whatever its weaknesses, had become increasingly undesirable. All knew that the situation was grave in the spring of 1998 as Canada prepared to hand over the chair position to the United States with much work unfinished and many details still disputed. The

Norwegians tried to fashion a compromise on the question of state and NGO observers, and the Finns produced a "non paper" recommending a broader commission to deal with the problem of an appropriate "umbrella" for the Arctic Council in an effort to evade the debate about sustainable development. To the Norwegian proposal, American official Tucker Scully replied that the proposal tended towards exclusion, particularly of those deemed "troublemakers." The United States, he averred, was "used to interacting with NGOS and their criticisms." A veto of the International Fund for Animal Welfare could not be justified simply because it brought different opinions into the council room.[10]

Seasoned Arctic official Ray Arnaudo of the U.S. State Department was friendly but blunt in late June 1998 when he responded to the Finnish "non paper." The commission idea proposed by the Finns was unacceptable: "The proposal gives an impression that outsiders (researchers, NGOs) will guide the work of the Council." He then said that the United States did not want a body where others ganged up to push their views on proposals "such as the trade of marine mammals" or the development of an Arctic free trade zone. "The United States holds the view," he said, "that governments of the member states take the initiatives, seek support from other member states, and then the Council makes the decisions." Setting up a commission to fuss over these details of the Council's responsibilities would lead nowhere. Arnaudo was suddenly blunt: "The United States is on the Arctic cooperation because of Alaska. Alaska is ready to cooperate but not in a way in which Alaska is told what to do." The United States, he continued, "is—for the time being—satisfied with the Council as [a] light framework for cooperation." He concluded by warning that the Canadian draft for upcoming ministerial was "unbalanced," presumably because it possessed a heavy framework.[11]

Although the Americans were not as blunt with their neighbour, Canadian officials knew that the Arctic Council had got off to a difficult start. They also knew that the United States by the mid-1990s was increasingly disillusioned with formal international organizations and more inclined to favour looser structures where issues could be sorted out without excessive rules and bureaucrats. With the end of the Canadian chairmanship of the Council approaching in 1998, Canadian Foreign Minister Lloyd Axworthy turned his attention more directly to the Arctic in an attempt to forge closer links with Russia, the recipient of much Canadian assistance, and to invigorate the Arctic Council. At a 1998 meeting of the Barents Euro-Arctic Council in Luleå, Sweden, he vigorously lobbied Deputy Secretary of State Strobe Talbott, a Clinton crony at Oxford, a Russia specialist, and a former *Time* journalist in Moscow, to assist in settling the disputes with the United States about the Arctic Council. He particularly emphasized the importance of the indigenous representatives, and Talbott was sympathetic.* By the time delegates came to Iqaluit for the ministerial on September 17, 1998, they had decided that the arguments over the rules of procedure and the terms of reference had to end even if the core problem, the meaning of "sustainable development," remained a source of difference. Prior to the meeting, the Permanent Participants and the Senior Arctic Officials debated the wording of the ministerial declaration and fished compromises out of the whirlpool of disagreement. The Aleut International Association, which represented about 6,000 aboriginals in the Aleutians and Russia, became the fourth Permanent Participant. The International Fund for Animal Welfare did not gain recognition as an observer, but the WWF, the International Union for Circumpolar Health, the Standing Committee of Parliamentarians of the Arctic Region, the International Arctic Science Committee, the United Nations Environment

---

*Talbott mentions the Luleå meeting in his memoirs but not the encounter with Axworthy. He stresses his discussions at Luleå with the Russians, with whom relations were souring, a serious liability for the operation of the Arctic Council. Talbott warned Russian foreign minister Yevgeny Primakov that his nation faced the possibility of sanctions because of its trade with Iran. The pressure came from House Speaker Newt Gingrich, who was being urged on by Israeli prime minister Benjamin Netanyahu. The Finns, whose counsel Talbott sought, warned that sanctions would be disastrous. *The Russia Hand: A Memoir of Presidential Diplomacy* (New York: Random House, 2002), 260.

Programme, the United Nations Economic Commission for Europe, the Northern Forum, and the Nordic Council joined Germany, Poland, the United Kingdom, and the Netherlands as observers. The air was cold, but the atmosphere had become much better.[12]

On the bay into which Martin Frobisher sailed in 1576 and in a town founded by the United States Air Force in 1942, Canadian foreign minister Lloyd Axworthy hosted the Iqaluit ministerial meeting. Beyond the treeline but outside the Arctic Circle, the town would soon be the capital of the new territory of Nunavut. Old military structures and even old Hudson's Bay Company buildings stood beside modern structures representing the town's new political life. Aware of the historical moment, Axworthy brought positive and even poetic enthusiasm to the task. "The North," he later wrote, "always has a mystical romantic quality for Canadians." The Arctic Council could be "a model for dealing with desert dust-storm problems afflicting East Asian residents; the water shortages in southern Africa; deforestation in Central America," and other such issues where intergovernmental collaboration was needed. Norway and Denmark sent their foreign ministers, Finland and Iceland their ministers of environment. The United States and Sweden sent officials, while Russia's delegate, the chairman of the State Committee for the Development of the North, arrived at the last moment because of the chaos in his country. Unfortunately, the Russian indigenous delegation was stranded in Moscow with neither air tickets nor visas because of bureaucratic confusion.[13]

In an interview given on September 15, Mary Simon had a wistful tone in talking about the Council she had done so much to create. She admitted that her people "haven't seen yet many results." The endless debates over words, commas, and observers had been tedious, but, she averred, "we had to get it right at the beginning." The meeting finally approved rules of procedure for the Council and terms of reference for the controversial Sustainable Development working group. Still, Simon reflected: "Part of me feels that we have been able to accomplish a lot in two years, but I also find that there's another part of me that says we could be doing a lot more." The first Arctic chair, the first Inuk to become a Canadian ambassador, and the veteran of aboriginal politics in Canada and more recently across the North, Simon was notably less ebullient than her minister Axworthy or Greenlander Alfred Jakobsen of the Inuit Circumpolar Council, who enthusiastically welcomed the Council as an emerging "harpoon-head" in support of Arctic peoples. To those who thought progress was slow, Jakobsen responded, "We're still dancing and developing, so we can really dance together." Iqaluit, for him, was the first dance of a promising evening.[14]

No one tripped on the floor, even if some of the Russians never made it to the dance hall, and the United States continued to choose to be a wallflower. Jane George, the superb reporter for the *Nunatsiaq News,* compared the Arctic Council to a "dysfunctional family." In George's opinion, "the Arctic Council ministerial meeting that wrapped up last Friday in Iqaluit resembled a bad made-for-TV mini-series." She caustically summed up the actors: "Russia, poor and delinquent, consistently offered up excuses for its behaviour and pleaded for help, but said little about doing anything to curb its bad habits. In response, the Nordic countries clucked about the need to be more morally responsible, while Canada, in its role of gracious enabler, pretended that everything was swell, pointing out that, after all, indigenous people were finally there with the big guys, too. The council's new leader, the United States, stood apart from the gang, aloof, a bit set in its ways, repeatedly mispronouncing its host's name as 'IKWALOOWEET.'"

According to George, "There was much bickering over whether the council should use indigenous 'people' or 'peoples,' with the United States asserting that an 's' made a great difference in international law and others disagreeing." Pekka Haavisto, the Finnish minister of environment and development, was unusually blunt: "The only problem is the United States. They want to keep the profile of the Arctic Council quite low."[15]

But spirits were nonetheless high after a ceremonial banquet with splendid Arctic fare complete with circumpolar entertainment featuring Saami dancers and Inuit throat-singers. Moreover, the Council could finally boast of some accomplishments. It proudly noted its support for a University of the Arctic, which David Stone of DIAND, Lars-Erik Liljelund of Sweden, and William Heal of the United Kingdom "thought up" at an early 1997 Arctic Monitoring and Assessment Programme (AMAP) meeting.* Moreover, the AMAP study on pollutants was gaining widespread attention because of its solid intellectual content and, within the Arctic Council, because it demonstrated how scientists could work with indigenous peoples to deal with a human problem. People in the North knew that pollutants were harming them; scientists who listened to their concerns proved that their fears were legitimate. Moreover, the pollutant study made specific recommendations for political action and international responses. Liljelund, who was present at Iqaluit, admitted that the Arctic eight did not share the same socio-economic problems even among their indigenous communities, but they did share environmental problems and, there, invaluable work could be done that would improve the lives of northern peoples. Although the United States would not endorse Canada's concept of sustainable development as an organizing instrument for Council work, the Americans did come forward with several projects with considerable promise for the future including telemedicine and technology transfer for sanitation. All agreed to support a Canadian program for the health of youth. The meeting ended with joyful toasts mingled with apprehension. The Arctic Council, in David Scrivener's words, had successfully reached its "perinatal" stage. Unfortunately, many did not trust its new American nurse.[16]

---

*The University of the Arctic is regarded as a concrete accomplishment of the Arctic Council. It is a cooperative network of institutions committed to research and higher education in the North. The eight Arctic Council nations cooperate, and the university encourages exchanges and circumpolar studies, although it does not have a central campus itself. Like many good ideas, rumour has it that it was born in a bar.

The United States had asked to be the second Arctic Council chair. In its own view, its new responsibility gave it the chance to wean the infant off dangerous temptations while maintaining its equilibrium and measured growth. After the dynamic but highly contentious years of Canadian leadership, American leadership brought a period of consolidation and study of what the Council's founders had created and where it might fit among the swelling number of Arctic actors. As befitted the greatest global power, the Arctic was treated as part of a broader process of international change. Many of the principal American officials involved in the Arctic Council had worked on Antarctica and with international environmental NGOS. They had also participated in the lively debates about the place of indigenous peoples in international law and organizations. By the end of the 1990s, the Arctic Council negotiations and the Finnish Initiative to create the AEPS had done much to develop a conceptual lens whereby the Circumpolar North became, for government officials, policy-makers, and increasingly social scientists, journalists, and NGOs, a region defined by its indigenous peoples and their political activism, its particular socio-economic challenges, and the Arctic's fundamental importance in global environmental challenges, most notably climate change. In focusing the new lens and integrating the new Arctic within the broader context of international change and collaboration, the Americans took on the chair at an appropriate moment.[17]

Although the United States often isolated itself in Arctic Council gatherings and, crucially, limited the scope of the Arctic Council, it possessed extraordinary resources that it could uniquely mobilize. Washington was the centre of the international environmental NGO movement and the great American foundations and research institutions that were central to research on the polar areas. Moreover, the Clinton administration had a strong environmental interest, notably in the office of Vice President Al Gore, and the 1997 Kyoto Accord ensured that the issue would remain in the forefront of American politics. These factors influenced the American approach to its chairing of the Council. First, the United States had consistently urged that the International Arctic Science Committee (IASC) be closer to the centre of the Arctic Council. In the course of Arctic Council negotiations, the IASC, which had been present and prominent in the early stages of the Finnish environmental initiative, moved to the sidelines, partly because indigenous representatives were suspicious of "pure science" as remote from their practical concerns, and partly because some scientists were highly skeptical about the relevance of "traditional environmental knowledge" to their Arctic work. Franklyn Griffiths, the co-chair of the Arctic Council Panel, had castigated the IASC in 1995 for its seeming reluctance to focus scientific work upon the human presence in the Arctic. Some IASC members resisted—one notable scientist publicly declared that the Arctic should be scientifically treated like Antarctica because the human presence was truly negligible in its vast geography. The United States as chair would move the Arctic Council closer to the IASC with its broader non-Arctic membership and to international science more generally.[18]

The second impact of the Council's move from Ottawa to Washington was a greater influence upon the Council of the climate change debate. In the late 1990s the debate over the commitments made in the Kyoto Accord had become deeply divisive within the Canadian government. Several government departments, particularly those dealing with natural resources and finance, believed that Canada had overcommitted at Kyoto, where, instructed by Prime Minister Chrétien to match the American pledge, the large Canadian delegation followed an American delegation led by environmental enthusiast Al Gore. In 1998, the government, worried about the Asian and Russian economic crises and the Canadian oil patch, abandoned plans to rally Canadians behind a massive effort to change their wasteful energy practices. In the United States, Congress similarly hesitated to take up the challenge represented by the Gore-inspired Kyoto pledge, but the administration remained firmly committed to confronting the challenge of climate change.

Moreover, a subtle shift was taking place as scientists began to warn that climate change was occurring more rapidly than had been expected and began to point to the Arctic as a bellwether. Could the change be halted? Should the focus become adapting to an inevitable and possibly catastrophic change?* The other Arctic states largely shared the Clinton administration's focus on climate change—including Norway, a major energy producer, and Russia, whose rapid and unfortunate deindustrialization made meeting Kyoto obligations easy.

The third major impact was, as expected, concentration on specific projects and an approach to the Sustainable Development working group that was project-oriented. It became apparent early in the American chairmanship that the work of the Arctic Monitoring and Assessment Programme, hosted and funded by Norway, was a model for future development of the Council. Essentially, the Arctic Council became, under American direction, more like the scientifically oriented Arctic Environmental Protection Strategy and less like the broader, more political body envisaged by the Canadians since the late 1980s and, especially, during the debates creating the Council.

When the Second Arctic Council ministerial met in Barrow at the northernmost tip of Alaska in October 2000, the mood was restrained and the Canadians noticeably less dominant. There were but two references to Canada in the ministerial declaration, one for organizing and supporting a future conference on capacity-building and the other for financing with Norway and Denmark the Indigenous Peoples' Secretariat in Copenhagen. Norway, which the United States had elbowed out of the chair position, received considerable praise, particularly for the

---

*The existence of satellites examining sea ice since the 1970s has given much more detailed evidence of the decline of Arctic ice coverage and Arctic sea volume. By the 1990s it appeared that coverage was declining significantly, as much as 2.2 percent per decade, but that figure has accelerated dramatically in the twenty-first century, pointing to the warming that occurs from the fact that ice reflects solar radiation more effectively than water. In short, the reduction of coverage multiplies the impact of warming.

work of the Oslo-based Arctic Monitoring and Assessment Programme (AMAP) in contributing scientifically to the Arctic Council Action Plan to Eliminate Pollution of the Arctic. This plan, ACAP as it became known, brought the Council its first major success, and in the words of the Barrow ministerial declaration, "ACAP, developed under the leadership of Norway, will be a basis for developing and implementing actions under the Council's auspices with respect to pollution prevention and remediation." Norway, it was agreed, would chair an ad hoc ACAP Steering Committee, which would guide the work "on the priority issues of persistent organic pollutants, heavy metals and radioactivity." The declaration further committed the ministers and their states to take a lead in advancing the work on persistent organic pollutants (POP) and, in particular, work towards the "completion and early ratification of a global convention on POPs." True to their word, seven Arctic states took the lead at Stockholm in May 2001 and signed the historic Stockholm Convention on Protecting Human Health and the Environment from Persistent Organic Pollutants. The Russians followed exactly one year later. It was, for the Arctic Council, the Arctic's indigenous peoples, and for AMAP, a long-awaited triumph.[19]

The Arctic Climate Impact Assessment

The Barrow ministerial planted important seeds for the Arctic Council's future by endorsing an Arctic Council Impact Assessment (ACIA), which was to be a joint project of AMAP and the Conservation of Arctic Flora and Fauna working group "in cooperation with the International Arctic Science Committee." The Americans agreed to finance a "substantial portion" of the ACIA secretariat. This project reflected American influence with its involvement of the International Arctic Science Committee, its confidence in AMAP, and, in its attention to climate change, a major preoccupation of the Clinton administration. The ministerial declaration, however, generally reflected the lower profile that Ray Arnaudo believed the Arctic Council must have and the focus on individual projects favoured consistently by the United States. While AMAP was praised generously and the work of CAFF duly noted, the working groups on Emergency Prevention, Preparedness and Response and Protection of the Arctic Marine Environment were essentially directed to examine existing arrangements and agreements and begin basic organization. The Sustainable Development working group was recognized for its work on Arctic children and youth, telemedicine, and cultural and eco-tourism. Its proposal to conduct a "Survey of Living Conditions in the Arctic" gained support, but the American emphasis on projects rather than an overarching sustainable development focus is clear. Indian Affairs and Northern Development official Jim Moore told a reporter that "it's still very much where a country takes the lead and the lion's share of the funding, and the others chip in." It was not the model that the Canadians had wanted, although Inuit leaders rightly complained about Ottawa's own reputation for parsimony.[20]

American influence was also felt in the addition of the Arctic Athabaskan Council and the Gwich'in Council International as Permanent Participants, making six in all with four—the others being the Inuit Circumpolar Council and the Aleuts—possessing an Alaskan base. What, finally, are we to make of this ministerial? There was a break from the tension, a sense of some accomplishment, but also a recognition that the lofty dreams of the previous decade had evaporated. When it came time to sign the "ministerial declaration," only two ministers (Justice from Finland and Environment from Iceland) signed. Mary Simon for Canada and Under Secretary of State Frank Loy for the United States signed for their nations. Most ministers, apparently, had other things to do.

The Barrow ministerial recognized that there was a need to review the structure of the Arctic Council organization, and Finland, as the new chair, asked Pekka Haavisto, a prominent Green politician and former Finnish minister of the environment, to carry out the study of Arctic Council structures and report on his findings at the Senior Arctic Officials meeting in Rovaniemi on June 12–13, 2001, with "finalization" at the

Arctic Council ministerial meeting in autumn 2002. At Iqaluit in 1998, it will be recalled that Haavisto had told a reporter that the United States was the principal problem for the Arctic Council. As expected, Haavisto was blunt. The document, particularly its early draft before states and others worked their influence upon it, is an invaluable portrait of the Council five years after its troubled creation. Not surprisingly, Haavisto spoke mainly to Europeans, and his analysis reflects their views. He drew upon a 2000 paper by Oran Young written for the Arctic parliamentarians that had urged the Council to concentrate on truly circumpolar issues and complained about a "cacophony of Arctic initiatives." Haavisto was even stronger in his criticisms of overlap, duplication, and political weakness. The outspoken Finn summarized the work of other bodies such as the Northern Forum and the activities of the working groups. The Arctic Monitoring and Assessment Programme received a high grade and the Emergency Preparedness, Prevention and Response failed. He wrestled with the question of where sustainable development fitted into the Arctic Council structure and then turned to the Council's "problems." He listed no fewer than seventeen.[21]

While recognizing that there were "no perfect organizations" and that "in all organizations personal likes and dislikes, gaps and overlaps, and some competition" will occur, Haavisto found that the Arctic Council fell far short of perfect. His titles describing the problems convey his impressions well: "Nobody knows exactly what is going on in the Arctic Council;" "No institutional memory"; "Problems in the funding"; "Lacking secretarial services"; "Participation of different ministries"; "The role of Observers is not defined"; "Co-operation with other Arctic actors is not structured"; "Bottom-up or top-down process?"; "Arctic policies made by the Working Groups"; "If there are overlaps, there are also probably gaps"; "Ownership of sustainable development"; "Sustainable development incoherent collection of projects"; "All projects don't have Circumpolar scope"; "Wild market for the project initiators"; "The working groups are competing of [*sic*] the same financial resources"; "PAME and ACAP competing in Russia"; and, finally, "EPPR's role unclear and weak." This list would not surprise readers of earlier chapters, but it does indicate the Council had not fulfilled the hopes of its early promoters.

As Haavisto conducted his interviews, he heard "some comments around on the 'good old days' of the Arctic Environmental Protection Strategy (AEPS) when the environmental ministries took the lead and gave coherence." However, as a former environment minister himself, he recognized that the Arctic's mounting challenges required the commitment of other departments, and there was no path leading back to the "good old days" of the AEPS. Indeed, Haavisto implicitly concluded that if the Arctic Council did not exist, it would have to be invented. The Arctic had become much more significant in "international politics, economics and communication" with the end of the Cold War and the advance of globalization. Haavisto's report urged restructuring, more funding, a secretariat, less overlap, and reducing the chaos of an organization with too many diverse projects of only local significance. But a compelling focus was emerging, one that would lead to a major project that would bring the Arctic Council into the forefront of international debate: the changing Arctic climate.

In 2012 Arctic historian John McCannon declared that "the most salient fact about the Arctic since the end of the Cold War has been its disappearing act—or at least its changing state of matter, from solid to liquid." While some still dispute the causes of global warming and the degree to which human activities are responsible, none can deny that, in McCannon's words, "the rate of melting [in the Arctic] has picked up speed like the rushing waters of a maelstrom as they near the vortex."[22] In navigating the rapid change, the Arctic states steered erratically in the nineties and the new millennium. At some points, they turned towards the beckoning shore of a newly "friendly Arctic" whose abundant mineral resources would became increasingly accessible as icebound waterways opened up. At other points, they hesitated when they realized that the Arctic thaw, which would warm oceans and release large quantities of methane from the permafrost, would have enormous implications for southern coastal communities and for human life generally. But nowhere was the impact on humans so great as upon northern people themselves. Across the North from the open summer waters of the Northwest Passage through the retreating glacier of Greenland to the ambitious resource developments of the Russian Arctic, northerners witnessed a rapid transformation of their lives.

"Nowadays snows melt earlier in the springtime. Lakes, rivers, and bogs freeze much later in the autumn. Reindeer herding becomes more difficult as the ice is weak and may give way ... Nowadays the winters are much warmer than they used to be. Occasionally during wintertime it rains. We never expected this; we could not be ready for this. It is very strange ... the cycle of the yearly calendar has been disturbed greatly and this affects the reindeer herding negatively for sure." The personal testimony of Larisa Avdeyeva of Lovozero, Russia, where she directed a Saami research centre, formed part of the powerful argument presented in the Arctic Climate Impact Assessment. Created when the Americans chaired the Arctic Council, with its administrative base at the International Arctic Research Center at the University of Fairbanks in Alaska, and with the United States the largest funder, the project took shape during the chairs of Finland (2002–2004) and Iceland (2002–2004). Its central body, the Assessment Integration Team, was chaired by Robert Correll of the American Meteorological Society and had six American members, three Norwegians (one, Jan Idar Solbakken representing Permanent Participants), two Canadians, and one each from Iceland and Sweden. There was no Russian member, although Russian science was strongly present in the analysis and, as with Avdeyeva, in the witness provided by indigenous peoples.[23]

The focus and title of the project reflect the character of the Arctic Council in its early years. The project was to concentrate on the impact of the changing climate in the Arctic specifically because the global impact was the responsibility of the UN-based Intergovernmental Panel on Climate Change (IPCC). The particular approach gave ample scope to the relevance of indigenous traditional environmental knowledge, an essential source because, as the ACIA acknowledged often in its opening pages, "the observational database for the Arctic is quite limited, with few long-term stations and a paucity of observations in general." As noted frequently in earlier chapters, the international debate on climate change, culminating in the Kyoto Accord of 1997, was largely absent from Arctic Council meetings in the 1990s. By the end of the decade, however, the controversies swirling around Kyoto, the growing testimony of northern observers like Avdeyeva, and IPCC research, which increasingly pointed to the Arctic as fundamentally important in understanding the global character of climate change, made the significance of a study of the impact much greater. The scientific credibility of AMAP work was strengthened by its persuasive research on persistent organic pollutants, and the International Arctic Science Committee had also turned to climate as a principal interest in the later nineties. With its circumpolar Arctic reach, scientific working groups, and commitment to biennial meetings of ministers who would participate in setting national policy goals, the Arctic Council seemed an ideal body to carry out an Arctic impact assessment. The project would be what AMAP chair David Stone had earlier said the new body badly needed: an important "deliverable."[24] The delivery did arrive, but its birth was unexpectedly difficult.

Between the conception of the ACIA in 1999 and its public emergence in 2004 came the administration of George W. Bush. Bush's Republicans disliked Kyoto, some because they denied the reality of climate change, others because they resisted the interventionist character of the Protocol, and still others because of their close ties with the fossil fuel industry that was the target of environmental activists. Climate change research and policy shops became unfashionable in official Washington, although not in most American universities and research centres, and certainly not in Iceland and Finland, the chairs of the Arctic Council during the first Bush administration. Except for Sweden, the remaining Arctic Council members were major producers of fossil fuels, and Canada's tar sands were becoming an increasing target for environmentalists who deplored their damage to the boreal forest and the high carbon emissions caused by production. Obviously between the science and the policy outcomes were many potential conflicts, and ACIA presented both opportunities and dangers for the Arctic Council in the first years of the new millennium. In an illuminating analysis of the ACIA and the Arctic Council, Swedish scholar and journalist Annika Nilsson has emphasized how that issue of climate change was "framed" within the ACIA. That framing drew upon the earlier work on the Arctic of the World Meteorological Organization and the UN Framework Convention on Climate Change and the Intergovernmental Panel on Climate Change. These efforts linked with the "emerging regional Arctic regime" as expressed in the Arctic Council to present the Arctic and its climate as globally significant. Nilsson notes three areas: first, the impact of physical processes in the Arctic; second, the impact on the Arctic habitat; and third, the understanding that "the Arctic is a bellwether or 'a canary in the mine shaft.'" The last, of course, has major climate policy possibilities and would potentially attract much attention.[25]

The Intergovernmental Panel on Climate Change report of 2001 had pointed to the Arctic as a region of particular significance to climate change scientists and gave impetus to the research work of ACIA, which came to involve over 300 scientists, indigenous representatives, and others. Over 160 independent experts and national scientific establishments provided peer review of their efforts. The report came in two parts: a shorter, readable survey for a general audience and a detailed, larger presentation for scientists. The evidence about changes that deeply affected Arctic life accumulated from northerners like Larisa Avdeyeva found compelling support in scientific research demonstrating that the Arctic had become much warmer in the last years of the twentieth century. There were uncertainties, regional differences, and much left unexplained, but the overall message was clear: "The Arctic climate is now warming rapidly and much larger changes are projected." And there could be no doubt: "Arctic warming and its consequences [would] have worldwide implications." During the course of the ACIA process, there had been many debates about the place in the report of the impacts upon humans and the extent to which social science should influence the final document. The linkages with AMAP's earlier work on pollutants became apparent during the steering committee meetings, as did the need for more research on human health in the Arctic. Not the least of the achievements of ACIA was the creation of new items for future Arctic Council agendas. "Deliverables" were no longer elusive.[26]

Under Correll's guidance, the scientific work proceeded well, and indigenous representatives reported satisfaction with the process. Problems appeared, however, when the Policy Drafting Team began its work; immediately differences became obvious, particularly between the United States and the rest. There were external factors that complicated the work. The Bush administration decision to attack Iraq divided the West and sharpened the differences between the United States on the one hand and Russia and Canada on the other. Among the Arctic Council states only Denmark supported the assault on Iraq in the spring of 2003, and the Bush administration's anger against Western countries that opposed their action was evident in all international forums. Moreover, the presidential race was beginning, and Bush faced a difficult fight against Democrat John Kerry, who strongly attacked Bush's environmental record. The timing was bad. Troubles first appeared when Senior Arctic Officials of the Arctic Council states met with members of the ACIA's Policy Drafting Team. The team faced tough comments from American representatives. On October 14, 2003, the Americans presented a paper to the Policy Drafting Team that threatened the entire plan. The so-called "US Statement on Policy Document" began with thanks to those who had worked on ACIA.

Then its mood changed: "As we have sought to review the draft Policy Document, we have come increasingly to the conclusion that there is a fundamental flaw in the process we are following—a process that is significantly different from that we have followed in the IPCC and other such efforts. Specifically, we are seeking here to develop the scientific assessment and its summary in tandem with policy recommendations that logically should flow from them."

The policy recommendations, the statement added, "should be developed only after *governments* [italics in original] have had an opportunity to consider the Scientific Document and the Synthesis Document on which they are based and draw their conclusions." "In effect," the statement somewhat ominously added, "we are putting the cart alongside the horse with the risk that neither cart nor horse will arrive at the destination."[27]

The American document is a single page and has an opaqueness that obscures precisely what was intended. But other governments knew what it meant: the United States wanted governments to have a much more intimate and directive part in the process. It was not for scientists or, for that matter, officials to dictate policy; governments—that is, politicians—should. The American document carefully avoided saying that ministers should be able to "choose" their science, but maintained that scientists should not be able to set out policy directly. They should offer opinions, not propose decisions. Of course, American politicians were not unique in these views, although the Bush administration's stance on climate change was a distinction that represented a difference from most others. In any event, the Senior Arctic Officials (SAO) halted the work of the Policy Drafting Team, and the Icelandic chair, Gunnar Pálsson, faced the difficult challenge of guiding the ACIA process towards the Arctic Council ministerial meeting in late fall 2004 in Reykjavik. Inevitably, the American presidential election intruded on the timetable, with a Washington newsletter reporting rumours that, within the SAO meetings, the Americans were pressing for delay in drafting any policy document dealing with the sensitive topic of climate change so close to the election. According to the newsletter, some "foreign officials and Native Americans" were suspicious of American activities and motivations. The rumours were true.[28]

The suspicion of the Permanent Participants turned to open anger in 2004, as they complained to Pálsson that they were being shunted to the side and that the Americans were bullying others to weaken the ACIA. The discontent became public at a ACIA workshop at Nuuk, Greenland, in April 2004 where the Americans argued that they did not oppose the so-called London document created by the Policy Drafting Team in itself, but rather the manner in which it had come forward, thereby essentially repeating the cart and horse metaphor. Faced with possible political embarrassment, the Americans agreed to let Pálsson take a lead in resuming negotiations, using the London draft as the basis once again. The Permanent Participants cooperated easily with ACIA chair Robert Correll, a prominent American environmental scientist, who in their view was sensitive, knowledgeable, and engaged. They clung to the Barrow ministerial declaration of the Arctic Council that, unlike the IPCC process, explicitly directed the ACIA to address "environmental, human health, social, cultural and economic impacts and consequences, *including policy recommendations* [italics in original]." On August 25, 2004, Inuit Circumpolar Council (ICC) chair Sheila Watt-Cloutier* wrote to Pálsson to remind him of the Barrow commitment and to express ICC concern about the draft policy document he had circulated.[29]

Watt-Cloutier began by thanking Pálsson for producing a proposal "in difficult intergovernmental circumstances." She then reminded him

---

*Watt-Cloutier was born in Kuujjuaq in Nunavik, Northern Quebec, in 1953. Her mother was a traditional healer and worked as an interpreter, and her father was an RCMP officer. She served as Canadian president of the ICC in the 1990s and as the international chair of the ICC between 2002 and 2006. She was particularly aggressive in promoting action against climate change, leading a group of indigenous hunters and trappers in charging the United States with contributing to the destruction of their way of life through the emission of greenhouse gases.

of the ACIA projections of the probable decline and possible extinction of marine life in the Arctic and the destruction of the Inuit "hunting and food sharing culture" that would result. The Pálsson draft was "declaratory not recommendatory," contrary to the Barrow instructions and contrary to the procedure followed with the AMAP report on Arctic pollution issues. She argued that "separation of recommendations by technical and policy specialists from political statements, commitments, and decisions by politicians is an important principle." The draft, however, was "a mix of different types of statements: declaratory, factual, key finding, conclusions and calls to action." It tried to be "all things to all people," while consistently avoiding policy recommendations. The draft pushed off analysis of adaptation and mitigation options to the United Nations Framework Convention on Climate Change (UNFCCC) and failed to indicate how ACIA would link with other international meetings and events. Watt-Cloutier told Pálsson that his text must be revised and objected to the restriction of the ICC to only one participant in the next meeting at which the states were permitted to have two. Finally, she warned Pálsson that the ICC was "not prepared to see the indigenous voice marginalized" and that it was "most unhelpful and inappropriate, in light of our extensive contribution to the ACIA, to restrict" the ICC's ability to participate at the last stage of the ACIA.[30]

Pálsson later told Annika Nilsson that he did not believe that Permanent Participants should have equal weight with the states at the table. His view may have reflected the fact that Iceland was the only Arctic Council state that lacked an indigenous population. Obviously, he did not share the closeness between indigenous leaders and government officials that existed in Canada, where land claim treaties required consultation, and Denmark, where Greenland was deeply integrated within Arctic Council decision-making. In the case of the other member states, indigenous representatives were closely linked with policy-makers either as members of national delegations or through Permanent

Participant membership. When, therefore, Pálsson worked on the chair's policy draft, he was neither compelled nor inclined to involve indigenous input because of domestic political influence or obligations. Conversely, Permanent Participants knew that political avenues to reach Pálsson, a highly respected career diplomat, did not exist, and this situation no doubt frustrated them. In a briefing book prepared for the Permanent Participants meeting in The Hague on August 29–30, the differences between the Pálsson draft and indigenous views are clear and numerous, as are the great hopes that the Permanent Participants and the Indigenous Peoples' Secretariat in Copenhagen placed upon the ACIA. They had limited resources but intended to use them to the maximum to put forward their views "to motivate Arctic and other states to take appropriate mitigation measures to attempt to slow the pace of climate change" and "to give Arctic indigenous peoples the resources required to adapt ..." Above all, the report noted, "there is an excellent chance that large parts of the ACIA will be leaked." With divisions deep, an election near, and anger rising, the prediction proved prescient.[31]

The Hague meeting of Senior Arctic Officials with Permanent Participants failed to reach agreement, and in September, Sheila Watt-Cloutier appeared before the United States Senate Committee on Commerce, Science, and Transportation, chaired by the powerful Republican senator John McCain, who was at odds with the Bush administration on the issue of climate change. Her testimony was emotional and striking: "We find ourselves at the very cusp of a defining event in the history of this planet." There would be "untold suffering" unless the emissions of greenhouse gases were quickly reduced. The Arctic was critical and would suffer greatly: "The ancient connection to our hunting culture may disappear within my grandson's lifetime," Watt-Cloutier lamented. "Protect the Arctic," she pleaded, "and you will save the planet." It was a brilliant presentation. McCain welcomed her comments and remarked that he had taken a trip to the Arctic himself.

Like her, he could testify that "these impacts are real." Watt-Cloutier joined Democratic senator Frank Lautenberg in criticizing the Bush administration for stalling. Shortly after the dramatic testimony that captured Washington's attention, she received a letter from Pálsson complaining about her remarks. They were, he claimed, "premature." The ICC responded that Watt-Cloutier and the organization were simply defending the integrity of the process and the Barrow ministerial declaration of 2000. On October 30, 2004, three days before the presidential election, the front page of the *New York Times* published large excerpts of the ACIA report, leaked to it by "European" sources. These sources told the *Times* that "the Bush administration had delayed publication until after the presidential election, partly because of the political contentiousness of global warning."[32]

Two days after George W. Bush was re-elected, the *Washington Post*'s front-page headline blared, "U.S. Wants No Warming Proposal: Administration Aims to Prevent Arctic Council Suggestions." Underneath a photograph of a snowmobile pulling a sledge on polar ice, the *Post* reported that the "study says sites such as the Arctic National Wildlife Refuge face historic temperature increases and weather changes."

For the Arctic Council, whose founding had been completely ignored in the *Post* and the *Times* and whose subsequent labours had remained obscure for American readers, the ACIA brought a historic change. The text under the photograph, with its specific reference to the Arctic National Wildlife Refuge, demonstrated that Arctic politics had at last become, in Congressman Tip O'Neill's historic description, "local" and meaningful.* The Council's work had penetrated the American political debate, the most important on the planet. With the ACIA, the Arctic became "the canary in the mineshaft," the harbinger of dramatic global

---

*Prior to ACIA, Canadian foreign minister Bill Graham was told by his department not to go to the Arctic Council ministerials unless American secretary of state Colin Powell was there. Powell never came, but Graham went nevertheless. (Source: Hon. William. C. Graham, February 2013).

climate changes, and a fuel for political battle. One European negotiator, the *Post* reported, claimed that the Bush administration was trying to "sidetrack the whole process so it is not confronted with the questions, 'do you believe in climate change or don't you?'" Pálsson told the *Post* that the controversy over the American position on climate change was "complicating his efforts to achieve a consensus among top ministers, who are supposed to sign off on the policy findings within a matter of weeks."[33]

The "complication" and a close deadline resulted in a consensus document, but one that nevertheless carried a clear message. It accepted that "climate change and other stressors present a range of challenges for Arctic residents, including indigenous peoples, as well as risks to Arctic species and ecosystems." The findings "will help inform government as they implement and consider future policies on global climate change." The policy recommendations, the ministerial declaration continued, would provide suggestions for "mitigation, adaptation, research, monitoring and outreach." Beneath its reassuring and collaborative tones lay profound differences: first, between states that accepted the need to move quickly to combat climate change and others who questioned rapid action and even the science itself; and second, between the Permanent Participants and states that had championed their interests within the Council and others who saw their role as lesser than the nation states at the council table. Faced with a diminished status, the Permanent Participants took their cause to Washington, raising a challenge to American policy in Congress and the media. They won a battle, but not a victory. Other states were hesitant to challenge the Americans' arguments. Canada, for example, had controversially refused to back the American war in Iraq and was itself a laggard in fulfilling its promises at Kyoto.[34]

Despite their misgivings about the final presentation of the ACIA, the 2004 Reykjavik ministerial was a high point for the Arctic indigenous peoples in shaping the major multilateral governance forum for the Arctic in the twenty-first century. The ACIA reflected and responded to the northern peoples' view that their climate was changing and their voices were heard. Chapter 3 of the ACIA dealt specifically with the impact upon them, and traditional environmental knowledge was given its full due. A survey published in 2012 ranked "scientific" assessments as the most important contribution of the Arctic Council, and among the assessments the ACIA was considered the most important by a wide margin. The ACIA report influenced the UN-based process and opinion makers throughout the world, and the Arctic became a "bellwether" of climate change for journalists, filmmakers, and climate change activists internationally. Suddenly, it mattered.

The 2004 ministerial also produced another of the top-ranked scientific assessments, the Arctic Human Development Report (AHDR). It was the first Arctic-wide scientific assessment of the human state of the Arctic, and it drew upon several of the first projects of the Arctic Council's controversial Sustainable Development working group (SDWG), such as telemedicine and children's health. As such, it gave new weight to SDWG, whose purposes had been hotly debated in the Council's early years. The University of the Arctic, very much a product of the Arctic Council negotiations, took the lead in the AHDR and appointed Oran Young to be the commission co-chair. While illustrating the hardships and challenges Arctic residents faced, the AHDR emphasized their resilience and innovative approaches, such as co-management for resources and, of course, the Arctic Council, a unique regional institution. Northerners were the principal contributors to the AHDR, whose base was at the Stefansson Arctic Institute in Iceland, unlike the ACIA, which despite its indigenous focus was primarily the product of southern scientists. Young and his co-chair Niels Einarsson of Iceland urged that Arctic indigenous peoples, other Arctic residents, regional bodies, the Arctic states, and the Arctic Council should find "explicit opportunities to coordinate and amplify the voice of the Arctic in broader policy areas." There were now many who harkened to that voice. As the Arctic became the canary in the mineshaft whose songs bore a haunting warning of a disappearing northern world and a global future of frightening uncertainty, the Arctic Council finally emerged from the diplomatic shadows. Still without a secretariat, lacking adequate funding, faced with interdepartmental rivalries within government, and reliant on southern political whims, the Arctic Council would nevertheless become the major forum for Arctic states and Arctic peoples shaping their northern fates in the twenty-first century.[35]

CONCLUSION

When eight Arctic nations gathered in Ottawa in the summer of 1996 to create the Arctic Council, their leaders, even Canada's, were absent. Most sent ministers, the United States only a senior official. Like the Arctic itself in those times, the new Council received notice on the back pages, if at all. Within governments, those working on Arctic matters occupied offices far from the narrow corridors of power. The Americans forced security off the Arctic Council agenda, emphasizing their point by attaching a bizarre asterisk announcing the exclusion to the forum's founding document. And it was only a forum, a place to meet, not to make international policy. By the time the Canadians once again took the chair in 2013, the Arctic and the Arctic Council had changed profoundly. Arctic sea ice had vanished more rapidly than even climate change pessimists of the late twentieth century had predicted. The summer ice cover of 7.5 million square kilometres of 1982 had shrunk to 5.36 in 2002 and an astonishingly low 3.41 in 2012. "Something very serious is going on in the Arctic," Arctic scientist David Barber warned in March 2013, "and we have to inform the planet about what it is." The planet was already watching, and foreign ministers now red-circled the date of Arctic Council meetings on their schedules. Like the Arctic itself, the Council was unready for the unexpected change.[1]

Sheila Watt-Cloutier's 2004 testimony before Senator John McCain's Congressional committee had been a triumph of the movement towards circumpolar collaboration that began with Eben Hopson's first Inuit Circumpolar Conference in Barrow, Alaska, in June 1977. There, the Inuit of Alaska, Canada, and Greenland had planted the seeds that were nurtured by Gorbachev and then carefully cultivated by remarkable leaders in the movement for circumpolar cooperation, such as Mary Simon and Jack Stagg in Canada, Esko Rajakoski and Mauno Koivisto in Finland, Aqqaluk Lynge in Greenland, and Thorvald Stoltenberg in Norway. When the still-embryonic Arctic Council seemed close to death in the mid-nineties, the Canadians with Simon as ambassador and Stagg as the hard-driving negotiator made sure it survived and, most significantly, that the Arctic peoples had a place at the table. The Council's future shape remained uncertain, its longevity unknown, but, after August 1996, it possessed the breath of life. With its unique structure whereby indigenous peoples sat with state representatives at the conference table with full rights to speak, consent, and be consulted, the Arctic Council pioneered new forms of international governance. For the peoples of the North—those who had long dwelt in the harsh, haunting, and isolated Arctic—the Arctic Council was an astonishing achievement. Shunted to the side by the southerners who explored and exploited the North for centuries, the indigenous peoples were the main architects of the principal international forum for a remarkable "Arctic awakening in the new millennium."[2]

For the eight Arctic states and its indigenous Permanent Participants, the Arctic Council had come to define the Arctic region, in the words of geographer Klaus Dodds, "as a fixed container, albeit one that is literally being cracked, melted, and transformed."[3] In the Arctic, nothing is fixed forever, not least the place of its indigenous peoples. They were mostly absent as southern nation states extended their imperium over the North in the first millennium but, as noted above, were fully present in the late twentieth century as new forms of Arctic governance emerged. After

2004, as the Arctic loomed ever larger not only in capitals of Arctic states but even in faraway Beijing, New Delhi, and Singapore, the Arctic Council moved rapidly beyond its initial preoccupations, concerns, and people. Mary Simon stepped down as Canada's Arctic ambassador in 2003, and the Harper government abolished the position in 2006, with Foreign Minister Peter MacKay declaring that "we didn't feel we were getting good value for money from that position." Jack Stagg died prematurely in August 2006, but a tribute in Parliament noted his work as deputy minister of the Department of Veterans Affairs, not his efforts to create the Arctic Council. Watt-Cloutier's eloquence in calling attention to climate change in the Arctic secured a Nobel Prize nomination in 2007, but the new attention concentrated upon the Arctic also brought unintended consequences. *Time*'s decision to place a polar bear apparently stranded on an ice floe on a 2006 cover with the dire warning, "Be worried. Be very worried." created a growing demand to list the bear as an endangered species, thereby threatening the hunting culture and economic life of the Arctic's peoples.[4]

Once again the Arctic was not what it seemed and what science deemed it to be. The polar bear, like Arctic peoples and mammals throughout history, was adapting. Although the bear was threatened by new dangers and faced an uncertain long-term fate, the elders were correct and the scientists, still learning about Arctic life, were probably wrong: the number of polar bears was not declining when *Time*'s cover appeared. But, as Mary Simon wistfully said in 2012 in speaking about the polar bear debate, the elders knew now that their world was changing so quickly that their wisdom was no longer so relevant and invaluable.[5]

When Brian Mulroney raised the possibility of an "arctic council" in Leningrad in November 1989, his government was soon to end military exercises in the Canadian North. The Cold War was quickly winding down, and the possibilities for demilitarization of the Arctic seemed real. The Canadian Arctic Council initiative gained much force in those times from the commitment of Arctic disarmament advocates such as John

Lamb, Tom Axworthy, Franklyn Griffiths, and especially the Walter and Duncan Gordon Foundation. Although their efforts and those of others from other Arctic states failed to incorporate "security" within the purview of the Arctic Council, the nineties were marked by a retreat from the intense militarization of the Arctic during the Cold War. The title of the 1992 book edited by Arctic Council Panel co-chair Franklyn Griffiths, *Arctic Alternatives: Civility or Militarism in the Circumpolar North*, captured the apparent Arctic choices of the time.[6] Throughout the decade, the military was in retreat in the North while concern for northern peoples grew and was reflected in international debates and organizations, most notably the Arctic Council. The Arctic Council became a symbol of a new civility, of a "friendliness" that marked rapidly increasing human encounters across the North.

In September 2001, a southern event, the terrorist attack on New York's World Trade Center, signalled that civility faced serious new challenges. In 2002 Canada resumed military exercises in the North, citing possible terrorist threats as a major justification. In 2003 the Iraq War shattered the pacific hopes of the previous decade and blocked the development of the human security movement that had nurtured the birth and development of the Arctic Council. While the 2004 Arctic Climate Impact Assessment (ACIA) drew attention to the problems northern peoples faced, it also spawned hopes for greater access to the potential riches of the Arctic through open waters and new sea lanes. Old boundary disputes flared up, even between Denmark and Canada, two of the leaders in the human security network. On August 1, 2003, HDMS *Triton* placed a Danish flag on contested Hans Island, which was located in the Nares Strait between Greenland and Ellesmere Island. Canadian soldiers responded on July 13, 2005, by placing a Canadian flag and an Inukshuk on the small island's rocks. Then, in a dramatic helicopter descent on July 20, Canadian defence minister Bill Graham landed on Hans Island, declaring to the Canadian Broadcasting Corporation that "it's part of Canada." Danish ambassador to Canada

Poul Kristensen immediately responded in the *Ottawa Citizen* that the remote, unpopulated, desolate island was actually part of Denmark.[7]

The two NATO allies bantered about Canadian Club whisky and Danish schnapps left on the island along with the national flags and symbols, but joking was set aside in August 2007 when the flamboyant Russian explorer–politician Artur Chilingarov planted a titanium Russian flag on the seabed directly beneath the North Pole. In reporting Chilingarov's daring feat, the British Broadcasting Corporation declared that it had put "Russia Ahead in [the] Arctic Gold Rush," an interpretation encouraged by Chilingarov's declaration that his team's goal was to "prove the North Pole is an extension of the Russian continental shelf."[8] Under Article 76 of the UN Convention on the Law of the Sea, the Arctic coastal states' Exclusive Economic Zones could extend 200 nautical miles and, for the seabed itself, 150 nautical miles beyond that point if there were a "natural prolongation" of its land territory. In a 2001 submission to the UN Commission on the Limits of the Continental Shelf, the Russians claimed that the Lomonosov Ridge was a "natural prolongation" as defined in Article 76. Meanwhile, the Danes eyed the ridge as an extension of Greenland. The Commission made no decision and asked for the Russians to resubmit their claim. Chilingarov said that he took soil from the seabed to prove that it possessed the same characteristics as Russia's continental shelf.*

Gold had beckoned Martin Frobisher to the Arctic in the sixteenth century, but in the twenty-first century the Arctic bonanza was principally oil and gas. In 2007 the UN Intergovernmental Panel on Climate Change fully accepted the warnings in ACIA and declared the polar regions "extremely vulnerable" and the most affected by climate change.[9] Much sooner than previously believed, the passages would

---

*Under the United Nations Convention on the Law of the Sea (UNCLOS), the coastal states should file their claim to the Commission on the Limits of the Continental Shelf within ten years after their ratification of UNCLOS. The relevant dates are Norway (2006), Russia (2007), Canada (2013), and Denmark (2014). The United States has not yet ratified.

open, Greenland's glacier would retreat, and the ice that had shielded the Arctic's treasures would become accessible. With Canadian prime minister Stephen Harper declaring that Canada could become an energy superpower and Russia's Vladimir Putin extolling the Arctic as the principal source of his nation's future wealth and greatness, the July 23, 2008, release by the United States Geological Survey (USGS) of the first trans-Arctic report on undiscovered but technically recoverable resources had a stunning impact. The Arctic, the respected USGS declared, held 90 billion barrels of oil and 1,670 trillion cubic feet of natural gas. This amounted to no less than 22 percent of the "undiscovered and technically recoverable resources in the world." With oil costing $147.30 per barrel when the report was released, the rush for resources seemed imminent.[10]

But the Arctic was not ready. Nor were the Arctic states. In particular, there were dangers for the so-called Arctic Five, the coastal states whose claims before the Continental Shelf Commission would restrict the area open to non-Arctic states to a small portion of the Arctic. Outsiders had noticed the Arctic states' grasp for control. The European Union Parliament, whose Arctic policies on seals, whales, and trapping had infuriated many northerners, began to debate the need for an international treaty to deal with environmental, shipping, and other Arctic concerns. In the prestigious American journal *Foreign Affairs*, Scott Borgerson spoke of coming "anarchy" in the Arctic where the Arctic Council "has remained silent on the most pressing challenges because the United States purposefully emasculated it at birth." The ideal solution, in his view, was an "overarching treaty" to guide the Arctic's future.[11] The Arctic coastal states disagreed. Facing this challenge and fearing that support for an Antarctic-treaty approach for most of the Arctic Ocean could attract wide backing, the Arctic Five met at Ilulissat in Greenland in May 2008 to counter what they termed the pressure for a new "international legal regime to govern the Arctic Ocean." On May 28, the five states issued a historic declaration:

The Arctic Ocean stands at the threshold of significant changes. Climate change and the melting of ice have a potential impact on vulnerable ecosystems, the livelihoods of local inhabitants and indigenous communities, and the potential exploitation of natural resources.

By virtue of their sovereignty, sovereign rights and jurisdiction in large areas of the Arctic Ocean, the five coastal states are in a unique position to address these possibilities and challenges. In this regard, we recall that an extensive international legal framework applies to the Arctic Ocean as discussed between our representatives at the meeting in Oslo on 15 and 16 October 2007 at the level of senior officials. Notably, the law of the sea provides for important rights and obligations concerning the delineation of the outer limits of the continental shelf, the protection of the marine environment, including ice-covered areas, freedom of navigation, marine scientific research, and other uses of the sea. We remain committed to this legal framework and to the orderly settlement of any possible overlapping claims.

The five clung to the UN Convention on the Law of the Sea to justify their claims and promised "more orderly" behaviour in the future.[12]

But the world itself was not orderly. By the end of 2008, oil cost less than $50 a barrel, the world financial system seemed to be collapsing, and Democrat Barack Obama was preparing to become president of the United States. Obama took climate change more seriously than the Bush Republicans, wanted a better relationship with Russia, and rejected the unilateralist approaches of the previous administration. In short, the Americans suddenly tilted towards "civility." In the new administration's first year in office, there was a major Arctic Council success: the Arctic Marine Shipping Assessment (AMSA), which responded to the ACIA and another Arctic Council 2004 report, the Arctic Marine Strategic Plan. Chaired by University of Alaska academic Lawson Brigham, a career United States Coast Guard officer who had sailed with the *Polar Sea* in historic voyages in the Arctic and Antarctic, AMSA reflected the practical impact of the dramatic changes in Arctic ice and waters. Its approach was to explore future possibilities in terms of governance and responsibilities in the event of different circumstances that might develop by 2050. Innovative, clearly written, wonderfully illustrated, and informed by the experience of sailors, the knowledge of indigenous peoples, the opinions of private business interests, and the work of Arctic scientists, the report was celebrated as a model of what the Arctic Council could do well. Shortly after the report's publication, Brigham attracted attention with a 2010 article in the influential American magazine *Foreign Policy* entitled "Think Again: The Arctic." Brigham set out to destroy Arctic myths, notably that the Northwest Passage and the Northern Sea Route would become the new Suez or Panama Canal. Not so, the seasoned sailor declared. The Arctic was warming, but the ice and dangers would remain for most of the year. How could a sea route be viable if not usable for most of the year?* It was time to dampen enthusiasm and exaggerated responses.[13]

Brigham began his article with Chilingarov's planting of the Russian flag on the seabed at the North Pole in August 2007 and angry reactions to that act. He correctly argued that whatever the fuss in Ottawa, Copenhagen, and Moscow, most disputes were being settled, notably the long-standing one between Norway and Russia in the Barents Sea. And then there was the Arctic Council. Although it lacked the legal bite of a treaty, "it has nonetheless been a force for good, getting everyone in the habit of discussing the future of the region in a diplomatic setting." As he wrote, a Council task force was actually negotiating a search-and-rescue treaty, the first careful foray into an area where the military held sway. Brigham later pointed out, after the treaty was in place, that the Americans not only had become active in the Council but, since the early part of the new century, were much greater funders than the Canadians and, in recent years, often stronger advocates of its utility.[14]

---

*This sober analysis of the difficulties of Arctic navigation was reflected in a 2011 comment by a naval commander, then my student at the Canadian Forces College. If it were left to the sailors, he claimed, Canadian naval strategy would not focus on finding terrorists in the Arctic but rather interdicting drugs in the Caribbean.

This background clarifies Hillary Clinton's sharply critical reaction to the Canadian government's decision to call the Arctic Five to Canada in spring 2010. At a moment when Canadian Arctic policy was to "Stand Up for Canada," and Russia blustered about its elongated Arctic boundaries, the Arctic Council had increasingly proven to be an effective "force for good."[15] Its gatherings and work dampened the nationalist fires that had flared up in the middle of the first decade of the new century. It had "calmed the waters" and, while not a place to settle territorial disputes, it had created an atmosphere where the eight Arctic states could, in Hillary Clinton's words, "showcase our ability to work together, not create new divisions."[16]

Unlike other American secretaries of state, Clinton decided to attend Council meetings and monitor its work, immediately raising the Council's profile. She had established ties with Alaskan indigenous leaders who probably inspired her attack on the Gatineau meeting's exclusion of the Permanent Participants. Declaring that the "world looks increasingly to the north," she also agreed to the establishment of a permanent secretariat for the Arctic Council. Although Canada had proposed to house and even fund the secretariat in its early Arctic Council proposals, the secretariat found its new home in Tromsø, Norway, an impressive and bustling northern capital that quickly embraced its new status. After Clinton's strong rebuke in 2010, she attended the Nuuk ministerial meeting in 2011. But it would be wrong to overemphasize Clinton's appearance at the Nuuk ministerial, the first by an American secretary of state. The meeting ended a productive Danish chairmanship and began a highly effective Swedish one.[17] It formalized approval of the new secretariat and of an Agreement on Cooperation on Aeronautical and Maritime Search and Rescue in the Arctic, the first legally binding agreement negotiated under the auspices of the Arctic Council.

In response to these meetings and other events, Canada began to tilt towards stronger support for the Arctic Council and multilateral cooperation. But a frequent lament in other foreign offices was that Canada had lost interest in the Arctic Council as it intensified its yearly military exercises in the Arctic in which Prime Minister Harper himself personally participated. When *The Economist* signalled the growing significance of the Arctic in a landmark special issue in June 2012, it noted Canada's military disposition while emphasizing that it was not in the interest of the Arctic states to have an Arctic bristling with weapons as the region's glorious resources became more accessible. Such conflicts attracted the attention of others, including the Chinese, the South Koreans, and the Indians, an outcome potentially dangerous to the common interests of Arctic states. They pulled together: by the summer of 2012, *The Economist* concluded, the "Arctic countries [had] decided to hold hands and gorge on resources." The Arctic Council was rapidly becoming the kitchen where the menu was most likely to be set.[18] But who would be the guests? Would they display good manners?

Faced with this challenge, the Swedish chairmanship responded with efficiency and skill. Foreign Minister Carl Bildt, a former prime minister and leading international diplomat, chaired the Council. His calls would be answered in ministers' offices not only in the Arctic Eight but in Brussels and other capitals throughout the world. Diplomat Gustaf Lind expertly guided the other Senior Arctic Officials in their work. Chief Michael Stickman of the Arctic Athabaskan Council, a veteran of many Council meetings, said that the Council was mainly a talk shop until the Swedes "started to get things done."[19] When they relinquished the chair at Kiruna in May 2013, they were able to report that a second legally binding agreement had been signed: the Agreement on Cooperation on Marine Oil Prevention Preparedness and Response. Five new observers were admitted: China, India, Japan, South Korea, and Singapore. Their new presence signalled that Arctic issues were now a global concern. But old issues persisted: the European Union's official presence was delayed until certain "concerns" were resolved. The Canadians, it was said, resisted the European Union's entry, a reflection of the indigenous opposition to EU policy on trapping and hunting. In contrast to the first

Arctic Council meeting in Ottawa in 1996, the *New York Times* not only covered the meeting but even sent a reporter, and coverage occurred in all corners of the planet. In 1996, only the Canadian foreign minister was present. At Kiruna, five foreign ministers, including John Kerry of the United States and Sergei Lavrov of Russia, signed the final declaration. Iceland's recent election meant that an official signed. Minister of Health Leona Aglukkaq signed for Canada and became Bildt's successor as the new Arctic Council chair.[20]

Some observers unfavourably compared Aglukkaq's international stature and political responsibilities with Bildt's diplomatic eminence. In the ministerial meeting, the precise and polished Bildt tapped his microphone four times when the diplomatic novice talked too long. But Aglukkaq's appointment was consistent with Canada's past, particularly her emphasis in her remarks on the importance of international collaboration for the health and well-being of those who lived in the north. Like Mary Simon, the first Arctic Council chair, she was an Inuk and had lived most of her life in the Arctic, and she had no hesitation in pushing away the EU from the Council, even if it was only temporary and offended an important Canadian trading partner then currently negotiating a free trade agreement with Canada. The Canadian chairmanship, she declared, would be marked by a stress on development in the Arctic, and a circumpolar business forum was at the top of the Canadian agenda for the "people of the north." While she talked about development and Arctic peoples, John Kerry, who reportedly negotiated the compromise on EU observer status, spoke eloquently and mainly about climate change. The difference reflected a tradition: Canada's Arctic policy grew from domestic needs, whereas American policy was shaped by global geopolitical concerns. There were other differences.

First, the Arctic Council was no longer an intimate affair. The days of small, lower-level delegations had ended. Ever larger conference halls hosted the meetings, and new voices and languages were heard. China, India, Korea, Singapore, and others now took their places at the table as observers at the Arctic Council. At the end of the Kiruna meeting, a "vision" statement was released that declared that the Council had "become the pre-eminent high-level forum of the Arctic Region." But its significance created complications. The question of observers had frustrated Arctic policy-makers since the Council's earliest days, but the sudden prominence of the Arctic made the topic compelling. At the Nuuk ministerial in May 2011, the Council announced criteria that potential observers must accept. Among them was acceptance of the sovereignty of the Arctic states and, significantly, the traditions and values of Arctic indigenous peoples. The Permanent Participants quickly pointed to the European Parliament's continuing hostility to the seal trade while others suggested that China's treatment of its own indigenous peoples made its observer status risible. But how could an effective Council exclude the world's most populous and soon-to-be economically largest nation not only from the table but even from the hallways? It could not, but the decision to admit China and others made the corridors more crowded and, perhaps, the chatter more confusing.

The second difference was the role of the Permanent Participants. The Harper government did choose an eminent Inuk to be the Arctic Council chair for 2013–2015 and expressed its commitment to a "greater understanding of the human dimension of the Arctic." Reflecting the bipartisan Canadian tradition, the government also said that it would "ensure that the central role of the Permanent Participants is not diminished or diluted."[21] However, on the eve of a Council meeting in Sweden in November 2012, the Russian Ministry of Justice announced that it was "closing the doors" of the Russian Permanent Participant, the Russian Association of Indigenous Peoples of the North (RAIPON), an action that the other Council members vigorously protested. Even before RAIPON was shut down, a RAIPON vice-president told a conference that his organization faced troubles whenever they raised questions about resource development. He also said that the government did not like its links with international indigenous groups and human rights activists.[22] Although a single RAIPON delegate appeared at Kiruna, the incident reflected a waning of the power of the Permanent Participant voice. In the early days of the Arctic Council, there was considerable support for a funding mechanism that would assure that Arctic voices were heard at the Council and in the working groups. Unlike many other hopes of earlier times, that promise remains unfulfilled, and in the more crowded rooms the indigenous voice is less powerful.*

The third difference apparent as the states came to the table in 2013 was the place of resource development on the Arctic menu. The debate over an indigenous presence had shaped the Arctic Council, and the participation of Permanent Participants with member states marked the Council as a unique international body, one that could be a model for indigenous peoples throughout the world. As the military retreated from the Arctic in the nineties, the Arctic Council became the congenial face of civility, of a "friendly Arctic" where cooperation replaced conflict and suspicion across the Polar North. It was not that the Permanent Participants rejected economic development; indeed, the debate over sustainable development reflected their interest in promoting economic growth that would benefit northern peoples. That was the important point that Jack Stagg made in support of the Arctic Council when he visited Washington to plead for its creation in 1996. But as Arctic waters melted, resources beckoned, and military ships and soldiers reappeared, the Arctic Council, with its critical asterisk preventing discussion of "security," faced fresh challenges. The Arctic Council's growing significance was apparent in its negotiation of the important agreement on search and rescue in 2011 and subsequently the agreement on marine

---

*The Kiruna meeting did not add non-governmental observer groups, although Greenpeace lobbied hard for acceptance. Once rejected, its members gathered outside the conference hall with megaphones and placards bearing the message "NO OIL." After their rejection, they wrote to their Canadian supporters claiming that "Prime Minister Harper will do anything it takes to accelerate oil development, muzzle scientists, gut environmental regulations, and deny indigenous rights." It claimed that "indigenous groups from every Arctic state signed a statement calling for a ban on offshore drilling in the Arctic."—Christy Ferguson to Greenpeace "supporters," May 2013.

oil pollution announced at Kiruna in May 2013.[23] But for many, doubts remained. "Preventing an Arctic Cold War" was the headline of a March 2013 *New York Times* article in which oceanographer Paul Berkman questioned whether the Arctic Council was up to the immense task it faced: "Whether it is through the Arctic Council or another entity, there needs to be a forum for discussing peace and stability, not just environmental and economic issues. We need 'rules of the road' to take us safely into the Arctic's future."[24]

It is a mark of the historic change that the growing prominence of the Arctic Council with its indigenous participants means that many rules will now be set not only in imperial southern capitals but often by northern peoples in Alaska, Nunavut, the Northwest Territories, the Saami Parliament, and, inevitably, northern Russia. Greenland with its indigenous majority, its growing independence from Denmark, and its great resource potential has become the focus of the debate about the Arctic future. The Indigenous Peoples' Secretariat moved from Copenhagen to Tromsø to join the new secretariat. Perhaps on a path to take its own seat at the Arctic Council table where its indigenous voice will be heard at heads of delegation Council meetings, Greenland captures the contradictions and promise of the region. In 2009 Kuupik Kleist, the leader of the autonomist Inuit Ataqatigiit Party, became prime minister. Son of a deaf and mute Inuk mother who was quickly abandoned by his Danish father, Kleist learned Danish at seventeen, became a gravelly voiced singer dubbed Greenland's Leonard Cohen, and became active in Greenland and circumpolar politics. As an Inuit Circumpolar Conference (ICC) leader, he attended many of the meetings in the mid-nineties when the Arctic Council took form and his fellow Inuit Ataqatigiit politician Aqqaluk Lynge was ICC president.

The poet-politician Lynge became ICC chair in 2009 just as Kleist became prime minister, and soon embarked upon a program to encourage rapid exploitation of resources to deal with the mounting social problems of the island and to free it from reliance on the massive Danish subsidy. By the summer of 2010 a monstrous drillship had appeared off Greenland's west coast, and Kleist was travelling the world seeking investment. Lynge reacted strongly: "Every night I pray they don't find oil and gas in the Greenland area because that will end the peace and calm heaven here." Lynge went to Kiruna in 2013 as the chair of the ICC. Kleist did not attend: he had been defeated in an election where his opponent Aleqa Hammond attacked, among other things, Kleist's plans to admit Chinese workers. Because the Swedes refused to grant a place at the table for Greenland beside Denmark, Hammond refused to go to Kiruna. She told a reporter: "It is not enough for Greenland to eat canapés with other countries' politicians, smile kindly, and be figureheads."[25]

Lynge was in Kiruna as the representative of the Inuit Circumpolar Council. Over a generation earlier, in Rovaniemi, Finland, Lynge had charmed the founding meeting of the Arctic Environmental Protection Strategy with his tale of how the Arctic was once an earthly paradise that became cold and most people went south. Now, people were returning. The legend, he claimed, "says that it is in the Arctic that we will find that the importance of our common humanity and concerns outweigh our differences."[26] The Arctic Council's fate will test that legend's truth.

APPENDIX:

DECLARATION OF THE ESTABLISHMENT OF THE ARCTIC COUNCIL

Ottawa, Canada   September 19, 1996

THE REPRESENTATIVES of the Governments of Canada, Denmark, Finland, Iceland, Norway, the Russian Federation, Sweden and the United States of America (hereinafter referred to as the Arctic States) meeting in Ottawa;

AFFIRMING our commitment to the well-being of the inhabitants of the Arctic, including recognition of the special relationship and unique contributions to the Arctic of indigenous people and their communities;

AFFIRMING our commitment to sustainable development in the Arctic region, including economic and social development, improved health conditions and cultural well-being;

AFFIRMING concurrently our commitment to the protection of the Arctic environment, including the health of Arctic ecosystems, maintenance of biodiversity in the Arctic region and conservation and sustainable use of natural resources;

RECOGNIZING the contributions of the Arctic Environmental Protection Strategy to these commitments;

RECOGNIZING the traditional knowledge of the indigenous people of the Arctic and their communities and taking note of its importance and that of Arctic science and research to the collective understanding of the circumpolar Arctic;

DESIRING further to provide a means for promoting cooperative activities to address Arctic issues requiring circumpolar cooperation, and to ensure full consultation with the full involvement of indigenous people and their communities and other inhabitants of the Arctic in such activities;

RECOGNIZING the valuable contribution and support of the Inuit Circumpolar Conference, Saami Council, and the Association of the Indigenous Minorities of the North, Siberia, and the Far East of the Russian Federation in the development of the Arctic Council;

DESIRING to provide for regular intergovernmental consideration of and consultation on Arctic issues.

HEREBY DECLARE:

1. The Arctic Council is established as a high level forum to:

    (a) provide a means for promoting cooperation, coordination and interaction among the Arctic States, with the involvement of the Arctic indigenous communities and other Arctic inhabitants on common Arctic issues,* in particular issues of sustainable development and environmental protection in the Arctic.

    (b) oversee and coordinate the programs established under the AEPS on the Arctic Monitoring and Assessment Program (AMAP), Conservation of Arctic Flora and Fauna (CAFF); Protection

---

*The Arctic Council should not deal with matters related to military security.

of the Arctic Marine Environment (PAME); and Emergency Prevention, Preparedness and Response (EPPR).

(c) adopt terms of reference for, and oversee and coordinate a sustainable development program.

(d) disseminate information, encourage education and promote interest in Arctic-related issues.

2. Members of the Arctic Council are: Canada, Denmark, Finland, Iceland, Norway, the Russian Federation, Sweden and the United States of America (the Arctic States).

The Inuit Circumpolar Conference, the Saami Council and the Association of Indigenous Minorities of the North, Siberia and the Far East of the Rusian Federation are Permanent Participants in the Arctic Council. Permanent participation equally is open to other Arctic organizations of indigenous peoples* with majority indigenous constituency, representing:

(a) a single indigenous people resident in more than one Arctic State; or

(b) more than one Arctic indigenous people resident in a single Arctic state.

The determination that such an organization has met this criterion is to be made by decision of the Council. The number of Permanent Participants should at any time be less than the number of members.

The category of Permanent Participation is created to provide for active participation and full consultation with the Arctic indigenous representatives within the Arctic Council.

3. Observer status in the Arctic Council is open to:

(a) non-Arctic states;

---

*The use of the term "peoples" in this Declaration shall not be construed as having any implications as regard the rights which may attach to the term under international law.

(b) inter-governmental and inter-parliamentary organizations, global and regional; and

(c) non-governmental organizations that the Council determines can contribute to its work.

4. The Council should normally meet on a biennial basis, with meetings of senior officials taking place more frequently, to provide for liaison and co-ordination. Each Arctic State should designate a focal point on matters related to the Arctic Council.

5. Responsibility for hosting meetings of the Arctic Council, including provision of secretariat support functions, should rotate sequentially among the Arctic States.

6. The Arctic Council, as its first order of business, should adopt rules of procedure for its meetings and those of its working groups.

7. Decisions of the Arctic Council are to be by consensus of the Members.

8. The Indigenous Peoples' Secretariat established under AEPS is to continue under the framework of the Arctic Council.

9. The Arctic Council should regularly review the priorities and financing of its programs and associated structures.

THEREFORE, we the undersigned representatives of our respective Governments, recognizing the Arctic Council's political significance and intending to promote its results, have signed this Declaration.

SIGNED by the representatives of the Arctic States in Ottawa, this 19th day of September 1996.

NOTES

PROLOGUE: CLINTON LOOKS NORTH

1. Clinton's remarks were reported in David Ljunggren, "Clinton Rebuke Overshadows Canada's Arctic Meeting," *Reuters*, March 29, 2010; Mary Beth Sheridan, "Clinton Rebukes Canada for Excluding Some from Arctic Talks," *The Washington Post*, March 30, 2010; "Clinton Bashes Canada for Limited Invitations to Northern Meeting," *The National Post*, March 30, 3010; Randy Boswell and Juliet O'Neill, "Clinton Blasts Canada for Exclusive Arctic Talks; Dresses Down Minister for Excluding Aboriginals, Three Northern Nations," *Ottawa Citizen*, March 30, 2010.
2. MacKay is quoted in Guy Faulconbridge, "Russian Sub Plants Flag Under North Pole," *Reuters*, August 2, 2007.
3. MacKay is quoted in Allan Woods, "'Back Off and Stay Out of our Airspace'; MacKay has Strong Words for Russia After Bombers Skirt Arctic; Russia Dismisses Response as a 'Farce'," *Toronto Star*, February 28, 2009.
4. Ljunggren, "Clinton Rebuke."
5. "Warm Weather, Heavy Snow Bring Skating Season on Rideau Canal to an End," *Canadian Press*, February 27, 2010.
6. The assessment was issued in two parts, the first in 2004 for broader distribution and the second, a much longer document for scientists. A summary is available at http://amap.no/acia. The full scientific report is now available at www.acia.uaf.edu/pages/scientific.html.
7. United States. U.S. Geological Survey, U.S. Department of the Interior, *Circum-Arctic Resource Appraisal and Estimate of Undiscovered Oil and Gas North of the Arctic Circle*, 2008, http://pubs.usgs.gov/fs/2008/3049/fs2008-3049.pdf (accessed February 14, 2013).

8. Mary Beth Sheridan, "Clinton Rebukes Canada at Arctic Meeting," *Washington Post*, March 30, 2010.

9. Ljunggren, "Clinton Rebuke." The Reuters report indicated that "Clinton's statement was the first open official rebuke of Ottawa since the months leading up to the 2003 Iraq War, which Canada refused to participate in." Cannon, it was reported, "spent much of his closing news conference responding to questions about Clinton's statement and insisting he was not trying to marginalize the Arctic Council."

10. Gloria Galloway, "Harper Rebukes U.S. Envoy over Arctic Dispute; Ambassador Reminded Panel That U.S. Doesn't Recognize Canada's Sovereignty," *Globe and Mail*, January 27, 2006.

11. Stephen Harper, Speech (Inuvik, Canada, August 28, 2008), http://pm.gc.ca/eng/media.asp?id=2258 (accessed November 2, 2011).

12. www.cbc.ca/news/canada/story/2011/05/12/wikileaks-cable-arctic-harper.html. Observed on November 2, 2011.

13. Documents and commentary found in Thomas Blanton and Dr. Svetlana Savranskaya, eds., *The Reykjavik File: Previously Secret Documents from U.S. and Soviet Archives on the 1986 Reagan-Gorbachev Summit*, National Security Archive Electronic Briefing Book No. 203, October 13, 2006, www.gwu.edu/~nsarchiv/NSAEBB/NSAEBB203/index.htm (accessed February 14, 2013).

14. Mikhail Gorbachev, "Speech in Murmansk at the Ceremonial Meeting on the Occasion of the Presentation of the Order of Lenin and the Gold Star to the City of Murmansk" (Murmansk, Soviet Union, October 1, 1987), www.barentsinfo.fi/docs/Gorbachev_speech.pdf (accessed February 12, 2013). The history of the idea for an Arctic Nuclear-Weapon-Free Zone is studied in Thomas S. Axworthy and Sara French, "A Proposal for an Arctic Nuclear-Weapon-Free Zone" (presented at the Interaction Council Expert Meeting on "Achieving a World Free of Nuclear Weapons," Hiroshima, Japan, April 15, 2010).

15. Quoted in Peter Mellen, *Landmarks of Canadian Art*, (Toronto: McClelland & Stewart, 1978), 22. Also, Obituary of Kenojuak Ashevak, *Globe and Mail,* January 12, 2013.

16. Quoted in Steven Loft, "Reflection on 20 Years of Aboriginal Art," *The Trudeau Foundation Papers 5*, no. 1 (2012), 17, www.trudeaufoundation.ca/sites/default/files/u5/reflections_on_20_years_of_aboriginal_art_-_steven_loft.pdf (accessed February 14, 2013).

17. Interviews with Lloyd Axworthy and Mary Simon. Mary Simon, *Inuit: One Future-One Arctic* (Peterborough, Ontario: The Cider Press, 1996), 14–16.

18. Simon, *Inuit*, 20. Interviews with Mary Simon and presentation to class at Trinity College, University of Toronto by Simon, February 2013.

19. Douglas Clarke, "Gorbachev's Arms Control Proposals for the Arctic," in *RFE Background Report 5* (October, 1987).

20. Ronald Purver, "Arctic Security: The Murmansk Initiative and its Impact," *Current Research on Peace and Violence* 11, no. 4 (1988), 153–156; Rob Huebert, "New Directions in Circumpolar Cooperation: Canada, the Arctic Environmental

Protection Strategy, and the Arctic Council," *Canadian Foreign Policy* 5, no. 2 (1998), 37–57.

21. Ronald Purver, "Arctic Security: The Murmansk Initiative and Its Impact," *Current Research on Peace and Violence* 11, no. 4 (1988), 150.

22. Thomas Axworthy, "Changing the Arctic Paradigm from Cold War to Cooperation: How Canada's Indigenous Leaders Shaped the Arctic Council," in *Yearbook of Polar Law,* (forthcoming).

23. Samuel Moyn, *The Last Utopia: Human Rights in History* (Cambridge, Massachusetts: Harvard University Press, 2010), 11. Jorge Luis Borges's essay, "Kafka and His Precursors" (originally published 1951), can be found in the compilation *Everything and Nothing* (New York: New Directions Publishing Corporation, 1999), 70.

24. Canada's foremost international affairs journal, *International Journal,* devoted two issues to the theme "The Arctic is hot": vol. 65, (Autumn, 2010) and vol. 66 (Autumn, 2011).

25. New York: The Macmillan Company, 1921. The book is freely available online at www.archive.org/stream/friendlyarctic017086mbp#page/n7/mode/2up (accessed December 13, 2011).

26. The photographs are available online from Dartmouth University, which houses Stefansson's papers at http://libarchive.dartmouth.edu/cdm/. An example is http://libarchive.dartmouth.edu/cdm/compoundobject/collection/stem229/id/3107/rec/83.

27. Stefansson discusses the diet in his article "Adventures in Diet," *Harper's Monthly Magazine* 171 (November 1935), 668–675.

28. The Canadian Museum of Civilization presented an extraordinary exhibition on the Canadian Arctic Expedition in 2011. The Exhibition extended the duration of the Expedition to 1918 rather than the more usual 1913–1916 and combined Stefansson's photographs with contemporary artifacts and detailed analysis. The comments by Amundsen and others are reported in W.R. Hunt, *Stef: A Biography of Vilhjalmur Stefansson* (Vancouver: University of British Columbia Press, 1996), 215–222.

29. Sherrill E. Grace, *Canada and the Idea of North* (Montreal and Kingston: McGill-Queen's University Press, 2007), 7.

30. Glyn Williams, *Arctic Labyrinth: The Quest for the Northwest Passage* (Toronto: Penguin Canada, 2009), 366.

ONE: PLACE: ICE AND WATER

1. United States Fish and Wildlife Service, *Towards an Ecologically Meaningful Definition of the Circumpolar Arctic,* Conservation of Arctic Flora and Fauna Workplan for 1993/1994 (Cambridge, UK: Scott Polar Research Institute, July 30, 1994).

2. J.L. Berggren and Alexander Jones, eds., *Ptolemy's Geography: An Annotated Translation of the Theoretical Chapters* (Princeton: Princeton University Press, 2001), 69.

3. Nicolás Wey Gómez, *The Tropics of Empire: Why Columbus Sailed South to the Indies* (Cambridge, Massachusetts: MIT Press, 2008), 18–22.

4. Discussion drawn from Glyn Williams, *Arctic Labyrinth: The Quest for the Northwest Passage* (Toronto: Penguin Canada, 2009), 2.

5. The myth of the Hyperboreans is discussed in Timothy Bridgman, *Hyperboreans: Myth and History in Celtic-Hellenic Contacts* (New York and London: Routledge, 2005).

6. Williams points out that the 1976 voyage of Tim Severin does prove that the type of ship used by St. Brendan could have travelled far in the Atlantic, in *Arctic Labyrinth,* 2.

7. Barry Lopez, *Arctic Dreams: Imagination and Desire in a Northern Landscape* (New York: Vintage Books, 2001), 317–318; Jared Diamond, *Collapse: How Societies Choose to Fail or Succeed* (New York: Viking, 2005), 270. A criticism of Diamond's claims about the Greenland Norse can be found in the following forum post: "Jared Diamond's claims about the Greenland Norse are completely wrong?" *Democratic Underground,* June 24, 2010, www.democraticunderground.com/discuss/duboard. php?az=view_all&address=247x29833 (accessed February 3, 2012).

8. Anthony Faulkes and Richard Perkins, eds., *A History of Norway and the Passion and Miracles of the Blessed Óláfr,* Viking Society for Northern Research Text Series 13 (London: Viking Society for Northern Research, 2001).

9. Robert McGhee, *The Last Imaginary Place: A Human History of the Arctic World* (Oxford: Oxford University Press, 2006), 44.

10. Ibid., 37–39.

11. Faulkes and Perkins, *A History of Norway,* 6.

12. This paragraph and the quotation follows McGhee's account in *Last Imaginary Place,* 54–55.

13. The quotation is found at the following website, http://libweb5.princeton.edu/ visual_materials/maps/websites/northwest-passage/mercator.htm (accessed February 9, 2012). The previous section draws from J.H. Parry, *The Age of Reconnaissance: Discovery, Exploration, and Settlement 1450–1650* (Berkeley: University of California Press, 1982). On Dee and Frobisher, the Canadian Museum of Civilization's exhibition on Frobisher's voyages assesses Dee's influence: Canadian Museum of Civilization, *John Dee,* www.civilization.ca/cmc/ exhibitions/hist/frobisher/frsub06e.shtml (accessed February 15, 2012).

14. Alan Cooke, "Frobisher, Sir Martin," in *Dictionary of Canadian Biography Online,* www.biographi.ca/009004-119.01-e.php?&id_nbr=230 (accessed February 16, 2012).

15. Richard Collinson, ed., *The Three Voyages of Martin Frobisher: In Search of a Passage to Cathaia and India by the North-West,* AD 1576–8 (London: The Hakluyt Society, 1867), 78. The original was written by George Best who accompanied Frobisher on his second and third voyages.

16. Ibid.

17. This calculation is for a "project" in 2013 compared to approximately 1570. The methods of comparison are found at www.measuringworth.com/ukcompare.

18. L.H. Neatby, "Martin Frobisher (ca. 1540–1594)," *Arctic* 36, no. 4 (1983), 374–375. A more critical evaluation of Frobisher is found in James McDermott, *Sir Martin Frobisher: Elizabethan Privateer* (New Haven, Connecticut: Yale University Press, 2001). McDermott reports the Spanish spy on the second voyage (192). The Canadian Museum of Civilization had an important exhibition on Frobisher's voyages and published an accompanying study in 1999: T.H.B. Symons, ed., *Meta Incognita: A Discourse of Discovery: Martin Frobisher's Arctic Expeditions 1576–1578* (Hull, Quebec: Canadian Museum of Civilization, 1999).

19. Clement Adams, "The Newe Nauigation and Discouerie of the Kingdome of Muscouia, by the North-East, in the Yeere 1553," in Richard Hakluyt, ed. *The Principall Navigations, Voyages and Discoveries of the English Nation* (London: The Hakluyt Society, 1589), lxiv, http://archive.org/stream/threevoyagesof wi00veerrich/threevoyagesofwi00veerrich_djvu.txt (accessed February 20, 2012).

20. Frances Jennings, *The Invasion of America: Indians, Colonialism and the Cant of Conquest* (New York: Norton, 1975), 168. David Quinn indicates that the source was Thomas Churchyard, who took part in the English campaigns in Ireland, in "Gilbert (Gylberte, Jilbert), Sir Humphrey," *Dictionary of Canadian Biography Online*, www.biographi.ca/009004-119.01-e.php?&id_nbr=307 (accessed February 22, 2012).

21. Williams, *Arctic Labyrinth*, 32–33; Margaret Montgomery Larnder, "Davis (Davys), John" in *Dictionary of Canadian Biography Online*, www.biographi. ca/009004-119.01-e.php?&id_nbr=161 (accessed February 23, 2012).

22. Jonathan Hart, *Empires and Colonies* (Malden, Massachusetts: Polity, 2008), 26; Shelagh Grant, *Polar Imperative: A History of Arctic Sovereignty in North America* (Vancouver: Douglas & McIntyre, 2010), 14–15.

23. Dr. Janice Cavell points out that "there was no clear-cut legal concept of *terra nullius* as such before the late nineteenth century, and the development of international law didn't follow a single linear path. Its origins were obscure, and even recently in the *Mabo v. Queensland* decision (1992) in Australia, the court was thought to have overturned the doctrine only to discover that the term itself had never been used. Janice Cavell to author, May 6, 2013.

24. Bruce Anderson, "Who Discovered the North Pole?" *Smithsonian*, April 2009, www.smithsonianmag.com/history-archaeology/Cook-vs-Peary.html (accessed February 28, 2012).

25. Renée Fossett, *In Order to Live Untroubled: Inuit of the Central Arctic, 1550 to 1940* (Winnipeg: University of Manitoba Press, 2001), 44–46.

26. Williams, *Arctic Labyrinth,* 47–53.

27. Ernest S. Dodge, "Baffin, William," in *Dictionary of Canadian Biography Online,* www.biographi.ca/009004-119.01-e.php?&id_nbr=38; Williams, *Arctic Labyrinth,* 43 (accessed March 1, 2012). The quotation is from Sir Clements R. Markham, *The Voyages of William Baffin* (London: The Hakluyt Society, 1881), 150.

28. Lydia Black, *Russians in America: 1732–1867* (Fairbanks: University of Alaska Press, 2004), 17–18. On the Little Ice Age and Greenland settlement: Grant, *Polar Imperative,* 81–86.

29. Mary Shelley, *Frankenstein or The Modern Prometheus* (London: George Routledge and Sons, 1891), 18.

30. In his history of Arctic exploration, Pierre Berton claims that the British of the Regency period forgot many of the explorations and "except for Hudson Bay and part of Baffin Island, the Arctic region was a blank on the map," in *The Arctic Grail: The Quest for the North West Passage and the North Pole, 1818–1919* (Toronto: Anchor Canada, 2001), 18.

31. Sir John Barrow, *Voyages of Discovery and Research within the Arctic Region From the Year 1818 to the Present Time* (London: John Murray, 1846), 6.

32. Janice Cavell, *Tracing the Connected Narrative: Arctic Exploration in British Print Culture* (Toronto: University of Toronto Press, 2008), 55.

33. Berton, *Arctic Grail*, 18.

34. McGhee, *Last Imaginary Place*, 218. McGhee draws upon Francis Spufford, *I May Be Some Time: Ice and the English Imagination* (New York: St. Martin's Press, 1997), which makes a similar argument at greater length.

35. Berton, *Arctic Grail*, 14–15.

36. Ibid., 34–44; and Robert E. Johnson, "Parry, Sir William Edward," in *Dictionary of Canadian Biography Online*, www.biographi.ca/009004-119.01-e.php?BioId=38245 (accessed February 28, 2012).

37. This section draws upon the excellent description of Parry's voyages and accomplishments in Williams, *Arctic Labyrinth*, 171–191, 223–226. The report on Lyon and the Inuit is found on 218–219.

38. George Francis Lyon, *The Private Journal of Captain G.F. Lyon, of H.M.S. Hecla, During the Recent Voyage of Discovery under Captain Parry* (London: John Murray, 1824), 233.

39. Cavell, *Tracing the Connected Narrative*, 15. Rae's reply is found in *Household Words* 10 (December 23, 1854). The description of the provisions on the *Erebus* and the *Terror* is found in Alexis S. Troubetzkoy, *Arctic Obsession: The Lure of the Far North* (Toronto: Dundurn Press, 2011), 163.

40. On the expedition's fate: Owen Beattie and John Geiger, *Frozen in Time: The Fate of the Franklin Expedition* (Vancouver: Douglas & McIntyre, 2004).

41. Barrow is quoted in Fergus Fleming, *Barrow's Boys: The Original Extreme Adventurers* (New York: Atlantic Monthly Press, 1998), 2. Murchison to Disraeli, March 2, 1860, quoted in Erika Behrisch, "Voices of Silence, Texts of Truth: Imperial Discourse and Cultural Negotiations in Nineteenth-Century Exploration Narrative" (unpublished doctoral dissertation, Kingston: Queen's University, 2002).

TWO: OWNING THE ARCTIC

1. The definition comes from the influential Robert Paul Wolff's *The Conflict Between Authority and Autonomy* (Oxford: Basil Blackwell, 1990), but further reflects the role of power as a necessary corollary to authority.

2. Quoted in Charles Emmerson, *The Future History of the Arctic* (New York: Public Affairs, 2010), 81–82. Original quotations in *New York Times*, September 6 and 8, 1909.

3. Shelagh Grant, *Polar Imperative: A History of Arctic Sovereignty in North America* (Vancouver: Douglas & McIntyre, 2010), 168.

4. Grant, *Polar Imperative*, 205–207.

5. Quoted in Janice Cavell, "'A Little More Latitude': Explorers, Politicians and Canadian Arctic Policy During the Laurier Era," *Polar Record* 47, no. 243 (2011), 291.

6. Admiralty as quoted in Glyn Williams, *Arctic Labyrinth: The Quest for the Northwest Passage* (Toronto: Penguin Canada, 2009), 362; Lewis Harcourt, "Colonial Secretary to Governor-General," May 10, 1913, RG 25, vol. 2668, Library and Archives Canada (LAC).

7. Pierre Berton, *The Arctic Grail: The Quest for the North West Passage and the North Pole, 1818–1909* (Toronto: Anchor Canada, 2001), 350ff.

8. Colin Summerhayes, "International Collaboration in Antarctica: The International Polar Years, the International Geophysical Year, and the Scientific Committee on Antarctic Research," *Polar Record* 44, no. 4 (2008), 321–334.

9. Trevor Levere, *Science and the Canadian Arctic: A Century of Exploration, 1818–1918* (Cambridge: Cambridge University Press, 1993), 9.

10. Bruce Henderson, "Who Discovered the North Pole?" *Smithsonian*, April 2009, www.smithsonianmag.com/history-archaeology/Cook-vs-Peary.html (accessed March 5, 2011). Comments on Peary based upon Lyle Dick, *Muskox Land: Ellesmere Island in the Age of Contact* (Calgary: University of Calgary Press, 2001).

11. The details of Stefansson's personal life in the Arctic is described well in Gísli Pálsson, *Travelling Passions: The Hidden Life of Vilhjalmur Stefansson*, trans. Keneva Kurz (Winnipeg: University of Manitoba Press, 2005).

12. David Gray, "Northern People, Northern Knowledge: The Story of the Canadian Arctic Expedition, 1913–1918," *Canadian Museum of Civilization*, October 27, 2003, www.civilization.ca/cmc/exhibitions/hist/cae/peo614e.shtml#fpannigabluk.

13. Diamond Jenness, "R.M. Anderson (1877–1961)," *Arctic* 14, no. 4 (1961), 268 (accessed March 10, 2012).

14. Robert McGhee, *The Last Imaginary Place: A Human History of the Arctic World* (New York: Oxford University Press, 2005), 105; and Janice Cavell and Jeff Noakes, *Acts of Occupation: Canada and Arctic Sovereignty, 1918–1925* (Vancouver and Toronto: University of British Columbia Press, 2010), 5.

15. Gísli Pálsson, "Hot Bodies in Cold Zones: Arctic Exploration," *The Scholar and Feminist Online* 7, no. 1 (2008), http://sfonline.barnard.edu/ice/palsson_01.htm (accessed May 14, 2012).

16. Sir Robert Borden, "Introduction," in Vilhjalmur Stefansson, *The Friendly Arctic: The Story of Five Years in Polar Regions* (New York: Macmillan, 1921), xxii.

17. Sherrill Grace, *Canada and the Idea of the North*, Paperback Edition (Montreal and Kingston: McGill-Queen's University Press, 2007), 29.

18. The historic judgment is found at the following website, www.worldcourts.com/pcij/eng/decisions/1933.04.05_greenland.htm (accessed March 30, 2012).

19. *Quoted* in Cavell and Noakes, *Acts of Occupation*, 232. This paragraph is based largely on this excellent study. See also Richard Diubaldo, "Wrangling over Wrangel Island," *Canadian Historical Review* 48, no. 3 (1967), 201–226.

20. International lawyer Michael Byers points out that Soviet limitation and the weakness of the sector theory in his book *Who Owns the Arctic: Understanding Sovereignty Disputes in the North* (Vancouver: Douglas & McIntyre, 2009), 43–44. On the White efforts, see Cavell and Noakes, *Acts of Occupation,* 75 and 258–259.

21. L.B. Pearson, "The Question of Ownership of the Sverdrup Islands," October 28, 1929, RG 85, vol. 347, Library and Archives Canada (LAC); Cavell and Noakes, *Acts of Occupation,* 245–246; and Grant, *Polar Imperative,* 237–238.

22. Cavell and Noakes, *Acts of Occupation,* 249.

23. John McCannon, *A History of the Arctic: Nature, Exploration, and Exploitation* (London: Reaktion Books, 2012), 198.

24. This section draws upon Ken S. Coates, P. Whitney Lackenbauer, William R. Morrison, and Greg Poelzer, *Arctic Front: Defending Canada in the Far North* (Toronto: Thomas Allen Publishers, 2008), 48–49. On the history and impact of residential schools, the finest study is J.R. Miller, *Shingwauk's Vision: A History of Native Residential Schools* (Toronto: University of Toronto Press, 1996), whose conclusions influence the discussion in this chapter and beyond.

25. The Soviet Arctic and Stalin's interest is discussed at length in Emmerson, *Future History of the Arctic,* ch. 2. See especially page 33 for a map of the gulag camps and other Arctic activities in the 1930s.

26. Ken S. Coates and William R. Morrison, *Strange Things Done: Murder in Yukon History* (Montreal and Kingston: McGill-Queen's University Press, 2004), 115–116.

27. Jay Bergman, "Valerii Chkalov: Soviet Pilot as New Soviet Man," *Journal of Contemporary History* 33, no. 1 (1998), 139.

28. The discussion of Byrd and Amundsen is found in McCannon, *A History of the Arctic,* 213–215. On Amundsen's airship ventures with American Lincoln Ellsworth: J.M. Scott, *The Private Life of Polar Expedition* (Edinburgh: William Blackwood, 1982), ch. 4.

29. The recent work of St. Petersburg historian Julia Lajus emphasizes the continuation of ties between Soviet scientists and Westerners. Source is Lajus, "The Circulation of Environmental Knowledge: Models of Development and Images of Northernness in 20th-c. Arctic Exploration in Scandanavia, Canada, and Russia" (keynote address presented at the Tri-University Annual History Conference, Wilfrid Laurier University, Waterloo, March 3, 2012).

30. On the wartime agreements and negotiations, see Coates et al., *Arctic Front,* 55–63.

31. Lt. Col. Charles Hubbard, "The Arctic Isn't So Tough," *Saturday Evening Post,* August 26, 1944.

32. Ibid.

33. *Time*, January 4, 1943; and Lester Pearson Diary, February 13, 1943, quoted in John English, *Shadow of Heaven: The Life of Lester Pearson. Volume One: 1897–1948* (London: Vintage UK, 1990), 258.

34. J. Peter Johnson, "The Establishment of Alert, N.W.T., Canada," *Arctic* 43, no. 1 (1990), 31.

THREE: THE COLD WAR CHILLS THE ARCTIC

1. Lester Pearson, "Canada Looks 'Down North,'" *Foreign Affairs* 24, no. 4 (1946), 638, 643–44, 647.

2. The DEW Line has attracted many scholars and popular writers. See Ken S. Coates, P. Whitney Lackenbauer, William R. Morrison, and Greg Poelzer, *Arctic Front: Defending Canada in the Far North* (Toronto: Thomas Allen Publishers, 2008), 70–76; and Joseph Jockel, *No Boundaries Upstairs: Canada, the United States, and the Origins of North American Air Defence, 1945–1958* (Vancouver: University of British Columbia Press, 1987).

3. The 1958 film *The Dew Line Story* is held at the National Archives of the United States and can be viewed at the following link, http://archive.org/details/gov. archives.arc.52896 (accessed February 19, 2013).

4. P. Whitney Lackenbauer and Peter Kikkert, eds., *The Canadian Forces and Arctic Sovereignty: Debating Roles, Interests and Requirements* (Waterloo: Wilfrid Laurier University Press, 2010), 7–8; and David Bercuson, "Continental Defense and Arctic Security, 1945–50: Solving the Canadian Dilemma," in K. Neilson and R.G. Haycock, eds., *The Cold War and Defense* (New York: Praeger, 1990), 153–170.

5. Olav Riste, "The Genesis of North Atlantic Defence Cooperation: Norway's Atlantic Policy, 1940–1948," *NATO Review* 29, no. 2 (1981), 19–23. See Philip Burgess, *Elite Images and Foreign Policy Outcomes: A Study of Norway* (Columbus: Ohio State University Press, 1968) for a discussion of the reasons why the Scandinavian defence option was not successful.

6. Philip Jowett and Brent Snodgrass, *Finland at War, 1939–45* (Botley, UK and New York: Osprey, 2006) is an excellent history of the three distinct wars Finland fought in this period.

7. This paragraph draws upon the excellent discussion of the militarization of the Arctic in John McCannon, *A History of the Arctic: Nature, Exploration, and Exploitation* (London: Reaktion Books, 2012), 239–245.

8. The background paper to the apology offered by Minister of Indian Affairs and Northern Development John Duncan in which this quotation is found is located at the following website: www.aadnc-aandc.gc.ca/eng/1100100015426 (accessed June 4, 2012). An account by a major Canadian public servant who became the responsible deputy minister supports the relocation on welfare grounds: Gordon Robertson, *Memoirs of a Very Civil Servant: Mackenzie King to Pierre Trudeau* (Toronto: University of Toronto Press, 2000), 121. A study which attempted to balance criticism with acceptance of the beneficent intentions of Canadian

policy-makers is Peter Kulchyski and Frank Tester, *Tammarniit (Mistakes): Inuit Relocation in the Eastern Arctic, 1939–1967* (Vancouver: University of British Columbia Press, 1994).

9. The film features devastating testimony from some who were relocated. It can be seen at the following website: www.isuma.tv/isuma-productions/exile-0 (accessed July 25, 2012).

10. Comment made by a former Ranger at a Munk–Gordon Arctic Security Program conference, January 29–30, 2013. Also, P. Whitney Lackenbauer, *The Canadian Rangers: A Living History* (Vancouver: University of British Columbia Press, forthcoming).

11. Renée Fossett, *In Order to Live Untroubled: Inuit of the Central Arctic, 1550–1940* (Winnipeg: University of Manitoba Press, 2001), 218–219.

12. Wayne's song, "North to Alaska," can be heard in its entirety at www.youtube.com/watch?v=JStONEESrUA (accessed September 18, 2012).

13. Sherrill Grace, *Canada and the Idea of the North* (Montreal and Kingston: McGill-Queen's University Press, 2007), 69. The Diefenbaker quotations can also be found in Grace, *Canada and the Idea of the North*. In footnote 9, page 9, she discusses different versions of the Diefenbaker speech and criticizes Peter Newman's cynical attitude towards Diefenbaker's northern vision.

14. Tim Querengesser, "Farley Mowat: Liar or Saint," *Up Here*, September 2009, www.uphere.ca/node/442 (accessed June 4, 2012). See also Grace, *Canada and the Idea of North,* 176–177.

15. J.R. Miller, *Shingwauk's Vision: A History of Native Residential Schools* (Toronto: University of Toronto Press, 1996), 10.

16. There is an excellent summary in W.W. Nassichuk, "Forty Years of Northern Non-Renewable Natural Resource Development," *Arctic* 40, no. 4 (1987), 274–284. It is the source of the quotation on canoes and foot. On Diefenbaker and Menzies, Denis Smith, *Rogue Tory: The Life and Legend of John G. Diefenbaker* (Toronto: MacFarlane Walter and Ross, 1995), 224ff.

17. Terence Armstrong, "Mining in the Soviet Arctic," *Polar Record* 10, no. 64 (1960), 16–22. Stefansson is quoted in Charles Emmerson, *The Future History of the Arctic* (New York: Public Affairs, 2010), 50. Emmerson describes the dreadful environmental legacy well (217ff).

18. This section draws upon the discussion in Shelagh Grant, *Polar Imperative: A History of Arctic Sovereignty in North America* (Vancouver: Douglas & McIntyre, 2010), 344–346.

19. Tucker Scully (former United States senior Arctic official), in discussion with the author, March 2012, Washington. Scully pointed out that there was, in most governments, a dual responsibility for both areas.

20. This comment is made in the United States National Academy of Sciences' history of the year, www.nas.edu/history/igy/ (accessed May 2, 2012).

21. The treaty gave full credit to the IGY in its opening declaration, which stated: "*Recognizing* that it is in the interest of all mankind that Antarctica shall continue for ever to be used exclusively for peaceful purposes and shall not become the

scene or object of international discord; *Acknowledging* the substantial contributions to scientific knowledge resulting from international cooperation in scientific investigation in Antarctica; *Convinced* that the establishment of a firm foundation for the continuation and development of such cooperation on the basis of freedom of scientific investigation in Antarctica as applied during the International Geophysical Year accords with the interests of science and the progress of all mankind ..." Initial signatories were Argentina, Australia, Belgium, Chile, France, Japan, New Zealand, Norway, United States, the Union of Soviet Socialist Republics, and the United Kingdom.

22. The distinguished legal scholar Donat Pharand of the University of Ottawa has urged a treaty, and produced a draft for the Canadian Arctic Resources Committee in 1991: "Draft Arctic Treaty: An Arctic Regional Council," Canadian Arctic Resources Committee papers (CARC), Wilfrid Laurier University Archives, Waterloo (WLU).

23. Lotz's book *Northern Realities: The Future of Northern Development in Canada* (Toronto: New Press, 1970) was an angry attack on Canadian ignorance of the North. Farley Mowat, *Canada North* (Toronto: McClelland & Stewart, 1969) has a similar tone. On the nationalism of the period, and in particular the role of Walter Gordon, see Stephen Azzi, *Walter Gordon and the Rise of Canadian Nationalism* (Montreal and Kingston: McGill-Queen's University Press, 1999).

24. Ivan Head, "Canadian Claims to Territorial Sovereignty in the Arctic Regions," *McGill Law Journal* 9, no. 3 (1963), 200.

25. There is an excellent selection of documents concerning this period in Lackenbauer and Kikkert, *The Canadian Forces and Arctic Sovereignty*, 47–144. Head discusses the approach in Ivan Head and Pierre Trudeau, *The Canadian Way: Shaping Canada's Foreign Policy, 1968–1984* (Toronto: McClelland & Stewart, 1995), 25ff.

26. House of Commons, *Debates*, October 24, 1969.

27. Ibid., April 16, 1970.

28. Head and Trudeau, *The Canadian Way*, 55.

29. House of Commons, *Debates*, June 2, 1972 (Hon. Jack Davis).

30. *United Nations Convention on the Law of the Sea*, 1982, Article 234, www.un.org/Depts/los/convention_agreements/texts/unclos/unclos_e.pdf (accessed June 4, 2012). On the importance and origins of Article 234: Michael Byers, *Who Owns the Arctic: Understanding Sovereignty Disputes in the North* (Vancouver: Douglas & McIntyre, 2009), 46–47. A detailed examination of the particular importance of the Arctic is found in Donald R. Rothwell, *The Polar Regions and the Development of International Law* (Cambridge: Cambridge University Press, 1996).

31. Mary Clay Berry, *The Alaskan Pipeline: The Politics of Oil and Native Land Claims* (Bloomington: Indiana University Press, 1975) describes the process well.

32. The broad sweep of the movement is covered in J. Edward de Steiguer, *The Origins of Modern Environmental Thought* (Tucson: University of Arizona Press, 2006). De Steiguer points out that politicians rarely mentioned environmental

issues before the 1960s and that the influence of Carson was "truly immense." On Trudeau, see John English, *Just Watch Me: The Biography of Pierre Trudeau, Volume Two: 1968–2000* (Toronto: Random House, 2009).

33. Greenpeace continued to have a strong Arctic focus. In the major environmental conference at Rio de Janeiro in June 2012, it concentrated its attention on the Arctic issue and had a large "Save the Arctic" on its opening webpage, www.greenpeace.org/international/en (accessed June 27, 2012).

34. John Hannigan and Walter Slipchenko, *Canada's Arctic Cooperation with the Soviet Union and Russia, 1965–2000*, 2010, http://walterslipchenko.com/pdf/FINAL%20REPORT%20WITH%20ATTACHMENTS_a.pdf (accessed February 21, 2013). Also, Walter Slipchenko, in discussion with the author, August 2010.

35. Hannigan and Slipchenko, *Canada's Arctic Cooperation*, viii. The full report on the Chrétien visit was written by Slipchenko and is an official document: *Siberia 1971: A Report on the Visit of The Honourable Jean Chrétien, Minister of Indian Affairs and Northern Development and Official Delegation to the Soviet Union, July–August 1971* (Ottawa: Information Canada, 1972).

36. The biography of Curley is found in Mark Nuttall, ed., *Encyclopedia of the Arctic: Volume I* (New York: Routledge, 2005), 456–457. Also, Nancy Karetak-Lindell, "Sovereignty–When Did This Become Our Cause?" in *Nilliajut: Inuit Perspectives on Security, Patriotism and Sovereignty* (Ottawa: Inuit Tapiriit Kanatami, 2013), 19–22, www.gordonfoundation.ca/sites/default/files/publications/NILLIAJUT_Inuit%20Perspectives%20on%20Security,%20Patriotism%20and%20Sovereignty.pdf (accessed February 20, 2013).

37. Stephanie Irlbacher-Fox, *Finding Dahshaa: Self-Government, Social Suffering and Aboriginal Policy in Canada* (Vancouver and Toronto: University of British Columbia Press, 2009), 16. The preface is by Dene leader Bill Erasmus.

38. Irlbacher-Fox, *Finding Dahshaa*, x–xi.

39. Billy Diamond, "Aboriginal Rights: The James Bay Experience," in Menno Boldt and J. Anthony Long, eds., *The Quest for Justice: Aboriginal Peoples and Aboriginal Rights* (Toronto: University of Toronto Press, 1985), 265–285. Diamond represented the Crees in the negotiations leading to the James Bay agreement.

40. Mary Simon, *Inuit: One Future—One Arctic* (Peterborough, Ontario: Cider Press, 1996). Young in commenting on Simon's importance said she "came out of the Makivik Corporation." Interview with Oran Young.

41. The finest study of the process remains the work of my late colleague at University of Waterloo: Sally Weaver, *Making Canadian Indian Policy: The Hidden Agenda 1968–70* (Toronto: University of Toronto Press, 1981). The most famous attack on the policy is Harold Cardinal, *The Unjust Society: The Tragedy of Canada's Indians* (Edmonton: M.G. Hurtig, 1969).

42. Thomas Berger, *Northern Frontier, Northern Homeland: The Report of the Mackenzie Valley Pipeline Inquiry, Volume I* (Ottawa: Supply and Services, 1977), 23. The second volume was published by the government later in the same year.

43. Berger, *Report of Pipeline Inquiry, Vol. 1*, vii. Hannigan and Slipchenko, *Canada's Arctic Cooperation* describes how cooperation in the seventies emerged around fauna.

44. Public opinion polls in Finland indicated that 90 percent of the population supported President Kekkonen's foreign policy of "active neutrality" even after he left office in 1982. Lee Miles, *The European Union and the Nordic Countries* (London: Routledge, 1996), 118.

45. The explanation is given in describing the Jane Glassco Fellowships, http://gordon-foundation.ca/node/516 (accessed May 12, 2012).

46. Lynge quoted in Jens Dahl, *IWGIA: A History* (Copenhagen: International Working Group for Indigenous Affairs, 2009), 38.

47. This excellent memorial website on Hopson has abundant detail on him and the ICC, www.ebenhopson.com/SecondOpeningPage.htm (accessed February 20, 2013). The quotation is taken from the original Lilly application. Other details in this section are also derived from the same source. See also Grant, *Polar Imperative*, 168–170.

48. Greenpeace claimed that modern hunting tools made a mockery of the claim of "traditional" hunting, in *Ottawa Citizen*, December 8, 1977.

49. The details are from Hopson's memorial website, which also contains a list of the 1977 delegates: see endnote 47. Also, Simon, *Inuit*, 13ff *Nunatsiaq News*, June 22, 1977.

50. Ronald Reagan, *United States Arctic Policy Statement*, April 14, 1983. Also, "General," sec. CARC papers, 3.10.5.11.1.8, WLU.

51. The quotation is from Benjamin B. Fischer, *A Cold War Conundrum: The 1983 Soviet War Scare* (Washington: CIA Center for the Study of Intelligence, 1997), summary, www.cia.gov/library/center-for-the-study-of-intelligence/csi-publications/books-and-monographs/a-cold-war-conundrum/source.htm#HEADING1-01 (accessed June 19, 2010).

52. On the period and, in particular, the Reagan policy of strengthening the Navy and its implication for Norway and the Arctic, see John Mearsheimer, "A Strategic Misstep: The Maritime Strategy and Deterrence in Europe," *International Security* 11, no. 2 (1986), 1–51. On Norway, see Olav Riste and Rolf Tamnes, *The Soviet Naval Threat and Norway* (Oslo: National Defence College of Norway, 1986). On the Canadian situation, Rob Huebert, "Steel, Ice and Decision-Making: The Voyage of the *Polar Sea* and its Aftermath" (unpublished doctoral dissertation, Halifax: Dalhousie University, 1994).

FOUR: THE FINNS MAKE A MOVE

1. An excellent contemporary analysis of the strategic arguments for Gorbachev, principally the imminent approval of a treaty limiting intermediate-range ballistic missiles, is found in Ronald Purver, "Arctic Security: The Murmansk Initiative and Its Impact," *Current Research on Peace and Violence* 11, no. 4 (1988), 147–158.

2. Gorbachev quotations in *New York Times*, October 1, 1987.

3. Mikhail Gorbachev, "Speech in Murmansk at the Ceremonial Meeting on the Occasion of the Presentation of the Order of Lenin and the Gold Star to the City

of Murmansk" (Murmansk, Soviet Union, October 1, 1987), www.barentsinfo.fi/docs/Gorbachev_speech.pdf (accessed April 10, 2012).

4. This paragraph is based on *Globe and Mail,* October 1, 1987; *New York Times,* October 1–3, 1987; *Reuters,* October 2, 1987; *Washington Post,* October 2, 1987; and an Associated Press report of October 2, 1987 that recounted the American reaction.

5. These were made to the United Nations General Assembly First Committee and at the United Nations Disarmament Commission and the Conference on Disarmament.

6. Thomas S. Axworthy, "A Brief History of the Arctic Council" (comments to symposium, University of Toronto, December 2, 2010). As a member of the board awarding grants, I was struck by the number of applications having an Arctic focus.

7. Akira Iriye, "A Century of NGOs," *Diplomatic History* 23, no. 3 (1999), 421–435; and Alison Van Rooy, *The Global Legitimacy Game: Civil Society, Globalization, and Protest* (Basingstoke: Palgrave Macmillan, 2004). Dr. Van Rooy's testimony to the Special Joint Committee Reviewing Canadian Foreign Policy (1995) drew upon her doctoral thesis in examining state support for NGOs.

8. The Inuit Tapirisat of Canada represented the Inuit. Their website (now the Inuit Tapiriit Kanatami) lists the important historical events. The number grew quickly in the eighties. www.itk.ca/historical-event (accessed June 10, 2012).

9. Paul Boyer, *By the Bomb's Early Light: American Thought and Culture at the Dawn of the Atomic Age* (New York: Pantheon, 1985), 359ff; and Sidney Tarrow, *The New Transnational Activism* (Cambridge and New York: Cambridge University Press, 2005), 219.

10. Obituary of J. Alan Beesley, *University of British Columbia Law School,* January 2009, www.law.ubc.ca/news/2009/feb/2_2_2009_beesley.html (accessed June 9, 2012).

11. Tom Siddon, Minister of Indian Affairs and Northern Development, *Building International Relations in the Arctic: 25 Years of Canada–USSR Cooperation* (Ottawa: Ministry of Supply and Services, 1991), 12. The description of Polar Bridge is found on page 22.

12. Jørgen Taagholt, "The International Arctic Science Committee," *Polar Record* 21, no. 150 (1988), 248. Also, confidential interviews conducted in the summer of 2011 provided clear evidence to me of the tension between some scientists and indigenous groups.

13. Pertti Torstila, deputy director general, Department of Foreign Affairs, Helsinki, "Nordic Security in 2000" (remarks to seminar, Kuhmo, Finland, July 21, 1988), 13.60, 13.61 Arktiset alueet, Finnish Ministry of Foreign Affairs (FMFA). Also, Satu Nurmi, in discussion with the author, May 3, 2012, Helsinki. The argument about the Finnish sense of the Arctic draws upon the important study by E.C.H. Keskitalo, *Negotiating the Arctic: The Construction of an International Region* (New York and London: Routledge, 2004).

14. Quotations are from Torstila, "Nordic Security."

15. There are three major studies of the late 1980s and early 1990s. Monica Tennberg completed her doctoral dissertation at the University of Lapland in 1998: "The Arctic Council: A Study in Governmentality" (unpublished doctoral dissertation); a revised version was subsequently published, as *Arctic Environmental Cooperation: A Study in Governmentality* (Aldershot: Ashgate, 2000). The third study is Keskitalo, *Negotiating the Arctic*. This chapter is very indebted to their work. Dr. Tennberg has also provided information directly to me.

16. Clive Archer, "Western Responses to the Murmansk Initiative," *Centrepiece* 14 (Spring 1989), 1, 31. Archer notes that Joe Clark "did not want to detach Canada's security position in the Arctic from its wider defence considerations" (16).

17. Satu Nurmi interview.

18. Kaj Bärlund and Kalevi Sorsa to Uffe Ellemann-Jensen, minister of foreign affairs, January 12, 1989, Denmark, 13.60 Arktiset alueet 1989, FMFA. I obtained another, earlier version of the note from Norwegian official Odd Rogne of the Norwegian Polar Institute, which he had received from Rajakoski before he toured the Nordic capitals. It does not mention Helsinki specifically and does note that the International Arctic Science Committee "now under discussion, might be instrumental to prepare scientific ground for concrete action." Rajakoski detailed his plan to a Canadian audience in 1989 in "The Arctic Multilateral Cooperation to Protect the Arctic Environment: The Finnish Initiative," in Thomas Berger and Douglas Roche, *The Arctic: Choices for Peace and Security* (Vancouver and Seattle: Gordon Soules, 1989), 54–55.

19. House of Commons Standing Committee on Foreign Affairs and International Trade, *Canada and the Circumpolar World: Meeting the Challenges of Cooperation in to the Twenty-First Century* (Ottawa: Public Works and Government Services, 1997), 225–226.

20. See the report in *New Scientist* 24 (February 25, 1989), 32.

21. Esko Rajakoski, "The Arctic: Choices for Peace and Security," Edmonton, March 18–19, 1989, 1.2031.3.1989 Arktiset alueet, 1989 II, FMFA. Other reactions are in the same file. The Rajakoski intervention was published in Berger and Roche, *The Arctic: Choices for Peace and Security*, 74–75.

22. Interview with Garth Bangay, February 2013.

23. United States Secretary of State to Jukka Robert Valtasaari, ambassador of Finland, March 20, 1989, 13.60 Arktiset alueet, 1989 II, FMFA. Risto Rautiainen, Counsellor, Memorandum, 13.60 Arktiset alueet, FMFA.

24. The Soviet document has no date, but its content suggests early 1989. 13.60 Arktiset alueet, 1989, FMFA. Arnaudo's reaction is described in Finnish Embassy, Washington, to Helsinki, January 13, 1989, 13.30 Arktiset alueet, FMFA. The other comments are from interviews, including Odd Rogne, in discussion with the author, July 2011, Oslo.

25. Ministry of Foreign Affairs, Finland, "Agenda," *Consultative Meeting on the Protection of the Arctic Environment* (Rovaniemi, 1989) 13.60 Arktiset alueet, 1989 IX, FMFA. The Americans had earlier indicated in August that there was insufficient time to prepare and had not sent "proper expert staffing" from

Washington. U.S. State Department to Ambassador of Finland, August 10, 1989, Arktiset alueet, 1989, FMFA.

26. Interview with Garth Bangay, February 2013.

27. Ministry of Foreign Affairs, Finland, *Consultative Meeting on the Protection of the Arctic Environment* (Rovaniemi, 1989). Visit to Rovaniemi, May 2012.

28. Interview with Garth Bangay, February 2013.

29. Deborah Mackenzie, "Arctic Protection Treaty Waits for American Involvement," *New Scientist* 24, no. 1688 (1989), 28.

30. American Arctic specialist Oran Young described American Arctic policy at the time as "vague and volatile" in the study *Arctic Politics: Conflict and Cooperation in the Circumpolar North* (Hanover, New Hampshire: University Press of New England, 1992), 86.

31. Interviews with several Finnish officials. Also, discussion by Douglas Nord of Mulroney's initiative is found in Patrick James, Nelson Michaud, and Marc J. O'Reilly, eds., *Handbook of Canadian Foreign Policy* (Lanham, Maryland: Lexington Books, 2006), 297, where Nord suggests the remark was casual. It was not: the government of Canada had been considering the initiative for many months.

32. There were continuing consultations with the Finns after Mulroney's remarks. Mary Vandenhoff, Canadian ambassador to Finland, to Pertti Paasio, Finnish foreign minister, January 29, 1991, 13.00 Arktinen neuvosto, Arctic Council f. 1990–1991, FMFA. Also, see the discussion about the changing definition of Arctic in Keskitalo, *Negotiating the Arctic*, chapters 2 and 3.

33. Risto Rautiainen, Ministry of Foreign Affairs, Finland, to Viktor Sebek, Advisory Committee on Pollution of the Sea, December 18, 1989, 13.60 Arktiset alueet, FMFA. This document indicates that Britain, West Germany, France, the Netherlands "and many others" had expressed "keen interest" to the Finns. The French were especially pointed in their objections.

34. Interview with Rosemarie Kuptana, January 30, 2013.

35. Simon to Pertti Paasio, December 5, 1989; and Paasio to Simon, March 14, 1990, 13.60 Arktiset alueet II, 1990, FMFA.

36. Interview with Garth Bangay, February 2013.

37. Mary Simon, in discussion with the author, March 9, 2012, and *Protecting the Arctic Environment* Report on the Yellowknife Preparatory Meeting (Yellowknife, Northwest Territories, April 18, 1990), 13.60 Arktiset alueet IV, FMFA. Interview with Garth Bangay, February 2013.

38. Ibid., Addendum 1. The comment on ecosystem being particularly Canadian was made to me by several Scandinavian officials. Also, Keskitalo, *Negotiating the Arctic,* 62–65; Rob Huebert, "The Canadian Arctic and the International Environmental Regime," in J. Oakes and R. Riewe, eds., *Issues in the North: Volume III* (Edmonton: Canadian Circumpolar Institute Press, 1997), 48; and Oran Young, *Creating Regimes: Arctic Accords and International Governance* (Ithaca: Cornell University Press, 1998), 88–90, 110–111. Bangay told me about Beesley's request that he become head of delegation.

39. Young, *Creating Regimes,* 111. Young calls them examples of "entrepreneurial leadership."

40. Drawn from the files in 13.60 Arktiset alueet, Puheenvuorot 13.6, 1991, Rovaniemi 12–14.6, 1991, FMFA.

41. Ibid. On Weinmann, the information is taken from Gerhard Peters and John T. Woolley, "Nomination of John Giffen Weinmann to be United States Ambassador to Finland," March 17, 1989, *The American Presidency Project,* www.presidency. ucsb.edu/ws/index.php?pid=16808#axzz201ryyKZ8 (accessed June 20, 2012).

42. Young, *Creating Regimes,* 109.

43. Ibid., 106.

44. 13.60 Arktiset alueet, FMFA. Roots's papers at Wilfrid Laurier University Archives trace his close links with international science organizations and his work with the Canadian government.

45. Ibid. Lynge was very active in the Home Rule movement in Greenland and, later, in international organizations.

46. This declaration is preserved on the Arctic Portal: *Arctic Environmental Protection Strategy* (Rovaniemi, Finland, June 14, 1991), http://library.arcticportal. org/1542/1/artic_environment.pdf (accessed June 30, 2012).

47. Tom Siddon to Robert Cameron, July 4, 1991, personal copy.

FIVE: THE CANADIAN INITIATIVE: THE ARCTIC COUNCIL

1. Terry Fenge, "Asserting Sovereignty in the Arctic: Inuit and the Nunavut Land Claims Agreement," in *Nilliajut: Inuit Perspectives on Security, Patriotism and Sovereignty* (Ottawa: Inuit Tapiriit Kanatami, 2013), 49–53.

2. E.C.H. Keskitalo, *Negotiating the Arctic: The Construction of an International Region* (New York and London: Routledge, 2004), 66–67, emphasizes how this expansion to eight Arctic states meant that the normal Canadian definition informed future discussions. Pharand had published extensively on the treaty and claimed that the response in Tromsø caused him to move forward with a treaty proposal.

3. Trudeau quoted in Ken S. Coates, P. Whitney Lackenbauer, William R. Morrison, and Greg Poelzer, *Arctic Front: Defending Canada in the Far North* (Toronto: Thomas Allen Publishers, 2008), 98–99.

4. Thomas S. Axworthy, "The Gordon Foundation and the Creation of the Arctic Council: Can the Past be Prologue?" (unpublished paper, 2011). Also, Axworthy, "Changing the Arctic Paradigm from Cold War to Cooperation: How Canada's Indigenous Leaders Shaped the Future Arctic Council" (paper prepared for the Fifth Polar Law Symposium, Arctic Centre, Rovaniemi, Finland. September 6–8, 2012).

5. The Canadian Broadcasting Corporation Digital Archives has made the relationship between Reagan and Mulroney clear as their duet, "When Irish Eyes are Smiling," is captured in a widely accessible video, www.cbc.ca/archives/categories/

economy-business/trade-agreements/canada-us-free-trade-agreement/sealing-the-friendship-with-a-song.html (accessed July 2, 2012).

6. *Toronto Star,* August 23, 1985. References to "uninvited" are common in letters to the editorial and news stories at the time. A Gallup Poll released on June 7, 1987, revealed that 85 percent of Canadians believed the Northwest Passage was not an international strait but in Canadian waters. The results were published in the *Toronto Star,* June 8, 1987. A good account of the *Polar Sea* is found in Coates et al., *Arctic Front,* 113–117. Rob Huebert, "Steel, Ice and Decision-Making: The Voyage of the *Polar Sea* and Its Aftermath" (unpublished doctoral dissertation, Halifax: Dalhousie University, 1994) is the fullest account. See also Huebert's "Canadian Arctic Security Issues: Transformation in the Post–Cold War Era," *International Journal* 54, no. 2 (1999), 203–229.

7. Franklyn Griffiths, "Arctic Authority at Stake," *Globe and Mail,* June 13, 1985. Griffiths and T.C. Pullen made these comments on a panel reported in the *Toronto Star*, July 30, 1985.

8. House of Commons, *Debates,* September 10, 1985. Quoted in Michael Byers, *Who Owns the Arctic: Understanding Sovereignty Disputes in the North* (Vancouver: Douglas & McIntyre, 2009), 53. Byers discusses the legal basis for Clark's comments on 52–54.

9. *Toronto Star*, August 8, 1985; *Globe and Mail,* August 8, 1985.

10. There is a good analysis of the meaning of the announcement in Byers, *Who Owns the Arctic,* 51–58. Also, Coates et al., *Arctic Front,* 116–118. Clark's announcement and comments are described in the *Toronto Star,* September 11, 1985. Also, House of Commons, *Debates,* September 10, 1985.

11. The reference to the "chattering class" is found in Coates et al., *Arctic Front,* 114. The description of the CARC meeting is found in *Toronto Star,* November 8, 1985, and the Gallup Poll in *Toronto Star,* October 28, 1985.

12. Mary Simon, "Militarization and the Aboriginal Peoples," in Franklyn Griffiths, ed., *Arctic Alternatives: Civility or Militarism in the Circumpolar North* (Toronto: Science for Peace/Samuel Stevens, 1992), 55–67.

13. Brian Mulroney, *Memoirs* (Toronto: Random House, 2007). On Beatty and American reaction, *Los Angeles Times,* June 6, 1987. Also, Derek Burney, *Getting It Done: A Memoir* (Kingston and Montreal: McGill-Queen's University Press, 2009), 97. Burney handled much of the interaction between the political and diplomatic in Mulroney's office and improved it considerably, although he does give an inaccurate date for the *Polar Sea* sailing (1986).

14. Brian Mulroney, "A Call for a New Northern Vision," *Policy Options* 27, no. 5 (2006), 9. Also, comments by Colin Powell, Washington, 2004, to School of Public Policy visitors.

15. This paragraph, including the quotation from Legault, is deeply indebted to Christopher Kirkey, "Smoothing Troubled Waters: The 1988 Canada–United States Arctic Co-operation Agreement," *International Journal* 50, no. 2 (1995), 401–426; Legault quotations are from page 425; conclusion from 426.

16. Ibid., 426.

17. Barry Lopez, *Arctic Dreams: Imagination and Desire in a Northern Landscape* (New York: Random House, 1986), 410–411.

18. Oran Young, "Arctic Futures: The Politics of Transformation," in James Kraska, ed., *Arctic Security in an Age of Climate Change* (Cambridge: Cambridge University Press, 2011), xxii. In an earlier work, Young and Gail Osherenko pointed to the support of MacArthur and Ford and commented that the "problem of fragmentation afflicting the efforts of the United States federal government to address a range of increasingly important Arctic issues is extraordinary even by these standards": Young and Osherenko, *The Age of the Arctic: Hot Conflicts and Cold Realities* (Cambridge: Cambridge University Press, 1989), 230.

19. Kyra Montagu to John Lamb, April 9, 1988, and John Lamb to Kyra Montagu, April, 26, 1988, John Lamb papers.

20. Willy Østreng, "Political–Military Relations among the Ice States: The Conceptual Basis of State Behaviour," in Franklyn Griffiths, ed., *Arctic Alternatives: Civility or Militarism in the Circumpolar North* (Toronto: Science for Peace/Samuel Stevens, 1992), 36. Science for Peace continues to maintain a description of the conference on its website, www.scienceforpeace.ca/international-conference-on-arctic-cooperation (accessed June 20, 2012). Account is also based on interviews with Tom Axworthy and Franklyn Griffiths as well as documents on the conference in the Gordon Foundation records. I was a member of the research committee of the Canadian Institute for International Peace and Security, which supported this conference.

21. Parliamentarians for Global Action, "The 'Montreal Appeal' on Arctic Security in the 1990s,"and "Strategy Session: Arctic Security and Cooperation," New York, November 13, 1989, Canadian Arctic Resources Committee papers (CARC), 3.10.5.10.1, Wilfrid Laurier University Archives, Waterloo (WLU). The second session involved McLean as convenor, Karl-Erik Svartberg and Karl-Erik Olsson, Swedish MPs; Terge Nyberge, MP of Norway; and Jaakko Ellisaari of Finland. Walter McLean, in discussion with the author, June 16, 2012. The McLean fonds at Library and Archives Canada (LAC) contain the files dealing with his activities.

22. Axworthy, "The Gordon Foundation." On McMillan, Ian MacDonald, "Brian's Brain," *National Post,* November 3, 2005.

23. Axworthy, "The Gordon Foundation," and "Changing the Arctic Paradigm"; Franklyn Griffiths, *Arctic Council Origins: A Memoir*, Franklyn Griffiths papers; and John Lamb to Ken Calder, Department of National Defence, April 20, 1989, Lamb papers.

24. Tom Axworthy, letter to author, n.d., November 2012.

25. Kyra Montagu to John Lamb, April 28, 1989, Lamb papers.

26. Office of the Prime Minister, "Notes for an Address by the Right Honourable Brian Mulroney, Prime Minister of Canada" (Arctic and Antarctic Institute, Leningrad, November 24, 1989); David Cox and Tariq Rauf, *Security Co-operation in the Arctic: A Canadian Response to Gorbachev's Murmansk Initiative* (Ottawa: CCACD, 1989). Ronald Purver describes the reaction to the CCACD proposals and comments on the Mulroney speech in detail in "The North in Canada's International Relations," in Fen Osler Hampson and Maureen Appel Molot,

eds., *Canada Among Nations 1989: The Challenge of Change* (Ottawa: Carleton University Press, 105–117.

27. Minutes of the Arctic Project Steering Committee Meeting, Ottawa, January 18, 1990, CARC papers 3.10.5.12.4, WLU. Also, Griffiths, "Arctic Council Origins."

28. Ibid. Dr. Griffiths is currently writing a study of the history of civility. Griffiths, in discussion with the author, Rosemarie Kuptana, in discussion with the author, January 30, 2013.

29. Stephen Hazell to Rosemarie Kuptana, September 4, 1990, enclosing reports of meetings in Iqaluit, August 22; and Rankin Inlet, August 28, CARC papers, 3.10.5.12.5, WLU. The reconstituted panel was made up of Franklyn Griffiths, Rosemarie Kuptana, Stephen Hazell, John Lamb, Cindy Gilday, John Amagoalik, Mary Simon, and Bill Erasmus, the last four and Kuptana being aboriginal. John Hannigan was the rapporteur.

30. Griffiths to Members of the Arctic Council Panel, September 20, 1990, enclosing Arctic Council Panel Report, Griffiths Papers. All references are from the attached report.

31. Ibid.

32. Griffiths, "Arctic Council Origins."

33. Secretary of State for External Affairs, "Notes for a Speech by The Secretary of State for External Affairs, The Right Honourable Joe Clark, P.C., M.P." (Conference on Canadian–Soviet Relations at the Government Conference Centre, Ottawa, November 28, 1990).

34. This rivalry was described to me by several individuals in a position to recognize it, including senior foreign affairs officials Paul Heinbecker, Wayne Lord, and Walter Slipchenko, who knew both departments well. It will emerge in later chapters in stronger form.

35. Minutes of the Arctic Project Steering Committee, Ottawa, November 30, 1990. Present: Tom and Roberta Axworthy, David Cox, Paul Joffe, Stephen Hazell, John Lamb, Charles McMillan, John Merritt, Kyra Montagu, Christine Lee, and Fred Roots.

36. Olli Mennander, Foreign Affairs, Finland, "Visit of Canadian Ambassador Mary Vandenhoff" (translation), November 29, 1990, No. 1118 Arktiset alueet; and Tom Grønberg, Director General, Foreign Affairs, Finland, "Canadian Plan for the Development of Cooperation" (translation), January 21, 1991.

37. Kai Granholm to Ministry of Foreign Affairs [MFA] (translation), Helsinki, November 29, 1990, Ibid., annex 2; and Granholm to MFA (translation), November 30, 2011, Ibid., annex 1.

38. "Arctic Council: Canadian Proposal for the Development of Cooperation," June 7, 1991. Ibid., Memo 640 (translation).

39. Kuptana, Griffiths, Simon, Lamb, and Hazell, draft letter to Rt. Hon. Brian Mulroney, February 26, 1991, Terry Fenge papers; and Hazell to Mulroney, March 28, 1991, Griffiths papers.

40. Arctic Council Panel, *To Establish an International Arctic Council: A Framework Report* (Ottawa: Canadian Arctic Resources Committee, 1991). The Griffiths

and Kuptana comments are contained, interestingly, in a press report from the Communications Branch of the Indian and Northern Affairs Canada found in Canadian Arctic Resources Committee, May 15, 1991, Fenge papers. The committee had apparently received this criticism of External Affairs from another government department. This summary is based on many discussions with individuals involved but, especially, interviews with Mary Simon, Tucker Scully, Odd Rogne, Satu Nurmi, Terry Fenge, and several Canadian officials.

41. Asko Numminen, Memorandum of discussion with R.F. Goff on "attitude of USA to the Canadian proposal for Arctic Council," November 29, 1990, Arktiset Political Department, POL-65, FMFA; and Secretary of State to American Embassies, Ottawa, Helsinki, Stockholm, Oslo, Moscow, Copenhagen, Reykjavik, August 15, 1991, Arktinen neuvosto, Arctic Council 1990–1991, FMFA. Obviously this was passed directly to Finnish officials. On Eagleburger's comments, John English, *Just Watch Me: The Life of Pierre Elliott Trudeau, Volume Two: 1968–2000* (Toronto: Random House, 2009), 600.

42. Mary Simon, in discussion with the author.

43. These documents are all translated from the Finnish and are found in the same archive as the Numminen reference in note 40. Specific details: Heinbecker (POL-60. DN ro 1990/25112. Reference OTT-0144); McCallion (Ibid., author Heinrichs); and Stagg (Ibid., Memo number 1393, author Risto Rautiainen).

44. The Finnish documents describe a discussion between Finn officials and Karen Mosher and Gilles Breton that occurred on March 20, 1992. Ibid. OTT0118, author Kuusela. The December 1991 document is Appendix 1 in Walter Slipchenko, *Arctic Council Panel: Analysis of the Results and Future Directions as a Result of the First Meeting of Representatives from the Eight Arctic Countries on the Canadian Proposal to Create an Arctic Council Held in Ottawa, May 4–5, 1992* (unpublished document, July 5, 1992).

45. Conference of the Foreign Ministers of the Baltic Sea, *Terms of Reference of the Council of the Baltic Sea States* (Copenhagen, March 5, 1992), Griffiths papers. On the initiative and the critical role of Stoltenberg, Oran Young, *Creating Regimes: Arctic Accords and International Governance* (Ithaca and London: Cornell University Press, 1998), 52–85.

46. Slipchenko, "Arctic Council Panel."

47. The press release and the other documents described are collected in Slipchenko, ibid. The Stagg remarks and the quotations from Wajda are found in Inuit Circumpolar Conference, *Experts Meeting on Arctic Council* (Ottawa, May 4–6, 1992). This record is found in the official documents of the Department of External Affairs (DEA), RG 25, vol. 1, A2011-00456, LAC.

48. Environics poll, May 1992, retrieved June 29, 2012, www.queensu.ca/cora/_trends/Ap_Voting.htm. "Arctic Council," discussion in Ottawa with Kathryn McCallion, OTT-0327/2. DN0.1990/25112, Arktiset Political, FMFA.

SIX: A WORTHWHILE CANADIAN INITIATIVE

1. Stephen Handelman, "Yeltsin, PM Sign Arctic Pact," *Toronto Star*, February 2, 1992. Later anecdotes suggest that Yeltsin was drunk, not tired.

2. Walter Slipchenko, *Arctic Council Panel: Analysis of the Results and Future Directions as a Result of the First Meeting of Representatives from the Eight Arctic Countries on the Canadian Proposal To Create an Arctic Council* (Ottawa, May 4–5, July 5, 1992). A letter from Barbara McDougall, secretary of state for External Affairs, to Whit Fraser, chairman, Canadian Polar Commission, February 12, 1993, gives election and constitutional crisis as the reason for the delay of the meeting. Department of External Affairs (DEA) files, Research Group (RG) 25, A2011-00456, vol. 1, Library of Archives Canada (LAC).

3. Finnish Embassy, Ottawa, (Erik Heinrichs) to Helsinki, "Arctic Council," October 19, 1992, NRO OTT-0349, DNo 1990/25112, MFA.

4. Slipchenko, *Arctic Council Panel*.

5. In an email exchange among Timo Koivurova, Piotr Graczyk, Terry Fenge, and the author, it was concluded that no earlier documents used the term "permanent participants." On the AEPS, the indigenous representatives were termed "AEPS Official Observer Organizations": Piotr Graczyk to Koivurova, Fenge, and English, March 2, 2012.

6. Gilles Breton, "The Case for an Arctic Council" (University of Alaska Fairbanks, August 14, 1992). The Young comment is contained in a report on the conference in the Terry Fenge papers where the Breton speech is also found.

7. Walter Slipchenko, "Meeting with External Affairs on Arctic Council," December 22, 1992, Fenge papers.

8. Terry Fenge to Arctic Council Panel, "Meeting in Anchorage with Alaskan and American Environmental Organizations," December 28, 1992, Fenge papers.

9. *Declaration on the Establishment of an Arctic Council*, January 14, 1993, DEA files, RG 25, A2011-00456, vol. 1, LAC. With handwritten comments.

10. "Summary Arctic Council Discussions" (Yellowknife, Northwest Territories, March 2, 1993), ibid. Several invited guests did not show up.

11. A letter from Mary Simon to Cindy Gilday, April 26, 1993, identifies the group. The Simon comments are kept in the same file: DEA, RG 25, A2011-00456, vol. 1, LAC.

12. "Meeting re: Arctic Council Negotiations," Wednesday, May 1993, DEA files, RG 25, A2011-00456, vol. 1, LAC. On Wajda, who was soon to retire, see www.emmitsburg.net/archive_list/articles/misc/cww/2011/diplomat.htm (accessed August 22, 2012).

13. Mary Simon in discussion with the author; Simon, *Inuit: One Future—One Arctic* (Peterborough, Ontario: Cider Press, 1996), 25; Inuit Circumpolar Council and the Arctic Council Panel, *Second Meeting of Representatives from the Eight Arctic Countries (Act II), on the Canadian Proposal to Create an Arctic Council* (Ottawa, May 19–20, 1993), DEA files, RG 25, A2011-00457, vol. 1, LAC.

14. Simon, *Inuit*, 21; 25.

15. Oran Young, *Creating Regimes: Arctic Accords and International Governance* (Ithaca and London: Cornell University Press, 1998), 66–67.

16. Simon is quoted in "Indigenous Peoples After UNCED," *Cultural Survival Quarterly* 18, no. 1 (1994). Available at www.culturalsurvival.org/publications/ cultural-survival-quarterly/brazil/indigenous-peoples-after-unced (accessed July 15, 2012).

17. Simon mentions the investigation as an ICC achievement in *Inuit*, 17. Thomas Berger, *Village Journey: The Report of the Alaska Native Review Commission* (New York: Hill & Wang, 1985). The description of the commission is taken from Mark Nuttall, ed., *Encyclopedia of the Arctic: Volume I* (New York: Routledge, 2005), 35. American motivations were described to me by senior official Tucker Scully.

18. On the Nuuk meeting, Monica Tennberg, *Arctic Environmental Cooperation: A Study in Governmentality* (Aldershot: Ashgate, 2000), 80–81. Tucker Scully, in discussion with the author, March 2012.

19. Simon, *Inuit*, 25.

20. Liberal Caucus Committee on Foreign Affairs, *Canada and the Circumpolar Arctic: Seeking an Agenda and an Action Plan*, 1992, Fenge papers.

21. Liberal Party of Canada, *Creating Opportunity: The Liberal Plan for Canada* (Ottawa: Liberal Party of Canada, 1993). As a member of Parliament elected in 1993, I was member of the foreign policy review and was later vice-chair of the Foreign Affairs and International Trade Committee. Some of the comments and assessments are, therefore, personal memories, as with the remark about Michael Pearson.

22. Gordon Barthos, "New Envoy Tackles Challenge of Canada's Last Frontier," *Toronto Star,* November 25, 1994. Mary Simon interview.

23. In 1997 Håken R. Nilson of the Norwegian Polar Institute undertook a report on the AEPS work, which was commissioned by the ministers of the environment of the eight Arctic states in 1996. The conclusions in this paragraph reflect that assessment. Nilson, *Arctic Environmental Protection Strategy (AEPS): Process and Organization, 1991–97: An Assessment* (Oslo: Norwegian Polar Institute, 1997).

24. A meeting of the Emergency Prevention, Preparedness and Response in the Arctic Group took place in Sweden in October 1992. A transcript of the meeting indicates that "The Inuit Circumpolar Conference (ICC) and the Russian Small Peoples' Association as well as the International Maritime Organization (IMO) and the United Nations Economic Commission for Europe (UNECE) were invited but did not attend." The Canadians sent four technical officials, as did the Danes, while the Finns sent one and the Russians only two, both from the Stockholm embassy. Ministry of Defence, "Meeting on Emergency Prevention, Preparedness and Response in the Arctic," Canadian Arctic Resources Committee Papers (CARC) 3.10.5.11.1.7, Wilfrid Laurier University Archives, Waterloo (WLU).

25. Ibid. Also, Tennberg discusses these questions throughout her invaluable study *Arctic Environmental Cooperation.* Lars-Otto Reiersen, AMAP, in discussion with the author.

26. Lars-Otto Reiersen, in discussion with the author. Several other Arctic scientists also expressed a similar view about AEPS operations.

27. Evan Bloom, a legal advisor at the State Department, noted in 1999 that the NGO participation was unusual but reflected "the critical role indigenous people play in regional matters." "Establishment of the Arctic Council," *The American Journal of International Law*, vol. 93 (July 1999), 712.

28. E.C.H. Keskitalo, *Negotiating the Arctic: The Construction of an International Region* (New York and London: Routledge, 2004). See also Oran Young's review in *Polar Research* 23, no. 2 (2004), 209–213, in which he suggests the evidence for Keskitalo's view is "not compelling" (212).

29. Franklyn Griffiths and Rosemarie Kuptana, "Arctic Council Discussion Paper," June 1990, Franklyn Griffiths Papers.

30. Terry Fenge to Hon. André Ouellet, March 28, 1994, CARC papers, 3.10.5.11.1.4, WLU.

31. The Presidential Decision Directive is attached to the Fenge document cited above. Also, "Agenda for Sustainability in the Arctic," n.d., CARC papers, 3.10.5.11.1.3, WLU.

32. This summary is derived from "AEPS Advisory Committee Meeting, Record of Discussion," December 14, 1994, personal copy. The account of the Simon's meeting with Finnish diplomat Heinrichs (translated) is found in NRO OTT002 DNo2990/25112, Pol-65, Ministry of Foreign Affairs (MFA). The description of Mary Simon's visit to Washington in late January 1995 and the American public response is found in a surprisingly long article in *Washington Times*, January 29, 1995. On the importance of the security breakthrough and the willingness of the Arctic Council Panel to pull back, Tom Axworthy to Author, n.d., January 2013.

33. The account is from *Toronto Star* and *Globe and Mail*, February 22–25, 1995.

34. Department of Foreign Affairs and International Trade, *Discussion Paper on the Establishment of an Arctic Council: A Collaborative Opportunity for the Eight Arctic States*, January 16, 1995, CARC papers, 3.10.5.12.7.3.4, WLU. Fenge to Marjory Loveys, February 1, 1995, ibid.

35. The background paper indicating responses to Canadian consultations is found in the Fenge papers. "Beyond 1996: Future AEPS Directions." Fax dating indicates it was received from the Environment Department at CARC offices on February 22, 1995. Also, Donald Rothwell, "International Law and the Protection of the Arctic Environment," *The International and Comparative Law Quarterly* 44, no. 2 (1995), 280–281, esp. endnote 4, 181, which lists several contemporary articles on the legal regime theme.

36. The "non paper" is described as such in the Canadian file on the Arctic Council. It is dated February 8, 1995, and can be found in Department of Foreign Affairs (DFA) files, RG 25, A2011-00458, LAC. On American attitudes towards "informal cooperation," see Evan Bloom, "Establishment of the Arctic Council," 712.

37. "Summary Notes of the Meeting of Arctic Countries' Senior Officials to Discuss the Establishment of an Arctic Council" (Ottawa, June 6–7, 1995). Also, Terry Fenge, circular document with attachment of Ottawa discussions, n.d., CARC papers, 3.10.5.12.7.3.5, WLU.

38. Robert Senseney, polar affairs chief, U.S. State Department, to Arctic Council negotiators, August 2, 1995, 13.00 Arktinen neuvisto, Arctic Council, vol. 1995, MFA. Following remarks are from interviews with Mary Simon, Terry Fenge, Tucker Sculley, Leslie Whitby, and several confidential interviews.

39. U.S. Arctic Network, National Audubon Society, The Wilderness Society, Alaska Marine Conservation Council, National Parks and Conservation Association, Alaska Natural Resources Center, Alaska Center for the Environment, Alaska Wildlife Alliance, Greenpeace, Trustees for Alaska, Northern Alaska Environmental Center, Alaska Friends of the Earth to Governor Tony Knowles, August 4, 1995, Juneau. Copy sent from U.S. Arctic Network to CARC. Fenge papers.

40. The account is based mainly on Finnish documents, especially Memo no. 1014, Washington to Helsinki, September 12, 1995, MFA. Also Christine Lee to Terry Fenge, September 8, 1995, CARC papers, 8.10.5.1.7.3.4, WLU.

41. Leslie Whitby, DIAND, to Robert Senseney, Department of State, October 18, 1995, Fenge papers. Mary Simon to Marie Bernard-Meunier, Jack Stagg, and John Rayner, January 17, 1996. "Re: Arctic Council: Towards Improved Collaboration on the Sustainable Development Agenda," DFA files, RG 25 A2011-00458, LAC.

42. Margie Gibson, executive director, U.S. Arctic Network to Terry Fenge, Tim Lash, Carole Saint Laurent, October 25, 1995, Fenge papers. Attachment. Gibson to Robert Senseney, October 25, 1995.

43. *Arctic Environmental Protection Strategy: Senior Arctic Affairs Officials' Meeting* (Iqaluit, Northwest Territories, March 15–17, 1995), DFA files, RG 25, A2011-00458. Interviews with Mary Simon, Leslie Whitby, and several confidential interviews.

SEVEN: THE SWIFT WINGS OF TRUTH

1. Quoted in Walter Slipchenko, "Multilateral Arctic Relations: The Arctic Council (1992–2000)," 163, endnote 14. Slipchenko worked as a consultant for the Government of the Northwest Territories of the time and Overvold was the chairman of the Deputy Ministers' Committee on International Circumpolar Relations.

2. Interview with Henry Huntington by Monica Tennberg, February 1996, quoted in Tennberg, "The Arctic Council: A Study in Governmentality" (unpublished doctoral dissertation, Rovaniemi: University of Lapland, 1998), 137.

3. Leslie Whitby announced a "new management structure for the AEPS in Canada" on February 22, 1996. She strongly defended the work of her "Team Canada" and asserted that the team had worked well with others including aboriginals. Document in Terry Fenge papers.

4. Tennberg, "The Arctic Council," 168.

5. For my own views on the role of NGOs and states, see John English, "The Ottawa Process: Paths Followed, Paths Ahead," *Australian Journal of International Affairs* 52, no. 2 (1998), 121–132.

6. Fen Osler Hampson and Dean Oliver, "'Pulpit Diplomacy': A Critical Assessment

of the Axworthy Doctrine," *International Journal* 53, no. 3 (1998), 379–406. The Arctic Council was not mentioned in the article.

7. "Meeting of Senior Officials to Discuss the Establishment of an Arctic Council" (Toronto, November 30, 1995, and December 2, 1995), 13:00 Arktinen neuvosto, Arctic Council 1995, Finnish Ministry of Foreign Affairs (FMFA).

8. Elizabeth Leighton, "Arctic Council Fast Track Derails?" *WWF Arctic Bulletin* 1.96 (1996): 4.

9. Wanja Tornberg to Mary Simon, January 19, 1996, Arktinen neuvosto, Arctic Council, 1996, FMFA. Note presence of Swedish document in Finnish papers. The Canadians paid little attention to the Swedish suggestion. RG 25, A2011-00458, Library of Archives Canada (LAC). Also, Will Martin to Mary Simon, March 13, 1996, ibid.

10. Michael Welsh, Canadian Embassy, Washington, to Ottawa, March 18, 1996, RG 25 A2011-00457, LAC.

11. Michael Welsh, Canadian Embassy, Washington to Ottawa, March 20, 1996, ibid.

12. Foreign Affairs, Ottawa, "Arctic Council: Proposed Date for Inaugural Meeting," April 1996, ibid.

13. "Arctic Council Meetings" (Ottawa, April 17–19, 1996), ibid. This file contains several drafts and accompanying documents. On the Americans missing the Arctic Parliamentarians meeting, *Globe and Mail,* March 15, 1996.

14. Comment in briefing paper prepared by Terry Fenge, executive director of CARC, for Sergio Marchi, the new minister of environment, March 17, 1996, Fenge papers.

15. "List of Issues," Arctic Council Negotiations, June 8–9, 1996, Fenge papers. There is no indication of the provenance of this document.

16. Robert Senseney to Mary Simon, May 22, 1996, Fenge papers.

17. Mary Simon, in discussion with the author. House of Commons Standing Committee on Foreign Affairs and International Trade, *Canada and the Circumpolar World: Meeting the Challenges of Cooperation into the Twenty-First Century* (Ottawa: Public Works and Government Services Canada, 1997). I was vice-chair of the committee and led the Eastern Arctic tour.

18. Robert Senseney, State Department, to Ambassador Mary Simon, June 3, 1996, Fenge papers.

19. Confidential copy of Robert Senseney to Arctic Advisory Group, April 12, 1996. The discussion of the differences between Canada and the United States draws deeply upon E.C.H. Keskitalo, *Negotiating the Arctic: The Construction of an International Region* (New York and London: Routledge, 2004), 140–145.

20. Pål Prestrud in *WWF Arctic Bulletin* 4 (1996): 7. Lloyd Axworthy in discussion with the author, November 2012; and Mary Simon in discussion with the author, December 2012.

21. His view is reported in Donald Rothwell, *The Polar Regions and the Development of International Law* (Cambridge: Cambridge University Press, 1996), 225n.

22. For a contemporary account of Scully's intervention, see Sheila Watt-Cloutier, Joe Kunuk, and Terry Fenge, "The Arctic Council, Sustainable Development, and the Inuit," *WWF Arctic Bulletin,* no. 4 (1996), 6–7.

23. Slipchenko, "Multilateral Arctic Relations," 161.

24. *Conservation of Flora and Fauna* (Anchorage, Alaska: U.S. Fisheries and Wildlife Service, 1994). Document at Scott Polar Research Institute, Cambridge, England.

25. *Globe and Mail,* August 15, 1996. Lloyd Axworthy to Franklyn Griffiths, July 12, 1996, Gordon Foundation papers.

26. Jane George, "Pomp and Ceremony for Arctic Council," *Nunatsiaq News,* September 28, 1996. Personal memory of event.

27. Anonymous (Clyde Sanger), "Hands across the Ice," *The Economist,* September 21, 1996, 48. The other press reports are from a check on the search engine ProQuest: twenty-two newspapers, the majority American, had some coverage.

28. "Persistent Organic Pollutants: Key Points to Note and Canadian Position," March 10, 1996, RG 25 A2011-00458, LAC. Terry Fenge, in discussion with author. A good history of the process is found in Keith Bull, "Protocol to the 1979 Convention on Long-Range Transboundary Air Pollution on Persistent Organic Pollutants: The 1998 Agreement for the UNECE," in H. Fielder, ed., *The Handbook of Environmental Chemistry* 3 (Berlin: Springer-Verlag, 2003). Bull was a UNECE employee. The document can be found at www.lu.lv/ecotox/publikacijas/ POP_LEGISLAT.PDF (accessed August 12, 2012).

29. Jane George, "What is the Arctic Council Anyway?" *Nunatsiaq News,* September 27, 1996.

30. Ibid.

31. House of Commons, *Canada and the Circumpolar World,* 44–48. Also, Oran R. Young, *The Arctic Council: Marking a New Era in International Relations* (New York: The Twentieth Century Fund, 1996); David Scrivener, *Environmental Cooperation in the Arctic: From Strategy to Council* (Oslo: Norwegian Atlantic Committee, 1996). Young also made comments on the future of the Arctic Council in Young, *Creating Regimes: Arctic Accords and International Governance* (Ithaca and London: Cornell University Press, 1998), especially 49–51.

32. "ICC Statement on the Arctic Council Sustainable Development Programme," Inuit Circumpolar Conference, Sept. 20, 1996, RG 25 A-2011-00458 (LAC); and Håken R. Nilson, *Arctic Environmental Protection Strategy (AEPS): Process and Organization, 1991–97: An Assessment* (Oslo: Norwegian Polar Institute, 1997).

33. "Delegation Report," Arctic Environmental Protection Strategy Meeting (Kautokeino, Norway, March 11–12, 1997), Canadian Arctic Resources Committee Papers (CARC), 3.10.5.16.1.1, Wilfrid Laurier University Archives, Waterloo (WLU).

34. Ibid. The Nilson AEPS report was scheduled to be presented at the ministerial meeting, Arctic Council, Senior Arctic Officials' Meeting, Kautokeino, Norway, March 12–13, 1997, Ministry of Foreign Affairs (MFA), RG 25, A2011-00458, LAC. This document contains the full record of the debate. Bernie Funston in discussion with the author, January 2013.

35. Johanne Forest, Environment Division, Foreign Affairs, Canada, to AEPS Advisory Committee, May 8, 1997. Enclosing U.S.A. and Greenland/Denmark Comments on the Ministerial Declaration. CARC papers, 3.10.5.11.1.2, WLU.

36. Franklyn Griffiths, "Canadian Priorities for the Arctic Council," March 31, 1997, Franklyn Griffiths papers. Terry Fenge, consultant to Christine Lee, Walter and Duncan Gordon Foundation, January 25, 1998, with attachment, "Canada and the Arctic Council," Gordon Foundation papers. Note: this is an "incomplete and unedited draft." It was prepared for the northern advisory group to Axworthy of which Fenge was a member.

37. The description of Fenge was given in 2011 by Harald Finkler, a senior DIAND official who was active on the Arctic Council file for over twenty years.

38. Simon did so to a parliamentary committee meeting that I chaired. House of Commons Committee on Foreign Affairs and International Trade, April 30, 1996.

39. Fenge, ibid. Confidential conversations on trade officials.

40. Fenge, ibid. Oran R. Young, "Arctic Governance: Preparing for the Next Phase" (paper prepared for Standing Committee of Parliamentarians of the Arctic Region, June 2002).

41. Lloyd Axworthy, *Navigating a New World: Canada's Global Future* (Toronto: Random House, 2003), 332–333.

42. Fenge, "Canada and the Arctic Council." The major documents in the RG 25 series of the Department of Foreign Affairs and International Trade Canada reflect the troubling disagreements, principally between Canada and the United States. The difficulties over sustainable development and the AEPS are illustrated in the document "Meeting of Senior Arctic Officials and Permanent Participants," October 7–9, 1997, RG 25, A2011-00458, LAC.

EIGHT: INTO THE NEW MILLENNIUM

1. Inuit Tapiriit Kanatami, *Social Determinants of Inuit Health in Canada: A Discussion Paper*, April 22, 2007. Available at http://ahrnets.ca/files/2011/02/ITK_Social_Determinants_paper_2007.pdf (accessed February 12, 2013).

2. House of Commons Standing Committee on Foreign Affairs and International Trade, *Canada and the Circumpolar World: Meeting the Challenges of Cooperation into the Twenty-First Century* (Ottawa: Public Works and Government Services Canada, 1997), 232–236. The committee pointed out that most Canadian development assistance concentrated on private projects in Russia, although some Canadian NGOs were also active. The Committee did not support Professor Oran Young's call for an Arctic "development bank," preferring to use existing institutions. John McCannon, *A History of the Arctic: Nature, Exploration, and Exploitation* (London: Reaktion Books, 2012), 271.

3. Ibid., 219.

4. E.C.H. Keskitalo, *Negotiating the Arctic: The Construction of an International Region* (New York and London: Routledge, 2004), 168. Professor Janice Stein, a member of the Walter and Duncan Gordon Foundation board, recalls lobbying Lloyd Axworthy for more resources for the Gordon-backed initiative. Conversation of August 31, 2012. Keskitalo's interviews were predominantly Nordic.

5. Keskitalo, *Negotiating the Arctic*, 160. "Revised Agenda," SAAO Meeting (Kautokeino, Norway, March 11–12, 1997), RG 25, A2011-00458, Library of Archives Canada (LAC). David Stone to J. Rayner, February 18, 1997, describes a proposed University of the Arctic and encloses a concept paper. It was a "further development of the idea for an Arctic Council 'deliverable' which three of us (Lars-Erik Liljelund of Sweden, Bill Heal of the UK, and myself) thought up during the recent AMAP. He asked that it be forwarded to Mary Simon with the request that she consider "distributing this paper to SAOs for their review and possible decision at Kautokeino." RG 25, A-2011-00459, LAC. The full history of the Canadian leadership on POPs is found in David Downie and Terry Fenge, eds., *Northern Lights Against POPs: Combatting Toxic Threats in the Arctic* (Montreal and Kingston: McGill-Queen's University Press, 2003). This book was published for the Inuit Circumpolar Commission.

6. Arctic Council SAO Meeting (Kautokeino, Norway, March 13, 1997), and "Revised Agenda," SAAO Meeting (Kautokeino, March 11–12, 1997), LAC.

7. Ambassador Mary Simon to Kåre Bryn, SAAO, Norway, February 19, 1997, and Robert Senseney, U.S. State Department, to Mary Vandenhoff, executive director, Canadian Arctic Council Secretariat, February 21, 1997, RG 25, A2011-0045, LAC. The complicated question of observers is covered best in Piotr Graczyk, "Observers in the Arctic Council—Evolution and Prospects," *Yearbook of Polar International Law* 3 (2011), 575–633.

8. "Message to Congress," February 10, 1997, in *Public Papers of the President of the United States: William J. Clinton: Book I* (Washington: Government Printing Office, 1997), 143–144.

9. Young makes the "dragging feet" comment in his review of E.C.H. Keskitalo's "Negotiating the Arctic" in *Polar Research* 23, no. 2 (2004), 212. More broadly, Young described the political and bureaucratic limitations in *Creating Regimes: Arctic Accords and International Governance* (Ithaca and London: Cornell University Press, 1998), 162–163, 196.

10. Scully made the comment to a Finn official. It was reported by the Washington embassy to the Finn Foreign Office on November 26, 1997 (translated). Ministry of Foreign Affairs (MFA), WASB120.

11. Embassy of Finland, Washington, to Helsinki, June 26, 1998 (translated). MFA, WASCO 19–27.

12. Lloyd Axworthy, *Navigating a New World: Canada's Global Future* (Toronto: Knopf Canada, 2003), 334–336. Lloyd Axworthy, in discussion with the author, March 2012. "The Iqaluit Declaration," The First Meeting of the Arctic Council (Iqaluit, Canada, September 18–19, 1998). This and other "declarations" are found on the Arctic Council website at www.arctic-council.org/index.php/en/about/documents/category/5-declarations (accessed August 28, 2012).

13. Axworthy, *Navigating a New World*, 334-335. Mary Simon is quoted in Jane George, "Mary Simon: the Arctic Council Is Taking the Time to Get it Right," *Nunatsiaq News*, September 17, 1998.

14. George, ibid.

15. Jane George, "Is the Arctic Council a Dysfunctional Family?" *Nunatsiaq News,* September 24, 1998.

16. David Stone to John Rayner, "Concept Paper from Canada and Sweden for a possible University of the Arctic," February 18, 1997, RG 25 A-2011-00459, LAC. David Scrivener, "Arctic Environmental Cooperation in Transition," *Polar Record* 35, no. 192 (1999), 51–58. Description from several interviews and *Nunatsiaq News.*

17. An idea of the rapidity of change and the extent to which the Arctic became of greater significance in international relations can be seen in a comparison between the influential American academic Oran Young's 1992 *Arctic Politics: Conflict and Cooperation in the Circumpolar North* (Dartmouth: University Press of New England), especially the preface, and his 1998 study *Creating Regimes: Arctic Accords and International Governance* (Ithaca and London: Cornell University Press), especially vii-ix and 46ff. Young writes: "Facilitated by the opening of the Arctic following the end of the Cold War and spearheaded by environmental advocacy groups fresh from a major victory involving mineral resources and environmental protection in the Antarctic, this campaign is likely to focus initially on environmental matters and to place heavy emphasis on the protection of ecosystems by placing them off limits to various kinds of human activities" (48–49).

18. Franklyn Griffiths, in discussion with the author.

19. On Stockholm and ratification dates, see http://chm.pops.int/Countries/ StatusofRatifications/tabid/252/Default.aspx (accessed August 31, 2012). As noted earlier, all ministerial declarations are available on the Arctic Council's website: www.arctic-council.org/index.php/en. The best account is the Inuit influence is Terry Fenge, "POPs and Inuit: Influencing the Global Agenda," in Terry Fenge and D.L. Downie, eds., *Northern Lights Against POPs: Combatting Toxic Threats in the Arctic,* 192–213. The assessment of its importance is from Terry Fenge to author, April 7, 2013.

20. Moore is quoted by Jane George in *Nunatsiaq News,* May 12, 2000.

21. Pekka Haavisto, assisted by Teemu Palosaari, "Review of the Arctic Council Structures," Draft, Helsinki 1.6. 2001, Gordon Foundation papers. The final report is on the Arctic Council website, www.arctic-council.org. Also, Oran R. Young, "The Structure of Arctic Cooperation: Solving Problems/Seizing Opportunities" (paper prepared for the Fourth Conference of Parliamentarians of the Arctic Region, Rovaniemi, August 27–29, 2000). This section also draws upon Olav Schram Stokke and Geir Hønneland, eds., *International Cooperation and Arctic Governance: Regime Effectiveness and Northern Region Building* (New York: Routledge, 2007).

22. McCannon, *A History of the Arctic,* 2.

23. *Arctic Climate Impact Assessment—Scientific Report* (Cambridge and New York: Cambridge University Press, 2005), 88. This section draws mainly from the outstanding assessment of the ACIA by Annika E. Nilsson, who had the opportunity to participate in several meetings and interviewed many of the participants. Annika E. Nilsson, "A Changing Arctic Climate: Science and Policy in the Arctic

Climate Impact Assessment," *Linköping Studies in Art and Science,* no. 386 (Linköping: Linköping University, 2007).

24. The IASC had published a 1995 report: *Effects of Increased Ultraviolet Radiation in the Arctic* (Oslo: IASC, 1995). The IPCC reports on the Arctic appearing in 2001 summarized earlier work: IPCC, *Climate Change 2001: Synthesis Report—A Contribution of Working Groups I, Ii, and II to the Third Assessment Report of the Intergovernmental Panel on Climate Change* (Cambridge and New York: Cambridge University Press, 2001).

25. Nilsson, *A Changing Arctic Climate,* 210.

26. The quotations are from the official summary at http://amap.no/acia/ (accessed September 6, 2012). Also, "Summary Report of the 5th Assessment Steering Committee Meeting," June 1–16, 2000.

27. U.S. Statement on Policy Document, n.d. [October 2003].

28. Nilsson quotes the newsletter, *Inside E.P.A.,* as having reported that "some foreign officials and Native American groups suspect the Bush administration is seeking the delay to avoid addressing the politically tricky issues a month before the 2004 presidential election." One of her interviews supported the view that politics were a factor. *A Changing Arctic Climate,* 138.

29. Comment on Correll in document written by ICC consultant Terry Fenge, n.d., Terry Fenge papers. Sheila Watt-Cloutier to Gunnar Pálsson, August 25, 2004, ibid.

30. Watt-Cloutier to Pálsson, ibid.

31. Nilsson describes the period and the debate over the Pálsson draft in detail in *A Changing Arctic Climate.* Also, "Permanent Participants ACIA Meeting" (The Hague, Netherlands, August 29–30, 2004), Fenge papers. See also the ICC account: Sheila Watt-Cloutier, Terry Fenge, and Paul Crowley, "Responding to Global Climate Change: The Perspective of the Inuit Circumpolar Conference on the Arctic Climate Impact Assessment," http://inuitcircumpolar.com/index. php?ID=267&Lang=En (accessed September 12, 2012).

32. There is an account of the testimony and of comments made later at www. ens-newswire.com/ens/sep2004/2004-09-16-10.aspc (accessed September 15, 2012). Also, *New York Times,* October 30, 2004. Full testimony of Watt-Cloutier is available on the ICC website, http://inuitcircumpolar.com/index. php?ID=261&Lang=En (accessed September 15, 2012).

33. *Washington Post,* November 4, 2004.

34. The Reykjavik Ministerial Declaration is available on the Arctic Council's website, www.arctic-council.org/index.php/en/about/documents/category/5-declarations (accessed September 15, 2012).

35. Niels Einarsson, Joan Nymand Larsen, Annika Nilsson, and Oran R. Young, *Arctic Human Development Report* (Akureyri, Iceland: Stefansson Arctic Institute, 2004), 238. Paula Kankaanpää and Oran R. Young, *The Effectiveness of the Arctic Council* (Rovaniemi: Arctic Centre, 2012). Paula Kankaanpää in discussion with the author, June 2012. Annika Nilsson, "Knowing the Arctic: The Arctic Council as a Cognitive Forerunner," in Thomas S. Axworthy, Timo Koivurova, and

Waliul Hasanat, *The Arctic Council: Its Place in the Future of Arctic Governance* (Toronto: Munk–Gordon Arctic Security Program, 2012), 190–224.

CONCLUSION

1. Ivan Semeniuk, "Why Is Arctic Sea Ice Vanishing Even Faster than Climate Models Predict?" *Globe and Mail*, March 16, 2013.

2. Pilita Clark, "Environment: Frozen Frontiers," *Financial Times*, February 6, 2013.

3. Klaus Dodds, "Anticipating the Arctic and the Arctic Council: Pre-emption, Precaution and Preparedness," in Axworthy et al., *The Arctic Council*, 23.

4. Peter MacKay as quoted in Randy Boswell, "Leaders Say Gov't Should Recreate Arctic Ambassador," August 4, 2007 at http://dl1.yukoncollege.yk.ca/agraham/stories/storyReader$4737?print-friendly=true (accessed September 12, 2012). Peter Stoffer in House of Commons, *Debates*, October 3, 2006; *Time*, April 3, 2006.

5. Interview with Mary Simon, 2012.

6. Franklyn Griffiths, *Arctic Alternatives: Civility or Militarism in the Circumpolar Arctic* (Toronto: Samuel Stevens, 1992).

7. "Disputing Boundaries," *CBC Newsonline*, October 11, 2005 (accessed February 27, 2013).

8. BBC *News*, August 1, 2007 (accessed February 27, 2013).

9. O.A. Anisimov, D.G. Vaughan, T.V. Callaghan, C. Furgal, H. Marchant, T.D. Prowse, H. Vilhjálmsson and J.E. Walsh, "Polar Regions" (Arctic and Antarctic) in M.L. Parry, O.F. Canziani, J.P. Palutikof, P.J. van der Linden, and C.E. Hanson, eds., *Climate Change 2007: Impacts, Adaptation and Vulnerability. Contribution of Working Group II to the Fourth Assessment Report of the Intergovernmental Panel on Climate Change* (Cambridge: Cambridge University Press, 2007), 653–685.

10. USGS Newsroom, Press Release, July 23, 2008. www.usgs.gov/newsroom/article.asp?ID=1980&from=rss_home#.UT9p56VgNFI (accessed March 7, 2013).

11. Scott Borgerson, "Arctic Meltdown: The Economic and Social Implications of Global Warming," *Foreign Affairs* vol. 87 (March–April 2008), 63–77.

12. The Ilulissat Declaration, May 28, 2008, at www.oceanlaw.org/downloads/arctic/Ilulissat_Declaration.pdf (accessed March 12, 2013).

13. Arctic Maritime Shipping Assessment 2009 at www.pame.is/images/stories/AMSA_2009_Report/AMSA_2009_Report_2nd_print.pdf (accessed September 15, 2012). Lawson Brigham, "Think Again: The Arctic," *Foreign Policy* (Sept/Oct 2010), www.foreignpolicy.com/articles/2010/08/16/think_again_the_arctic?page=0,4 (accessed September 15, 2012).

14. Brigham, ibid. Interview with Lawson Brigham, January 2011.

15. On "Stand Up for Canada," Ken Coates, Whitney Lackenbauer, William R. Morrison, and Greg Poelzer, *Arctic Front: Defending Canada in the Far North* (Toronto: Thomas Allen, 2008), 214. "Calming the waters" is the description in

John McCannon, *A History of the Arctic: Nature, Exploration and Exploitation* (London: Reaktion Books, 2012), 282.

16. Supra, 14–16.

17. Documents on the meeting are found at www.arctic-council.org/index.php/en/document-archive/category/20-main-documents-from-nuuk# (accessed May 24, 2013).

18. The special issue of *The Economist* of June 16, 2012, which used this description as its headline describing the political state of the Arctic, reflected and strengthened the intense interest in the Arctic at the time.

19. Comment to author, May 15, 2013.

20. Kiruna documents are found at www.arctic-council.org/index.php/en/document-archive/category/425-main-documents-from-kiruna-ministerial-meeting (accessed May 25, 2013).

21. The Canadian positions and several links to Canadian sites are provided by the Arctic Council at www.arctic-council.org/index.php/en/canada (accessed March 14, 2013).

22. The conference remarks are reported in Thomas S. Axworthy, "Russia Turns Back the Clock," January 20, 2013. Walter and Duncan Gordon Foundation News Release.

23. The full title is The Agreement on Cooperation on Aeronautical and Maritime Search and Rescue in the Arctic.

24. Paul Berkman, "Preventing an Arctic Cold War," *New York Times,* March 12, 2013.

25. Quoted in www.nunatsiaqonline.ca/stories/article/65674greenland_walks_away_from_the_arctic_council (accessed May 25, 2013).

26. Lynge is quoted in Michael T. Klare, *The Rest for What's Left: The Global Scramble for the World's Last Resources* (New York: Picador, 2013), 72–73. Klare's chapter is entitled "Invading the Arctic."

BIBLIOGRAPHY

ACIA. *Arctic Climate Impact Assessment—Scientific Report.* Cambridge and New York: Cambridge University Press, 2005.

Adams, Clement. "The Newe Nauigation and Discouerie of the Kingdome of Muscouia, by the North-East, in the Yeere 1553." In *The Principall Navigations, Voyages and Discoveries of the English Nation,* edited by Richard Hakluyt. London: The Hakluyt Society, 1589. http://archive.org/stream/threevoyagesofwi00veerrich/three-voyagesofwi00veerrich_djvu.txt (accessed February 20, 2012).

Anderson, Ian, and Fred Pearce. "Is There an Ozone Hole over the North Pole?" *New Scientist,* February 25, 1989.

Anonymous (Clyde Sanger). "Hands Across the Ice." *The Economist,* September 21, 1996.

Archer, Clive. "Western Responses to the Murmansk Initiative." *Centrepiece* 14 (Spring 1988).

Arctic Council Panel. *To Establish an International Arctic Council: A Framework Report.* Ottawa: Canadian Arctic Resources Committee, 1991.

Arctic Council SAO Meeting. Kautokeino, Norway, March 13, 1997.

Arctic Environmental Protection Strategy. Rovaniemi, Finland, June 14, 1991. http://library.arcticportal.org/1542/1/artic_environment.pdf (accessed June 30, 2012).

Armstrong, Terence. "Mining in the Soviet Arctic." *Polar Record* 10, no. 64 (1960), 16–22.

Axworthy, Lloyd. *Navigating a New World: Canada's Global Future.* Toronto: Random House, 2003.

Axworthy, Thomas S. "A Brief History of the Arctic Council." Comments to symposium, University of Toronto, December 2, 2010.

———. "Changing the Arctic Paradigm from Cold War to Cooperation: How Canada's Indigenous Leaders Shaped the Future Arctic Council." Paper prepared for the Fifth Polar Law Symposium, Arctic Centre, Rovaniemi, Finland, September 6–8, 2012.

Axworthy, Thomas S., and Sara French. "A Proposal for an Arctic Nuclear-Weapon-Free Zone." Presented at the Interaction Council Expert Meeting on "Achieving a World Free of Nuclear Weapons", Hiroshima, Japan, April 15, 2010.

Azzi, Stephen. *Walter Gordon and the Rise of Canadian Nationalism.* Montreal and Kingston: McGill-Queen's University Press, 1999.

Barrow, Sir John. *Voyages of Discovery and Research Within the Arctic Region From the Year 1818 to the Present Time.* London: John Murray, 1846.

Beattie, Owen, and John Geiger. *Frozen in Time: The Fate of the Franklin Expedition.* Vancouver: Douglas & McIntyre, 2004.

Behrisch, Erika. "Voices of Silence, Texts of Truth: Imperial Discourse and Cultural Negotiations in Nineteenth-Century British Arctic Exploration Narrative." Unpublished doctoral dissertation, University of Michigan, 2002.

Bercuson, David. "Continental Defense and Arctic Security, 1945–50: Solving the Canadian Dilemma." In *The Cold War and Defense,* edited by K. Neilson and R.G. Haycock, 153–170. New York: Praeger, 1990.

Berg Bentzrød, Sveinung. "Vi Er Amundsens Etterkommere." www.aftenposten.no/nyheter/iriks/article2081918.ece (accessed December 5, 2011).

Berger, Thomas. *Northern Frontier, Northern Homeland: The Report of the Mackenzie Valley Pipeline Inquiry, Volume I.* Ottawa: Supply and Services, 1977.

———. *Village Journey: The Report of the Alaska Native Review Commission.* New York: Hill & Wang, 1985.

Berggen, J.L., and Alexander Jones, eds. *Ptolemy's Geography: An Annotated Translation of the Theoretical Chapters.* Princeton: Princeton University Press, 2001.

Bergman, Jay. "Valerii Chkalov: Soviet Pilot as New Soviet Man." *Journal of Contemporary History* 33, no. 1 (1998), 135–152.

Berton, Pierre. *The Arctic Grail: The Quest for the North West Passage and the North Pole, 1818–1909.* Toronto: Anchor Canada, 2001.

Black, Lydia. *Russians in America: 1732–1867.* Fairbanks: University of Alaska Press, 2004.

Blanton, Thomas, and Dr. Svetlana Savranskaya, eds. "The Reykjavik File: Previously Secret Documents from U.S. and Soviet Archives on the 1986 Reagan-Gorbachev Summit." National Security Archive Electronic Briefing Book No. 203, 2006. www.gwu.edu/~nsarchiv/NSAEBB/NSAEBB203/index.htm (accessed February 20, 2013).

Bloom, Evan. "Establishment of the Arctic Council," *American Journal of International Law* 93 (July 1999), 712–732.

Borgerson, Scott, "Arctic Meltdown: The Implications of Global Warming," *Foreign Affairs* 87 (March–April 2008), 63–77.

Borges, Jorge Luis. "Kafka and His Precursors" (1951). In *Everything and Nothing,* 70–73. New York: New Directions Publishing Corporation, 1999.

Boyer, Paul. *By the Bomb's Early Light: American Thought and Culture at the Dawn of the Atomic Age.* New York: Pantheon, 1985.

Breton, Gilles. "The Case for an Arctic Council." Conference proceedings, *Changing*

Roles of the United States in the Circumpolar North conference, University of Alaska, Fairbanks, August 12–14, 1992.

Bridgman, Timothy. *Hyperboreans: Myth and History in Celtic-Hellenic Contacts*. New York and London: Routledge, 2005.

Bull, Keith. "Protocol to the 1979 Convention on Long-Range Transboundary Air Pollution on Persistent Organic Pollutants: The 1998 Agreement for the UNECE." In *The Handbook of Environmental Chemistry*, edited by H. Fielder. Vol. 3, 1–11. Berlin: Springer-Verlag, 2012. http://www.lu.lv/ecotox/publikacijas/POP_LEGISLAT.PDF (accessed August 12, 2012).

Burgess, Philip. *Elite Images and Foreign Policy Outcomes: A Study of Norway*. Columbus: Ohio State University Press, 1968.

Burney, Derek. *Getting It Done: A Memoir*. Montreal and Kingston: McGill-Queen's University Press, 2009.

Byers, Michael. *Who Owns the Arctic: Understanding Sovereignty Disputes in the North*. Vancouver: Douglas & McIntyre, 2009.

Cardinal, Harold. *The Unjust Society: The Tragedy of Canada's Indians*. Edmonton: M.G. Hurtig, 1969.

Cavell, Janice. *Tracing the Connected Narrative: Arctic Exploration in British Print Culture*. Toronto: University of Toronto Press, 2008.

Cavell, Janice, and Jeff Noakes. *Acts of Occupation: Canada and Arctic Sovereignty*. Vancouver and Toronto: University of British Columbia Press, 2010.

Clarke, Douglas. "Gorbachev's Arms Control Proposals for the Arctic." *RFE Background Report 5* (October 1987).

Clay Berry, Mary. *The Alaskan Pipeline: The Politics of Oil and Native Land Claims*. Bloomington: Indiana University Press, 1975.

Coates, Ken S., P. Whitney Lackenbauer, William R. Morrison, and Greg Poelzer. *Arctic Front: Defending Canada in the Far North*. Toronto: Thomas Allen Publishers, 2008.

Coates, Ken S., and William R. Morrison. *Strange Things Done: Murder in Yukon History*. Montreal and Kingston: McGill-Queen's University Press, 2004.

Collinson, Richard, ed. *The Three Voyages of Martin Frobisher: In Search of a Passage to Cathaia and India by the North-West, AD 1576-8*. London: The Hakluyt Society, 1867.

Cox, David, and Tariq Rauf. *Security Co-operation in the Arctic: A Canadian Response to Gorbachev's Murmansk Initiative*. Ottawa: CCACD, 1989.

Dahl, Jens. *IWGIA: A History*. Copenhagen: International Working Group for Indigenous Affairs, 2009.

De Steiguer, J. Edward. *The Origins of Modern Environmental Thought*. Tucson: University of Arizona Press, 2006.

The DEW Line Story. U.S. Information Agency, 1958. http://archive.org/details/gov.archives.arc.52896 (accessed February 19, 2013).

Diamond, Billy. "Aboriginal Rights: The James Bay Experience." In *The Quest for Justice: Aboriginal Peoples and Aboriginal Rights*, edited by Menno Boldt and J. Anthony Long, 265–285. Toronto: University of Toronto Press, 1985.

Diamond, Jared. *Collapse: How Societies Choose to Fail or Succeed*. New York: Viking, 2005.

Dick, Lyle. *Muskox Land: Ellesmere Island in the Age of Contact*. Calgary: University of Calgary Press, 2001.

Diubaldo, Richard. "Wrangling over Wrangel Island." *Canadian Historical Review* 48, no. 3 (1967), 201–226.

Einarsson, Niels, Joan Nymand Larsen, Annika E. Nilsson, and Oran R. Young. *Arctic Human Development Report*. Akureyri, Iceland: Stefansson Arctic Institute, 2004.

Emmerson, Charles. *The Future History of the Arctic*. New York: Public Affairs, 2010.

English, John. *Just Watch Me: The Biography of Pierre Trudeau, Volume Two: 1968–2000*. Toronto: Random House, 2009.

———. "The Ottawa Process: Paths Followed, Paths Ahead." *Australian Journal of International Affairs* 52, no. 2 (1998), 121–132.

———. *Shadow of Heaven: The Life of Lester Pearson. Volume One: 1897–1948*. London: Vintage UK, 1990.

Faulconbridge, Guy. "Russian Sub Plants Flag under North Pole." *Reuters*, August 2, 2007.

Faulkes, Anthony, and Richard Perkins, eds. *A History of Norway and the Passion and Miracles of the Blessed Óláfr*. Translated by Carl Phelpstead. Viking Society for Northern Research Text Series 13. London: Viking Society for Northern Research, 2001.

Fenge, Terry. "Asserting Sovereignty in the Arctic: Inuit and the Nunavut Land Claims Agreement." In *Nilliajut: Inuit Perspectives on Security, Patriotism and Sovereignty*, edited by Carrie Grable, Karen Kelley, James Kuptana, Martin Lougheed, and Scot Nickels, 49–53. Ottawa: Inuit Tapiriit Kanatami, 2013.

———. "POPs and Inuit: Influencing the Global Agenda." In *Northern Lights Against POPs: Combatting Toxic Threats in the Arctic*, edited by D.L. Downie and Terry Fenge, 192–213. Montreal and Kingston: McGill-Queen's University Press, 2003.

Fenge, Terry, Paul Crowley, and Sheila Watt-Cloutier. "Responding to Global Climate Change: The Perspective of the Inuit Circumpolar Conference on the Arctic Climate Impact Assessment." http://inuitcircumpolar.com/index.php?ID=267 &Lang=En (accessed September 12, 2012).

Fischer, Benjamin B. *A Cold War Conundrum: The 1983 Soviet War Scare*. Summary. Washington: CIA Center for the Study of Intelligence, 1997. www.cia.gov/library/center-for-the-study-of-intelligence/csi-publications/books-and-monographs/a-cold-war-conundrum/source.htm#HEADING1-01 (accessed June 19, 2010).

Fleming, Fergus. *Barrow's Boys: The Original Extreme Adventurers*. New York: Atlantic Monthly Press, 1998.

Fossett, Renée. *In Order to Live Untroubled: Inuit of the Central Arctic, 1550–1940*. Winnipeg: University of Manitoba Press, 2001.

Gorbachev, Mikhail. "Mikhail Gorbachev's Speech in Murmansk at the Ceremonial Meeting on the Occasion of the Presentation of the Order of Lenin and the Gold Star to the City of Murmansk." Murmansk, October 1, 1987. www.barentsinfo.fi/docs/Gorbachev_speech.pdf (accessed February 21, 2013).

Grace, Sherrill. *Canada and the Idea of the North*. Paperback. Montreal and Kingston: McGill-Queen's University Press, 2007.

Graczyk, Piotr. "Observers in the Arctic Council—Evolution and Prospects." *Yearbook of Polar International Law* 3 (2011), 575–633.

Grant, Shelagh. *Polar Imperative: A History of Arctic Sovereignty in North America*. Vancouver: Douglas & McIntyre, 2010.

Gray, David. "Northern People, Northern Knowledge: The Story of the Canadian Arctic Expedition." *Canadian Museum of Civilization* (October 27, 2003). www.civilization.ca/cmc/exhibitions/hist/cae/peo614e.shtml#fpannigabluk (accessed March 10, 2012).

Griffiths, Franklyn. "Arctic Council Origins: A Memoir," Draft, March 20, 2011. Franklyn Griffiths papers. http://gordonfoundation.ca/sites/default/files/images/Jan18%20-%20Griffiths_ArcticCouncilOrigins.pdf (accessed March 1, 2013).

Hannigan, John, and Walter Slipchenko. *Canada's Arctic Cooperation with the Soviet Union and Russia, 1965-2000*, 2010. http://walterslipchenko.com/pdf/FINAL%20REPORT%20WITH%20ATTACHMENTS_a.pdf (accessed March 1, 2013).

Harper, Stephen. Speech at Inuvik, Northwest Territories, August 28, 2008. http://pm.gc.ca/eng/media.asp?id=2258 (accessed November 2, 2011).

Hart, Jonathan. *Empires and Colonies*. Vancouver: Douglas & McIntyre, 2010.

Head, Ivan. "Canadian Claims to Territorial Sovereignty in the Arctic Regions." *McGill Law Journal* 9, no. 3 (1963), 200–226.

Head, Ivan, and Pierre Trudeau. *The Canadian Way: Shaping Canada's Foreign Policy, 1968-1984*. Toronto: McClelland & Stewart, 1995.

Henderson, Bruce. "Who Discovered the North Pole?" *Smithsonian*, April 2009. www.smithsonianmag.com/history-archaeology/Cook-vs-Peary.html (accessed March 5, 2011).

Honderich, John. *Arctic Imperative: Is Canada Losing the North?* (Toronto: University of Toronto Press, 1987)

Hønneland, Geir, and Olav Schram Stokke. *International Cooperation and Arctic Governance: Regime Effectiveness and Northern Region Building*. New York: Routledge, 2007.

House of Commons Standing Committee on Foreign Affairs and International Trade. *Canada and the Circumpolar World: Meeting the Challenges of Cooperation in to the Twenty-First Century*. Ottawa: Public Works and Government Services, 1997.

Huebert, Rob. "The Canadian Arctic and the International Environmental Regime." In *Issues in the North: Volume III*, edited by J. Oakes and R. Riewe. Edmonton: Canadian Circumpolar Institute Press, 1997.

———. "Canadian Arctic Security Issues: Transformation in the Post–Cold War Era." *International Journal* 54, no. 2 (1999), 203–229.

———. "New Directions in Circumpolar Cooperation: Canada, the Arctic Environmental Protection Strategy, and the Arctic Council." *Canadian Foreign Policy* 5, no. 2 (1998), 37–57.

———. "Steel, Ice and Decision-Making: The Voyage of the *Polar Sea* and Its Aftermath." Unpublished doctoral dissertation, Dalhousie University, 1994.

Hunt, W.R. *Stef: A Biography of Vilhjalmur Stefansson*. Vancouver: University of British Columbia Press, 1996.

"ICC Statement on the Arctic Council Sustainable Development Programme." Presented at the Inuit Circumpolar Conference, September 20, 1996.

"Indigenous Peoples after UNCED." *Cultural Survival Quarterly* 18, no. 1 (1994). www.culturalsurvival.org/publications/cultural-survival-quarterly/brazil/indigenous-peoples-after-unced (accessed July 15, 2012).

Intergovernmental Panel on Climate Change. *Climate Change 2001: Synthesis Report—A Contribution of Working Groups I, Ii, and II to the Third Assessment Report of the Intergovernmental Panel on Climate Change*. Cambridge and New York: Cambridge University Press, 2001.

International Arctic Science Committee. *Effects of Increased Ultraviolet Radiation in the Arctic*. Oslo: IASC, 1995.

Inuit Circumpolar Conference. *Experts' Meeting on Arctic Council*. Ottawa, May 4, 1992.

Inuit Tapiriit Kanatami. *Social Determinants of Inuit Health in Canada: A Discussion Paper*, April 22, 2007. http://ahrnets.ca/files/2011/02/ITK_Social_Determinants_paper_2007.pdf (accessed February 12, 2013).

"The Iqaluit Declaration." The First Meeting of the Arctic Council. Iqaluit, September 16, 1998.

Iriye, Akira. "A Century of NGOs." *Diplomatic History* 23, no. 3 (1999), 421–435.

Irlbacher-Fox, Stephanie. *Finding Dahshaa: Self-Government, Social Suffering and Aboriginal Policy in Canada*. Vancouver and Toronto: University of British Columbia Press, 2009.

James, Patrick, Nelson Michaud, and Marc J. O'Reilly, eds. *Handbook of Canadian Foreign Policy*. Lanham, Maryland: Lexington Books, 2006.

Jenness, Diamond. "R.M. Anderson (1877–1961)." *Arctic* 14, no. 4 (1961), 268.

Jennings, Frances. *The Invasion of America: Indians, Colonialism and the Cant of Conquest*. New York: Norton, 1975.

Jockel, Joseph. *No Boundaries Upstairs: Canada, the United States, and the Origins of North American Air Defence, 1945–1958*. Vancouver: University of British Columbia Press, 1987.

Johnson, J. Peter. "The Establishment of Alert, N.W.T., Canada." *Arctic* 43, no. 1 (1990), 21–34.

Jowett, Philip, and Brent Snodgrass. *Finland at War, 1939–45*. Botley, UK, and New York: Osprey, 2006.

Kankaanpää, Paula, and Oran R. Young. *The Effectiveness of the Arctic Council*. Rovaniemi: Arctic Centre, 2012.

Karetak-Lindell, Nancy. "Sovereignty—When Did This Become Our Cause?" In *Nilliajut: Inuit Perspectives on Security, Patriotism and Sovereignty*, 19–22. Ottawa: Inuit Tapiriit Kanatami, 2013. www.gordonfoundation.ca/sites/default/files/publications/NILLIAJUT_Inuit%20Perspectives%20on%20Security,%20Patriotism%20and%20Sovereignty.pdf (accessed February 20, 2013).

Keskitalo, E.C.H. *Negotiating the Arctic: The Construction of an International Region.* New York and London: Routledge, 2004.

Kirkey, Christopher. "Smoothing Troubled Waters: The 1988 Canada–United States Arctic Co-operation Agreement." *International Journal* 50, no. 2 (1995): 401–426.

Kulchyski, Peter, and Frank Tester. *Tammarniit (Mistakes): Inuit Relocation in the Eastern Arctic, 1939–1967.* Vancouver: University of British Columbia Press, 1994.

Kunuk, Zacharias. *Exile.* Documentary. www.isuma.tv/isuma-productions/exile-0 (accessed July 25, 2012).

Lackenbauer, P. Whitney. *The Canadian Rangers: A Living History.* Vancouver: University of British Columbia Press, forthcoming.

Lackenbauer, P. Whitney, and Peter Kikkert, eds. *The Canadian Forces and Arctic Sovereignty: Debating Roles, Interests and Requirements.* Waterloo: Wilfrid Laurier University Press, 2010.

Lajus, Julia. "The Circulation of Environmental Knowledge: Models of Development and Images of Northernness in 20th-c. Arctic Exploration in Scandinavia, Canada, and Russia." Keynote address presented at the Tri-University Annual History Conference, Wilfrid Laurier University, Waterloo, March 3, 2012.

Leighton, Elizabeth. "Arctic Council Fast Track Derails?" *WWF Arctic Bulletin* no. 1.96 (1996), 4.

Levere, Trevor. *Science and the Canadian Arctic: A Century of Exploration, 1818–1918.* Cambridge: Cambridge University Press, 1993.

Liberal Party of Canada. *Creating Opportunity: The Liberal Plan for Canada.* Ottawa: Liberal Party of Canada, 1993.

Ljunggren, David. "Clinton Rebuke Overshadows Canada's Arctic Meeting." *Reuters,* March 29, 2010.

Loft, Steven. "Reflection on 20 Years of Aboriginal Art." University of Victoria, February 8, 2012. www.trudeaufoundation.ca/sites/default/files/u5/reflections_on_20_years_of_aboriginal_art_-_steven_loft.pdf (accessed February 14, 2013).

Lopez, Barry. *Arctic Dreams: Imagination and Desire in a Northern Landscape.* New York: Vintage Books, 2001.

Lotz, Jim. *Northern Realities: The Future of Northern Development in Canada.* Toronto: New Press, 1970.

Lyon, George Francis. *The Private Journal of Captain G.F. Lyon of H.M.S. Hecla, During the Recent Voyage of Discovery Under Captain Parry.* London: John Murray, 1824.

MacEachern, Alan. "J.E. Berniér's Claims to Fame." *Scientia Canadensis: Canadian Journal of the History of Science, Technology and Medicine* 33, no. 2 (2010), 43–73.

Mackenzie, Deborah. "Arctic Protection Treaty Waits for American Involvement." *New Scientist,* October 28, 1989.

Markham, Sir Clements R. *The Voyages of William Baffin.* London: The Hakluyt Society, 1881.

McCannon, John. *A History of the Arctic: Nature, Exploration, and Exploitation.* London: Reaktion Books, 2012.

McDermott, James. *Sir Martin Frobisher: Elizabethan Privateer.* New Haven, Connecticut: Yale University Press, 2001.

McGhee, Robert. *The Last Imaginary Place: A Human History of the Arctic World.* Oxford: Oxford University Press, 2006.

Mearsheimer, John. "A Strategic Misstep: The Maritime Strategy and Deterrence in Europe." *International Security* 11, no. 2 (1986), 1–51.

Mellen, Peter. *Landmarks of Canadian Art.* Toronto: McClelland & Stewart, 1978.

"Message to Congress," February 10, 1997. In *Public Papers of the President of the United States: William J. Clinton: Book I,* 143–144. Washington: Government Printing Office, 1997.

Miles, Lee. *The European Union and the Nordic Countries.* London: Routledge, 1996.

Miller, J.R. *Shingwauk's Vision: A History of Native Residential Schools.* Toronto: University of Toronto Press, 1996.

Mowat, Farley. *Canada North.* Toronto: McClelland & Stewart, 1969.

Moyn, Samuel. *The Last Utopia: Human Rights in History.* Cambridge, Massachusetts: Harvard University Press, 2010.

Mulroney, Brian. "A Call for a New Northern Vision." *Policy Options* 27, no. 5 (2006), 5–9.

———. *Memoirs.* Toronto: Random House, 2007.

Nassichuk, W.W. "Forty Years of Northern Non-Renewable Natural Resource Development." *Arctic* 40, no. 4 (1987), 274–284.

Neatby, L.H. "Martin Frobisher (ca. 1540–1594)." *Arctic* 36, no. 4 (1983), 374–375.

Nilson, Håken R. *Arctic Environmental Protection Strategy (AEPS): Process and Organization, 1991-97: An Assessment.* Oslo: Norwegian Polar Institute, 1997.

Nilsson, Annika E. *A Changing Arctic Climate: Science and Policy in the Arctic Climate Impact Assessment.* Linköping Studies in Art and Science. Linköping: Linköping University, 2007.

———. "Knowing the Arctic: The Arctic Council as a Cognitive Forerunner." In *The Arctic Council: Its Place in the Future of Arctic Governance,* edited by Thomas S. Axworthy, Waliul Hasanat, and Timo Koivurova, 190–224. Toronto: Munk–Gordon Arctic Security Program, 2012.

Nuttall, Mark, ed. *Encyclopedia of the Arctic: Volume I.* New York: Routledge, 2005.

Office of the Prime Minister. "Notes for an Address by the Right Honourable Brian Mulroney, Prime Minister of Canada." Arctic and Antarctic Institute, November 24, 1989.

Osler Hampson, Fen, and Dean Oliver. "'Pulpit Diplomacy': A Critical Assessment of the Axworthy Doctrine." *International Journal* 53, no. 3 (1998), 379–406.

Østreng, Willy. "Political-Military Relations among the Ice States: The Conceptual Basis of State Behaviour." In *Arctic Alternatives: Civility or Militarism in the Circumpolar North,* edited by Franklyn Griffiths, 26–45. Toronto: Science for Peace/Samuel Stevens, 1992.

Pálsson, Gísli. "Hot Bodies in Cold Zones: Arctic Exploration." *The Scholar and Feminist Online* 7, no. 1 (2008). http://sfonline.barnard.edu/ice/palsson_01.htm.

———. *Travelling Passions: The Hidden Life of Vilhjalmur Stefansson.* Translated by Keneva Kurz. Winnipeg: University of Manitoba Press, 2005.

Parry, J.H. *The Age of Reconnaissance: Discovery, Exploration, and Settlement 1450–1650.* Berkeley: University of California Press, 1982.

Pearson, Lester B. "Canada Looks 'Down North.'" *Foreign Affairs* 24, no. 4 (1946), 638–647.

Peters, Gerhard, and John T. Woolley. "Nomination of John Giffen Weinmann to Be United States Ambassador to Finland." *The American Presidency Project*, March 17, 1989. www.presidency.ucsb.edu/ws/index.php?pid=16808#axzz201ryyKZ8 (accessed June 20, 2012).

Protecting the Arctic Environment. Report on the Yellowknife Preparatory Meeting. Yellowknife, Northwest Territories, April 18, 1990.

Purver, Ronald. "Arctic Security: The Murmansk Initiative and Its Impact." *Current Research on Peace and Violence* 11, no. 4 (1988): 147–158.

———. "The North in Canada's International Relations." In *Canada Among Nations 1989: The Challenge of Change*, edited by Maureen Appel Molot and Fen Osler Hampson, 105–118. Ottawa: Carleton University Press, 1990.

Querengesser, Tim. "Farley Mowat: Liar or Saint." *Up Here*, September 2009. www.uphere.ca/node/442 (accessed June 4, 2012).

Rajakoski, Esko. "Multilateral Cooperation to Protect the Arctic Environment: The Finnish Initiative." In *The Arctic: Choices for Peace and Security*, edited by Thomas Berger and Douglas Roche. Vancouver: Gordon Soules, 1989.

"Reykjavik Ministerial Declaration," November 23, 2004. www.arctic-council.org/index.php/en/about/documents/category/5-declarations (accessed September 15, 2012).

Riste, Olav. "The Genesis of North Atlantic Defence Cooperation: Norway's Atlantic Policy, 1940–1948." *NATO Review* 29, no. 2 (1981), 19–23.

Riste, Olav, and Rolf Tamnes. *The Soviet Naval Threat and Norway.* Oslo: National Defence College of Norway, 1986.

Robertson, Gordon. *Memoirs of a Very Civil Servant: Mackenzie King to Pierre Trudeau.* Toronto: University of Toronto Press, 2000.

Rothwell, Donald R. "International Law and the Protection of the Arctic Environment." *The International and Comparative Law Quarterly* 44, no. 2 (1995), 280–312.

———. *The Polar Regions and the Development of International Law.* Cambridge: Cambridge University Press, 1996.

Scott, J.M. *The Private Life of Polar Expedition.* Edinburgh: William Blackwood, 1982.

Scrivener, David. "Arctic Environmental Cooperation in Transition." *Polar Record* 35, no. 192 (1999), 51–58.

———. *Environmental Cooperation in the Arctic: From Strategy to Council.* Oslo: Norwegian Atlantic Committee, 1996.

Secretary of State for External Affairs. "Notes for a Speech by the Secretary of State for External Affairs, the Right Honourable Joe Clark, P.C., M.P." Conference on Canadian–Soviet Relations at the Government Conference Centre, Ottawa, November 28, 1990.

Shelley, Mary. *Frankenstein or The Modern Prometheus*. London: George Routledge and Sons, 1891.

Siddon, minister of Indian Affairs and Northern Development, Tom. *Building International Relations in the Arctic: 25 Years of Canada–USSR Cooperation*. Ottawa: Ministry of Supply and Services, 1991.

Simon, Mary. *Inuit: One Future—One Arctic*. Peterborough, Ontario: Cider Press, 1996.

———. "Militarization and the Aboriginal Peoples." In *Arctic Alternatives: Civility or Militarism in the Circumpolar North*, edited by Franklyn Griffiths, 55–67. Toronto: Science for Peace/Samuel Stevens, 1992.

Slipchenko, Walter. *Siberia 1971: A Report on the Visit of The Honourable Jean Chrétien, Minister of Indian Affairs and Northern Development and Official Delegation to the Soviet Union, July–August 1971*. Ottawa: Information Canada, 1972.

Smith, Denis. *Rogue Tory: The Life and Legend of John G. Diefenbaker*. Toronto: MacFarlane Walter and Ross, 1995.

Spufford, Francis. *I May Be Some Time: Ice and the English Imagination*. New York: St. Martin's Press, 1997.

Stefansson, Vilhjalmur. "Adventures in Diet, Part I." *Harper's Monthly Magazine* 171 (November 1935), 668–675.

———. "Adventures in Diet, Parts II and III." *Harper's Monthly Magazine* 172 (May 1935), 46–54.

———. *The Friendly Arctic: The Story of Five Years in Polar Regions*. New York: Macmillan, 1921.

Summerhayes, Colin. "International Collaboration in Antarctica: The International Polar Years, the International Geophysical Year, and the Scientific Committee on Antarctic Research." *Polar Record* 44, no. 4 (October 2008), 321–334.

Symons, T.H.B. *Meta Incognita: A Discourse of Discovery: Martin Frobisher's Arctic Expeditions 1576–1578*. Hull, Quebec: Canadian Museum of Civilization, 1999.

Taagholt, Jørgen. "The International Arctic Science Committee." *Polar Record* 21, no. 150 (1988), 248.

Tarrow, Sidney. *The New Transnational Activism*. Cambridge and New York: Cambridge University Press, 2005.

Tennberg, Monica. "The Arctic Council: A Study in Governmentality." Unpublished doctoral dissertation, University of Lapland, 1998.

———. *Arctic Environmental Cooperation: A Study in Governmentality*. Aldershot: Ashgate, 2000.

www.arctic-council.org/index.php/en/about/documents/category/5-declarations (accessed August 28, 2012).

Troubetzkoy, Alexis S. *Arctic Obsession: The Lure of the Far North*. Toronto: Dundurn Press, 2011.

U.S. Fisheries and Wildlife Service. *Conservation of Flora and Fauna*. Anchorage, Alaska: Scott Polar Research Institute, 1994.

United States Fish and Wildlife Service. *Towards an Ecologically Meaningful Definition of the Circumpolar Arctic*. Conservation of Arctic Flora and Fauna Workplan for 1993/1994. Cambridge, UK: Scott Polar Research Institute, July 30, 1994.

United States Geological Survey, U.S. Department of the Interior. *Circum-Arctic Resource Appraisal and Estimate of Undiscovered Oil and Gas North of the Arctic Circle*, 2008. http://pubs.usgs.gov/fs/2008/3049/fs2008-3049.pdf (accessed February 14, 2013).

Van Rooy, Alison. *The Global Legitimacy Game: Civil Society, Globalization, and Protest*. Basingstoke: Palgrave Macmillan, 2004.

Watt-Cloutier, Sheila, Joe Kunuk, and Terry Fenge, "The Arctic Council, Sustainable Development, and the Arctic Council," *WWF Arctic Bulletin*, no. 4 (1996), 6–7.

Weaver, Sally. *Making Canadian Indian Policy: The Hidden Agenda, 1968–70*. Toronto: University of Toronto Press, 1981.

Wey-Gómez, Nicolás. *The Tropics of Empire: Why Columbus Sailed South to the Indies*. Cambridge, Massachusetts: MIT Press, 2008.

Williams, Gwyn. *Arctic Labyrinth: The Quest for the Northwest Passage*. Toronto: Penguin Canada, 2009.

Wolff, Robert Paul. *The Conflict Between Authority and Autonomy*. Oxford: Basil Blackwell, 1990.

Young, Oran R. *The Arctic Council: Marking a New Era in International Relations*. New York: The Twentieth Century Fund, 1996.

———. "Arctic Futures: The Politics of Transformation." In *Arctic Security in an Age of Climate Change*, edited by James Kraska, xxi. Cambridge: Cambridge University Press, 2011.

———. "Arctic Governance: Preparing for the Next Phase." paper prepared for the Standing Committee of Parliamentarians of the Arctic Region, June 2002.

———. *Arctic Politics: Conflict and Cooperation in the Circumpolar North*. Hanover, New Hampshire: University Press of New England, 1992.

———. *Creating Regimes: Arctic Accords and International Governance*. Ithaca: Cornell University Press, 1998.

———. "Review of Negotiating the Arctic: The Construction of an International Region, by E. C. H. Keskitalo." *Polar Research* 23, no. 2 (2004), 211–213.

———. "The Structure of Arctic Cooperation: Solving Problems/Seizing Opportunities." Paper prepared for the Fourth Conference of Parliamentarians of the Arctic Region, Rovaniemi, Finland, August 27–29, 2000.

Young, Oran R., and Gail Osherenko. *The Age of the Arctic: Hot Conflicts and Cold Realities*. Cambridge: Cambridge University Press, 1989.

ARCHIVAL SOURCES AND INTERVIEWS

One of the perils of writing contemporary history is the lack of archival documents. When I began *Ice and Water*, I feared that I would have to rely principally on interviews, which I have found to be valuable mainly for anecdotal colour and personal details. Although this information is important, documentary evidence provides a much more solid base. Fortunately, the Finnish government granted me access to its invaluable files on the Arctic Environmental Protection Strategy, the forerunner of the Arctic Council, and some materials on the early years of the Arctic Council. Subsequently, with the assistance of archivists, I filed Access to Information requests for Canadian material dealing with the Arctic Council and received over 5,000 pages of documents, principally on the period 1990–2000. These two collections have provided the core for the analysis of the formation of the Arctic Council.

My work was also greatly assisted by several individuals who played a major part in the creation of the Arctic Council, who gave me access to their own papers. I would like to thank Tom Axworthy, Franklyn Griffiths, John Lamb, and Terry Fenge. Terry's papers complemented the excellent collection of the Canadian Arctic Resources Committee, which are held at Wilfrid Laurier University. Tom Axworthy also provided access to the papers of the Walter and Duncan Gordon Foundation, which was a key player not only in the creation of the Arctic Council but also in Canadian Arctic policy more generally after 1980. I have received other documents from individuals, including Mary Simon, Odd Rogne, Walter McLean, Whitney Lackenbauer, and Shelagh Grant. Students in the two courses I taught on the Arctic, one at the Canadian Forces College, the other at Trinity College at the University of Toronto, gave me new insights into the Arctic, and I profited greatly from their essays and the discussions.

The following list of interviews does not include many conversations with individuals about the Arctic Council. The Munk–Gordon Arctic Security Program at the University of Toronto has held annual conferences whose participants spoke freely about Arctic affairs. One of the conferences concentrated on the Arctic Council, and it offered me the opportunity to speak with many of the leading actors in the Council about its work.

Lloyd Axworthy, November 22, 2012
Tom Axworthy, January 10, 2012
Garth Bangay, March 31, 2012
Lawson Brigham, January 12, 2012
Berndt Bull, June 27, 2011
Harald Finklar, March 21, 2012
Terry Fenge, May 17, 2012, and December 3, 2012
Bernie Funston, December 3, 2012
Bill Graham, November 28, 2012
Odmund Graham, June 29, 2011
Shelagh Grant, January 9, 2013
Franklyn Griffiths, June 9, 2011
Paul Heinbecker, November 22, 2012
Paula Kankaanpää, May 8, 2012
Timo Koivurova, May 7, 2012
Rosemarie Kuptana, January 30, 2012

Gustaf Lind, May 17, 2012
Wayne Lord, October 22, 2012
Charles McMillan, June 8, 2013
Gunngjorg Nåvik, June 28, 2011
Satu Nurmi, May 3, 2012
Lars-Otto Reiersen, June 28, 2011
Eskon Riepula, May 7, 2012
Douglas Roche, June 16, 2012
Odd Rogne, June 28, 2011
Tucker Scully, March 23, 2012
Mary Simon, March 20, 2012, and February 27, 2013
Monica Tennberg, May 7, 2012
Leslie Whitby, March 21, 2012
Oran Young, June 23, 2011

ACKNOWLEDGMENTS

Ice and Water is part of a series edited by two good friends, Bob Bothwell and Margaret MacMillan. I'd like to thank them for supporting the book and for their many helpful comments. At Penguin, Diane Turbide, Sandra Tooze, Patricia Jones, and Justin Stoller provided editorial and other assistance, particularly in the final months before publication.

Tom Axworthy, president of the Walter and Duncan Gordon Foundation, initially suggested the book to me, and Janice Stein of the Munk School of Global Affairs offered me a role in the important Munk–Gordon Arctic Security Program, which is ably directed by Sara French with the assistance of the talented Meredith Kravitz. The program's annual conferences, notably the 2012 conference on the Arctic Council, provided me with many contacts and a wealth of information relevant to the study. I am deeply grateful to Janice and Tom for their constant encouragement. Tom has been a guest lecturer in the contemporary history course I have taught at Trinity College with the Hon. Bill Graham and Jack Cunningham. The classes have had significant Arctic content.

I would like to thank our many fine students for their contributions to my understanding of the North. Bill's own experience as Canada's defence and foreign minister provided me with insight and wise comment over the past few years as we have worked together at Trinity, which has been my wonderful academic home during this study. I also continued to benefit from the advice of many colleagues from the University of Waterloo where I taught for twenty-eight years, notably Whitney Lackenbauer, a former student who has become one of the leading academic specialists on the Arctic. In 2010–11, I was a visiting professor at the Canadian Forces College in Toronto, and several of my students wrote essays on the Arctic and the Canadian military. They gave me an important military perspective on current events in the Canadian Arctic.

After I began this book, the History Department at Western University invited me to give the annual Joanne Goodman lectures. I chose the development of the Arctic Council as my subject, and the lectures formed the base for the book that followed. I'm deeply grateful to Western, the department, and, especially, the very gracious and efficient Shelley McKellar, who organized the lecture and the logistics. The Arctic Athabaskan Council appointed me as a consultant to their delegation to the 2013 Arctic Council ministerial meeting, which permitted me to see how the Council functioned at its highest level. I'd like to thank delegation members Chief Gary Harrison and Chief Bill Erasmus, and the delegation head, Michael Stickman, for providing me this opportunity.

An Arctic Council veteran described Terry Fenge as the "historical memory" of the Arctic Council. He was exceptionally helpful opening his papers to me, shrewdly analyzing events and people, and carefully reading the manuscript. A central figure in this book, Mary Simon was generous with her time and candid in her assessments. I have identified several others in the list of interviews who gave freely of their time. John Lamb, Frank Griffiths, Tom Axworthy, and the Gordon Foundation gave me full access to their papers. Thanks to the excellent assistance I had from Library and Archives Canada staff, I managed to identify and receive a truly astonishing amount of documentary material on the creation of the Arctic Council. This was complemented by a remarkable decision by the Finnish government to allow me full access to the papers of their foreign ministry for the 1990s. Professor Timo Koivurova worked out this arrangement and also found an excellent translator for me, Pirjo Kleemola-Juntunen, who worked closely with me in the Finnish Archives. Rare is the historian of recent events who has such extensive access to primary documents. I am deeply grateful to those who made it possible.

I have also benefited from excellent assistants. The Gordon Foundation lent me Alice Bothwell, a remarkable and cheerful young woman, who greatly aided my research. Meredith Kravitz also helped out in many different ways. Annie Donolo pored over periodicals and other sources during one summer, and John Yolkowski assisted in various ways at different times. During the writing of this book, I served as general editor of the *Dictionary of Canadian Biography*, and I'd like to thank Professor Réal Bélanger, directeur general adjoint, Robert Fraser, Willadean Leo, Julia Armstrong, and Chris Pennington for their patience with my schedule and other commitments. My partner, Irene Sage, was always supportive, even giving up a holiday while I immersed myself in the Arctic. My son Jonathan English was consistently encouraging and his partner, the writer Elena Vardon, cleaned up my prose and errors and created the index. I have been blessed with wonderful friends, relatives, and colleagues.

INDEX